Fate, Providence and Free Will: Philosophy and Religion in Dialogue in the Early Imperial Age

Ancient Philosophy & Religion

VOLUME 4

The titles published in this series are listed at *brill.com/aphr*

Fate, Providence and Free Will: Philosophy and Religion in Dialogue in the Early Imperial Age

Edited by

René Brouwer
Emmanuele Vimercati

BRILL

LEIDEN | BOSTON

Cover illustration: The posthumous encounter of the deceased with the philosophers (1950 NAM 90), relief from the funeral sacrificial table (mensa) in the "House of Proclus" on the Southern slope of the Acropolis at Athens, excavated in 1955, used by courtesy and permission of the New Acropolis Museum in Athens.

Library of Congress Cataloging-in-Publication Data

Names: Brouwer, René, editor. | Vimercati, Emmanuele, editor.
Title: Fate, providence and free will : philosophy and religion in dialogue in the early imperial age. / edited by René Brouwer, Emmanuele Vimercati.
Description: Leiden ; Boston : Brill, 2020. | Series: Ancient philosophy and religion, 2542-3576 ; volume 4 | Includes index. |
Identifiers: LCCN 2020023486 (print) | LCCN 2020023487 (ebook) | ISBN 9789004435667 (hardback) | ISBN 9789004436381 (ebook)
Subjects: LCSH: Philosophy and religion–History. | Philosophy, Ancient. | Theology, Doctrinal–History–Early church, ca. 30-600. | Free will and determinism–History. | Providence and government of God–History.
Classification: LCC BL51 .F355 2020 (print) | LCC BL51 (ebook) | DDC 123.093–dc23
LC record available at https://lccn.loc.gov/2020023486
LC ebook record available at https://lccn.loc.gov/2020023487

Typeface for the Latin, Greek, and Cyrillic scripts: "Brill". See and download: brill.com/brill-typeface.

ISSN 2542-3576
ISBN 978-90-04-43566-7 (hardback)
ISBN 978-90-04-43638-1 (e-book)

This book is printed on acid-free paper and produced in a sustainable manner.

Contents

Notes on Contributors

René Brouwer
Assistant Professor in Legal Theory, University of Utrecht.

Ludovica De Luca
Research Fellow in the History of Ancient Philosophy, University of L'Aquila.

Pia De Simone
Research Fellow in the History of Ancient Philosophy, Università Cattolica del Sacro Cuore, Milan.

Mark Edwards
Professor of Early Christian Studies, Tutor in Theology, Christ Church, University of Oxford.

Troels Engberg-Pedersen
Professor Emeritus of New Testament Exegesis, University of Copenhagen.

Maria Luisa Gatti
Associate Professor in the History of Ancient Philosophy, Università Cattolica del Sacro Cuore, Milan.

George Karamanolis
Associate Professor in Ancient Philosophy, University of Vienna.

Péter Lautner
Professor of Philosophy, Pázmány Péter Catholic University, Budapest.

Aldo Magris
Professor of Theoretical Philosophy, University of Trieste.

Claudio Moreschini
Professor Emeritus of Latin Literature, University of Pisa.

Carlo Natali
Honorary Professor of History of Ancient Philosophy, University Ca' Foscari, Venice.

Enrico Peroli
Professor of Moral Philosophy, University of Chieti-Pescara.

Roberto Radice
Professor of History of Ancient Philosophy, Università Cattolica del Sacro Cuore, Milan.

John Rist
Professor Emeritus of Classics and Philosophy, University of Toronto.

Ricardo Salles
Researcher in Ancient Philosophy, Universidad Nacional Autónoma de México.

Emmanuele Vimercati
Professor of History of Ancient Philosophy, Pontifical Lateran University, Rome.

Introduction

René Brouwer and Emmanuele Vimercati

The topic of this book is the debate about fate, providence and freedom in the early Imperial age. With "early Imperial" we refer to the period between 31 BCE and 250 CE: it starts with Augustus' imperial rule, during whose reign the debate among philosophers about fate and freedom was rekindled, and ends with Plotinus and Origen, when the different positions in the debate were more or less fully developed. The aim of this book is to show how in this period the notions of fate, providence and freedom were developed and debated, not only within and between the philosophical schools, but also in the interaction with other "religious" movements, here understood in the general sense of people sharing beliefs in and worship of (a) superhuman controlling power(s), such as Gnosticism, Hermetism and – of course – Judaism and Christianity. The word "religious" may well be considered problematic: Boys-Stones (2017, 21–22) avoids the word "religious" altogether (presumably since it can also be applied to Platonism itself, as he had argued in his 2016), speaking of "contemporary movements with intellectual affinities." If only for practical reasons, with regard to these movements in which the focus is on sharing beliefs about worshipping god(s), we stick to the traditional term "religious" here.

The early Imperial period is especially important for the development of the notions of fate, providence and – as it will come to be known – free will. In the Hellenistic period the debate among philosophers had started with Stoics and Epicureans, who took up the opposite positions in the debate: determinism vs. libertarianism respectively. The Academic Sceptics joined in by attacking their dogmatic positions. In the early Imperial period the debate was broadened. Platonists and Aristotelians, explicitly referring back to the writings of the founders of their schools, now venerated as "authorities", developed their own dogmatic positions in the controversy. The debate broadened in another way, too: members of the different religious sects, Jews, Christians, but also Hermetics and Gnostics, became interested in the debate among philosophers, if only to give as much as possible a rational justification of their beliefs. They hence started to rethink their own doctrines in terms of this debate, eagerly picking up on the philosophers' terminology related to the emerging notion of the free will.

The early Imperial debate turned out to be influential. In late antiquity, the discussion was continued by the Greek and Latin church fathers, among whom can be singled out Gregory of Nyssa (c. 335–395), especially in his *Against*

 | DOI:10.1163/9789004436381_002

Fate,[1] and Augustine of Hippo (354–430), in e.g. his *On Free Will*. In this context, Boethius (c. 477–524) was a transitional figure between antiquity and the middle ages: in his writings the ancient tradition culminated and a new era begins. In his *On the Consolation of Philosophy* (see Sharples 1991 for text and commentary) he joined in the discussion and in so doing advanced it considerably. In the high middle ages "voluntarists", like Henry of Ghent (1217–1293) and Duns Scotus (1266–1308), argued for the independence of the will from the intellect, whereas "intellectualists", like Thomas Aquinas (1225–1274), defended the subordination of the will to the intellect – Aquinas seeking a more balanced relationship between the two faculties. In the early modern period the debate about determinism and freedom continued with thinkers like Erasmus, Luther, Hobbes, Descartes, Spinoza, Locke, Leibniz and Hume. Even if the notion of providence has received less attention these days (cf. Lloyd 2008), the discussion between determinists (now often invoking recent insights in neuroscience concerning the operations of the brain as evidence) and libertarians still rages on (for overviews see De Caro et al. 2014, Keil 2017).

In recent years the ancient origins of the debate have attracted the attention of a considerable number of scholars. Mention should be made of Frede's lecture series, published posthumously in 2011 after his untimely death, but also the volumes edited by Natali and Maso 2005, Masi and Maso 2013, De Caro, Mori and Spinelli 2014, D'Hoine and Van Riel 2014, Destrée, Salles and Zingano 2014. This volume differs from these studies in a couple of aspects. First, the volume does not cover the whole of period of ancient philosophy, from the earliest Greek thinkers to the "closure" of Plato's Academy by Justinian, but is restricted to the early Imperial age, when the debate about determinism and freedom develops in now familiar, "modern" terms. Second, the interaction between the philosophical and religious movements in the early Imperial period has attracted less attention thus far. The interaction is yet again important for the "modern" debate. In this volume we therefore seek to present the debate about determinism and freedom among philosophers and religious thinkers, Jewish, Christian, Gnostic and Hermetic. In introducing or clarifying most of the aspects of the problem, the early Imperial discussion set the stage for the later debate.

In two joint conferences held at the Pontifical Lateran University (Rome, 28–29 September 2017) and at the Università Cattolica del Sacro Cuore (Milan, 16–17 November 2017), organized by Emmanuele Vimercati and Maria Luisa Gatti, scholars from both ancient philosophy and religious studies presented

1 For a modern translation see Meredith 1999, 64–73, for a recent study see Motta 2008.

their research on different aspects of the debate and thus discussed the development of the notions of fate, providence and free will together. This volume is the result thereof: the papers at the conference were all revised in the light of these discussions. The contributions have become linked to one another, such that – so the editors hope – the volume can serve as a compact introduction to the topic.

1 The Archaic and Classical Premises

Fate already occurs in the earliest Greek texts. Different words are used to refer to it, such as *moira*, *heimarmenē*, and *anankē*. *Moira* and *heimarmenē* are nouns related to *meiromai*, "to receive one's share." *Moira* is used not only with regard to the power that distributes but also to the share thus allotted to a human being. Homer already uses it in both meanings (see *Iliad* 24.209: "In this way for him did resistless *Moira* spin with her thread at his birth", 7.52: "Not yet is it your fate to die", respectively), in Greek tragedy Aeschylus (c. 525–455) uses *Moira* prominently in a choir song in the *Eumenides*, at lines 335–336: "This is the office that ever-determining *Moira*, when it span the thread of our life, assigned unto us to hold unalterably."[2] *Heimarmenē* is the participle of *meiromai*, used as an adjective in tragedy, by e.g. Aeschylus, *Agamemnon* 913: "decreed by fate" (είμαρμένα). From the Hellenistic thinkers onwards, *heimarmenē* would be used as a noun, and become the standard expression for fate. *Anankē* is used by Aeschylus in the first part of his *Oresteia*, at l. 218: in order to sacrifice his daughter Agamemnon "had to put on the harness of necessity" (ἀνάγκας ἔδυ λέπαδνον). With the world divinely ordered, human beings will thus do whatever is ordained; at best they can recognize what fate has in store for them. In such a context, it is "unhelpful" (Williams 1993, 133) to discuss Agamemnon's response in modern terms of freedom of the will.

Also among the earliest Greek thinkers – or "Presocratics", as they are often referred to in Diels' not altogether felicitous neologism, since many of the Pre-Socratics are in fact contemporaries of Socrates –, fate is discussed. As far as it is possible to reconstruct from the pithy remains of their writings, the debate among these thinkers was about the order of the world: whether it is the result of fate as a divine force or whether it is the product of mechanical necessity. The doctrine that fate is the divine power that orders all things was held by Anaximander and Heraclitus among others. Both thinkers maintained

2 τοῦτο γὰρ λάχος διανταία Μοῖρ' ἐπέκλωσεν ἐμπέδως ἔχειν.

that all things occur "according to necessity" (κατὰ τὸ χρεών). Anaximander of Miletus (c. 610–545) maintained that the coming-into-being and destruction of all things occurs "according to necessity, for they pay penalty and retribution to each other."[3] Heraclitus of Ephesus (c. 525–475) spoke of "according to strife and necessity" (Origen, *Against Celsus* 6.42, fr. 80 DK, D63 LM: κατ' ἔριν τὸ χρεών), which in the presumably Stoicised doxography in Diogenes Laertius, at 9.7 (fr. A1 DK, R46 LM), is formulated as "All things come about by fate" (πάντα δὲ γίνεσθαι καθ' εἱμαρμένην), with human beings usually not recognizing their place ordained by this power. The order of the world as the result of mechanical necessity is the doctrine held by the 5th century thinkers Leucippus (see e.g. Aëtius 1.25.4, fr. 2 DK, D73 LM) and Democritus of Abdera (see e.g. Aristotle, *On the Generation of Animals* 5.8 789b2–4, fr. A66 DK, D74 LM).

In Plato's dialogues, the notions of providence, fate and human responsibility are usually brought up in "stories" (μύθοι), in which we are told that the gods care for human beings, especially with regard to those who have chosen to live the good life. In the *Republic*, at 10.614a–621b, Socrates tells the tale of Er, a soldier from Pamphylia killed in battle, but who miraculously came to life again: Er tells about how human beings who have chosen to live a virtuous life are rewarded by the gods in their afterlife. In the "likely" account in the *Phaedrus* 246a–249d, Socrates compares a human being to the combined power of a winged team of horses and charioteer: here again rewards befall upon human beings who as much as possible have chosen to follow the charioteer in themselves, which stands for reason. Also in the "stories" or "mythic incantations" (in Mayhew's 2010 translation) in the *Laws* 10.903a–907b about "the care (ἐπιμέλεια) of the gods for the world", yet again those human beings are rewarded who have chosen the good life. The most important among these stories for the early Imperial period is the "likely" story (εἰκός) in the *Timaeus*, at 29d, about the coming into being of the universe by the god's providence for the world and the human beings therein.

With regard to Aristotle, neither providence nor fate figures prominently in his extant writings: the notions are only referred to in passing (Sharples 2011, 206, against Verdenius 1960). Instead, in his *Physics* 2.4–6, Aristotle discusses the notions of 'luck' (*tuchē*), 'chance' (*automaton*), and 'mechanical necessity' (*matēn*). However, in his psychology of action he discusses freedom of decision in the book 3 of his *Nicomachean Ethics*, chapters 1–7. In his logic, in *On Interpretation*, ch. 9, with its well-known example of the sea battle, he discusses the

3 Simplicius, *Commentary on the Physics* 24.19–20, fr. 110 DK, D6 LM: κατὰ τὸ χρεών, διδόναι γὰρ αὐτὰ δίκην καὶ τίσιν ἀλλήλοις τῆς ἀδικίας.

modal notions of necessity and possibility. In the Imperial era Plato's "stories" as well as Aristotle's discussions of luck, chance and (ontological) necessity in his physics, of freedom of decision in his ethics, and of possibility and necessity in logic, will be used again and rise to prominence, placed in the context of the Hellenistic debate about fate and freedom.

2 The Hellenistic Debate

In the Hellenistic period the notion of fate and its relation to freedom becomes already a central topic, especially with the Epicureans and the Stoics, who are usually regarded as the game changers here. The centrality of these notions, though, does not yet imply that the debate between Stoics and Epicureans is already conducted in terms of the problem of "free will." It has even been refreshingly argued that the problem as such has a later origin (see Bobzien 1998b, cf. Bobzien 2000 and 1998a on Epicurus and the Stoics respectively).

While building on to Leucippus' and Democritus' atomism, Epicurus of Samos (341–270) maintained that human beings are not subjected to mechanical necessity, but can have things "in their power." In his *On the Nature of the Gods* 1.69 Cicero formulated it in the following manner: "He [Epicurus] invented a way to escape from necessity, which clearly had escaped Democritus: he said that the atom [...] makes a very slight swerve,"[4] in the Lycian inscription the 2nd century Epicurean Diogenes of Oenoanda fr. 54.3.1–7 Smith (LS 20G) put it like this: "There is a free movement in atoms, which Democritus failed to discover but Epicurus brought to light."[5] This free movement Epicurus called the swerve, *parenklisis*, or *clinamen* in Lucretius' Latin translation (see Greenblatt 2011). See Cicero, *On Fate* 22 (LS 20E3): "Epicurus thinks that the necessity of fate is avoided by the swerve of an atom."[6] According to Cicero's account in his *On the Nature of the Gods*, at 1.69, the swerve would allow that "we" as human beings have things "in our power" (*in nostra potestate*).[7] It follows that human beings need not be bothered by the traditional accounts about the gods or about fate. In his *Letter to Menoeceus*, preserved by Diogenes

4 *invenit quo modo necessitatem effugeret, quod videlicet Democritum fugerat: ait atomum* [...] *declinare paululum.*

5 ἐλευθέραν τινὰ ἐν ταῖς ἀτόμοις κείνησιν εἶναι, ἣ[ν] Δημόκριτος μὲν οὐχ εὗρεν, Ἐπίκουρος δὲ εἰς φῶς ἤγαγεν.

6 *Epicurus declinatione atomi vitari necessitatem fati putat.*

7 For further discussion of the relation between atomism and Epicureanism, especially in relation to Cicero's reports thereof, see Vimercati 2018.

Laertius, at 10.133 (LS 20A), Epicurus writes that he rejects fate as ordering power: "As for fate, which some have posited as ruler over all things, he laughs at the notion, and claims instead that some things occur by chance, others through our own agency."[8] (Tr. Mensch.)

Rather than rejecting fate, the Stoics stressed its importance: for them fate is, first and foremost, an aspect of the divine, immanent principle that orders the world. According to the Stoics, the world as a whole should be understood as a living being. Its order is a product of two "principles", one active, the other passive. The active principle orders the world by going through the passive principle of matter. This active principle is given different names: in terms of popular religion the Stoics refer to it as Zeus, but also as fate and providence, in philosophers' terms they refer to it as fire or reason. The different names given to the active principle bring out its different aspects. Fate relates to the causal aspect of the active principle that orders the world. Since the world is a living being, the sequence of causes is best understood in a biological sense: rather than one cause having one effect, multiple causes have different effects (Sauvé Meyer 2009). Providence relates to another aspect of the rational principle: it refers to the divine plan, in which everything that exists and occurs has its place and its meaning.

In the interconnectedness of Stoic thought, these doctrines on physics (including theology) are closely related to the other two parts of philosophy distinguished by the Stoics, logic (including epistemology) and ethics. In their epistemology, the Stoics hold that only the sage as the perfectly rational being will always deal correctly with his (or her) sense-impressions: building on these impressions and with the help of his correctly functioning faculty of reason, the sage will thus be able to have knowledge. In their ethics, they hold that the good life consists in living according to nature, that is the life in which one has brought one's own nature in accordance with the nature of the whole. Since it is only the sage that can have knowledge, also of the operations of his own nature in relation to the nature of the whole, it is only the sage who can live the good life. Human beings, who have not yet developed their rationality to perfection, are not always able to understand the order of things, let alone able to consistently live in accordance with it. The non-sages' incorrect judgments about the course of things will affect their lives in a negative manner. The Stoics call these incorrect judgments emotions, which include anger and fear. They thus analyse anger as the non-sage's incorrect judgment about how

8 τὴν δὲ ὑπό τινων δεσπότιν εἰσαγομένην πάντων ἂν γελῶντος ⟨εἱμαρμένην⟩, ἃ δὲ ἀπὸ τύχης, ἃ δὲ παρ' ἡμᾶς. The text follows Dorandi 2013, reading Sedley's ἂν γελῶντος for ἀγγέλλοντος.

he or she is affected by the order of things, and fear as an incorrect judgment about how he or she may be affected.

Like the Epicureans, the Stoics also discussed human freedom in relation to fate and providence, but in a radically different manner. According to the Stoics, the Epicurean conception of freedom as doing what one pleases does not imply freedom at all. Different from all other animated human beings, by virtue of their rational faculty human beings have the power to discover the course of things and their place within this course. As we have seen already, such a tying in is the prerogative of the perfect human being only. Hence – in terms of their para-doxes (literally: unconventional opinions) – the Stoics maintained that only the sage is free. Freedom rather consists in living according to nature, that is contributing to or otherwise following the course of things. All non-sages are dragged along, like – in Cleanthes' famous metaphor – dogs tied to a cart. In the Stoics' paradoxical formulation the sage is free, the inferior person is enslaved.

In modern terminology regarding the problem of the free will, the Epicureans could be labelled as libertarians, the Stoics as determinists, or perhaps better yet as "soft determinists" (Sharples 1983, 7–10, Keil 2017). According to Epicurus, the causes of their actions can be with human beings themselves. According to the Stoics, unlike all other beings in the world human beings have the freedom to align themselves (or not) with the order of things by virtue of their faculty of reason.

Stoic determinism was not only challenged by the Epicureans. The debate between Stoics and Epicureans was taken to another level by the Academic Sceptics, by Arcesilaus and especially Carneades, who criticised the dogmatic positions of both schools. These sceptics were especially critical of the Stoics' conceptions of knowledge and causality. For their challenge on Stoic determinism Cicero, *On Fate* 26–33 (LS 70G) can be consulted.

3 The Early Imperial Debate

The debate in the early Imperial period was characterised both by continuity as well as by change. As for continuity, the Stoics remained a driving force in the debate about determinism and freedom. The members of the school retained the determinist doctrines of the founders of the school (see Brouwer's chapter), but not without developing it further. Here Epictetus must be singled out: in his chapter Salles shows how Epictetus' conception of "what is up to us" can be considered to fit in within Stoic causal determinism, whereas Brouwer, following Frede 2011, suggests that Epictetus' notion of *prohairesis*, which he may have taken over from Aristotle, appears to be functioning in the modern sense of a faculty of "will".

As for the change, two changes need to be highlighted here. The first change is the interest among religious thinkers in the debate. Already at the beginning of the Imperial period the Stoic determinist position proved to be a catalyst for both Jewish and Christian thinkers. In their chapters, De Luca, Radice and Engberg-Pedersen make a case for the influence of the Stoics on Philo's and Paul's thinking on providence, fate and freedom.

A further change occurs with the entry of Platonists and Aristotelians into the debate. The entry of each schools has a different background. In Plato's Academy, already in the first century BCE the sceptical approach endorsed by Arcesilaus and Carneades had been abandoned: the school had become dogmatic. Its members now regarded Plato's writings as authoritative and interpreted his dialogues – and the stories therein – in a dogmatic manner. Emulating the Stoics in their systematic accounts of philosophy (Engberg-Pedersen 2017), these Platonists wrote systematic accounts of Plato's doctrines in teaching manuals. With regard to Aristotle's Lyceum, also in the first century BCE, this school underwent a revival, due to the fact that Aristotle's lecture notes had become readily available again in an edition published by Andronicus of Rhodes. Like the Platonists, Aristotelians thus started to read, interpret and comment upon these authoritative texts, too. Since Aristotle's writings are already in themselves systematic accounts of particular topics, commentaries rather than teaching manuals would become the Aristotelians' favourite genre. Against this background, students of Plato and Aristotle joined in the continuing debate about determinism and freedom, while taking the writings of their respective founders into account. In this manner Platonists and Aristotelians formulated their own doctrinal positions on fate, providence and freedom, while attributing them to either Plato or Aristotle.

In the scholarly literature the earliest Imperial Platonists are usually referred to as "Middle Platonists",[9] the Platonists in between the sceptical Academics on the one hand and Plotinus and his followers (often referred to as "Neoplatonists") on the other. In developing their doctrines on fate, providence and freedom they used Plato's stories from the *Republic*, *Phaedrus* and the *Timaeus*, which we already encountered above. They took them as expressions of Plato's authoritative opinions or even of more ancient wisdom (Boys-Stones 2001, cf. Vimercati 2015, 28–36). In interpreting these stories, often with the help of the allegorical methods already developed by the Stoics, the Platonists could thus reveal the underlying doctrines about providence and fate.

9 See e.g. Dillon 1996, the modern classic on Middle Platonism.

The Middle Platonists argued against the Stoics on notably two points, their conception of god and on how to understand the relation between providence and fate. With regard to god, they attacked the Stoic doctrines of the immanence and corporality of the divine active principle that pervades and thus orders the world. The Platonists, using the story in the *Timaeus*, defended the transcendence of god as the "demiurge" or "craftsman", who has created the world. This transcendent god not only creates, but remains interested in his creation, caring about it and intervening in it. However, since the Platonic god is not interested in individual beings, he is interested in creation in an indirect manner by means of providence and fate. With regard to providence and fate, the Middle Platonists attacked the Stoics for taking providence and fate to be but different aspects of the divine rational active principle. Rejecting the Stoic doctrine that this corporeal principle is coextensive with passive matter, they distinguished between two types of causality: natural (or physical) causality that can be found in the sensible world on the one hand and supernatural (or metaphysical) causality that can be found in the realm of ideas on the other. Fate operates in the sensible world, providence operates in the world of Platonic ideas. According to the Middle-Platonists, then, as Vimercati makes clear in chapter 7, fate becomes subordinated to providence.

Among the early Imperial Aristotelians, Alexander of Aphrodisias (c. 150–c. 230 CE), deserves special attention. Just like other Aristotelians, Alexander of Aphrodisias wrote above all commentaries on Aristotle's writings. Since Aristotle did not deal with the topic, with regard to fate, providence and freedom, he could not rely on an Aristotelian treatise; he thus joined in the debate by writing a separate treatise, *On Fate*, in which he nevertheless declared to set out "Aristotle's opinion about fate and what is up to us."[10] In fact, Alexander made use of the Aristotelian passages in moral psychology and in logic, and placed them in the context of the debate about fate and freedom, as Natali makes clear in chapter 8.

Like the Platonists, the Aristotelians also attacked the Stoic conception of the immanent divine principle: starting from Aristotle's conception of god as the unmoved mover, and using his distinction between the heavenly and the sublunary regions, Aristotelians inferred that divine providence only operates in the heavenly realm.[11] In a deist manner god thus remains aloof from the earthly realm: relying upon Aristotle's discussion in the *Nicomachean Ethics* Aristotelians like Alexander of Aphrodisias could thus present Aristotle as an

10 1,164.13–14 Bruns: τὴν δόξαν τὴν Ἀριστοτέλους […] περί τε εἱμαρμένης καὶ τοῦ ἐφ' ἡμῖν.

11 For the evidence Sharples 2010, frs. 18DHINO, can be conveniently consulted.

antideterminist, defending a conception of freedom as freedom of decision, that is of having the choice between alternative courses of actions. In chapter 9 Lautner deals with the epistemological and psychological implications of this antideterminism.

In the early Imperial debate among the philosophical schools two conceptions of freedom thus emerge: on the one hand we find Aristotelians defending a conception of freedom of decision as the ability to choose between different courses of action, on the other hand we find Stoics and Platonists defending a conception freedom that is in different ways related to the divine. For both the Stoics and the Platonists human beings are free as long as they act like god. The difference between Stoics and Platonists lies in the fact that the Stoic sage, who has perfected his or her reason, always acts according to the divine active principle of reason, since he or she has become an active part of that principle, while the Platonist sage becomes like god as much as is possible in this sensible world.

With Plotinus, Platonism enters into a different phase. Plotinus could reinterpret Plato's writings by profiting from the debate between Stoics and Aristotelians, also with regard to the Stoic doctrine of determinism and the Aristotelian defense of freedom of decision. In his version of Platonism Plotinus no longer accepts the Middle Platonists' dualism between god and matter, nor their explanation of divine causality. Plotinus still presents god as omniscient and free, but different from the Middle Platonists' conception of god, who first acts as a demiurge and thereafter as a sort of spectator of future events, Plotinus' god is self-sufficient, free from any reference to natural ends and does not "create" or govern. In his chapter Peroli discusses Plotinus' Platonism starting out from the divine point of view, whereas in her discussion of *Ennead* 3.1 Gatti does so from the human point of view.

Just as in the beginning of the early Imperial period with Philo and Paul, the debate continued to attract the attention of religious movements, now also including Gnosticism and Hermetism. The relevance of the debate in philosophy for the development of their beliefs can be classified under four headings: first, the nature of god, second, the original human condition, third, the good life, and fourth, the afterlife. With regard to the nature of god: does god care for his creation, as Platonists maintained against the Aristotelians? If he does, does he care for individual human beings or rather for the human species? Another question is how god cares: does god intervene directly or does he operate through some intermediaries, such as other divine powers, lower gods, or demons? With regard to human nature: are all human beings equal or should a distinction be made between different kinds of human beings? With regard to the good life: what do men need to be able to live the good life? Is virtue sufficient or is more needed? With regard to the afterlife: Is there such a thing? Is it restricted in time or eternal? If so, what does it look like: e.g. salvation or condemnation? To whom does it apply? The influence from the philosophical schools on the religious movements is especially strong on the side of the Platonists. These religious movements in their turn exerted influence on the schools, where yet again the Imperial Platonists need to be singled out. Platonism, Gnosticism and Christianity came to share – in different ways – a hierarchy of ontological levels and different orders of causation, which refer to the different ways in which god acts upon the world.

The philosophical-religious debate about fate and freedom arguably culminated in the discussion between the anti-Christian Celsus and Origen. Their respective positions are the subject of the two final chapters. De Simone shows how Celsus' view supports a (Middle) Platonist understanding of providence, though possibly influenced by the Aristotelian debate and addressed against the supposed divine power of Jesus – as proclaimed by Christians –, whereas Edwards shows how Origen defends a Platonist conception of providence, though adhering to Christian belief.

4 Plan of the Volume

The chapters in this volume are presented as much as possible in chronological order. John Rist's discussion of the importance of the debate (chapter 1) is followed by two chapters on the Stoics and a couple of chapters on the influence these Stoics exerted on religious thinkers. In chapter 2 Brouwer discusses the notion of will in Stoicism, in chapter 3 Salles addresses Epictetus' notion of what is "up to us." In chapters 4 and 5 De Luca and Radice deal with the Stoics' influence on Philo's cosmology and ethics respectively; in chapter 6 Engberg-Pedersen makes a case for their influence on Paul. While the influence of Plato's writings is also discussed in De Luca's and Radice's chapters, it is the main focus of Vimercati's chapter on the Middle-Platonists (chapter 7). The Aristotelian Alexander of Aphrodias is dealt with by Natali and Lautner: in chapter 8 Natali shows how Alexander made use of Aristotle's writings, whereas in chapter 9 Lautner deals with the epistemological and psychological implications of Alexander of Aphrodisias' rejection of fate. The influence exerted by Stoicism and Platonism alike on Gnostics, Hermetics, and Christians is discussed in chapters 10–12 by Magris, Moreschini and Karamanolis respectively. The new phase in Platonism, starting with Plotinus, who had been able to take into account the debate between Stoics and Aristotelians, is discussed in chapter 13 by Peroli (from the divine point of view) and in chapter 14

Gatti (from the human point of view). The culmination of this philosophical-religious debate with Celsus' defense of freedom as discussed by De Simone in chapter 15 and Origen's Platonist conception of providence – discussed by Edwards in chapter 16 – rounds off the volume.

Bibliography

Bobzien, Susanne. 1998a. *Determinism and Freedom in Stoic Philosophy*. Oxford: Oxford University Press.

Bobzien, Susanne. 1998b. "The Inadvert and Late Birth of the Free-Will Problem." *Phronesis* 43: 133–175.

Bobzien, Susanne. 2000. "Did Epicurus Discover the Free Will Problem?" *Oxford Studies in Ancient Philosophy* 19: 287–337.

Boys-Stones, George. 2001. *Post-Hellenistic Philosophy. A Study of Its Development from the Stoics to Origen*. Oxford: Oxford University Press.

Boys-Stones, George. 2016. "Providence and Religion in Middle Platonism." In *Theologies of Ancient Greek Religion*, edited by Esther Eidinow, Julia Kindt and Robin Osborne, 317–338. Cambridge: Cambridge University Press.

Boys-Stones, George. 2017. *Platonist Philosophy 80 BC to 250 AD: The Greek and Latin Texts*. Cambridge: Cambridge University Press.

D'Hoine, Pieter, and Gerd van Riel, eds. 2014. *Fate, Providence and Moral Responsibility in Ancient, Medieval and Early Modern Thought*. Leuven: Leuven University Press.

Destrée, Pierre, Ricardo Salles and Marco Zingano, eds. 2014. *What is Up to Us? Studies on Agency and Responsibility in Ancient Philosophy*. Sankt Augustin: Academia.

De Caro, Mario, Massimo Mori and Emidio Spinelli, eds. 2014. *Libero arbitrio. Storia di una controversia filosofica*. Rome: Carocci.

Dillon, John. 1996. *The Middle Platonists. A Study of Platonism 80 B.C. to A.D. 220* [1977], 2nd edn. London: Duckworth.

DK: Diels, Hermann, and Walther Kranz, eds. 1952. *Die Fragmente der Vorsokratiker*, 6th edn. Berlin: Weidmann.

Dorandi, Tiziano, ed. 2013. *Diogenes Laertius. Lives of Eminent Philosophers*. Cambridge: Cambridge University Press.

Engberg-Pedersen, Troels, ed. 2017. *From Stoicism to Platonism. The Development of Philosophy 100 BCE–100 CE*. Cambridge: Cambridge University Press.

Frede, Michael. 2011. *A Free Will. Origins of the Notion in Ancient Thought*, edited by Anthony A. Long. Berkeley: University of California Press.

Greenblatt, Stephen. 2011. *The Swerve. How the World Became Modern*. New York: Norton.

Keil, Geert. 2017. *Willensfreiheit* [2007]. 3rd edn. Berlin: De Gruyter.

Lloyd, Geneviève. 2008. *Providence Lost*. Cambridge (Mass.): Harvard University Press.

LM: Laks, André, and Glenn W. Most. 2016. *Early Greek Philosophy*. Cambridge (Mass.): Harvard University Press.

LS: Long, Anthony. A., and David N. Sedley. 1987. *The Hellenistic Philosophers*. Cambridge: Cambridge University Press.

Magris, Aldo. 2016. *Destino, provvidenza, predestinazione. Dal mondo antico al cristianesimo* [2008]. 2nd edn. Brescia: Morcelliana.

Masi, Francesca G., and Stefano Maso, eds. 2013. *Fate, Chance, and Fortune in Ancient Thought*. Amsterdam: Hakkert.

Mayhew, Robert, tr. 2008. *Plato. Laws 10*. Oxford: Clarendon.

Meredith, Anthony. 1999. *Gregory of Nyssa*. London: Duckworth.

Motta, Beatrice. 2008. *Il* Contra fatum *di Gregorio di Nyssa nel dibattito tardo-antica sul fatalismo e sul determinismo*. Pisa: Fabrizio Serra.

Natali, Carlo, and Stefano Maso, eds. 2005. *La catena delle cause. Determinismo e antideterminismo nel pensiero antico e contemporaneo*. Amsterdam: Hakkert.

Sauvé-Meyer, Susan. 2009. "Chain of Causes." In *God and Cosmos in Stoicism*, edited by Ricardo Salles, 71–89. Oxford: Oxford University Press.

Sharples, Robert W., tr. 1983. *Alexander of Aphrodisias. On Fate*. London: Duckworth.

Sharples, Robert W., tr. 1991. *Cicero: On Fate (De fato) & Boethius: The Consolation of Philosophy (Philosophiae consolationis) IV.5–7, V*. Warminster: Aris and Phillips.

Sharples, Robert W. 2010. *Peripatetic Philosophy 200 BC to AD 200. An Introduction and Collection of Sources in Translation*. Cambridge: Cambridge University Press.

Smith, Martin F., ed., tr. 1993. *Diogenes of Oinoanda. The Epicurean Inscription*. Naples: Bibliopolis.

Verdenius, Willem J. 1960. "Traditional and Personal Elements in Aristotle's Religion." *Phronesis* 5: 56–70.

Vimercati, Emmanuele, ed. 2015. *Medioplatonici. Opere, frammenti, testimonianze*. Milan: Bompiani.

Vimercati, Emmanuele. 2018. "Cicéron et les atomistes." In *Les présocratiques à Rome*, edited by Sylvie Franchet d'Espérey and Carlos Lévy, 57–84. Paris: PUPS.

Williams, Bernard. 1993. *Shame and Necessity*. Berkeley: University of California Press.

CHAPTER 1

Fate, Providence, and Free Will: Why Bother?

John Rist

As ever, the studies in the present collection are built on earlier academic labours. I think particularly of *Greek and Roman Philosophy* 100 B.C.–200 A.D. edited by Richard Sorabji and Robert Sharples and *What is up to us?* edited by Pierre Destrée, Ricardo Salles and Marco Zingano. In this first chapter I shall appropriate these and other recent writings without much apology, since I have interpreted my task as not primarily to engage in the exposition of particular texts, whether Platonic, Aristotelian, Stoic, Epicurean or early Christian – though I can hardly avoid a little such exposition – but rather to try to identify common ground between the varying schools, even when they seem a long way apart. That might point us beyond merely dialectical – even eristic – considerations towards something more permanent – indeed still philosophically interesting – below and behind the sweeping claims which various thinkers advanced in the gladiatorial atmosphere in which much ancient philosophy was fought out.

Above all I want to ask a "meta-question": why bother about these ancient debates at all? Have we not put all that behind us? In order to respond to that challenge, I will raise three more specific questions. The first is whether it still matters what the ancients have to say about what we are tempted to call a free will; the second is what we are to make of the ethical usefulness of the belief that there is some sort of divine activity in the world which, according to our theistic preferences, we may call fate or providence; the third is whether contemporary analysis of freedom, moral obligation, and responsibility is always helpful – rather than often confusing – in approaching what went on in the ancient world. But the overriding challenge remains: does the study of what the ancients thought about fate, providence or free will have any lasting philosophical value, or does it reveal that those who busy themselves with it are engaged in cultural archaeology at best and at worst in some higher form of data-accumulation of less importance than asking how many lies a politician uttered in a recent speech but more important than discovering how many camels there are in Saudi Arabia.

I shall tackle these questions in turn, starting with general comment on what we, *as contemporaries*, have in mind when we think about free will, before trying to see whether philosophers in the Hellenistic and Imperial Ro-

 | DOI:10.1163/9789004436381_003

man eras were starting from more or less similar assumptions. In raising that methodological problem, I note that Richard Sorabji believes that much ancient discussion, especially of philosophical psychology, was a good deal more sophisticated than what we often meet with among our contemporaries.[1] If he is right – even in some cases – we ought to ask why we are doing less well than the ancients, and particularly whether it has anything to do with the fact that we have, over the centuries, got ourselves into the position of asking the wrong questions, indeed perhaps at times even empty questions: questions, that is, to which there is no possibly useful answer agreeable or even available.[2] Perhaps it is as though we are often unwittingly debating how to square the circle. But any attempt to resolve so genuine and fundamental a puzzle is beyond my immediate remit.

1 Freedom

First then a few facts about contemporary discussions, not least about terminology. The title of this collection points to freedom, but we cannot assume that what we (as contemporary philosophers) think about the obvious or more natural understanding of that concept would command anything like universal acceptance in antiquity. Hence it will be useful to start with a few comments about ancient and modern uses of "free", since in many earlier discussions of freedom in antiquity such clarification would have been helpful.

In most modern debates about the freedom of the "will" – whatever that is, a question to which I will return, however briefly – the reader does not have to wait long before hearing about the Principle of Alternative Possibilities (or PAP). That principle explains that for an action to be called 'free' the agent has to be able, when performing it, to have the genuine option of doing something different, perhaps even the opposite of what he actually chooses to do. But for many ancient thinkers, this would seem a very odd way to understand the word "free". Many of them, from Plato to Plotinus and Augustine, would say that a free act is an act targeted on the good; the free and virtuous agent would not wish even to dream of doing the opposite.

This position is well reflected in the language Augustine uses to describe the state of the saints in heaven. They are subject to *desideranda necessitas* (*Unfinished Work* 5.61): that means – and it was not until the fourteenth century

1 See his extended comments in Sorabji 2000, 1–7.

2 See Rist 2014, 1–2 and *passim*.

that any Christian would have denied it; but then Duns Scotus did[3] – that it would not occur to them as desirable even to be capable of choosing any alternative possibility than the morally and spiritually best available. Not much choice-theory there – the Good still trumps the Chosen or Preferred – and to see why Augustine (and for that matter Plato and many other ancients) would want to say something like that, consider the following: I am in possession of the ring of Gyges; I know that I can commit crimes as I choose with no fear of punishment – assuming, of course, that there is no God to wield the big stick, as the vast majority of ancients would consider unlikely.

God being absent, or if present able to be suborned (cf. Plato, *Laws* 10.885b), suppose I decline the suggestion that I would have no problem with holding up a bank if I possessed the ring of Gyges. I laugh it off, but my interlocutor persists until I say: "Look, I am just not that kind of person; I just could not bring myself to do that." And let us look at that "could not". I don't decline to hold up the bank because I have insufficient physical strength to pull the trigger of my Saturday-night special; the "could not" is a moral "could not". I don't even debate, consider the alternative possibilities and then finally come down in favour of refusing to rob the bank; I just refuse to rob. And there is a way of universalizing this non-necessity of agonizing over some kinds – hopefully eventually as many as possible – of moral choices. If God is good, he does not weigh up whether to spread malaria; he just doesn't spread malaria. My action, then – and the attitude I have attributed to God – points to the normal pre-modern way of talking about what we call freedom of the will. For most ancients (and medievals) to be free is to be able to pursue only the right course, by the right means, for a good end; "to be freed" (*liberatus*) from unruly desires which get in the way of doing the right thing in pursuit of that good end.

Before proceeding further, it is worth giving somewhat more consideration to the linguistic problems which regularly arise in discussions of ancient debates about freedom and related themes, the problematic words – not all of which I shall inspect now – including *boulēsis, prohairesis, voluntas, eleutheria, autexousios*. I have little original to say about them, but sometimes what is well known is forgotten and a brief reminder will do no harm. Let me start with *boulēsis*. It may at times be translated as "wish", but something more like "rational will" is often more helpful, not least because *boulēsis* sometimes seems to do the work of more obvious words for that "will" which is absent in Plato and Aristotle.

---

3 Cf. Rist 2014, 144.

One of the earliest and most helpful passages about *boulēsis* is to be found in Plato's *Gorgias* (466a9ff.) where the translation "rational willing" is appropriate: that is, for a wanting which is not merely a desire but a desire for an intelligible good. But we must also remember that for Plato (even if not in the *Gorgias*, at least soon after) desires and willings are always somehow related not only to goods but to goods that we *love* – since it becomes a Platonic axiom that we cannot know a genuine good without loving it and we cannot love it without knowing it. And by analogy the same applies to improper but still longed-for "goods". We think we know them (because we believe something about them) and we assume we love them – though we would be better described as lusting after them, as one might lust after power or someone's body (while not bothering about the soul, unless perhaps it is important and exciting to corrupt that first, or as well). So, when we think about what Plato, at least after the *Symposium*, would mean by *boulēsis* – rational willing – we need to recognize that rational willing must somehow be understood in terms of loving. To go further on that, however, is a story for another day; all we need recognize now is that it is radically unplatonic (even if implied by some latter-day Platonists) to separate "willing" from loving, that is, from some form of *eros*.

So far so comparatively straightforward, but when we move to *prohairesis* more substantial difficulties begin, though recent writing by Michael Frede and others has pointed us in the right direction.[4] In Aristotle, the sense of *prohairesis* is clear; the word refers to the choice of means best suited to secure the varying ends identified by whatever moral vision we possess (*Nicomachean Ethics* 3.5, 1114b7): that is, to our disposition, itself the product of previous choices made as a result of training, education, and more generally experience, which normally but not necessarily determine what we do. But in the Imperial Roman age, things change and in Epictetus in particular there is a degree of uncertainty as to how the word *prohairesis* is best translated. Some of us believe that we can get help from *voluntas* which seems the roughly parallel word in Latin, especially as *voluntas* is used by Epictetus' fellow Stoic Seneca.

But there is also the possibility that though the two words come close together, their semantic fields are not identical but merely overlapping. Hence some think that the best Greek equivalent for *voluntas* would not be *prohairesis* but our old friend *boulēsis*, which (in a Stoic context where anything like a Platonic "passionate" *eros* is to be rigorously excluded) might tempt us to translate it simply as "will." I leave Seneca aside, however, having only introduced him as a possible assistant in interpreting Epictetus.

4 Frede 2014, 360–363.

Frede translated *prohairesis* in Epictetus (in my view more or less rightly) as the "*disposition* to choose",[5] emphasizing the disposition rather than the resulting occurrent willing, and thus raising the problem of whether we form our own dispositions or whether they are the result of causes outside our control. Here, however, we again run into problems about "free", for a "free *prohairesis*" (on which Epictetus insists – as at *Dissertations* 3.5.7) could either point to a disposition from which could only emerge choices of what is good and right – which, in my view, is what Epictetus wants to say – or to a state of mind whereby we can choose whatever we like, in the spirit of our own Principle of Alternative Possibilities: in that modern sense we would only be free if we could choose not only what is right but rather what is either right or wrong; that immediate decision, that is, would be up to us. Of course, Epictetus might interject, our decision would depend on whether we are sages or not: for the sage would only choose the right, while the ordinary bloke, even if he "meant well", could make serious mistakes, whether or not out of mere malice (in the ordinary sense of that word).

Frede seems at least unclear about how he wants to resolve the problem. On the one hand he says that for Epictetus, "to become free we have to change our way of thinking about things by scrutinizing our thoughts"; as we shall see, that might require outside assistance, especially if our disposition is more or less fixed by our past experiences. On the other hand, also according to Frede, Epictetus, in wanting our disposition to be "free" (*eleuthera*), seems at least "very close to the idea of a free *will*": but to what sense of "free" is Frede *now* referring? If he means in the normal 'ancient' sense, he would seem to be right; if by "free" he refers to the Principle of Alternative Possibilities, then surely that cannot be what Epictetus (or any other Stoic) could intend.

Nevertheless, the association of "free" with *prohairesis* is important, whether or not we translate that term as disposition or limit ourselves to the effect of our disposition as revealed by willed choices. And, as Frede observes, very similar language appears in early Christian texts (Justin, *Apology* 1.43 and Tatian, *Against the Greeks* 7.1: ἐλευθερία τῆς προαιρέσεως). These writers want our *prohairesis* to be free because our choices are to be subject to God's just judgments. A free *prohairesis* – perhaps it matters little in these contexts whether we are talking about the disposition or the choices that result from it – must indicate that we can (or somehow should have been able to) choose the right and reject the wrong. That claim is more disturbing than anything Epictetus needs, for in Christian writers the risks entailed by responsibility are greater: we may be saved or damned.

5 Frede 2014, 360.

Justin and Tatian would to some extent agree with Epictetus; it is up to us, they would say, to attend to Christian preachers. But is it? That would depend on how they understand the necessity of a grace that we need to help us along the road to proper choices and in general to a righteous disposition. And when we come to Origen (whom Frede notes uses similar language – *eleuthera prohairesis* in *On Principles* 3.1), the problem is greater, since Origen is aware not merely of the problems of providence (how God arranges all things, including our dispositions and choices, for the best), but also of predestination: God not only knows how we shall behave, but *decides* somehow in advance of all our behaviours whose heart will be hardened (or left hardened), and thus who will not be saved, and to whom he will give the opportunity to mend his own ways. For present purposes, however, I leave predestination aside.

That said, we notice that Christians who talk about a free *prohairesis* have this in common with Stoics like Epictetus: we may be in moral trouble, but help is at hand, either from the availability of Stoic teachers, or for Christians from the helping grace of a providential and philanthropic divinity. But the latter option may be rejected, as by Plotinus, as a mere excuse for moral laziness (*Enneads* 3.2.8.43 ff.). Does that mean that, for at least some Platonists, there is no obvious recourse for us miserable humans who have "forgotten their father"? How can such forgetfulness be overcome?

For Plotinus a specific remedy is at hand, and that not simply in the form of a suggestion that you listen to what we teach you. For we have not entirely fallen: something of our soul, in Plotinus' language, has remained above (*Enneads* 2.9.2, 4.3.12, 4.8.8, 5.1.10). We are not entirely corrupt; indeed, we retain the moral strength to hang on to our better selves and hence learn from teachers, this time Platonists, how to identify our "empirical" selves with our real 'self' above: we can learn to pull ourselves up by our own bootstraps. According to a thesis which may seem something of a precursor of the Kantian will – that noumenal self which remains free of the chain of the mechanistic and determined physical universe – we can live at a higher and non-choice-ridden level; we are free in that our higher self has no time for Alternative Possibilities, but will always seek, indeed know, the good and the good alone.

Perhaps I should add (as I have argued elsewhere)[6] that this confidence about the moral strength of our unfallen self – genuinely Platonic in spirit though it appears to be – lapsed almost entirely after Plotinus. Porphyry characteristically sat on the fence; Iamblichus and his successors had recourse precisely to that help from the gods – obtainable by theurgy – which Plotinus had

6 Rist 1992.

damned as moral laziness. And in any case, Plotinus' "way out" only works, if, as a pure Platonist must hold, you are to be identified as your soul alone: which Christians of course could not accept (though they often tried – and try – to do so).

2 Moral Obligation

After freedom let us turn to a second (related) dogma of much contemporary moral philosophy, the origin of which, in its strictest form, goes back especially to Kant. According to Kant, "ought" implies "can." That implies that there is no point in prescribing a moral rule which I simply cannot obey. Despite its wide contemporary acceptance, however, the Kantian dogma is rather strange. Suppose you are trying to break a habit; the case of smoking is particularly revealing. If you think self-harm is morally wrong, you would not smoke, but many admit that it is – and that smoking enormously increases the risk of serious illness – but they go on smoking. "Ought" for them does not imply 'can', though it may imply a second-order desire: I want to want to give up smoking.[7] Augustine's "Give me chastity, but not yet", is a good ancient parallel. And the problem cannot simply be dismissed by saying that smoking is an "addiction"; for so are other vices, such as gambling and watching pornography; and both Plato and Aristotle had indicated the problem of 'acratic' behaviour more generally.

In antiquity, most pagan philosophers think not that "ought" implies "can", but that for most of us "ought" *ought* to imply "can." But why are they entitled even to that much of the Kantian claim? Only presumably because they are optimistic about human nature, though that optimism is not normally buttressed on metaphysical claims about the possession of a Plotinian "soul above" (or a Kantian noumenal self). For although the Stoics insist that the wise man will always do what he ought, they admit that he is as rare as the phoenix. For most of us "ought" does not imply "can" (or at least "can yet"); most of us are moral failures. But according to Plotinus, as we have seen – and in this he is in some sense typical of his pagan philosophical predecessors – our failure is a mark not of inevitable moral weakness, but of moral laziness. And that insistence on our moral capacity – whether or not backed by some sort of metaphysical explanation – points to a substantial disagreement in antiquity between pagans and Christians (and probably members of some other religious groups as

7 Frankfurt 1971.

well, though that is beyond my comparative expertise). Nevertheless, it is interesting – and demands explanation – that Plotinus is the last pagan Platonist to uphold the older more "humanistic" view.

3 Responsibility: Aristotle

The principal problem for those of us who after reflection on the human condition deny that "ought" always implies "can" but also deny that there is anything unreasonable in giving moral instruction about what I should do when I cannot (at least as a rule) do it, is that where "ought" does not imply "can", I may be held responsible (but by whom? – that is important) for failing to do what I cannot do.

Let us approach this difficulty obliquely. It is a serious problem for moralistic accounts of "ought" that philosophers find it easier to formulate rules of correct behaviour than to explain why it seems impossible consistently to obey them. Thus, utilitarians think we should pursue the greatest good of the greatest number, whether in all our acts or in certain kinds of acts, but they are not, in practice, stupid enough as to suppose that anyone can consistently follow such a demanding (and logically confused) rule in their own lives. There is, it seems, a curiously unrealistic, indeed unworldly, strain in much moral philosophy. As C.O.A. Coady noted, "I, for one, would no more think of consulting your average moral philosopher over a genuine moral problem than of consulting a philosopher of perception about an eye complaint."[8]

After freedom and obligation, then, we have passed to responsibility, for, as already noted, it seems odd to suppose that we should be held responsible for what we cannot decline – though in practice criminal justice systems are often built on that premise. Indeed, despite being told not to judge, we regularly judge and condemn, sometimes erroneously, since we believe that society could not survive unless we take that kind of risk. The problem gets worse as the cases become more complex or more ideologically tainted; not least because defence lawyers regularly try to confuse the jury by what often amounts to more or less blatant deception and omission in their presentation of the evidence. I pass over the practice of jury selection in some jurisdictions which has become a device to ensure that as few jurors as possible can understand the complexities of the case, being thus the more readily bamboozled.

8 Cited by Gregory 2012, 220. For extended discussion of the reductionist unreality of much contemporary moral philosophy see Chappell 2014.

In ancient accounts who is to be counted responsible? The problem was first formally set up by Aristotle, whose criteria are very strict. We are to be held responsible for our acts unless we are the victims of unavoidable ignorance or overwhelming external pressure (*Nicomachean Ethics* 3.1, 1110a1). Thus, drunkenness would be no excuse – and presumably not even torture – though being drugged against one's will would relieve one of responsibility – for there are some things which no one should knowingly do under any circumstances: such as murder one's mother (*Nicomachean Ethics* 3.1, 1110a29).

It is often claimed, however, that Aristotle's account is impossibly strict because it limits itself to external pressures. Why does he not say anything about internal constraints, such as predetermined psychological conditions over which we have no control? Indeed, such conditions might include being in such a state that all one's decisions are the result of preceding chains of causes; that might seem to make a particular decision unavoidable, whether it can be said to derive "from me" or not. But Aristotle does have answers to such questions.

We get near the problem when we ask whether certain actions should be treated as our responsibility in all circumstances, provided, that is, that they arise from us, that is, from our decision. That could look like a hard determinism which cannot be attributed to Aristotle since he is not a hard determinist about future contingent events (*On Interpretation* 9, 19a30 ff.). Objectively, he seems to claim, the possibility of acting in one way or another – but be careful about the weasel-word "possibility" (theoretical or actual?) – is always available with regard to future acts. We shall do what we shall do, that is, but we shall not do what we shall do under compelling necessity. A somewhat similar attitude can be detected in Stoic claims as well. Of course, though this is not hard determinism, it is not indeterminism either.

4 Responsibility: the Stoics

Turning then to the Stoics, we note that they differ from earlier thinkers in one very important respect; they introduce the notion of assent, absent in both Plato and Aristotle, and assent might seem to involve positing what we call the "will", however that is to be explained. And the late second-century Aristotelian Alexander of Aphrodisias seems to have been so impressed by assent as willed that he thought that Aristotle too must have assumed it – and therefore presented his master with a theory somewhat similar to that of the Stoics.

Philosophically, however, assent – even when not coupled with ideas about a "will" – has its own problems, and we may wonder whether that is why many of the ancients ignored it. And historically the introduction of a *faculty* of the "will" – bolstered by the attribution of such an idea to Augustine – made things worse, perverting much subsequent discussion of human persons, as of moral action, throughout the medieval period and beyond.[9] For the following difficulty arises: Is it I who decide to perform some action or – to put it a bit crudely – is it my will? Or as Hume understood the problem, is the mind some sort of theatre in which competing faculties, primarily the intellect and the will, somehow battle for supremacy?

Much of the difficulty, I think, is caused by reifying the concept of "will" (*voluntas*/*prohairesis*); such terms should better be taken to apply to the state of the agent which then reveals itself in the occurrent actions he or she undertakes. But where did the mistake, if that is what it is, begin? Must it be laid at the door of *any* of the ancients. Perhaps Epictetus is the guilty party (or for some the "worthy" party); see *Dissertations* 3.5.7 on *eleuthera prohairesis*. But no, in light of what seemed a correct reading of his *prohairesis*, he is not!

I have already touched on the idea that "ought" need not entail "can", as well as on essential features of early Christian theology which already depend on denying even the "modified" version of the "Kantian" axiom prevalent among most of the pagans. But complications in seeing the problem in terms of assent lie beneath the ancient surface. The Stoics distinguish between a *pathos* and a *propatheia*. A *pathos*, in the official definition, is an impulse which has got out of control; a *propatheia* is a natural, strictly instinctive reaction which, so long as it is not assented to, is outside the moral domain and for which – so the claim runs – we are therefore not to be held responsible. For if we were, "ought" would not imply "can" in a much stronger sense.

Examples: even recalling the army of Hannibal approaching the walls of Rome is enough to produce an involuntary shudder (Seneca, *On Anger* 2.2.5 ff).[10] But – and here we see where the notion of assent *might* sometimes do useful philosophical work – if the shudderer does not assent to the proposition that death is to be feared and at all costs avoided, he is morally kosher. That might seem to settle problems about pain (broadly understood), pain being one of the standard enemies of the good life in the ancient world; but there is also pleasure, and there are similar possibly non-moral reactions possible here too. An unusually interesting one appears in the early Christian text known as the *Shepherd of Hermas*, at 1: the writer sees a lady bathing naked in the Tiber and reacts with: "Lucky the man who is married to her!" From the reference

9 Rist 2014, *passim*.

10 Graver 2007, 85–108.

to marriage, that sounds a more Christian and generally more moral reaction than: "I wouldn't mind going through her on a Saturday night", but ancient Cynics (capital C) ask whether the instinctual desire really is morally-neutral, while later Christians might see it as an effect of Original Sin. If they are right, then '"ought" implies "can"' looks to be in even worse philosophical straights.

According to the Cynics, to experience a *propatheia* indicates an (unexplained) failure at a deeper level to be morally good. Perhaps complete insensibility is the answer: only that can relieve one of moral responsibility. Unsurprisingly, that has appealed to many ascetics in many traditions. The Christians, for their part, relying on traditions both biblical and Hellenic, developed a more psychologically plausible, if to many moderns a no more edifying – though challenging – alternative: a theory of Original Sin which reminds us that living up not merely to Kantianism but to most (if not all) moral schemes offered by philosophers – implies either that we need divine assistance or that we are superhuman. But to go for the superhuman option might raise questions about transcending good and evil which (incoherent Gnostic fantasies apart) hardly surface in antiquity and which although of great interest, I shall leave aside.[11]

Let us then return to the possible *merits* of Stoic assent, and to the classic example: a soldier sees Hannibal's army approaching; that is, he receives an impression, and that impression comes with a proposition which will govern the morality of his subsequent behaviour. For with the *phantasia* comes the suggestion – after the initial non-moral shudder – that death is to be feared. The sage should not even *dream* of assenting to that, the vicious man may well do so – and perhaps desert his post, thus showing himself as unfree and cowardly.

This is an interesting example even if we discount the Stoic story of how we come to be presented with the fateful proposition. For since virtually none of us are likely to become sages, we may have to *decide* what to do; for our disposition is inadequately stable, liable, as the Stoics would put it, to give weak assents. In fact, even Stoics could plausibly recognize wider possibilities, where the sage too may be unable to rely immediately on his disposition in a novel situation but will still attempt – and succeed – to take the right decision. The Stoics can explain this in terms of their two kinds of cause: the original cause, in this case our disposition which will give us general answers, and the triggering cause which invites our character to respond characteristically, in our immediate case to the phantasm of the approach of Hannibal's army. For a

11 But see my comments on Plato's Thrasymachus in Rist 2002, 10–23.

new circumstance might offer even the sage a genuine dilemma; he has never seen anything quite like this, so he may have to take an explicit decision, that is, to articulate to himself some kind of assent. We might add, however, that the Stoics err if they suppose (like some existentialists) that *all* moral action, at least by non-sages, depends on explicit rather than implicit decisions – based on past experience – of this kind.

Such comment on the usefulness but not the general usefulness of the Stoic notion of assent may more generally indicate that too many of the ancient debates about freedom and determinism (as elsewhere, but moderns often hardly do better) turn on the recognition of an unnoticed fact, helpful in more fully explaining human decision-making, but also on an exaggeration of its importance. For although even sages may sometimes need explicit assent, that is no general situation and cannot be universalized by anyone – such as Aristotle as well as the Stoics themselves – who holds that the better we become, the less agonizing decision-making we shall experience, and that when we are perfect (if that is possible) all our decisions will be not only be fated and predictable (at least by God), but also "instinctively" right.

But as we have seen, the introduction of an *exaggerated* concept of assent might encourage the development of another undesirable philosophical consequence: the notion of a reified will, as distinct from willing being seen as the expression of an underlying disposition: in the Platonic traditions a disposition determined by our loves – and hates. Happily, some of us (Bernard Williams and Michael Frede among others) are beginning to see that the whole thing was a terrible mistake. Plato and Aristotle were right to have no truck – or perhaps even to imagine truck – with anything like our still fashionable talk of a will or a faculty of the will or (*a fortiori*) of a free *will*: a will, that is, as distinct from a mere capacity, whether rational or irrational, to be stubborn in our characteristic moral habits or habitual delusions.

None of this implies that we should give up the idea of personal responsibility and neither Plato, nor Aristotle nor the Stoics supposed we should do so. I have already indicated one way in which responsibility can be approached – as indeed it had been by philosophers from Plato via Aristotle and the Stoics to Plotinus. We can be counted as free (or at least undetermined) so long as we are willing and able to listen to someone who purports to teach us – though inexplicably, as it might seem, many of us are not! Be that as it may, man is an interrelating and dialoguing animal – from birth and even before. Hence it is not hard to see why Plato and Aristotle in particular were so hostile to sophists; for sophists abuse the only method we have of making ourselves better and becoming capable of being responsible for our actions. For to reject sophistry – that is, the poisoning of the wells of intelligent discourse – is essential if we are to avoid getting ourselves into a position where – if only to provide social glue – we think we must hold people responsible who are not really responsible at all: that is, of treating them as "virtually" responsible. But perhaps Plato and Aristotle (and many other ancients) were too ready to believe that sophistry could so easily be defeated: they might be less cavalier in our age of propaganda and fake news.

I am not, then, claiming (as does Galen Strawson[12]) that responsibility is a delusion – still less that any ancient philosophers would have thought it so – nor that we should, as philosophers, encourage people to think that they have a free will (and are therefore responsible for their actions) when in fact they have no such thing (as does Smilansky).[13] Rather I am trying to focus on how in their varying ways a number of ancient thinkers tried to face the problem of how we can escape from what they might call necessity: the threat, that is, that we are ruled entirely by the dispositions we inevitably acquire. And as we follow these debates, we should look back to the question whether and what we can learn from the ancients: that is, before we had made so many mistakes that we find it difficult to know where it might be profitable to begin to think about philosophical psychology, hence ethics.

Were what I have argued about common ancient accounts of our dispositions, their authority, and how they can be improved, correct, then whatever the strength (or more likely weakness) of the apparent libertarianism and resort to something like a Principle of Alternative Possibilities introduced by Alexander of Aphrodisias as an "obvious" necessity for Aristotle, or the attempts of a number of Platonists (such as Plutarch)[14] to claim that the power of fate is merely limited, then any such desperate measures would be unnecessary. What we would need, however, would be the ability to keep our minds open enough to allow ourselves to learn from some sort of teacher, whoever – divine or human – we judge to be adequate. A striking example of such necessary open-mindedness might be recognized in the decision of Plotinus, recorded by Porphyry, to link his philosophical fortunes to those of an obscure Ammonius, a man apparently very different from the standard professional Platonists of his day (*Life of Plotinus* 3). Indeed, he even joined the Emperor Gordian's expedition eastwards in the hope of learning something from the more remote thinkers of those parts: whether as a member of the retinue of the Emperor or, as Hilary Armstrong once suggested, as a bartender

12 Strawson 1994.

13 Smilansky 2002.

14 Cf. Boys-Stones 2007.

supplying the more material wants of the Roman troops. But that might be mere desperation rather than any possibly mistaken optimism.

5 Fate and Providence

We can finally turn to our fourth (but still related) theme: fate and providence; if you are a Stoic there is little difference. In ancient philosophy, we can divide thinkers and schools in different ways, but one of the more interesting is between providentialists and non-providentialists. Among the former are the Platonists and the Stoics, among the latter Aristotle (despite his later Neoplatonic and medieval remake) and the Epicureans. The Platonists tend to follow Plato's law in *Republic* 10.617e, where in the myth of Er we read that we choose our own destiny, that virtue has no master and that god is not responsible. That certainly looks like a claim that our actions, though worked out in a providentialist universe, are not *determined* by god. If so, it might bring Plato and Platonists closer to Stoics than is often supposed, since in Stoicism the aim, as Cicero puts it, at *On Fate* 41, is 'to escape necessity and retain fate'. For I argued long ago[15] – and am still inclined to believe – that what the Stoics in general (and Chrysippus in particular) want to emphasize when they talk about "fate" (εἱμαρμένη, *fatum*) is that whatever is going to happen is going to happen. That is a god's eye comment, and does not imply determinism, though it need not rule it out. Chrysippus, in this like Plato, wants to retain providence but to allow a certain apparently choice-based "freedom" for the individual – at least for the bad individual – to decide, however fruitlessly, what he does.

For we should recall what we identified as the normal (but not universal) sense of "freedom" – and related words – in antiquity; "political" *libertas* (as of the Roman people) aside,[16] freedom is only to be able to do the right thing for a good end. The freer you are, the less choice you have. Hence the Stoic sage (who succeeds in living in accordance with the divine "fragment" (ἀπόσπασμα) that he is) will be free to do what providence requires of him, while the worse we are, the more we are compelled, the more we are dragged – despite external appearances – behind the cart of fate (*SVF* 2.975; cf. Seneca, *Letters to Lucilius* 107.11). Either we freely choose – that is allow ourselves to follow providence and become virtuous – or we *choose* (Principle of Alternative Possibilities) not to be free (in the proper sense of "free"); then we appear unfree.

15 Rist 1969, 127, 132.

16 For Roman political *libertas* see especially Syme 1939, 154–156.

There are few sages but, as we have seen, that does not imply the rest of us miserable specimens are condemned never to get better, that is, determined to get worse – more enslaved – or at least to remain worse? That is not the Stoic view – nor for that matter that of Platonists and Aristotelians – because (for Stoics) although acts "preferred" (προηγμένα) are not virtuous and the non-sage is still technically a fool and a slave, he can reform, if he goes to the Stoic school. Hence the only real benefit a good Stoic can confer on anyone else is to teach him Stoicism, for since we have something divine about us, we are able to take in the right thoughts and ultimately the right dispositions. Long ago I argued that Plotinus too, as a Platonist, thought that the only really worthwhile thing a wise man can do for his fellows is to teach them *Platonic* philosophy[17] – so that they relearn who they really are, by learning, as Plotinus puts it (*Enneads* 5.1), who is their metaphysical father – as has been well explained by Gerson.[18] So, both Stoics and some Platonists think we cannot improve ourselves; we need a teacher or perhaps at the political level an enforcer; we may be bound to what we have made of ourselves, but we are not bound beyond providential liberation.

Neither fate nor providence is problematic for the Aristotelians and Epicureans, so I can leave them aside. Of course, it is not that they have nothing to say about either of them; they can use them as a stick with which to beat philosophical opponents. While for Stoics and Platonists providence has to be defended, for the others it can only be ignored or mocked as a delusion.

For the Stoics providence is the name for what a philanthropic and immanent deity (of whom we are each an operative part) knows what will be and knows that it will be for the best. God's providential foreknowledge is no barrier to human responsibility and need not be viewed as predetermining events. But when we come to the Christians – as we have already noted with Origen – the problems become more serious if we move from foreknowledge to predestination: that is, to God's plan, not merely about the benefits to be obtained from recognizing that we are members of his orderly universe, but about how his grace – necessary for free action – is bestowed, and to whom, and whether in a manner intelligible to us. Happily, as noted above, that is beyond my present remit; in any case it turns on problems about God's omnipotence – and is therefore beyond the bounds of pagan philosophy altogether – rather than human capacities. What is not beyond my remit, however, is whether we can learn anything still philosophically valuable from the thinkers and themes

17 Rist 1967, 163; cf. *Enneads* 6.9.7.22.

18 Gerson 2014, 262–263.

we have just glanced at. I hope I have shown that on freedom, human capacities, responsibility and providence we certainly can, hence that we should ignore the siren voices that often urge us to debase much challenging ancient thinking by treating it as a primitive version of what "we" now better comprehend.

Bibliography

Boys-Stones, George. 2007. "Middle Platonism on Fate and Human Autonomy." In *Greek and Roman Philosophy 100 B.C.–200 A.D.*, edited by Robert W. Sharples and Richard Sorabji, 431–447. London: Institute of Classical Studies.

Chappell, Timothy. 2014. *Knowing What to Do: Imagination, Virtue and Platonism in Ethics*. Oxford: Oxford University Press.

Destrée, Pierre, Ricardo Salles and Marco Zingano, eds. 2014. *What is Up to Us? Studies on Agency and Responsibility in Ancient Philosophy*. Sankt Augustin: Academia.

Frankfurt, Harry G. 1971. "Freedom of the Will and the Concept of the Person." *Journal of Philosophy* 68: 5–20.

Frede, Michael. 2014. "The eph' hemin in Ancient Philosophy." In *What is Up to Us? Studies on Agency and Responsibility in Ancient Philosophy*, edited by Pierre Destrée, Ricardo Salles and Marco Zingano, 351–363. Sankt Augustin: Academia.

Gerson, Lloyd P. 2014. "Moral Responsibility and What is Up to Us in Plotinus." In *What is Up to Us? Studies on Agency and Responsibility in Ancient Philosophy*, edited by Pierre Destrée, Ricardo Salles and Marco Zingano, 251–264. Sankt Augustin: Academia.

Graver, Margaret. 2007. *Stoicism and Emotion*. Chicago: Chicago University Press.

Rist, John M. 1967. *Plotinus: The Road to Reality*. Cambridge: Cambridge University Press.

Rist, John M. 1992. "Pseudo-Dionysius, Neoplatonism and the Weakness of the Soul." In *From Athens to Chartres: Neoplatonism and Medieval Thought. Studies in Honour of Edouard Jeauneau*, edited by Haijo J. Westra, 135–161. Leiden: Brill. Reprinted in his 1996 *Man, Soul and Body: Essays in Ancient Thought from Plato to Dionysius*. Aldershot: Variorum.

Rist, John M. 2002. *Real Ethics: Rethinking the Foundations of Morality*. Cambridge: Cambridge University Press.

Rist, John M. 2014. *Augustine Deformed: Love, Sin and Freedom in the Western Moral Tradition*. Cambridge: Cambridge University Press.

Sharples, Robert W., and Richard Sorabji, ed. 2007. *Essays in Greek and Roman Philosophy 100 B.C.–200 A.D.* London: Institute of Classical Studies.

Smilansky, Saul. 2002. "Free Will, Fundamental Dualism and the Centrality of Illusion." In *The Oxford Handbook of Free Will*, edited by Robert Kane, 489–505. Oxford: Oxford University Press.

Sorabji, Richard. 2000. *Emotion and Peace of Mind: From Stoic Agitation to Christian Temptation*. Oxford: Oxford University Press.

Strawson, Galen. 1994. "The Impossibility of Moral Responsibility." *Philosophical Studies* 75: 5–24.

Syme, Ronald. 1939. *The Roman Revolution*. Oxford: Oxford University Press.

CHAPTER 2

Divine and Human Will in Imperial Stoicism

René Brouwer

1 Introduction

In this paper I discuss the Stoic understanding of *boulēsis*, in the vernacular often translated as "will." In the modern tradition will is often understood as a faculty on the basis of which one can act independently from reason or emotion.[1] This understanding of *boulēsis* as a faculty is a later development, as has been made clear in recent work by above all Michael Frede.[2] Here I want to show that this later development will have to be understood against the background of the Stoics' paradoxical understanding of *boulēsis*, that is – literally – in deliberate contrast with its ordinary usage in the Greek language. I thus want to contribute to a better understanding of the emergence of the modern notion of the faculty of human will and the conception of freedom that goes with it.

As we will see, in early Stoicism the notion of *boulēsis* is used both with regard to beings already perfectly rational by nature, i.e. gods (or the god for that matter), as well as with regard to human beings, who have managed to bring their rational capacities to perfection. In both cases *boulēsis* is put on a par with – or made redundant to – perfect or perfected reason. This usage is in line with the Stoics' monistic physics, according to which both the nature of the world and that of human beings are guided by reason.

Only with later Stoics the connection between will and perfect reason is loosened, with regard to human beings that is. It is here that a different understanding of will could emerge. This different understanding allows for the introduction of a more modern conception of will, in the sense of a faculty of willing. Rather than *boulēsis* this comes to be referred to, at least with Epictetus, as *prohairesis*, a related but less used, and hence perhaps less controversial, term in the Stoics' technical vocabulary.

As for the structure of this chapter, I start out from the early Stoic evidence on *boulēsis*, and then pay most attention to later Stoic thinkers, above

1 See Dihle 1982, 20.
2 Frede 2011, cf. Frede 2014.

 | DOI:10.1163/9789004436381_004

all Seneca and Epictetus, but also Marcus Aurelius, and discuss how they dealt with *boulēsis*, both in relation to the divine and in relation to human beings.

2 Early Stoicism

The early Stoics proposed controversial meanings of ethical terms such as goodness, virtue, freedom and indeed will. This is in line with their intellectual ancestry, which included both Socrates as well as the Cynics: already Zeno of Citium on Cyprus, the founder of Stoicism, was educated by the Cynics and inspired by Socrates. His biographer or better doxographer Diogenes Laertius nicely captured this in the little anecdote with which he almost immediately starts his account of the life and doctrines of Zeno, at 7.2–3:

> Zeno went up into Athens and sat down in a bookseller's shop, being then a man of thirty. As he heard the bookseller reading from Book 2 of Xenophon's *Memorabilia*, he was so pleased that he inquired where men like Socrates were to be found. Crates [of Thebes, the Cynic] happened to pass by, so the bookseller pointed to him and said: "Follow that man (τούτῳ παρακολούθησον)." [...] For a certain time, then, he was instructed by Crates, and when at this time he had written his *Republic* some said in jest that he had written it on the dog's tail.

As for the Socratic ancestry, an important account is offered by Plato, *Apology* 30e–31a, in which Socrates characterised himself as a horsefly of Athens, making its citizens rethink their answers to questions as to what is good, what is just etc.:

> Just as such [as a horsefly], it seems to me, the god has attached me to the city – the kind of person who wakes you up, prevails upon you and reproaches each one of you and never stops landing on you all day long all over the place.

It is this Socrates that inspired the Cynics. Diogenes of Sinope, the first among the Cynics, the 'doggish ones', also made the Athenians' rethink conventional values, nicely expressed in the little anecdote from Diogenes Laertius, at 6.20–21, in which the Delphic oracle brings Diogenes of Sinope to philosophy, suggesting that "Diogenes of Sinope alter the currency." The expression should be understood both in its conventional and metaphorical sense. Diogenes or his father, a banker, literally defaced coins, but he also metaphorically rethought political vocabulary and incited others do so, too. In this Socratic-Cynic tradition, Zeno, a student of Crates of Thebes, himself a pupil of Diogenes of Sinope, but also Cleanthes and Chrysippus, followed suit.[3] They gave controversial meanings to traditional vocabulary, which as Cicero, in the preface of his *Paradoxes of the Stoics*, informs us goes against the common opinion of all human beings, at 4:

> Because these opinions are surprising and go contrary to the opinion of all human beings (the Stoics themselves call these hence "paradoxes"), I want to find out whether it is possible to bring these into the light. (Tr. Wright, modified)

From Cleanthes, Zeno's successor as head of the Stoic school, a saying to the same effect has been preserved by Arrian in his notes of the lectures by the Stoic Epictetus (1st century CE), at 4.1.173 (*SVF* 1.619):

> You will perceive that, as Cleanthes used to say: "Possibly the philosophers say what goes against common opinion (παράδοξα), but absolutely not what goes against reason (παράλογα)."

It is against this background of rethinking common opinion, so I submit here, that the Stoic terms with regard to human conduct, including will, have to be understood. As for the terms with regard to human conduct, these Stoic paradoxes were nicely put together by Cicero in his *Paradoxes of the Stoics*: the first paradox is that virtue is the only good;[4] the second paradox is that only virtue can make one happy,[5] the third paradox is that all mistakes are equal,[6] the fourth paradox is that all non-virtuous beings are mad,[7] and the fifth paradox is that only the perfect human being is free, all imperfect human beings are slaves.[8]

As for the Stoics' paradoxical understanding of *boulēsis*, let us first look at some instances of the common meaning of *boulēsis*, as intention or wish.[9] Two

---

3 For the evidence see esp. Philodemus, *On the Stoics*, edited by Dorandi 1982.

4 For further evidence on the early Stoics see Plutarch, *On Stoic Self-Contradictions* 13.1039C (*SVF* 3.29), Diogenes Laertius 7.101 (*SVF* 3.30).

5 For Zeno see Diogenes Laertius 7.127 (*SVF* 1.187), Cicero, *On Ends* 5.79 (*SVF* 1.187).

6 For Zeno see Diogenes Laertius 7.120 (*SVF* 1.224).

7 For Zeno see Diogenes Laertius 7.32 (*SVF* 1.226), cf. Stobaeus 2.99.3 (*SVF* 1.216).

8 For Zeno see Diogenes Laertius 7.33 (*SVF* 1.222), for the Stoics in general see Cicero, *On Ends* 3.75 (*SVF* 3.591), Stobaeus 2.101.14–20 (*SVF* 3.593). On the paradoxes see further Brouwer 2020.

9 Cf. Vasiliou 2016, 8.

examples should suffice here. In his *History*, at 3.39.3, Thucydides uses *boulēsis* in the sense of wish or intention:

> Becoming over-confident as to the future, and conceiving hopes which, though greater than their power, were less than their intention (ἐλάσσω δὲ τῆς βουλήσεως), they [*sc*. the Mytilenians] started a war against us.

Like Thucydides, in his *On the Soul* 3.10, at 433a23, Aristotle presents *boulēsis* as wish or intention, as a kind of desire, connected with reasoning: "*Boulēsis* is a desire (ὄρεξις); and whenever one is moved according to reasoning (κατὰ τὸν λογισμὸν), one is also moved according to *boulēsis*." (Tr. Miller.)

In the extant evidence on the early Stoics – and it has to be said: that is preciously little indeed – *boulēsis* occurs in discussions of their account of the highest good or end. According to the Stoics, the end consists in living in accordance, that is living in accordance with one's own nature and the nature of the universe. This end of living in accordance with nature can be found in Diogenes Laertius 7.88 (*SVF* 3.4, LS 63A):

> Living in accordance with nature is living in accordance with our own nature and the nature of the universe, doing nothing which is forbidden by the law common to all things, that is right reason, pervading all things, and is identical with this Zeus, leader and administrator of all that is.[10]

The pivotal notion here is reason. According to the Stoics, reason as the physical force of fire pervades the world, going through all things,[11] and it is with this reason that human beings will have to bring their own rational capacity in accordance, and thus achieve the end.[12] The Stoics give the different aspects of their understanding of reason in the world different names: in the Diogenes Laertius passage law and Zeus bring out its normative aspect. Elsewhere, they identify reason with "fate" (εἱμαρμένη), and "providence" (πρόνοια). Fate they understand as reason in its causal aspect, as the cause of all things that are and of the manner in which they are ordered in time, past, present,

---

10 τὸ ἀκολούθως τῇ φύσει ζῆν, ὅπερ ἐστὶ κατά τε τὴν αὑτοῦ καὶ κατὰ τὴν τῶν ὅλων, οὐδὲν ἐνεργοῦντας ὧν ἀπαγορεύειν εἴωθεν ὁ νόμος ὁ κοινός, ὅσπερ ἐστὶν ὁ ὀρθὸς λόγος, διὰ πάντων ἐρχόμενος.

11 For Zeno see e.g. Stobaeus 1.35.9, Augustine, *Against the Academics* 3.38 (both in *SVF* 1.157), cf. Brouwer 2014, 47.

12 For an account of the end in physical terms see Brouwer 2014, 74–79.

and future.[13] Providence relates to the aspect of divine foresight or of the divine plan, according to which everything has happened, happens and will happen.[14] The relevance of the Stoics' monistic conception of reason with its accompanying aspects of fate and providence for the subsequent ancient debate about the determinist character of the world order, which started immediately with Epicurus, who vehemently rejected Stoic determinism,[15] and continued well into the early imperial period, can hardly be underestimated.[16] By then the writings of thinkers earlier than the Stoics, such as Aristotle, who may not yet have been concerned with determinism,[17] were discussed in this key.

Boulēsis is yet another name given to reason pervading the whole, for which the continuation of the Diogenes Laertius passage quoted on p. 34 provides the evidence:

> And the virtuous disposition of the happy man and his good flow of life are just this: always doing everything on the basis of the concordance of each man's guardian spirit with the *boulēsis* of the administrator of the whole.[18]

According to the Stoics, the end of following nature can thus also be understood in terms of acting in accordance with the *boulēsis* of the administrator of the whole. The Stoics thus used *boulēsis* in the sense of the will of Zeus, who as perfect reason pervades the world.

If this understanding of *boulēsis* as divine reason pervading common nature is already "paradoxical", the Stoics made a further remarkable use of *boulēsis* with regard to human beings. For the Stoics *boulēsis* is one of the three "good emotions" of the sage, this rare perfect human being that has brought his rational faculty in accordance with the reason that pervades the world.[19] "Good

---

13 See e.g. Diogenes Laertius 7.149 (*SVF* 1.175). Cf. Frede 2003, Sauvé-Meyer 2009. For the Stoic conception of sympathy as the resulting interconnectedness of the things in the world see Brouwer 2015.

14 See Aëtius 1.27.5 (*SVF* 1.176). Cf. Reydams-Schils 1999, Lloyd 2008, 90–128, Algra 2014.

15 For the evidence see LS 20. For the debate in terms of luck see Brouwer 2019, 37.

16 For the Stoics as setting the debate for the Platonists in the Imperial age see Engberg-Pedersen 2017, for the Platonist conceptions of fate, providence and free will see Bonazzi 2014, Magris 2016, 209, and Vimercati's chapter in this volume.

17 See Natali's chapter in this volume.

18 εἶναι δ' αὐτὸ τοῦτο τὴν τοῦ εὐδαίμονος ἀρετὴν καὶ εὔροιαν βίου, ὅταν πάντα πράττηται κατὰ τὴν συμφωνίαν τοῦ παρ' ἑκάστῳ δαίμονος πρὸς τὴν τοῦ τῶν ὅλων διοικητοῦ βούλησιν.

19 For living in accordance see further Brouwer 2014, ch. 1, for the rarity of the sage ch. 3 and 4.

emotions" is the standard translation of *eupatheiai*.[20] This translation conveys both the adverb *eu*, good, as well as *pathos*, emotion. (It should be noted that *pathos* is often less felicitously rendered by the term *passion*, which in English refers to more violent emotions like jealousy etc.) The extant sources on these good emotions are once again limited: they include passages from Ps.-Andronicus, Diogenes Laertius, and – more elaborate, but in his Latin translation – Cicero. In the first source, Ps.-Andronicus, *On Emotions* 6 Glibert-Thirry (SVF 3.432), three good emotions are distinguished and defined:

> There are three kinds of good emotions: *boulēsis* is perfectly rational striving, joy is perfectly rational swelling, caution is perfectly rational shrinking.[21]

The physiological terminology of swelling and shrinking fits the Stoic understanding of reason in the physical sense and of hence of virtue as a physical disposition on the basis of which the perfect human being participates in the force that orders the world. *Boulēsis* or will as swelling has to be understood as contributing to the course of reason, caution as shrinking means holding back from active participation.[22] In the second source, Diogenes Laertius, at 7.115–116 (SVF 3.413, LS 65F), these definitions are repeated, and the good emotions are contrasted with their opposites:

> They say that there are three good emotions: joy, caution, will. Joy, they say, is the opposite of pleasure, consisting in perfectly rational swelling; and caution is the opposite of fear, consisting in perfectly rational shrinking. For the wise man will not be afraid at all, he will rather be cautious. They say that will is the opposite of desire, consisting in perfectly rational striving.[23]

Finally, our most elaborate source is Cicero, *Tusculan Disputations* 4.12 (SVF 3.438). As elsewhere in his philosophical writings, also here Cicero makes

20 See Graver 2007, 51.

21 εὐπαθείας εἴδη γ'· [...] βούλησις μὲν οὖν ἐστιν εὔλογος ὄρεξις. χαρὰ δὲ εὔλογος ἔπαρσις. εὐλάβεια δὲ εὔλογος ἔκκλισις.

22 For caution as respect for the divine order see van Herten 1934, 36, Graver 2007, 53.

23 εἶναι δὲ καὶ εὐπαθείας φασὶ τρεῖς, χαράν, εὐλάβειαν, βούλησιν. καὶ τὴν μὲν χαρὰν ἐναντίαν φασὶν εἶναι τῇ ἡδονῇ, οὖσαν εὔλογον ἔπαρσιν· τὴν δ' εὐλάβειαν τῷ φόβῳ, οὖσαν εὔλογον ἔκκλισιν. φοβηθήσεσθαι μὲν γὰρ τὸν σοφὸν οὐδαμῶς, εὐλαβηθήσεσθαι δέ. τῇ δ' ἐπιθυμίᾳ ἐναντίαν φασὶν εἶναι τὴν βούλησιν, οὖσαν εὔλογον ὄρεξιν.

Greek thought available to the Romans, by translating technical terminology into Latin.[24] Like Ps.-Andronicus and Diogenes Laertius, Cicero not only gives us the definitions of the Stoic good emotions, and of their opposites, by choosing the translation "consistencies" (*constantiae*),[25] he also emphasises the connection of the good emotions with the life that is lived in accordance with nature:

> By nature, all people pursue those things which they think to be good and avoid their opposites. Therefore, as soon as someone receives an impression of a thing which he thinks is good, nature itself urges him to reach out after it. When this is done in accordance with practical wisdom and in a consistent manner, it is the sort of striving which the Stoics call a *boulēsis*, and which I shall term *voluntas*. They think it can be found in wise persons only, and define it as follows: *voluntas* is what one strives for with reason.[26] (Tr. Graver 2005, modified)

So to sum up the early Stoic understanding of *boulēsis*: the Stoic formulation of the goal of life as living in accordance with reason (ὁμολογία) is also expressed in terms of "will", which the Stoics – contrary to the common understanding as we found it in Thucydides and Aristotle – understood as perfect reason, both with regard to reason pervading the world as well as with regard to human being, who has brought his rational faculty to perfection. The will of the perfect human being can thus said to be in agreement with the will of Zeus. The sage, in his good state of willing, can thus actively contribute, together with Zeus, to governing the world.

Before moving to the use of *boulēsis* by later Stoics, it may be helpful to return briefly to the early Stoic conception of freedom or – for that matter – to Cicero's fifth paradox that only the virtuous human being is free and that all others are slaves.[27] The sage's freedom consists in following cosmic reason, in having a rational disposition out of which he or she will always take the right

24 On Cicero as a translator of the Greek philosophical vocabulary see his *On Divination* 2,.1–6, and further Kilb 1939, Hartung 1970.

25 In the Western tradition this translation would become popular in the Renaissance, esp. with Lipsius' influential *On Constancy* (1584).

26 *natura enim omnes ea, quae bona videntur, secuntur fugiuntque contraria; quam ob rem simul obiecta species est cuiuspiam, quod bonum videatur, ad id adipiscendum impellit ipsa natura. id cum constanter prudenterque fit, eius modi adpetitionem Stoici* βούλησιν *appellant, nos appellemus voluntatem, eam illi putant in solo esse sapiente; quam sic definiunt: voluntas est, quae quid cum ratione desiderat.*

27 See above n. 8.

decision. All non-virtuous beings who are not able to follow cosmic reason are by contrast enslaved.

3 Later Stoics: Seneca, Epictetus, Marcus Aurelius

Let us now move on to the use of *boulēsis* by the Stoics from the early Imperial period, notably Seneca, Epictetus and Marcus Aurelius. Do they stick to the early Stoic "paradoxical" understanding of divine and human will?

Like the early Stoics, Seneca speaks of the end of living in accordance with the nature of the universe, using the notion of *voluntas* with regard to this nature. See Seneca, *Letter* 66.39:

> To put it briefly: the material of the good is sometimes contrary to nature; but the good never is, since there is no good without reason, and reason follows nature. What, then, is reason? The imitation of nature. What is the highest good of the human being? Behaving according to the will of nature (*ex naturae voluntate se gerere*).[28] (Tr. Graver and Long, modified)

Likewise Seneca, at *Letter* 20.5, uses *voluntas* with regard to the perfect human being:

> What is wisdom (*sapientia*)? Always willing the same thing, always rejecting the same thing (*idem velle atque idem nolle*). You do not even have to add the proviso that what you want should be right: only with what is right one can always be satisfied.

Different from the early Stoic sources, in Seneca's *Letters* also the common usage of *voluntas* can be found.[29] *Letter* 81.13 offers a good example. There Seneca speaks of the imperfect, inferior person, who can will, but not know:

> He is deficient in knowledge rather than in willing, for willing is not something that has to be learned.[30]

The common meaning of *voluntas* can be illustrated with a couple of examples from Cicero. In the *Topics*, in which he deals with types of arguments, as

28 Cf. Bourbon 2019, 262.

29 Cf. Rist 1969, 225, Fuhrer 2010, Bourbon 2019, 284.

30 *scientia illi potius quam voluntas desit: velle non discitur.*

part of his overall plan to discuss the theoretical underpinnings of rhetoric,[31] Cicero makes the distinction between *scripta* and *voluntas* in the context of an enumeration of types of conflicts about written documents, at 96:

> There are three types of possible disagreement (*controversia*) about every written document: ambiguity, discrepancy between letter and intention (*discrepantia scripti et voluntatis*), and contradictory texts.

The second, here still theoretical difference between letter and intention is instantiated in a famous case, known as the *Causa curiana*, which was brought before the courts in the late nineties BCE. The legal point of contention was whether the testament should be interpreted literally (as argued for by Q. Mucius Scaevola Pontifex, whose contribution to the development of Roman law above all consisted in producing the first general compendium of Roman law[32]) or according to the intention of the testator (as argued for by Crassus). Cicero discusses the case several times. In his *Brutus* 196 he describes the crux of the case in the following manner:

> What a deception was set for people if the letter (*scriptum*) of the testament were ignored, and if intentions (*voluntates*) were to be determined by guess-work, and if the written words of simple-minded human beings were to be perverted by the interpretation [of clever lawyers].[33] (Tr. Hendrickson)

In comparison with the early Stoics Seneca still uses *voluntas* in the early Stoic sense as reason, both in relation to the world and to the sage.[34] However different from the early Stoics, Seneca also uses *voluntas* in a common-sensical manner, outside the domain of the perfectly rational sage, applying it to imperfect, ordinary mortals.[35] According to Brad Inwood, Seneca may even have

31 See Reinhardt 2003, 7.

32 Pomponius, *Handbook ap. Digest* 1.2.41, cf. Brouwer (forthcoming).

33 For another account of the *causa Curiana* in terms of see Cicero, *On the Orator* 1.242, cf. 1.180.

34 See e.g. Monteils-Laeng 2014, 394–410.

35 Perhaps Seneca's use was influenced by the first 'Roman' Stoics, that is Greek thinkers who presented themselves in Rome in the first second century BCE. In comparison with the early Stoics they focus less on the perfectly rational human being: Panaetius is prepared to discuss virtue in a second-rate manner, on the level of the Roman 'good man' (*vir bonus*) rather than that of the perfect sage. Unfortunately, the evidence about these Middle Stoics is limited: no trace of the use of *boulēsis* or *voluntas* has survived. On these 'Roman' Stoics see further Brouwer (forthcoming).

contributed to the development towards a more modern understanding of will as volition. Inwood points at Seneca's interest in self-knowledge, self-control and the moment of making a causally efficacious judgment.[36] However, as Inwood himself acknowledges, these interests are not yet discussed under a single heading, let alone of *voluntas*.

A similar, broadening approach can be discerned in Epictetus' thought. In good early Stoic fashion, Epictetus discusses the end in terms of common and human nature. See Arrian, *Epictetus' Dissertations* 1.20.14 (*SVF* 1.182):

> All the same, what is most essential in the teaching of the philosophers can be stated very briefly. If you want to know, read Zeno's works, and you'll see. For does it take in fact long to say that "our end lies in following the gods, and the essence of the good in the correct use of impressions"? If you ask, '"What, then, is God, and what is an impression? And what is nature in the individual and nature in the universe?" (καὶ τί ἐστι φύσις ἡ ἐπὶ μέρους καὶ τί ἐστι φύσις ἡ τῶν ὅλων), the discussion is already beginning to drag out.[37]

Again, like the early Stoics or Seneca for that matter, Epictetus also discusses the nature of the universe in terms of will. See Arrian, *Epictetus' Dissertations* 1.17.13–18 (*SVF* 2.29, part):

> What is in fact admirable? To understand the will of nature (τὸ βούλημα τῆς φύσεως). What, then, do you follow (παρακολουθεῖς) that by yourself? If so, what need do you have of anyone else? For if it is true that all who do wrong do so involuntarily (ἄκοντας), and you for your part have come to know the truth, it necessarily follows that you must already be acting rightly. – No, by Zeus, I don't follow the will of nature. (Tr. Hard, modified)

This is how Epictetus himself put it in his *Handbook*, at 26: "The will of nature (βούλημα τῆς φύσεως) may be learned from those events in life in which we don't differ from one another." It should perhaps be noted, however, that Epictetus uses *boulēma* rather than *boulēsis* here. This implies a shift in focus from the act of willing (as the ending *-is* denotes) to the actual product of willing (as the ending *-ma* denotes). The shift seems a change of empha-

36 Inwood 2005 [2000], 155, followed by Fuhrer 2010.

37 The translation used here (and below) is Hard 2014.

sis rather than in substance: in these passages Epictetus does not stress that nature wants, but rather on what it is that nature wants.

Like Seneca, Epictetus uses will with regard to the sage and also with regard to ordinary mortals. With regard to the sage we read, at Arrian, *Epictetus' Dissertations* 2.14.7:

> The striver for wisdom needs to bring his own will into harmony with what happens, so that neither anything that happens happens without him wanting to, nor anything that fails to happen when we want it to happen.[38]

With regard to the inferior person, see Arrian, *Epictetus' Dissertations* 1.12.13–14:

> Do I write the name "Dion" just as I want? Of course not, I'm taught to want to write it as it ought to be written. (βούλομαι γράφειν ὡς θέλω τὸ Δίωνος ὄνομα; οὔ· ἀλλὰ διδάσκομαι θέλειν, ὡς δεῖ γράφεσθαι.) And when it comes to music? The same applies. And in general, with regard to any of the arts and sciences? The same applies. Otherwise there would be no point in trying to gain knowledge of anything, if it could be adapted to fit as everyone wanted it.

In his focus on ordinary human beings Epictetus appears to go a step further than Seneca: he not only uses the term of *boulēsis* in relation to ordinary human beings, he also appears to have been the first to have used the modern understanding of volition.[39] He speaks of the ability of human beings to do what they want, to make the correct or incorrect decision. For this disposition out of which ordinary human beings make a choice, Epictetus introduces the notion of *prohairesis*, as the three following passages from Arrian, *Epictetus' Dissertations* attest:

> 1.25.1: The good of man, and likewise his ill, lies in his ability to choose (ἐν προαιρέσει), while everything else is nothing to us.

38 καὶ ἐνταῦθα τὸ μὲν ἔργον τοῦ φιλοσοφοῦντος τοιοῦτόν τι φανταζόμεθα, ὅτι δεῖ τὴν αὑτοῦ βούλησιν συναρμόσαι τοῖς γινομένοις, ὡς μήτε τι τῶν γινομένων ἀκόντων ἡμῶν γίνεσθαι μήτε τῶν μὴ γινομένων θελόντων ἡμῶν μὴ γίνεσθαι.

39 This practical focus may have been inspired by his teacher Musonius Rufus (1st century CE). For his extant lectures see Hense 1905, still the standard edition, and Lutz 1947 and King 2011 for translations in English.

> 3.1.40: For you yourself are neither flesh nor hair, but the ability to choose (προαίρεσις), and if you render that virtuous, then you yourself will be virtuous.
>
> 3.9.2: The ability to choose cannot be hindered or harmed by anything that lies outside the sphere of choice, but only by choice itself.[40]

Where does the term come from? In the extant evidence on the Stoics before Epictetus the word occurs in an account that is usually taken to go back to Arius Didymus, a philosopher befriended by the emperor, Augustus (see Inwood 1989, 346, with references to the extant sources). It survived in Stobaeus 2.87.14 (*SVF* 3.173):

> There are numerous species of practical impulse, including these: proposal, inclination, preparation, undertaking, choice, pre-choice, will and willingness. Proposal is an indication of completion; inclination is an impulse before an impulse; preparation is an action before an action; undertaking is an impulse towards something that is now in hand; choice is will from comparison; pre-choice is a choice before a choice; will is well-reasoned desire; willingness is an unforced will.[41]

It occurs again in Stobaeus, at 2.99.14–15 (*SVF* 3.567), where the sage is said to be "great, because he is able to accomplish things in accordance with his pre-choice."[42]

It may well be that the term may have been taken from Aristotle's lecture notes both by Arius Didymus as well as by Epictetus.[43] These notes, that is Aristotle's works as we know them, had become available from the first century BCE onwards. In the *Nicomachean Ethics* 3.3, 1113a3–6 ("Each of us stops inquiring about what way to act when he brings back the starting-point to himself, and within himself, to the leading element, since this is what he deliberately chooses (τοῦτο γὰρ τὸ προαιρούμενον)", tr. Reeve), but also in his *Eudemian Ethics* 2.11, 1228a2 ("It is on the basis of his decision (*prohaeresis*) that we judge

40 προαίρεσιν γὰρ οὐδὲν δύναται κωλῦσαι ἢ βλάψαι ἀπροαίρετον εἰ μὴ αὐτὴ ἑαυτήν.

41 τῆς δὲ πρακτικῆς ὁρμῆς εἴδη πλείονα εἶναι, ἐν οἷς καὶ ταῦτα· πρόθεσιν, ἐπιβολήν, παρασκευήν, ἐγχείρησιν, αἵρεσιν, προαίρεσιν, βούλησιν, θέλησιν. πρόθεσιν μὲν οὖν εἶναι λέγουσι σημείωσιν ἐπιτελέσεως· ἐπιβολὴν δὲ ὁρμὴν πρὸ ὁρμῆς· παρασκευὴν δὲ πρᾶξιν πρὸ πράξεως· ἐγχείρησιν δὲ ὁρμὴν ἐπί τινος ἐν χερσὶν ἤδη ὄντος· αἵρεσιν δὲ βούλησιν ἐξ ἀναλογισμοῦ· προαίρεσιν δὲ αἵρεσιν πρὸ αἱρέσεως· βούλησιν δὲ εὔλογον ὄρεξιν· θέλησιν δὲ ἑκούσιον βούλησιν.

42 μέγαν μέν, ὅτι δύναται ἐφικνεῖσθαι τῶν κατὰ προαίρεσιν ὄντων αὐτῷ καὶ προκειμένων.

43 Rapp 1995, 114, Forschner 2013, 107–108.

someone to be of a certain character,"[44] tr. Inwood and Woolf), Aristotle connects *prohaeresis* with character development: such choices can make one's character good or bad. To the basic meaning of pre-choice, Epictetus would thus have added the meaning of ability to choose or even moral character itself.[45] With Aristotle's writings available and brought into in the debate about (in-)determinism, Epictetus may have considered *prohairesis* a good term to designate the ability to make a choice out of an imperfect disposition, contrasting it with *boulēsis* in the early Stoic understanding as the perfectly rational disposition. The contrast is preshadowed in the Stobaeus-passage, where *boulēsis* as well-reasoned desire is also mentioned. Out of this imperfect disposition choices are made, also, as Spinelli and Verde suggested, on the basis of imperfectly rational opinions.[46] With this understanding of *prohairesis* as the ability to choose, also out of an imperfect disposition, we may well find the origin of the faculty of will.[47]

With this notion of the ability to choose, freedom in a more common sensical understanding comes back into play. Of course, for the sage his or her "freedom" consists in following reason that pervades nature, thus in having a rational disposition out of which he or she will take the right decision.[48] With regard to the non-sage or inferior person, who does not have this disposition, freedom can now also be understood as the ability to make a decision out of an imperfectly rational disposition. True freedom still consists in having a rational disposition and making the correct decisions; however, having the ability to make a preliminary decision allows one to make the incorrect decision, and thus allow for the faculty of will to be called "free."[49] It is against the combined background of these developments in the understanding of will and freedom that the modern notion of free will can be said to have emerged.

This common-sensical background is at least in line with, perhaps even inspired by the Roman understanding of freedom as a faculty. This meaning is attested for in book 9 of the *Teaching Manual* written by the Roman lawyer Florentinus (2nd century BCE), and that survived in the *Digest* 1.5.4 prooemium (fr. 25 Lenel): "Freedom (*libertas*) is one's natural ability (*naturalis facultas*) of

---

44 καὶ διὰ τοῦτο ἐκ τῆς προαιρέσεως κρίνομεν ποῖός τις.

45 On Epictetus' understanding of *prohairesis* as choice, the ability to choose, and moral person see further Gourinat 2005.

46 Spinelli and Verde 2014, 85–86.

47 Frede 2011, 85, 2014, 360. Cf. Voelke 1973, Bobzien 1998, 411–412, Gourinat 2005, Frede 2011, 85, Bourbon 2019, 142–197.

48 See above n. 8. Cf. Bobzien 1997, Mikeš 2016.

49 On freedom in Stoicism (and Paul) see Engberg-Pedersen's contribution to this volume.

"doing what one pleases" (*facere libet*), as long as the law or some other force does not prevent him." This Roman understanding presumably goes back to the *patria potestas*, the "unrestricted rule of the father within his own home", including the *ius vitae necisque*, the (in-)famous right of the father over life and death of the family members.[50] Of course, this is not the place to pursue this Roman influence further.

I move on to Marcus Aurelius, as the last among the late Stoics under discussion here. Does the emperor follow Seneca and Epictetus in their use of *boulēsis/voluntas* with regard to ordinary human beings? The answer is negative: with Marcus Aurelius we are firmly back to the early Stoic understanding,[51] with two differences, which can easily be explained.

As with the early Stoics, Marcus Aurelius describes *homologia* as living in accordance with common (or universal) nature, at 5.3.2: "Keep to a straight course, follow your own nature and common nature; for the path of both is but a single path",[52] and 8.7.1–2: "It [a rational nature] is part of it [common nature], just as the nature of the leaf is part of the plant's nature."[53]

Likewise, at 9.1.1, Marcus Aurelius also expresses the end of *homologia* in terms the will of universal nature or god:

> Whoever commits injustice acts irreverently; for since the nature of the whole has created rational beings for the sake of one another, to benefit their fellows according to their deserts and in no way to do them harm, it is plain that one who offends against nature's will is guilty of irreverence towards the most venerable of the gods.[54]

With regard to the divine, Marcus uses *boulēma* rather than *boulēsis*, as already Epictetus had. The focus is simply on the result, rather than the process: *boulēma*, rather than *boulēsis*. The focus is thus on choice as result (expressed in the ending *-ma*), rather than the actual process of willing (with ending *-sis*).

---

50 Kaser, Knütel, Lohsse 2017, 352: "Die *patria potestas* unterwirft die Haussöhne und Haustöchter einer in alten Zeit nahezu unbeschränkten Herrschaft ihres Gewalthabers." Cf. Wenger 1924, Voci 1980, Saller 1991, 144–165, Krause 2003, Frier and McGinn 2004, Hartmann 2007, 132.

51 Voelke 1973, 109.

52 ἀλλ' εὐθεῖαν πέραινε ἀκολουθῶν τῇ φύσει τῇ ἰδίᾳ καὶ τῇ κοινῇ, μία δὲ ἀμφοτέρων τούτων ἡ ὁδός. The translation used here and below is by Hard 2011.

53 μέρος γὰρ αὐτῆς ἐστιν ὡς ἡ τοῦ φύλλου φύσις τῆς τοῦ φυτοῦ φύσεως.

54 ὁ ἀδικῶν ἀσεβεῖ· τῆς γὰρ τῶν ὅλων φύσεως κατεσκευακυίας τὰ λογικὰ ζῷα ἕνεκεν ἀλλήλων, ὥστε ὠφελεῖν μὲν ἄλληλα κατ' ἀξίαν βλάπτειν δὲ μηδαμῶς, ὁ τὸ βούλημα ταύτης παραβαίνων ἀσεβεῖ δηλονότι εἰς τὴν πρεσβυτάτην τῶν θεῶν.

With regard to the sage Marcus Aurelius uses *boulesthai*, at 10.11.4: "He wants nothing else than to walk the straight path according to the law, and by walking the straight path, to follow god."[55] Next to *boulesthai*, he also uses *thelein*, at 5.25.2:

> Another does wrong. What is that to me? [...] As for me, I have what common nature wills that I should have, and I am doing what my own nature wills that I should do.[56]

Does *thelein* imply a deviation from the early Stoics? It seems not: in late antiquity *boulesthai* has become antiquated and is thus often replaced by *thelein*.[57] Despite some terminological differences, Marcus Aurelius thus sticks to the early Stoic use of will with regard to the divine or of the sage.

4 Conclusion

In sum: how should we understand the notion of will in later Stoicism? With regard to the divine will, later Stoics do not differ from the early Stoics: the notion of will as perfect reason can still be found with later Stoics. Throughout the history of the school the Stoics kept using *boulēsis* as the perfectly rational willing of common nature or god, and of the rare sage, who lives in accordance with common nature. However, with regard to the human will, we see that among the later Stoics will starts to get separated from perfect reason. With Seneca we find *boulēsis*/*voluntas* used in its ordinary sense as intention, unconnected to perfect reason. With regard to imperfect human beings, Epictetus makes the further move of using *prohairesis*, a term until then little used in Stoicism, in the sense of the imperfect disposition out of which a decision can be made. This decision can go with or against that order, but makes one in a common sense feel free, and thus allows for a more modern understanding of the faculty of free will. The early Stoics would have been stunned.

55 οὐδὲν ἄλλο βούλεται ἢ εὐθεῖαν περαίνειν διὰ τοῦ νόμου καὶ εὐθεῖαν περαίνοντι ἕπεσθαι τῷ θεῷ.

56 ἐγὼ νῦν ἔχω, ὅ με θέλει νῦν ἔχειν ἡ κοινὴ φύσις, καὶ πράσσω, ὅ με νῦν πράσσειν θέλει ἡ ἐμὴ φύσις.

57 See Monteils-Laeng 2014, 378, cf. Wifstrand 1942, 16–46, Voelke 1973, 110, Dihle 1982, 146.

Bibliography

Algra, Keimpe A. 2014. "Plutarch and the Stoic Theory of Providence." In *Fate, Providence and Moral Responsibility in Ancient, Medieval and Early Modern Thought*, edited by Pieter d'Hoine and Gerd van Riel, 117–135. Leuven: Leuven University Press.

Bobzien, Susanne. 1998. *Determinism and Freedom in Stoic Philosophy*. Oxford: Clarendon.

Bonazzi, Mauro. 2014. "Middle Platonism on Fate and Autonomy: A Confrontation with the Stoics." In *Fate, Providence and Moral Responsibility in Ancient, Medieval and Early Modern Thought*, edited by Pieter d'Hoine and Gerd van Riel, 283–294. Leuven: Leuven University Press.

Bourbon, Marion. 2019. *Penser l'individu. Genèse stoïcienne de la subjectivité*. Turnhout: Brepols.

Brouwer, René. 2014. *The Stoic Sage. The Early Stoics on Wisdom, Sagehood and Socrates*. Cambridge: Cambridge University Press.

Brouwer, René. 2015. "Stoic Sympathy." In *Sympathy*, edited by Eric Schliesser, 15–35. New York: Oxford University Press.

Brouwer, René. 2019. "The Stoics on Luck." In *The Routledge Handbook on the Philosophy and Psychology of Luck*, edited by Ian Church and Robert Hartman, 34–44. London: Routledge.

Brouwer, René. 2020. "Stoic Ethics and Socratic Ignorance." In *The Routledge Handbook to Hellenistic Philosophy*, 107–118. New York: Routledge.

Brouwer, René. *Law and Philosophy in the Late Roman Republic*. Cambridge: Cambridge University Press (forthcoming).

Dihle, Albrecht. 1982. *The Theory of Will in Classical Antiquity*. Berkeley: University of California Press.

Dorandi, Tiziano, ed., tr. 1982. "Filodemo. *Gli Stoici* (PHerc. 155 e 339)." *Cronache ercolanesi* 12: 92–133.

Engberg-Pedersen, Troels, ed. 2017. *From Stoicism to Platonism. The Development of Philosophy, 100 BCE–100 CE*. Cambridge: Cambridge University Press.

Forschner, Maximilian. 2013. "Epiktets Theorie der Freiheit im Verhältnis zur klassischen stoischen Lehre." In *Epiktet. Was ist wahre Freiheit?*, edited by Samuel Vollenweider, 97–118. Tübingen: Mohr Siebeck.

Frede, Dorothea. 2003. "Stoic Determinism." In *The Cambridge Companion to the Stoics*, edited by Brad Inwood, 179–205. Cambridge: Cambridge University Press.

Frede, Michael. 2011. *A Free Will. Origins of the Notion in Ancient Thought*, edited by Anthony A. Long. Berkeley: University of California Press.

Frede, Michael. 2014. "The *eph' hêmin* in Ancient Philosophy." In *What is Up to Us. Studies on Agency and Responsibility in Ancient Philosophy*, edited by Pierre Destrée,

Ricardo Salles, and Marco Zingano, 351–363. Sankt Augustin: Academia.

Frier, Brian W., and Thomas A.J. McGinn. 2004. *A Casebook on Roman Family Law*. New York: Oxford University Press.

Fuhrer, Therese. 2010. "Wollen oder Nicht(-)Wollen. Zum Willenskonzept bei Seneca." In *Wille und Handlung in der Philosophie der Kaiserzeit und Spätantike*, edited by Jörn Müller and Roberto Hofmeister Pich, 69–94. Berlin: De Gruyter.

Gourinat, Jean-Baptiste. 2005. "La 'prohairesis' chez Épictète: décision, volonté, ou 'personne morale'?" *Philosophie antique* 5: 93–134.

Graver, Margaret. 2005 *Cicero on the Emotions*. Chicago: University of Chicago Press.

Graver, Margaret. 2007. *Stoicism & Emotion*. Chicago: University of Chicago Press.

Graver, Margaret, and Anthony A. Long, tr. 2015. *Seneca. Letters on Ethics to Lucilius*. Chicago: University of Chicago Press.

Hard, Robin, tr. 2011. *Marcus Aurelius. Meditations*. Oxford: Oxford University Press.

Hard, Robin, tr. 2014. *Epictetus. Discourses, Fragments, Handbook*. Oxford: Oxford University Press.

Hartmann, Elke. 2007. *Frauen in der Antike*. Munich: Beck.

Hartung, Hans-Joachim. 1970. *Ciceros Methode bei der Übersetzung griechischer philosophischer Termini*. diss. Hamburg.

Hense, O., ed. 1905. *C. Musonii Rufi reliquiae*. Leipzig: Teubner.

van Herten, Joseph C.A. 1934. θρησκεία εὐλάβεια ἱκέτης. Amsterdam: Paris.

Inwood, Brad. 1989. "Areios Didymos." In *Dictionnaire des philosophes antiques*, vol. 1, edited by Richard Goulet, 346–349. Paris: CNRS.

Inwood, Brad. 2005. *Reading Seneca*. Oxford: Clarendon.

Inwood, Brad, and Raphael Woolf, tr. 2013. *Aristotle. Eudemian Ethics*. Cambridge: Cambridge University Press.

Kaser, Max, Rolf Knütel and Sebastian Lohsse. 2017. *Römisches Privatrecht*, 21th edn. Munich: Beck.

Kilb, Georg. 1939. *Ethische Grundbegriffe der alten Stoa und ihre Übertragung durch Cicero im dritten Buch de finibus bonorum et malorum*. Freiburg i. Br.: Herder.

King, C., tr. 2011. *Musonius Rufus. Letters and Sayings*. s.l.: CreateSpace.

Krause, Jens-Uwe. 2003. "Antike." In (eds.), *Geschichte der Familie*, edited by Andreas Gestrich, Jens-Uwe Krause, and Michael Mitterauer, 1–159. Stuttgart: Kröner.

Lenel, Otto. 1889. *Palingenesia iuris civilis*. Leipzig: Tauchnitz.

Lloyd, Geneviève. 2008. *Providence Lost*. Cambridge (Mass.): Harvard University Press.

LS: Long, Anthony A. and David N. Sedley. 1987. *The Hellenistic Philosophers*. Cambridge: Cambridge University Press.

Lutz, Cora E. 1947. "Musonius Rufus 'The Roman Socrates.'" *Yale Classical Studies* 10: 3–147.

Magris, Aldo. 2016. *Destino, provvidenza, predestinatione* [2008]. 2nd edn. Brescia: Morecelliana.

Mikeš, Vladimír. 2016. *Le paradoxe stoïcien: liberté de l'action déterminée*. Paris: Vrin.

Monteils-Laeng, Laetitia. 2014. *L'agir sans vouloir*. Paris: Garnier.

Reeve, C. David C., tr. 2014. *Aristotle. Nicomachean Ethics*. Indianapolis: Hackett.

Reinhardt, Tobias, ed., tr. 2003. *Cicero's Topica*. Oxford: Oxford University Press.

Reydams-Schils, Gretchen. 1999. *Demiurge and Providence. Stoic and Platonist Readings of Plato's* Timaeus. Turnhout: Brepols.

Rist, John M. 1969. *Stoic Philosophy*. Cambridge: Cambridge University Press.

Saller, Richard. 1991. "Corporeal Punishment, Authority and Obedience in the Roman Household." In *Marriage, Divorce, and Children in Ancient Rome*, edited by Beryl Rawson, 144–165. Oxford: Clarendon.

Sauvé-Meyer, Susan. "Chain in Causes." In *God and Cosmos in Stoicism*, edited by Ricardo Salles, 71–89. Oxford: Oxford University Press.

Spinelli, Emilio, and Francesco Verde. 2014. "Alle radici del libero arbitrio? Aporie e soluzioni nelle filosofie ellenistiche." In *Libero arbitrio. Storia di una controversia filosofica*, edited by Mario De Caro, Massimo Mori, and Emidio Spinelli, 59–98. Rome: Carocci.

SVF : von Arnim, Hans, ed. 1903–1905. *Stoicorum veterum fragmenta*. Leipzig: Teubner.

Vasiliou, Iakovos, ed. 2016. *Moral Motivation*. New York: Oxford University Press.

Voci, Pasquale. 1980. "Storia della patria potestas da Augusto a Diocleziano." *Iura* 31: 37–100.

Voelke, André-Jean. 1973. *L'idée de volonté dans le stoïcisme*. Paris: PUF.

Wenger, Leopold. 1924. "Hausgewalt und Staatsgewalt im römischen Altertum." In *Miscellanea Francesco Ehrle*, vol. 2, 1–55. Rome: Bibliotheca Apostolica Vaticana.

Wright, Maureen R., tr. 1991. *Cicero on Stoic Good and Evil. De finibus bonorum et malorum liber III and Paradoxa Stoicorum*. Warminster: Aris and Phillips.

CHAPTER 3

Epictetus on What Is in Our Power: Modal versus Epistemic Conceptions

Ricardo Salles

There is a modal conception of what is "in our power" (ἐφ' ἡμῖν) often attributed to Epictetus according to which an activity φ is in our power (ἐφ' ἡμῖν) only if nothing external 'can' hinder our φ-ing in the modal sense that nothing external *could* hinder it even if nothing external actually does so. I call this conception "MC." For instance, If I walk now but you could hinder my walking, then, even if you do not actually hinder it, walking now is *not* in my power. The attribution of MC to Epictetus goes back at least to Simplicius,[1] and has strong advocates in modern scholarship.[2] In this short paper I contend, however, that MC ought to be rejected as an interpretation of Epictetus. As I shall argue in section 1, MC has no strong textual support and, in addition, it presupposes a problematic notion of counterfactual possibility. In section 2, I claim that there is an alternative conception of what is in our power, the Epistemic Conception or "EC" that we may attribute to Epictetus. It is well supported by textual evidence and does not lead to the problems of MC. Its key notion is

1 See *Commentary on Epictetus' Manual* 4.1–4: "By "in our power" he means that of which we are in control and over which we have authority. For we say that those things are in the power of each person which the person does not have from someone else, and which cannot be thwarted by someone else" (ἐφ' ἡμῖν ἐκεῖνα λέγει, ὧν κύριοί ἐσμεν, καὶ ὧν τὴν ἐξουσίαν ἔχομεν. ταῦτα [γὰρ] καὶ ἐπ' αὐτῷ ἑκάστῳ λέγομεν, ἃ μὴ παρ' ἄλλου ἔχει, μηδὲ ὑπ' ἄλλου τινὸς ἐμποδίζεσθαι δύναται).

2 See Bobzien 1998, 332: "For Epictetus [walking] does not seem to [be in our power: ἐφ' ἡμῖν], since in principle something *could* prevent [us] from walking, even if in this case nothing does", Long 2002, 219: "Epictetus is saying that something is "ours" or "up to us" [ἐφ'ἡμῖν] only if it cannot be externally impeded. Taking a step can be externally impeded. Therefore, even when we voluntarily walk, we should not say that the only causal factor was our *prohairesis*, because our body's parts do not strictly belong to 'us' and so do not fall within the unequivocal scope of our agency. In order for something fully to depend on us, Epictetus claims, it must be the kind of thing that is in our power under all possible circumstances, including bodily paralysis or a tyrant's seizure of all our limbs. The only kinds of thing that qualify are the two mental functions of *prohairesis*, assent and impulse", and more recently Coope 2016, 251: "For Epictetus, something only counts as depending on the agent [= ἐφ'ἡμῖν] if nothing external to the agent could interfere with it."

 | DOI:10.1163/9789004436381_005

not modal, but epistemic: an activity φ is in our power only if we know that our φ-ing will not be hindered.[3] As will be seen, *EC* imposes a very demanding condition for an activity to be in our power, but less demanding than the counterfactual condition imposed by *MC*. In section 3, I mention two questions connected to this very issue that I shall leave open. Firstly, why does Epictetus associate what is in our power with what we *know* that will not be hindered? A weaker and philosophically more plausible view would be that what is in our power is what will not be hindered, independently of whether or not we know it. The reasons that led Epictetus to uphold the stronger view may be related to his conception of the role of knowledge in ethics. Secondly, of all the activities that we normally perform, are there any such that can we genuinely *know* that they will not be hindered? Epictetus' answer to this question is that there are, namely, our purely mental activities, e.g. assent: activities that do not involve, as actions such as walking do, the intentional use of our limbs or our organs because they occur inside the soul. In relation to this question, I shall argue that this answer seems to conflict with Stoic corporealism, and explore whether, given Stoic corporealism, Epictetus is truly entitled to claim that we know that our purely mental activities will never be hindered.

1 Against the Counterfactual Conception

The main evidence for the attribution of *MC* to Epictetus – the contrast he often sets out between activities that something external "can" (δύναται) hinder and activities that something external 'cannot' hinder – is questionable.[4] In itself, the term "can" is ambiguous. It may be used, in principle, to express two different claims: (a) the *modal* claim that it is possible that something external hinders the action even if it does not actually do so, and (b) the *epistemic* claim that I do not know whether something external will hinder it. But (b) does not imply (a). For example, I do not know whether my walk this afternoon will be hindered by something external. Therefore, my action "can" be hindered in the epistemic sense. But suppose that, as a matter of fact, nothing external will hinder my walk and that this proposition – *nothing external will*

3 This complements Salles 2014, 174, according to which for Epictetus an activity is in our power if and only if we are the cause of it. *EC* does not exclude that the causal condition is also necessary (i.e. that I must be the cause of φ in order for it be in my power), but as I argue here it is not sufficient on its own: the knowledge that φ will not be hindered is also necessary.

4 One relevant passage here is *Dissertations* 4.1.68–71 cited below as T3 and discussed in section 2.

hinder it – is *necessary*. If so, then it is *impossible* that something will hinder it and, hence, it is *false* that something could hinder it. Therefore, something external "can" hinder my action in the epistemic sense (since I do not know yet whether something will hinder it) but nothing external "can" hinder it in the modal sense (since it is necessary that nothing will hinder it). I will argue in section 2 that as a matter of fact Epictetus' use of the term "can" in this context is not modal, but epistemic.

In addition, MC implies a counterfactual notion of possibility according to which there are things that could occur even if they never actually do so, that is in itself problematic for two reasons. Firstly, it is contrary to Stoic determinism. According to Stoic determinism there is only one possible world, the actual one, inasmuch as every actual event and state is necessitated by prior causes. Surely, determinism is not conspicuous in Epictetus. However, there are clear references to determinism in his work.

> T1: Stobaeus 4.44.60, fr. 8 Schenkl (= Musonius Rufus, fr. 42 Hense):
> Ῥούφου ἐκ τῶν Ἐπικτήτου περὶ φιλίας.
> ὅτι τοιαύτη ἡ τοῦ κόσμου φύσις καὶ ἦν καὶ ἔστι καὶ ἔσται καὶ οὐχ οἷόν τε ἄλλως γίγνεσθαι τὰ γιγνόμενα ἢ ὡς νῦν ἔχει· [...] ἐὰν πρὸς ταῦτά τις ἐπιχειρῇ ῥέπειν τὸν νοῦν καὶ πείθειν ἑαυτὸν ἑκόντα δέχεσθαι τὰ ἀναγκαῖα, πάνυ μετρίως καὶ μουσικῶς διαβιώσεται τὸν βίον.
> Of Rufus from the writings of Epictetus *On Friendship*.
> That such was, and is, and will be, the nature of the cosmos, and that it is not possible for the things that come into being to come into being otherwise than they actually do [...] If someone attempts to direct his mind to these things and to persuade himself to accept voluntarily the things that are necessary, he will have a very balanced and harmonious life.[5]

Even if this passage is read as a quotation by Epictetus of his teacher Musonius Rufus rather than as a statement of his own views on the matter, there is no reason for thinking that Epictetus departed from his teacher on this specific issue.[6] At least, his moral psychology is fully consistent with determinism, and it is wrong to think that for him our mind is free from necessitating causes.[7]

5 Unless otherwise stated all translations are my own.

6 On this question see Long 2002, 176.

7 As is noted in Bobzien 1998, 335, Brennan 2001, 275–9, Long 2002, 221 and 229–230, Salles 2005, 110, Frede 2007, 119, Braicovich 2010, 205–210, and Frede 2011, 44–48. For a different, somewhat indeterministic interpretation, see Dobbin 1991, 121 discussed in Long 2002, 229.

Secondly, although Chrysippus proposed a notion of counterfactual possibility designed to be consistent with determinism, there is no evidence that Epictetus followed him on this. Chrysippus' notion of counterfactual possibility is attested in Diogenes Laertius.[8]

> T2: Diogenes Laertius 7.75 (*SVF* 2.201, LS 38D, BS 19.22[9]):
> δυνατὸν μὲν τὸ ἐπιδεκτικὸν τοῦ ἀληθὲς εἶναι, τῶν ἐκτὸς μὴ ἐναντιουμένων πρὸς τὸ ἀληθὲς εἶναι, οἷον ζῇ Διοκλῆς.
> Possible is that which is susceptible of being true and which is not prevented by external factors from being true, such as *Diocles is alive*.

Here "possible" qualifies a proposition, e.g. the proposition *Diocles is alive*. This proposition is possible because it is "susceptible" of being true and nothing external prevents it from being true. But what is "susceptible of" being true? One adequate answer, first proposed by Long and Sedley, is that the proposition *A does Φ* is "susceptible of" being true if and only if *A* – the subject of the proposition – is "susceptible of" doing φ; and *A* is "susceptible of" doing φ if and only if *A* is physically fit, or strong enough, to φ. For instance, the proposition *I rob the bank* is "susceptible of" being true because I am susceptible of robbing the bank in the sense that I am physically fit to rob it.[10] This notion of modal counterfactual possibility is fully consistent with causal determinism. For instance, I am physically fit to rob a bank and nothing external prevents me to do so, even though it is causally necessitated by my moral character that I refrain from doing so. Thus, my action is counterfactually possible in a modal sense, but its non-occurrence is nevertheless causally necessitated. However, there is no evidence that Epictetus ever used Chrysippus' notion of counterfactual possibility to explain how something can or cannot be hindered. In

8 The ancient sources other than Diogenes Laertius that report Chrysippus' modal theory are listed in Bobzien 1998, 112 n. 39.

9 I use the following abbreviations. *SVF*: von Arnim 1903–1905; LS: Long-Sedley 1987; BS: Boeri-Salles 2014.

10 1987, 1:235. Other construals have been proposed, which do not affect the point I want to make. See for example Coope (2016, 253 and 243 n. 20, based on Bobzien 1998, 112–116, 310–313): "According to Chrysippus, the claim "X is F" is possible just in case (1) being something of X's kind is compatible with being F (that is, the claim "admits of being true") and in addition (2) there are no external factors preventing X from being F (that is, the claim "is not prevented by external factors from being true"). For example, "Dio is walking today" is possible just in case (1) being human (that is, being the kind of thing Dio is) is compatible with walking (in a way that, say, being a tree or a fish would not be) and (2) there is nothing external that prevents Dio from walking today (for example, he is not chained down)."

fact, Epictetus' ethics, and notably his theory of moral progress, does not require counterfactual possibilities.[11] I return to this issue at the end of the next section.

2 The Epistemic Conception

I now turn to the epistemic conception of what is in our power (EC): an activity φ is in our power only if we know that our φ-ing will not be hindered. If I am currently walking from *A* to *B* and know that my walk will not be hindered, then my walk from *A* to *B* is in my power. Otherwise, if something *will* hinder my walk at some point between *A* and *B*, or if nothing will but I do not *know* it, then the walk is not in my power. EC does not involve any counterfactual modality as MC does. In EC, what is in our power is determined through considerations regarding what we know of what *actually* happens. There is no need to appeal to counterfactual possibilities.

Unlike MC, EC is well supported by the evidence. In fact, my attribution of EC to Epictetus is based on an epistemic reading of 'can' in the very passages that the advocates of MC normally cite in support of their interpretation, and to which I have already referred in section 1. Here is one of them, from Epictetus' lengthy discourse 4.1 "On Freedom."[12]

> T3: Epictetus, *Dissertations* 4.1.68–71:
> πότερον οὖν οὐδὲν ἔχεις αὐτεξούσιον, ὃ ἐπὶ μόνῳ ἐστὶ σοί, ἢ ἔχεις τι τοιοῦτον; – οὐκ οἶδα. – ὅρα οὖν οὕτως καὶ σκέψαι αὐτό. μή τις δύναταί σε ποιῆσαι συγκαταθέσθαι τῷ ψεύδει; – οὐδείς. – οὐκοῦν ἐν μὲν τῷ συγκαταθετικῷ τόπῳ ἀκώλυτος εἶ καὶ ἀνεμπόδιστος. – ἔστω. – ἄγε, ὁρμῆσαι δέ σε ἐφ' ὃ μὴ θέλεις τις δύναται ἀναγκάσαι; – δύναται. ὅταν γάρ μοι θάνατον ἢ

11 Moral progress – a key feature of Epictetus' ethical teaching – requires alternative courses of action, but the kind of alternative courses it requires does not presuppose counterfactual possibility. For it requires diachronic, not synchronic, alternative courses of action, i.e. it does not demand that when I φ at a time *t*, I have the possibility of not φ-ing at *t*, but just that when I φ at *t*, I have the possibility of not φ-ing at some future time t^*. If I currently act cowardly, my moral progress does not require the possibility that I act courageously *now*, but just the possibility that I act courageously *in the future*. And diachronic possibility, in contrast with synchronic possibility, does not presuppose counterfactual possibilities. In fact, it is fully compatible with necessitating causes: the necessity of my acting cowardly now is compatible with the necessity of my acting courageously in the future.

12 See also T7 and T8 below.

δεσμὰ ἀπειλῇ, ἀναγκάζει μ' ὁρμῆσαι. – ἂν οὖν καταφρονῇς τοῦ ἀποθανεῖν καὶ τοῦ δεδέσθαι, ἔτι αὐτοῦ ἐπιστρέφῃ; – οὔ. – σὸν οὖν ἐστιν ἔργον τὸ καταφρονεῖν θανάτου ἢ οὐ σόν; – ἐμόν. – σὸν ἄρα ἐστὶ καὶ τὸ ὁρμῆσαι ἢ οὔ; – ἔστω ἐμόν. – τὸ δ' ἀφορμῆσαι τίνος; σὸν καὶ τοῦτο.

– Do you have nothing autonomous, which is in your power alone, or do you have something of this kind? – I do not know. – Well, look at it in this way, and examine it. Is anyone capable of making you assent to what is false? – No one. – In the realm of assent, then, you are unrestrained and unhindered. – Let us suppose I am. – Now, is there anyone capable of forcing you to exercise an impulse for what you do not wish? – Yes, there is. For when someone threatens me with death or prison, he forces me to exercise an impulse. – If, however, you disdain dying or being imprisoned, would you still pay attention to him? – No. – Is disdaining death, then, your own act, or not? – My own. – And is the exercise of an impulse towards something your own act, or not? – Let us suppose it is. – And the exercise of an aversion to something? That is your own act, too.

This passage is a clear statement of the view that assent and refusal are "our own act" (Epictetus uses the second person singular: ἔργον σόν) and "in our power" (ἐφ' ἡμῖν) because they "cannot" be hindered. Now, consider another passage that also discusses what it is for something to be "our own (act)."

T4: Epictetus, *Dissertations* 2.6.8–10 (LS 58J):

ἀεὶ μεμνημένος ὅ τι σὸν καὶ τί ἀλλότριον [καὶ] οὐ ταραχθήσῃ. διὰ τοῦτο καλῶς ὁ Χρύσιππος λέγει ὅτι 'μέχρις ἂν ἄδηλά μοι ᾖ τὰ ἑξῆς, ἀεὶ τῶν εὐφυεστέρων ἔχομαι πρὸς τὸ τυγχάνειν τῶν κατὰ φύσιν· αὐτὸς γάρ μ' ὁ θεὸς ἐποίησεν τούτων ἐκλεκτικόν. εἰ δέ γε ᾔδειν ὅτι νοσεῖν μοι καθείμαρται νῦν, καὶ ὥρμων ἂν ἐπ'αὐτό· καὶ γὰρ ὁ πούς, εἰ φρένας εἶχεν, ὥρμα ἂν ἐπὶ τὸ πηλοῦσθαι.'

Being always reminded of what is your own, and what is another's, you will not be troubled. For this reason, Chrysippus rightly says: "As long as what comes next is unclear to me, I always cling to the things naturally fitted to attain what is in accordance with nature, for god himself created me as a selector of these things. At any rate, if I knew that I am destined to be ill now, I would exercise an impulse for being so; for the foot too, if it had a mind, would aspire to be muddied."

Epictetus quotes Chrysippus with approval and connects Chrysippus' ideas with his own views about what is "our own." Now, just as **T3** is a clear statement of the view that an activity, or "act" (ἔργον), φ is "our own" or "in our power" only if our φ-ing "cannot" be hindered, so too **T4** is a clear statement of the view that an act φ is "our own" (and hence "in our power") only if we *know* that our φ-ing will not be hindered. These two necessary conditions could hardly be meant by Epictetus to be independent from one another. In particular, he seems to rule out a situation where we know that our φ-ing will not be hindered, but in which god "can" hinder it anyway. And this entails, in favour of the epistemic reading of "can", that our φ-ing "cannot" be hindered by god if we know that our φ-ing will not be hindered by him. The example given in **T4** is of a *state*, not an action. But this does not affect my argument. *EC* concerns activities, but it may apply equally well to states if, following the Stoics, we look at activities and states as two different species of events understood as the exemplification of properties: activities are the exemplification of dispositions whereas states are the exemplification of qualities.[13] Thus a more general statement of *EC* would be: for any exemplification by us of a property *P*, this exemplification is in our power only if we know that this exemplification will not be hindered. In sum, **T3** and **T4** support the epistemic reading of "can" and constitute strong evidence that Epictetus does not have a modal conception of what is in our power (*MC*), but rather an epistemic one (*EC*).

To be sure, this epistemic conception stipulates a very demanding condition for an action to be in our power. This is so for two reasons. The first one is that in Stoic epistemology, knowledge is a strong cognitive state, difficult to come by. In **T4**, the term used by Epicetus (or Chrysippus, whom he quotes) is the verb εἰδέναι. In a similar passage, **T5**, Epictetus uses προειδέναι and προγιγνώσκειν:

T5: *Dissertations* 2.10.5–6:

διὰ τοῦτο καλῶς λέγουσιν οἱ φιλόσοφοι ὅτι εἰ προῄδει ὁ καλὸς καὶ ἀγαθὸς τὰ ἐσόμενα, συνήργει ἂν καὶ τῷ νοσεῖν καὶ τῷ ἀποθνῄσκειν καὶ τῷ πηροῦσθαι, αἰσθανόμενός γε, ὅτι ἀπὸ τῆς τῶν ὅλων διατάξεως τοῦτο ἀπονέμεται, κυριώτερον δὲ τὸ ὅλον τοῦ μέρους καὶ ἡ πόλις τοῦ πολίτου. νῦν δ' ὅτι οὐ προγιγνώσκομεν καθήκει τῶν πρὸς ἐκλογὴν εὐφυεστέρων ἔχεσθαι, ὅτι καὶ πρὸς τοῦτο γεγόναμεν.

For this reason, the philosophers rightly say that the fine and good man foreknew the things that will happen, he would contribute even to becoming ill, dying or being mutilated, perceiving that this is allotted in accordance with the ordering of the whole, and that the whole is more authoritative than the part and the city than the citizen. But since that we do not currently know in advance [what will happen], it is appropriate

13 I develop this point fully in Salles 2018, 142–150.

that we hold fast to those things that are more naturally suited to be selected, for this is that for which we were generated.

It is not evident whether the use of these verbs is intended to refer to "knowledge" in the strictest sense (ἐπιστήμη) or to mere "cognition" (κατάληψις), which is weaker than ἐπιστήμη, but a demanding kind of epistemic grasp nonetheless.[14]

The second reason has to do with the specific *content* of the state of knowledge referred to in these passages. In the example chosen by Epictetus, the content of the knowledge – be it knowledge proper or mere cognition – is especially elusive. Unlike other contents, e.g. 2 + 2 = 4, my actions and states in the future are determined by a highly complex conjunction of elements. In Stoic physics, everything that occurs in the cosmos occurs for the preservation of the current cosmic order. Given Epictetus' views on divine "providence" (προνοία), this completely general proposition is for him a truth that anyone well trained in Stoic philosophy will easily grasp.[15] But it may not be manifest which particular actions or states are, in a given situation, required for this preservation. For something that is beneficial to the cosmos as a whole may, in a given situation, be harmful to one of its parts. This view is implied by Epictetus in a passage that complements **T4** and **T5**:

T6: *Dissertations* 2.5.24–25:

πῶς οὖν λέγεται τῶν ἐκτός τινα κατὰ φύσιν καὶ παρὰ φύσιν; ὥσπερ ἂν εἰ ἀπόλυτοι ἦμεν. τῷ γὰρ ποδὶ κατὰ φύσιν εἶναι ἐρῶ τὸ καθαρῷ εἶναι, ἀλλ', ἂν αὐτὸν ὡς πόδα λάβῃς καὶ ὡς μὴ ἀπόλυτον, καθήξει αὐτὸ⟨ν⟩ καὶ εἰς πηλὸν ἐμβαίνειν καὶ ἀκάνθας πατῆσαι καὶ ἔστιν ὅτε ἀποκοπῆναι ὑπὲρ τοῦ ὅλου· εἰ δὲ

---

14 See e.g. Sextus Empiricus, *Against the Professors* 7.151 (LS 41C, BS 7.8): "cognition" (κατάληψις) is "assent belonging to a cognitive impression, and a cognitive impression, so they claim, is one which is true and of such a kind that it could not turn out false" (καταληπτικῆς φαντασίας συγκατάθεσις· καταληπτικὴ δὲ φαντασία κατὰ τούτους ἐτύγχανεν ἡ ἀληθὴς καὶ τοιαύτη οἵα οὐκ ἂν γένοιτο ψευδής) and "knowledge" (ἐπιστήμη) is "cognition which is secure and firm and unchangeable by reason" (τὴν ἀσφαλῆ καὶ βεβαίαν καὶ ἀμετάθετον ὑπὸ λόγου κατάληψιν). For a discussion of the evidence and the intermediate position of cognition see Meinwald 2005, 226–231 and, more recently, Brouwer 2014, 29–41 and 70–72.

15 See e.g. the first lines of *Dissertations* 1.6 "On Providence" commented on in Long 2002, 150: "Whether he speaks of Nature (as in 1.6.21 and 1.16.9), or of Zeus or God (as in 1.6.3 and 1.19.11), Epictetus takes it to be completely certain that human beings are equipped to understand how this cosmic principle excellently governs the world and how, in particular, it has made human beings not only social animals but also "world citizens" (1.9.1, 1.19.13, 2.10.3, 3.24.11)." See also 2.14.23–28 discussed in Magrin 2018, 301–302.

> μή, οὐκέτι ἔσται πούς. τοιοῦτόν τι καὶ ἐφ' ἡμῶν ὑπολαβεῖν δεῖ. τί εἶ; ἄνθρωπος. εἰ μὲν ὡς ἀπόλυτον σκοπεῖς, κατὰ φύσιν ἐστὶ ζῆσαι μέχρι γήρως, πλουτεῖν, ὑγιαίνειν. εἰ δ' ὡς ἄνθρωπον σκοπεῖς καὶ μέρος ὅλου τινός, δι' ἐκεῖνο τὸ ὅλον νῦν μέν σοι νοσῆσαι καθήκει, νῦν δὲ πλεῦσαι καὶ κινδυνεῦσαι, νῦν δ' ἀπορηθῆναι, πρὸ ὥρας δ' ἔστιν ὅτ' ἀποθανεῖν.
>
> What is the meaning of the statement that some external things are natural and others unnatural? It is as though we took ourselves to be detached beings. For while I admit that it is natural for the foot to be clean, yet if you take it as a foot and not as something detached, it will be appropriate for it to step into mud and trample on thorns, and sometimes be amputated for the sake of the whole. Otherwise it will no longer be a foot. That is the way we should also view ourselves. What are you? A human being. If you view yourself as something detached, it is natural for you to live to old age, to be wealthy, and healthy. But if you view yourself as a human being and a part of some whole, for the sake of that whole it is appropriate for you now to be sick, now to set sail and take risks, now to be in need, and maybe even die before your time.[16]

I have argued that EC is well attested in our sources and that it is a demanding conception of what is in our power: it requires knowledge of god's providential plan, which may itself require, in connection with the same person, different actions or states at different times. But however demanding EC may be, it is surely less demanding than MC. If we accept counterfactual possibilities at all, there always seems to be something that could hinder our actions even if it actually does not, no matter how we interpret the counterfactual modality involved in this claim. Suppose, for example, that we interpret this modality in Chrysippean terms and say that an activity φ is in our power if and only there is nothing X such that (i) nothing external to X prevents X from hindering our φ-ing and (ii) X is physically fit, or strong enough, to hindering it. But if so, then surely the Stoic god could always interfere with my activities with the result that nothing would be in my power? I return to this question shortly.

3 Closing Remarks: Two Open Questions

In this final section, I address two connected general questions dealing with the interpretation of Epictetus. I will have to leave them open because they are

16 Long tr. in 2002, 200–201.

very broad, and a full discussion of them would take us way beyond the scope of this paper.

Firstly, why does Epictetus associate what is in our power with what we *know* that will not be hindered? Why does not he propose the simpler, and weaker, association of what is in our power with what will not be hindered, independently of whether we know or not? For example, if I am walking from *A* to *B* and nothing will hinder my action (because it is in god's plan), but I do not know this, then why is my walk not in my power? In other words, why do I have to *know* this in order for the walk to be in my power? One hypothesis that would require further investigation is that for Epictetus the simple fact that nothing will hinder my action, in isolation from my knowledge of it, is of no use for the guidance of my life. Purely theoretical enquiries are ethically worthless.

> T7: Stobaeus 2.1.31, Epictetus, fr. 1 Schenkl:
> τί μοι μέλει, φησί, πότερον ἐξ ἀτόμων ἢ ἐξ ἀμερῶν ἢ ἐκ πυρὸς καὶ γῆς συνέστηκε τὰ ὄντα; οὐ γὰρ ἀρκεῖ μαθεῖν τὴν οὐσίαν τοῦ ἀγαθοῦ καὶ κακοῦ καὶ τὰ μέτρα τῶν ὀρέξεων καὶ ἐκκλίσεων καὶ ἔτι ὁρμῶν καὶ ἀφορμῶν καὶ τούτοις ὥσπερ κανόσι χρώμενον διοικεῖν τὰ τοῦ βίου, τὰ δ' ὑπὲρ ἡμᾶς ταῦτα χαίρειν ἐᾶν, ἃ τυχὸν μὲν ἀκατάληπτά ἐστι τῇ ἀνθρωπίνῃ γνώμῃ, εἰ δὲ καὶ τὰ μάλιστα θ⟨εί⟩η τις εἶναι καταληπτά, ἀλλ' οὖν τί ὄφελος καταληφθέντων; οὐχὶ δὲ διακενῆς πράγματα ἔχειν φατέον τοὺς ταῦτα ὡς ἀναγκαῖα τῷ τοῦ φιλοσόφου λόγῳ προσνέμοντας;
>
> Why (he says) should I care whether existing things are compounded from atomic or incomposite elements, or from fire and earth? Isn't it enough to learn the essence of good and bad and the measures of desires and aversions and also of positive and negative impulses, to run our lives using these as rules; and not to bother about those things that are beyond us? Perhaps they cannot be known by the human mind, and even if one were to suppose that they are perfectly knowable, what is the advantage of such knowledge? Shouldn't we say that people who make this *essential* to a philosopher's discourse are wasting their time?[17]

So, in an enquiry into what is in our power, it is not enough to know what is in our power *in abstracto*. We must also know, for each activity that we want to perform, whether this activity is in our power.

The second question is connected to the first: how many of the activities that we perform are such that can we genuinely *know* that they will, or that

17 Long tr. in 2002, 149.

they will not, be hindered? Very few given the reason mentioned in section 2. But there is at least one specific set of activities such that, according to Epictetus, we do know that they will not be hindered, namely the set of our "purely mental" activities. These are activities that do not involve, as actions such as walking do, the intentional use of our limbs or our organs because they occur inside the soul. This is suggested for instance in the following passage also extracted, like **T3**, from "On Freedom."[18]

> **T8**: *Dissertations* 4.1.72–73:
> τί οὖν, ἂν ἐμοῦ ὁρμήσαντος περιπατῆσαι ἐκεῖνός με κωλύσῃ; – τί σου κωλύσει; μή τι τὴν συγκατάθεσιν; – οὔ· ἀλλὰ τὸ σωμάτιον. – ναί, ὡς λίθον. – ἔστω· ἀλλ' οὐκέτι ἐγὼ περιπατῶ. – τίς δέ σοι εἶπεν τὸ περιπατῆσαι σὸν ἔργον ἐστὶν ἀκώλυτον;
>
> Yes, but what if my impulse is to walk freely and another person hinders me? – What part of you can he hinder? Not your assent, surely? – No, but my little body. – Yes, as he could a stone – So be it; but I no longer walk – And who told you that walking was an activity of your own that cannot be hindered?

As before, I read the "can" in an epistemic sense: we know that nothing will ever interfere with our acts of assents; in contrast, we do not know whether something will interfere with my actions. For example, every time I assent to the proposition *nothing will hinder my walk from A to B*, the assent, according to Epictetus, is never hindered. In contrast, it may happen that, when I assent, something does hinder my action. When this happens, the assent does not fail: it is successfully completed. What fails is just the action involved in the proposition to which I successfully assent.

Now, what is the basis of this difference according to Epictetus? Why, if we do not know whether our actions will be hindered, we do know that our mental activities will not? This is a difficult question that Epictetus does not address in clear terms and that modern Epictetus scholars normally bypass,[19]

18 For further references, see Bobzien 1998, 333 n. 6.

19 See for instance Bobzien 1998, 333–334: "For nearly every activity that involves intentional bodily movements however small, we can imagine some external obstacles that will prevent it from being carried out. With (positive) actions such as walking, eating, or escaping one's enemy, we can never be sure whether they will be in our power. [In contrast] external hindrances are not conceivable [in the case of assent and intention]. Neither natural nor human force can prevent them from occurring, as Epictetus never tires of repeating. For Epictetus, assent, intention, and refraining from action depend on us, because

with few exceptions.[20] In some contexts, for instance, Epictetus intimates that the reason why our mental activities "cannot" be hindered is that not even the Stoic god has the *strength* needed to hinder them. Consider for instance the following passage (a parallel passage is *Dissertations* 1.1.3).

> **T9**: *Dissertations* 1.6.40:
> καίτοι ὅ γε θεὸς οὐ μόνον ἔδωκεν ἡμῖν τὰς δυνάμεις ταύτας, καθ' ἃς οἴσομεν πᾶν τὸ ἀποβαῖνον μὴ ταπεινούμενοι μηδὲ συγκλώμενοι ὑπ' αὐτοῦ, ἀλλ' ὃ ἦν ἀγαθοῦ βασιλέως καὶ ταῖς ἀληθείαις πατρός, ἀκώλυτον τοῦτο ἔδωκεν, ἀνανάγκαστον, ἀπαραπόδιστον, ὅλον αὐτὸ ἐφ' ἡμῖν ἐποίησεν οὐδ' αὑτῷ τινα πρὸς τοῦτο ἰσχὺν ἀπολιπών, ὥστε κωλῦσαι ἢ ἐμποδίσαι.
> However, god has not only given us these capacities [e.g. the capacity of examining impressions and of assenting to, or refusing them], in virtue of which we will endure everything that happens without being abased or stunted by it, but, as is characteristic of a good king and a true father, he has given them to us free of all restraint, compulsion, or hindrance, and has put them totally in our power, not even reserving any strength for himself to hinder or restrain them.

It is far from obvious why a Stoic would accept the idea that not even god is strong enough to hinder our mental activities. For what is "strength"? The term ἰσχύν is not defined in **T9**. But it probably denotes – as it does in other places in Epictetus – the power of a body to stretch in order to act on another body.[21] Now in Stoicism the soul is, just like the body, a *corporeal* entity, i.e. something that is by nature affected by the action of other bodies.[22] So one consequence of Stoic corporealism is that the mere fact that an activity is purely mental

---

we have the general ability to perform them, and no one and nothing external to us has the power of interfering and keeping us from performing them." See also Dobbin 1998, 101–113, and Coope 2016, 250–252.

20 See Graver 2002, 349–355 and especially Sharples 2005, 203–213.

21 See e.g. *Dissertations* 2.23.3 on the Stoic theory of vision, according to which, when we see, a portion of breath extends from our eyes to the objects that we see, touches it, and transmits back to our soul the form of the object. Epictetus uses here the term ἰσχυρόν to point out that this breath is so 'strong' that it has the power to stretch out very long distances without being destroyed: "Has god given you eyes for nothing? Was it for nothing that he has infused into them a breath of such strength and ingenuity that it can reach far out and model the imprints of whatever is seen?" (εἰκῇ οὖν σοι ὁ θεὸς ὀφθαλμοὺς ἔδωκεν, εἰκῇ πνεῦμα ἐνεκέρασεν αὐτοῖς οὕτως ἰσχυρὸν καὶ φιλότεχνον, ὥστε μακρὰν ἐξικνούμενον ἀναμάσ⟨σ⟩εσθαι τοὺς τύπους τῶν ὁρωμένων;) Tr. Hard-Gill, slightly modified.

22 As is implied in the Stoic definition of body as things that offer "resistance" (ἀντιτυπία) to touch, for which see Galen in *SVF* 2.381 (>LS 45F) and Sextus Empiricus in *SVF* 2.501.

does not guarantee, all by itself, that it will be immune from the action of god or even that it will be *more* immune than actions to external coercion in general.

Corporealism is at the core of early Stoic physics, e.g. in Chrysippus, according to whom any body – including the soul – is subject to the action of external factors. In one his key arguments for moral responsibility, however, he argues that the way in which our soul reacts to an impression we receive from outside and, in particular, whether or not our will gives assent to the impression, is not determined by the impression, but by the intrinsic properties of our soul. Of course, our soul is a body that was generated at some point in the past. So its acquisition of the properties that currently determine how we react to present impressions is ultimately fully determined by external factors in the past. At any rate our assent to a given impression is not determined in the present by *that* impression. But the same holds true of our body. The way in which our body reacts to coercion depends on its intrinsic properties. The heavier I am, the less easy it is to push me. In fact, the example used by Chrysippus to illustrate how the reaction of our soul is not determined by our impressions is that of the motion of an *inanimate* body, a cylinder or spinning cone. Their motion is not fully determined by an external push, which merely triggers the motion, but by their intrinsic properties.[23] To recapitulate, corporealism does not warrant the difference Epictetus vindicates between soul and body with respect to coercion. It is certainly true that in Epictetus corporealism is not as prominent as in early Stoicism. But there are sure signs that he is a corporealist. On his view, for example, the soul is made of "breath" (πνεῦμα), the early Stoic term for expressing their corporealist view that the soul is a body.[24] And he refers with approval to strongly corporealist early Stoic physical theories, such as the theory of vision.[25] For this reason it remains an open question why, according to Epictetus, if we do not know whether our actions will be hindered, we do know that our mental activities will not.[26]

23 The two main sources for Chrysippus' cylinder argument are Cicero, *On Fate* 42–43 and Aulus Gellius, *Attic Nights* 7.2.11 thoroughly discussed in Bobzien 1998, 258–271.

24 See notably *Dissertations* 2.23.3 (cited above) and 3.3.22, both identified by Long (2002, 158) as evidence for corporealism in Epictetus.

25 In *Dissertations* 2.23.3 (cited above twice).

26 Earlier versions of this paper were presented at the Ancient Philosophy Workshop in Oxford in October 2016 and at the colloquium "Fate, Providence and Free Will. Philosophies and Religions in Dialogue in the Early Imperial Age (20 B.C.–A.D. 250)" held at the Università Cattolica del Sacro Cuore in Milan in November 2017. I am thankful to Terry Irwin and Emmanuele Vimercati for their invitation and to the audiences for the discussion. I am especially grateful to Richard Sorabji, Sophie Cartwright, Gretchen Reydams-Schils and

Bibliography

Bobzien, Susanne. 1998. *Determinism and Freedom in Stoic Philosophy*. Oxford: Clarendon.

Braicovich, Rodrigo S. 2010. "Freedom and Determinism in Epictetus' *Discourses*." *Classical Quarterly* 60: 202–220.

Brennan, Ted. 2001. "Fate and Free Will in Stoicism: A Discussion of Susanne Bobzien, *Determinism and Freedom in Stoic Philosophy*." *Oxford Studies in Ancient Philosophy* 21: 259–86.

Brouwer, René. 2014. *The Stoic Sage. The Early Stoics on Wisdom, Sagehood and Socrates*. Cambridge: Cambridge University Press.

BS: Boeri, Marcello D., and Ricardo Salles. 2014. *Los filósofos estoicos: ontología, lógica, física y ética, traducción, comentario filosófico y edición anotada de los principales textos griegos y latinos*. Sankt Augustin: Academia.

Coope, Ursula. 2016. "Rational Assent and Self-Reversion: a Neoplatonist Response to the Stoics." *Oxford Studies in Ancient Philosophy* 50: 237–287.

Dobbin, Robbin. 1991. "Prohairesis in Epictetus." *Ancient Philosophy* 11: 111–135.

Dobbin, Robbin. 1998. *Epictetus. Discourses I*. Oxford: Clarendon.

Frede, Michael. 2014 [2007]. "The *eph'hêmin* in Ancient Philosophy." In *What is Up to Us? Studies on Agency and Responsibility in Ancient Philosophy*, edited by Pierre Destrée, Ricardo Salles, Marco Zingano, 351–363. Sankt Augustin: Academia. (Originally published in ΦΙΛΟΣΟΦΙΑ 37: 110–23.)

Frede, Michael. 2011. *A Free Will. Origins of the Notion in Ancient Thought*, edited by Anthony A. Long. Berkeley: University of California Press.

Graver, Margaret. 2003. "Not Even Zeus: A Discussion of A.A. Long, *Epictetus: A Stoic and Socratic Guide to Life*." *Oxford Studies in Ancient Philosophy* 24: 343–359.

Hard, Robin, tr., and Christopher Gill, ed. 2014. *Epictetus. Discourses, Fragments, Handbook*. Oxford: Oxford University Press.

Long, Anthony A. 2002. *Epictetus. A Stoic and Socratic Guide to Life*. Oxford: Clarendon.

LS: Long, Anthony A., and David N. Sedley. 1987. *The Hellenistic Philosophers*. Cambridge: Cambridge University Press.

Magrin, Sara. 2018. "Nature and Utopia in Epictetus." *Phronesis* 63: 293–350.

Meinwald, Constance. 2005. "Ignorance and Opinion in Stoic Epistemology." *Phronesis* 50: 215–231.

the editors of the present volume for their written comments. The research for this paper received support from two projects, CONACYT CB 2013 221268 and PAPIIT-UNAM IN403620, a sabbatical grant from PASPA-UNAM, and a GlaxoSmithKline Fellowship from the National Humanities Center in North Carolina.

Salles, Ricardo. 2014. "Epictetus and the Causal Conception of Moral Responsibility and What is in Our Power." In *What is up to us? Studies on Causality and Responsibility in Ancient Philosophy*, edited by Pierre Destrée, Ricardo Salles, and Marco Zingano, 169–182. Sankt Augustin: Academia.
Salles, Ricardo. 2018. "Two Classic Problems in the Stoic Theory of Time." *Oxford Studies in Ancient Philosophy* 55: 133–183.
Sharples, Robert. 2005. "Ducunt volentem fata, nolentem trahunt." In *La catena delle cause: Determinismo e antideterminismo nel pensiero antico e contemporaneo*, edited by Carlo Natali and Stephano Maso, 197–216. Amsterdam: Hakkert.
SVF: von Arnim, Hans. 1903–1905. *Stoicorum veterum fragmenta*. Leipzig: Teubner.

CHAPTER 4

Providence and Cosmology in Philo of Alexandria

Ludovica De Luca

1 Introduction

Philo's conception of providence has two main implications, one cosmological, the other ethical.[1] The first implication concerns the action of God in creating and governing the world, whereas the second deals primarily with human responsibility. Whereas the ethical implications are discussed by Roberto Radice in the next chapter of this volume, I will here focus on the cosmological ramifications of providence, which in Philo are related to the coming-into-being and the corruption of the world.[2]

The cosmological relevance of providence is attested especially in the works written by Philo after his participation in the delegation to the Emperor Gaius Caligula in 38 CE. In Rome, he actively sought more protection for the Alexandrian Jewish community, which, under the prefect Flaccus, had been suffering unsustainable forms of abuse.[3] Recently, Maren Niehoff suggested that the period spent in Rome would also have influenced him from a cultural and philosophical point of view.[4] In the works which Philo wrote during and after his stay, he paid more attention to issues such as that of providence which were widely discussed in Rome. Even though providence is a topic that can be found in all of Philo's works, in the works which are considered to have been written after the Roman embassy, it resurfaces as "freed" from the dense allegorical accounts in the *Allegorical Commentary* and in the *Questions and Answers*, where the philosophical issues are more difficult to extract.[5] After

1 For providence in Philo of Alexandria and its consequences on ethics and theodicy, see Frick 1999, 139–175. The standard edition of Philo's works is Cohn-Wendland 1896–1930.

2 Frick 1999, 89–118. For providence in Philo, see also Dragona-Monachou 1994, 4456–4461.

3 Schwartz 2009, 14–31.

4 See Niehoff 2018, 1–22.

5 According to Niehoff 2018, 245–246, Philo was born ca. 20 BCE in Alexandria, where he wrote the *Allegorical Commentary* and the *Questions* between ca. 10–35 CE. After the pogrom in the autumn of 38 CE, he travelled to Rome as the head of the Jewish embassy to Gaius (cf. Josephus, *Antiquities of the Jews* 18.259). Between 38–41 CE Philo was active in Rome as ambassador and author and, according to Niehoff, even probably led the negotiations with Claudius after Gaius' assassination in 41 CE. Between 40–49 CE, Philo started to write a new series of works, addressing a wider Graeco-Roman audience, which include his historical

 | DOI:10.1163/9789004436381_006

the embassy, Philo – like Seneca a few years later – would devote a whole treatise to providence, dealing with the connection between *pronoia* and theodicy in a more substantial manner.[6] Also in *On the Creation of the World* (part of the *Exposition of the Law*) he assigned to providence a fundamental role within his cosmology.[7]

The Roman embassy also affected Philo's approach to cosmology, in which providence allows for a specific form of communication between God and the cosmos which He created. In Philo's conception of *pronoia* the Jewish tradition, Platonism and Stoicism converge.[8] Philo's providence is a "synthetic" concept, in the sense that it not only refers to the divine "premeditation" that precedes the creative act, but also to God's "care" towards the world. Philo develops from a Jewish perspective doctrines that can already be found in the *Timaeus* and in the Stoic readings of this dialogue. Philo's conception of *pronoia* shows a remarkable continuity with the conception that permeates the Jewish-Hellenistic literature of his time. Although Philo's cosmology is functional to his ethics, in the works which he wrote after the embassy, providence is no longer considered solely in relation to man's responsibility, as it had been in the *Allegorical Commentary*. *Pronoia* starts to assume the role of "guarantor" of a cosmology aimed at reconciling Judaism, Platonism and Stoicism. Philo's providence is a philosophical answer to questions regarding the perpetual existence of the cosmos.[9]

2 Providence in *On the Creation of the World*

Already at the beginning of *On the Creation of the World* Philo explicitly refers to *pronoia*. At 9, he attacks those who – like Aristotle and Epicurus – had

---

and philosophical writings and the *Exposition of the Law*. According to Niehoff, Philo died in ca. 49 CE.

6 *On Providence* 1.77–88 Aucher. See Niehoff 2018, 76–77, cf. Kaiser 2007, 134–146, where, in the light of the Stoic tradition, the Wisdom of Ben Sirach is compared with Seneca's *On Providence*, Philo's *Every Good Man is Free* and Cicero's *On the Paradoxes of the Stoics*, with a focus on analogies/divergences between human action and divine providence. For Philo and Seneca see also Radice 1989, 281–319 and Scarpat 1977, 64–65. For Philo's *On Providence* see Runia 2017, 159–178 and Radice in this volume.

7 Niehoff 2018, 74–77, cf. Runia 2017, 177. Frick 1999, 185–189; 194 underlines how in *On the Embassy to Gaius* and *Against Flaccus* Philo identifies providence with justice and with the divine protection which the Alexandrian Jewish community was seeking more urgently than in previous years. In these two works Philo appears to have elaborated a notion of providence aimed at encouraging and instilling hope in the Jewish people.

8 Runia 1986, 241–242. Cf. Frick 1999, 92–94.

9 Frick 1999, 102–108, and Runia 1986, 494. Cf. Sterling 1992, 15–41.

believed that the cosmos was ungenerated. Philo has no doubts in considering providence as indispensable for an explanation of the origin of the world:

> But the passive object, which of itself was without soul and unmoved, when set in motion and shaped and ensouled by the intellect, changed into the most perfect piece of work, this cosmos. Those who declare that it is ungenerated are unaware that they are eliminating the most useful and indispensable of the contributions to piety, the (doctrine of) providence (πρόνοιαν).[10]

In his commentary on the passage Runia states: "The doctrine of providence has to be seen as the obverse of the doctrine of creation."[11] The existence of *pronoia*, in fact, guarantees the whole creative process which involves both macrocosm (world) and microcosm (man).[12] Although from several passages of *On the Creation of the World* it is clear that providence must be taken for granted, Philo refers again to it only at the end of his work. Nevertheless, Philo, following Genesis and Plato's *Timaeus*, highlights that God is like a father who takes care of the sons which He has generated.[13] According to Philo, the world is not left to chance but is subject to a divine will, which, in line with the Stoic tradition, corresponds to the law of God and the law of nature.[14] God, like a king and a commander, rules over the cosmos by making sure that everything follows His providential plan which aims at avoiding a "power-vacuum"

10 Cf. *On Providence* 1.6–8. All translations of *On the Creation of the World* in this chapter are taken from Runia 2001. Runia offers the parallels of Cicero, *On the Nature of the Gods* 1.18–20, where the Epicurean Velleius attacks *Pronoia* presented as "the old woman predicting future of the Stoics" (*anus fatidica Stoicorum*), and of Atticus, fr. 4 Des Places (= Eusebius, *Preparation for the Gospel* 15.6.1–17), where the existence of providence in the universe is safeguarded in an anti-Aristotelian key (Runia 2001, 117–118). For a discussion of *On the Creation of the World* 9, see also Radice 1987, 234–236; cf. Trabattoni 2009, 113–122.

11 Runia 2001, 117–118.

12 See also Radice 1987, 235.

13 For God as father see *On the Creation of the World* 46, 74–75, 84, 89, 145, 171.

14 In *On the Creation of the World*, at 143, Philo states: "But since every well-governed city has a constitution, it was the case that the citizen of the world necessarily made use of the constitution which belonged to the entire cosmos. This is the right reason of nature, which is named with a more appropriate title "ordinance" (θεσμός), a divine law, according to which obligations and rights have been distributed to each creature." Radice underlines that, despite Stoic influence, Philo's thoughts here are original. Even if Philo is using a Stoic lexicon, the law of nature corresponds to the Torah (cf. Radice 1987, 302). For the law in Philo and some possible connections with Platonic-Stoic authors (such as Antiochus of Ascalon), see Koester 1970, 521–541 and Horsley 1978, 35–59.

(ἀναρχία) in this world.[15] On a metaphorical level, the divine plan corresponds to a blueprint which an architect would draw up in order to build the "great city" of the cosmos (μεγαλόπολις).[16] From a cosmological point of view, therefore, providence does not consist only in divine thoughtfulness and care for the perpetual existence of the cosmos, it also expresses the foresight of God: everything happens as has already been inscribed in the Architect's project. The corruption of the cosmos, however, does not form a part of this divine blueprint. Runia has made clear that the connection between providence and the indestructibility of the world in Philo is to be understood against the background of Plato's *Timaeus*, at 41a6–b6, where Plato writes that the things which the demiurge has assembled are not dissolvable unless he wants.[17] Following Plato, in *On the Eternity of the World* Philo argues against the theory of *ekpurōsis*, which – so he stresses – the Stoics Boethus of Sidon and Panaetius of Rhodes also did not accept.[18] More specifically, in *On the Eternity of the World* 25–26 Philo defends the indestructibility of the cosmos by referring this time

---

15 In *On the Creation of the World*, at 11, Philo states: "It is a worthless and unhelpful doctrine, bringing about a power-vacuum (ἀναρχία) in this cosmos, just like (what happens) in a city, because it does not then have a ruler or magistrate or judge, by whom everything is lawfully administered and regulated." In his commentary Runia 2001, 139 explains his preference for translating *power-vacuum* rather than *anarchy* "because this would obscure the meaning of a lack of legitimate authority. But of course when this is missing, anarchy in the modern sense ensues. As a Jewish inhabitant of Alexandria, Philo knew at first hand what civil anarchy could mean. Witness the dreadful pogrom of 38 CE. Implicit here is the apologetic theme of the monarchic rule of the God of Israel."

16 In *On the Creation of the World* 17–20 Philo compares the paradigm, in which the ideas are contained, to a νοητὴ πόλις and this cosmos to a μεγαλόπολις. For Philo's simile of God as an architect, see Runia 2003, 89–106 (cf. his 1990, 398–412, 2000, 361–379 and Decharneux 2017, 11–26). My forthcoming monograph *Il Dio architetto di Filone di Alessandria* (Opif. 17–20) is dedicated to an analysis of *On the Creation of the World* 17–20.

17 Runia 1986, 494 stresses that Philo is best brought in connection with the Middle Platonists. A common aspect is that God is not considered as responsible for the evil in the cosmos (see Emmanuele Vimercati's contribution to this volume). According to Runia, the Stoic tradition seems to be dominant in comparison to the Platonic tradition. See e.g. *On Providence*, where Plato's thought plays a secondary role in comparison with Stoicism. In *On the Heavens* 1.10, 279b4–282b7 Aristotle, referring to the *Timaeus* and its interpreters, had already criticized those who believed in both a generated and an indestructible cosmos. Cf. Frick 2001, 102–108.

18 *On the Eternity of the World* 76–78. Von Arnim inserts this passage into *SVF* as Boethus, fr. 7. In the collections on Panaetius, scholars usually only regard section 76 as Panaetian: see fr. 65 Van Straaten, fr. 131 Alesse, fr. A59 Vimercati (who takes 76–84 on board as uncertain: fr. C1). It should be remembered that Philo's authorship of *On the Eternity of the World* has been doubted: see further Runia 1981, 105–151. For Philo as a "doxographer", see Runia 2008 (for *On the Eternity of the World*, see 34–39).

to *Timaeus* 32c5–33b1, where the universe is described as "ageless and without sickness" (ἀγήρως καὶ ἄνοσος).

In Frick's words, "the doctrine of providence functions as an essential pillar within the structure of Philonic thought as a whole",[19] or put differently: *pronoia* holds everything together. On the one hand, *pronoia* is the "divine forethought" in which the creation – and, more generally, everything will happen – is planned. On the other hand, *pronoia* is the law which governs the world as a city. Due to providence the world can persist even after the sixth day when God stopped creating and embellishing it. At the end of the *On the Creation of the World*, at 170–171, Philo illustrates the key-points of his cosmology:

> By means of the creation account which we have discussed he [Moses] teaches us among many other things five lessons that are the most beautiful and excellent of all.
>
> The first of these is that the divinity is and exists, on account of the godless, some of whom are in doubt and incline in two directions concerning his existence, while others are more reckless and brazenly assert that he does not exist at all, but is only said to exist by people who overshadow the truth with mythical fictions.
>
> The second lesson is that God is one, on account of those who introduce the polytheistic opinion, feeling no shame when they transfer the worst of political systems, rule by the mob, from earth to heaven.
>
> The third lesson is, as has already been said, that the cosmos has come into existence, on account of those who think it is ungenerated and eternal, attributing no superiority to God.
>
> The fourth lesson is that the cosmos too is one, since the creator is one as well and he has made his product similar to himself in respect of its unicity, expending all the available material for the genesis of the whole. After all, it would not have been a complete whole if it had not been put together and constituted of parts that were themselves whole. There are those who suppose there to be multiple cosmoi, and there are others who think their number is boundless, whereas they themselves are the ones who are really boundlessly ignorant of what it is fine to know.
>
> The fifth lesson is that God also takes thought (προνοεῖ) for the cosmos, for that the maker always takes care of what has come into existence is a necessity by the laws and ordinance of nature, in accordance with which parents too take care of their children.

19 Frick 2001, 1.

At 172, Philo summarizes the five lessons by stating:

> He, then, who first has learnt these things not so much with his hearing as with his understanding, and has imprinted their marvelous and priceless forms on his own soul, namely that God is and exists, and that he who truly exists is one, and that he made the cosmos and made it unique, making it, as was said, similar to himself in respect of its being one, and that he always takes thought (προνοεῖ) for what has come into being, this person will lead a blessed life of well-being, marked as he is by the doctrines of piety and holiness.[20]

From these five lessons or "doctrines" (δόγματα) it can be inferred that providence occupies an intermediate position, between the existence of God and that of the cosmos. Providence, in fact, originates in God but represents a sort of "bridge" between the Creator and mankind. In addition to guaranteeing the existence of the cosmos, providence includes the care of the Father for what has been created.

The doctrines have been understood as decrees of faith. According to Goodenough, these five doctrines corresponded to "the first creed in history".[21] Against Goodenough, Runia argued that this summary of the Mosaic/Philonic doctrine – which might have didactic goals – cannot consist in "a creed or articles of faith in which one must believe before one can belong to Judaism."[22] Rather, they are "the fundamental or preliminary doctrines (δόγματα) of which one must be intellectually convinced in order to embark on an understanding of the scriptures that embrace both the Mosaic legislation and the wider Jewish tradition."[23] Runia suggested that these doctrines could have a pre-Philonic origin, even if "the strong philosophical emphasis makes it likely that Philo decisively contributed to their formulation."[24]

These doctrines, in fact, should be contextualized not only within Hellenistic Judaism, but also within the contemporary debate among philosophers, because they contain answers to the "standard philosophical questions of Philo's

20 Frick 1999, 2 translates: "(1) God is and is from eternity, and (2) that He who really IS is One, and (3) that He has made the world and (4) has made it one world, unique as Himself is unique, and (5) that He ever exercises providence for his creation."

21 Runia 2001, 392 against Goodenough 1962, 37.

22 Runia 2001, 394.

23 Runia 2001, 394. Cf. Radice 1987, 312, for a comparison between *On the Creation of the World* 172, *On the Special Laws* 3.189, *On Rewards and Punishments* 42 and *Questions and Answers* 2.34.

24 Runia 2001, 394.

time."[25] Excluding God's uniqueness, in his *Placita* Aëtius testifies to divine existence (1.7), to the corruptibility/incorruptibility of the cosmos (2.4), to its uniqueness (1.5 and 2.1), and, finally, to the presence of providence in the world (2.3).[26] Aëtius reports that, according to all philosophers – with the exception of the Atomists, Epicurus, Ecphantus and Aristotle –, it is providence which animates and administers the world.[27] Philo, as we will see, stresses the emblematic role of *pronoia* within the five doctrines as being in harmony with the Platonic and Stoic traditions, implicitly brought up by Aëtius, and coherent with the Stoic reading of the *Timaeus*.[28]

3 *Pronoia* in Hellenistic Judaism: from Royal Care to Divine Providence

Like other concepts in the *corpus Philonicum*, providence has a double meaning, which is theological and philosophical at the same time. According to Philo, no conflict is to be assumed between Judaism and Hellenistic philosophy: he even introduces Moses as the first philosopher.[29] Philo's concept of providence, elaborated from a cosmological perspective, is part of a general need to reformulate philosophical topics in a Judaic key.[30] This need has its roots in Judaic-Hellenistic thought. As soon as Jewish thinkers starts to write in Greek, they also adopt philosophical issues discussed in this language. As is well known, Philo, who most probably did not know Hebrew, used the *Septuagint*, the Greek translation of the Scriptures. The "seventy translators" thus already imported typically Greek notions in their translations.

In general, the seventy translators rarely used the term *pronoia* in the sense of "divine providence". Only in the books of the *Septuagint* which were composed directly in Greek and where the influence of Stoicism is more manifest

25 Runia 2001, 392–393.

26 See Runia 2001, 392–393, cf. Runia 2009, 341–373. Mansfeld and Runia 1997–2018, vol. 1, 321–323 suggest that the *Placita* could have been writing during the first century CE.

27 Mansfeld and Runia 1997–2018, vol. 1, 337–346.

28 See Reydams-Schils 1999 for the readings of the *Timaeus* from the ancient Stoics to Calcidius. See also Reydams-Schils 2013, 29–58 and Alesse 2018, 46–57 (for the *Timaeus* especially 49–50).

29 *On the Creation of the World* 8: "Moses, however, had not only reached the very summit of philosophy, but had also been instructed in the many and most essential doctrines of nature by means of oracles." Cf. *On the Creation of the World* 131, where Philo compares Moses with the "other philosophers" (ἄλλοι φιλόσοφοι).

30 For the notion of "Judaic-Hellenistic thought", see Calabi 2010, 5–14. See also Wendland 1912, 192–211 and Momigliano 1975, 74–96.

does this word start to mean "providence". In the second book of Maccabees an embryonic sense of providence can be found, not yet related to the celestial government of the cosmos, but to the terrestrial authority of kings.[31] Two examples should suffice here: at 2 Maccabees 4.6 the "regal decision" (βασιλικὴ πρόνοια) of king Seleucus IV Philopator re-establishes peace, and at 2 Maccabees 14.9 his son Demetrius, once having become king, is asked "to take care" (προνοεῖν) of his people and, in particular, of the Jews. According to Arnaldo Momigliano, the *Letter to Aristeas*, where the origin of the *Septuagint* is celebrated in a solemn manner, would have been written around the same time as the second book of *Maccabees*. Both of them are to be connected to the same cultural ambience.[32] Also in the *Letter of Aristeas*, in fact, *pronoia* is a typical characteristic of kings.[33] In particular, at 30.5 mention is made of "royal care" (βασιλικὴ πρόνοια) that warranted the translation of the Torah.[34] Two further examples can be found at 80.3 and 190.3. At 80.3 *pronoia* is king Ptolemy's "forethought" towards the temple furnishings, which he has donated to the High priest Eleazar. At 190.3, the hope is expressed that every king will exercise "great care" (πολλὴ πρόνοια) towards the people which they govern.[35]

However, in the *Letter*, at 201.2, *pronoia* is used in the sense of divine providence. This use is attributed to Socratic Menedemus of Eretria (4th–3rd century BCE), apparently also present at the celebration of the translation of the *Septuagint* in the presence of the king, who in his answer pronounces these words:

> Indeed, O King. For since all things are governed by providence (προνοίᾳ), and assuming this correctly, that human beings are created by God, it follows that all sovereignty and beautiful speech have a starting point in God.[36] (Tr. Wright)

31 According to Momigliano 1987, 41–51, the second book of *Maccabees* should be dated around 124 BCE. Cf. Sacchi 2012–2019, 1434 n. 9. For the use of the verb προνοέω and of the substantive πρόνοια in the *Septuagint*, see Moulton-Milligan 1930, 543.

32 Sacchi 2012–2019, 1434.

33 Philo frequently describes God as king (e.g. *On the Creation of the World* 71 and 88). He seems to invert the process of the divinization of the sovereigns, typical of the Hellenistic age, with Alexander the Great as the standard example: Wendland 1912, 123–127.

34 Wright 2015, 154. Cf. Calabi 2011, 60–61 n. 28.

35 Wright 2015, 342–343.

36 See Diogenes Laertius 2.140. Wright 2015, 351–352 remarks that the Menedemus quotation could be due not only to his reputation as philosopher but also as a host of symposia, where he was often one of the last to leave. Cf. Gruen 2013, 2711–2768, especially 2749.

Unlike the earlier occurrences of *pronoia* in the *Letter*, here it no longer characterizes the actions of kings, but refers to the divine government of the cosmos. A similar meaning can also be found in the *Septuagint*, in relation to the heavenly sovereign. In 3 Maccabees 4.21 and 5.30, God helps and protects the Jewish people, using invincible, divine providence.[37] Also, in 4 Maccabees *pronoia* is an exclusive characteristic of God and represents the silent "director", who guides all the events narrated in the book.[38] In 4 Maccabees 17.22 only providence could save Israel from oppression and could protect the Jewish people from the misfortunes which fall upon them.

In the Book of Wisdom a similar notion of providence as "divine protection" can be found. According to Scarpat, this book would have been composed within the Alexandrian Jewish community by an author who was well-skilled in Platonic and Stoic traditions.[39] At 6.7, with reference to the severe judgment which awaits powerful men, it is said that not only does God create everything, whether big or small, He also "provides" (προνοεῖ) equally to everything.[40] At 14.3, in the metaphor of a ship at the mercy of stormy waves, it is said that only the providence of the Father guides everything: "but your foresight, oh Father, pilots it" (ἡ δὲ σή, πάτερ, διακυβερνᾷ πρόνοια).[41]

According to Otto Kaiser, providence is also implicit in the Wisdom of Sirach – a Greek translation of a text originally written in Hebrew, probably in Jerusalem at the beginning of 2nd century BCE. There it is connected to the creation of the world.[42] At 39.12–35 – so Kaiser – Ben Sirach is concerned with ensuring the responsibility of man and there are no doubts about the finalistic character of the divine action.[43] The God of Ben Sirach predicts how human beings will behave, by making sure that they will have the means at their disposal to do well, such that He can do good to right people and the evil to the bad one (Wisdom of Sirach 39.16–21). In the Wisdom of Sirach, providence serves divine justice, which finds expression in God's punishment or reward.

37 Sacchi 2012–2019, vol. 2.2, 1537–1538.

38 See e.g. 4 Maccabees 9.24 and 13.19.

39 Scarpat 1989, vol. 1, 18. Cf. Winston 1979, 25–59 and Sacchi 2012–2019, vol. 3, 864.

40 Sacchi 2012–2019, vol. 3, 893 n. 83, where, in the context of Stoicism the connections between the use of the verb προνοεῖν and the verb ποιεῖν are discussed.

41 In Wisdom of Sirach 17.2 αἰώνια πρόνοια concerns all people, except blasphemous men who are excluded from perpetual providence and who are prisoners of darkness. In the *Septuagint pronoia* is also mentioned in the Greek version of the book of Daniel, at 6.19, where it is said that God, in "taking care of him" (πρόνοιαν ποιούμενος αὐτοῦ), closes the lion's jaws in order that they do not disturb Daniel ever again.

42 Kaiser 2007, 96–112. For Wisdom of Sirach see Sacchi 2012–2019, vol. 3, 955–960.

43 Kaiser 2007, 96.

As Kaiser notes, despite his debt to Stoicism throughout the work, Ben Sirach's conception of providence lacks the aspect of "necessity" (ἀνάγκη), which according to the Stoics determines the fate of man.[44] God gives human beings what they deserve: He is benevolent towards good people and punitive to the bad.[45] Therefore, the Creator does not determine the course of things in the world in their entirety, but from the beginning He provides men with the means they will need to do good. For this reason, according to Kaiser, the hymn at 39.12–35 can be understood as a sort of celebration of God, who created the world and the human beings in it, and who governs over them.[46]

Philo developed his conception of providence against this Judaic-Hellenistic background, where Platonic and Stoic traditions had already merged with Judaism. On the basis of the *Timaeus*, however, Philo emphasized the cosmological role of *pronoia*, which becomes part of the five doctrines expressed in his "Mosaic philosophy."[47] Aristoboulus (2nd century BCE) was a Peripatetic of Jewish descent, who, like Philo, lived in Alexandria and used Greek philosophy in order to interpret the Scripture. Unfortunately, only a very limited part of his work survives. For this reason, it is difficult to ascertain the role of providence in Aristoboulus' thought and to know, in particular, if he held that providence guaranteed the creation of the world as did Philo. Although in these fragments Plato is quoted by name, it is not possible to establish with certainty whether the *Timaeus* may have represented a stable point of reference for his works.[48] Runia, in particular, sees some traces of divine providence in fr. 4 Radice (Eusebius of Caesarea, *Preparation for the Gospel* 13.12.4) and in fr. 5 (Eusebius of Caesarea, *Preparation for the Gospel* 13.12.12), where God preserves what He has produced according to His original arranging.[49] Even if it is not possible to exactly establish the role of providence according to Aristoboulus, Philo

44 Kaiser 2007, 107.

45 Kaiser 2007, 107.

46 Kaiser 2007, 109–110.

47 For "the essence of Mosaic philosophy", see Radice 1987, cxxxviii–cxxxix.

48 For Aristoboulus and the *Timaeus*, see Reydams-Schils 1999, 137–139. Also Niehoff 2013, 90–91 (cf. her 2011, 58–74) highlights a possible role of the *Timaeus* in Aristobulus' thought. According to Radice 1995, 97–119, 181–182, however, Aristoboulus does not refer at all to the *Timaeus*. The imprint of this Platonic dialogue would have emerged from the few and short, but – so Radice – not insignificant, fragments. Radice also notes that in Aristoboulus, furthermore, there are no echoes of the Platonic doctrine of ideas, which will later be fundamental in Philo. See also Runia 1986, 410.

49 Runia 2001, 118. The presence of the divine providence in Aristoboulus would be evidenced by the verb συνέχειν. In fr. 4 Radice, Aristoboulus embraces the idea, which he attributes also to Pythagoras, Socrates and Plato, of the possibility of listening to the "voice of god." According to Aristoboulus, the three philosophers described nature as a divine

seems to be aware of being part of the hybrid process which had been established between Judaism and Graeco-Roman philosophy. This process started in Alexandria: there *pronoia* came to mean not only royal care but also the divine design in which everything has its place. God is not responsible for evil actions but He can reward those who act rightly in conformity with the divine law. In this way human actions are in accordance with God's plan, in which everything – including the creation of the cosmos – is inscribed.

4 The *Timaeus* and Stoicism: the Philosophical Sources of Philo

The role of *pronoia* in *On the Creation of the World* must also be discussed in relation to the *Timaeus*. As the studies by Radice and Runia have shown, Philo's work on the creation of the cosmos seems to be nothing more than an attempt to give a double "exegesis" of both the book of Genesis and the *Timaeus*.[50] Philo offers a Stoic interpretation of the *Timaeus* with continuous reference to the creation in Genesis. As I already noted in the Introduction, with regard to the *Timaeus* Philo would most likely have been influenced by a Stoic reading of this Platonic dialogue.[51] Gretchen Reydams-Schils has underlined how in the development of different interpretations of the *Timaeus* (she speaks of a "hermeneutic circle") the Stoics played a central role.[52] Despite their overall hostile attitude towards this Platonic dialogue, the Stoics assimilated some of its doctrines.[53] Philo, as well as other authors before him (such as Posidonius

creature "held together" (συνεχομένη) by the Creator. In fr. 5 Radice, Aristoboulus underlines that, when God gives an order (τάξις), He also "maintains" (συνέχει) and "remodels" (μεταποιεῖ) it. Cf. Radice 1995, 200–201, 214–215.

50 Radice 1989, 125–186, 373–378, Runia 1987, 384–388, 399–411, 426–433, 461–467, 535–546. Cf. Niehoff 2007, 161–191, where she suggests that Philo could have played a decisive role within the "textual community" which was born around the *Timaeus*. Philo attributes a certain "sacredness" to Plato and attributes to his works an authority similar to that of the Torah. For Philo's explicit and implicit quotations of Plato, see Koskenniemi 2019, 102–106.

51 The Stoics themselves could have accessed it through collections of *vetusta placita* or through transmitted memorizations: cf. Reydams-Schils 1999, 16, 35–36, 41–83, Reydams-Schils 2008, 169–195, Reydams-Schils 2013, 29–58. Cf. Mansfeld 1990, 3167–3177, Mansfeld and Runia 1997–2018, vol. 2.1, 27–41.

52 Reydams-Schils 1999, 16. For a summary of the reception of *Timaeus* until Philo, see Runia 1987, 38–57. For the general reception of *Timaeus* see Reydams-Schils 2003, Sheppard and Sharples 2003, Steel and Leinkauf 2005, Napolitano 2007, Celia and Ulacco 2015.

53 See Alesse 2018, 46–57. Cf. Sedley 2007, 225–230 for the dependence of the Stoics on the *Timaeus*. For their use of *Timaeus* 30b1–c1 Sedley 2007, 229–233 points to Sextus Empiricus, *Against the Professors* 9.104 and Cicero, *On the Nature of the Gods* 2.21 (both in *SVF* 1.111).

and Antiochus of Ascalon, as they are known to us via Cicero's writings), could have formulated his conception of *pronoia* on the basis of this kind of readings of the *Timaeus*.[54] In Philo's "Stoic reading of *Timaeus*" the Judaic-Hellenistic tradition remains, however, crucial.

In the *Timaeus*, at 30b8–c1, Timaeus, recognizing the demiurge's benevolence as the starting point for the creation of the world, states that the universe, which is like a living being endowed with soul and thought, had been generated "thanks to divine providence" (διὰ τὴν τοῦ θεοῦ πρόνοιαν). A similar notion of providence can also be found in book 10 of Plato's *Laws*,[55] in particular at 901d–902c, where the idea that the gods do not care about human affairs is rejected, since the gods understand, see and listen to everything that happens.[56] The *Timaeus*, however, goes one step further than the *Laws*: *pronoia* not only preserves and takes care of human beings but also has a generative character. When Philo considers *pronoia* in relation to the demiurge, who in *On the Creation of the World* becomes one of ways by which Philo refers to God, his point of reference is obviously the *Timaeus*.[57] In the Philonic image of God as an architect, this world is perfect, because it was built by the Creator according to the blueprint which He had previously designed. The generative character of *pronoia* in the *Timaeus* can be found also in Stoics like Chrysippus who also conferred to it the capacity of shaping matter.[58] In Stoicism, *pronoia* is identified with the nature of the whole. According to Diogenes Laertius 7.138 (SVF 2.634), Chrysippus and Posidonius stated that providence coincides with *nous*, which permeates the cosmos as a "force of cohesion".[59] Philo takes up this aspect of Stoic *pronoia*, in order to reconcile the transcendent and the immanent roles of the Creator. He lives in the world which He has built, ruling it not only "from above" but also "from within". Different from the Stoics' conception, Philo's *pronoia* has no value in itself and can exist only if God "activates"

54 Reydams-Schils 1999, 117–133 (cf. her 2013, 25–43). According to Radice 1989, 267–275, however, neither in Antiochus nor in Posidonius traces of Philo's theory of ideas as thoughts of God can be found. Ideas as thoughts God is thus to be attributed to Philo. Cf. Runia 1987, 46–49.

55 In the *Laws*, however, Plato does not use a specific lexicon focused on *pronoia* which is possible to find only through adverbial connotations or in connection with human forethought. For instance, see *Laws* 4.721c7, 8.838e7, 9.871a2, 873a6.

56 Cf. *Phaedrus* 254e7, where *pronoia* is the foresight of the charioteer. For *pronoia* in Plato, see Dragona-Monachou 1994, 4419–4422, cf. Ferrari 2010, 177–192.

57 E.g. *On the Creation of the World* 36, 68, 138–139, 146, 171. Cf. Powers 2013, 713–722.

58 Cicero, *On the Nature of the Gods* 3.92 (SVF 2.1107). For *pronoia* in Stoicism, see Dragona-Monachou, 1976, 1994, 4424–4452, as well as Brouwer and Salles in this volume.

59 Plutarch, *On the Contradictions of the Stoics* 34.1049F (SVF 2.937) also reports that, according to Chrysippus, both universal nature and universal reason are to be identified with providence and Zeus.

it. For this reason, *pronoia* becomes part of the five Philonic doctrines, occupying an intermediate position between God and the cosmos: providence both originates in God and acts on the world.

5 Conclusions

Philo's debt towards Stoicism concerns the role which divine immanence plays in his theology, where it is harmonized with God's transcendence.[60] As Maren Niehoff has pointed out, both the politics of the Empire and Stoicism represent the context for the emergence of a "monotheistic creation theology", which can be found not only in Philo but also in later Jewish authors such as Flavius Josephus.[61] Therefore the cosmological meaning of *pronoia*, which emerges in *On the Creation of the World* must be understood in relation to these political and philosophical influences which Judaism encountered at the dawn of the new era. Philo's interpretation of the *Timaeus* in a Stoic-Jewish key is emblematic of the new air which Philo inhaled in Rome. In *On the Creation of the World* providence becomes a symbol of the encounter between Judaism and Greco-Roman Hellenistic philosophy and Philo elaborates this concept in order to prove that the cosmos will be governed in the best possible way.

Bibliography

Alesse, Francesca. 2018. "The Influence of the Platonic Dialogues on Stoic Ethics from Zeno to Panaetius of Rhodes." In *Brill's Companion to the Reception of Plato in Antiquity*, edited by Harold Tarrant, Danielle A. Layne, Dirk Baltzly, and François Renaud, 46–57. Leiden: Brill.

Calabi, Francesca. 2010. *Storia del pensiero giudaico ellenistico*. Brescia: Morecelliana.

Calabi, Francesca, tr. 2011. *Lettera di Aristea a Filocrate*, 2nd edn. Milan: Rizzoli (BUR).

Celia, Francesco, and Angela Ulacco, eds. 2015. *Il* Timeo. *Esegesi greche, arabe, latine*. Pisa: Pisa University Press.

60 Niehoff 2018, 99–100: "Following his immersion in Stoic philosophy, Philo interprets Plato's *Timaeus* with emphasis on divine immanence. [...] Plato's god remains separate from the world, enjoying a perfection that is impossible in the material realm. Philo's creator God, by contrast, has become astonishingly close to humans and the world, sharing his very essence in the creation."

61 Niehoff 2013, 85–106 (I owe the reference to this article to Prof. Runia). Cf. Radice 2008, 124–145.

Cohn, Leopold, and Paul Wendland, eds. 1896–1930. *Philonis Alexandrini opera quae supersunt*, 7 vols. Berlin: Reimer.

Decharneux, Badouin. 2017. “L'Architecture comme paradigme philosophique dans le *De opificio* de Philon d'Alexandrie (*Opif.* 17–22).” *Diversitate si identitate culturala in Europa* 14: 11–26.

Dragona-Monachou, Myrto. 1976. *The Stoic Arguments for the Existence and the Providence of the Gods*. Athens: National and Capodistrian University of Athens.

Dragona-Monachou, Myrto. 1994. “Divine Providence in the Philosophy of the Empire.” In *Aufstieg und Niedergang der römischen Welt*, edited by Wolfgang Haase, vol. 2.36.7, 4417–4490. Berlin: De Gruyter.

Ferrari, Franco. 2010. “Provvidenza platonica e autocontemplazione aristotelica in Plutarco.” In *Gods, Daimones, Rituals, Myths and History of Religions in Plutarch's Works: Studies Devoted to Professor Frederick E. Brenk*, edited by Luc Van der Stockt, Frances B. Titchener, Heinz G. Ingenkamp and Aurelio Pérez Jiménez, 177–192. Málaga: Universidad de Málaga.

Frick, Peter. 1999. *Divine Providence in Philo of Alexandria*. Tübingen: Mohr Siebeck.

Goodenough, Erwin R. 1962. *An Introduction to Philo Judaeus*. 2nd edn. New Haven: Yale University Press.

Gruen, Erich. 2013. “The Letter of Aristeas.” In *Outside the Bible: Ancient Jewish Writings Related to Scripture*, edited by Louis H. Feldman, James L. Kugel, and Lawrence H. Schiffman, 2711–2768. Lincoln: University of Nebraska Press.

Horsley, Richard A. 1978. “The Law of Nature in Philo and Cicero.” *Harvard Theological Review* 71: 35–59.

Kaiser, Otto. 2007. *Der Menschen Glück und Gottes Gerechtigkeit. Studien zur biblischen Überlieferung im Kontext hellenistischer Philosophie*. Tübingen: Mohr Siebeck.

Koester, Helmut. 1970. “*Nomos physeos*: The Concept of Natural Law in Greek Thought.” In *Religions in Antiquity. Essays in Memory of Erwin Ramsdell Goodenough*, edited by Jacob Neusner, 521–541. Leiden: Brill.

Koskenniemi, Erkki. 2019. *Greek Writers and Philosophers in Philo and Josephus. A Study of Their Secular Education and Educational Ideals*. Leiden: Brill.

Mansfeld, Jaap. 1990. “Doxography and Dialectic: The *Sitz im Leben* of the Placita.” In *Aufstieg und Niedergang der römischen Welt*, edited by Wolfgang Haase, vol. 2.36.4, 3167–3177. Berlin: De Gruyter.

Mansfeld Jaap and David T. Runia, eds. 1997–2018. *Aëtiana. The Method and Intellectual Context of a Doxographer*, 3 vols. Leiden: Brill.

Momigliano, Arnaldo. 1975. *Alien Wisdom. The Limits of Hellenization*. Cambridge: Cambridge University Press.

Momigliano, Arnaldo. 1987. *Pagine ebraiche*. Turin: Einaudi.

Moulton, James H. and George Milligan, eds. 1930. *The Vocabulary of the Greek Testament*. London: Hodder and Stoughton.

Napolitano, Linda, ed. 2007. *La sapienza di Timeo. Riflessioni in margine al "Timeo" di Platone*. Milan: Vita e Pensiero.

Niehoff, Maren R. 2007. "Did the Timaeus Create a Textual Community?" *Greek, Roman, and Byzantine Studies* 47: 161–191.

Niehoff, Maren R. 2011. *Jewish Exegesis and Homeric Scholarship in Alexandria*. Cambridge: Cambridge University Press.

Niehoff, Maren R. 2013. "The Emergence of Monotheistic Creation Theology in Hellenistic Judaism." In *Jewish and Christian cosmogony in Late Antiquity*, edited by Lance Jenott and Sarit Kattan Gribetz, 85–106. Tübingen: Mohr Siebeck.

Niehoff, Maren R. 2018. *Philo of Alexandria. An Intellectual Biography*. New Haven: Yale University Press.

Powers, Nathan. 2013. "Plato's Demiurge as Precursor to the Stoic Providential God." *Classical Quarterly* 63: 713–722.

Radice, Roberto, tr. 1987. *Filone di Alessandria. La filosofia mosaica. La creazione del mondo secondo Mosè; Le allegorie delle leggi*. Milan: Rusconi.

Radice, Roberto. 1989. *Platonismo e creazionismo in Filone di Alessandria*. Milan: Vita e Pensiero.

Radice, Roberto. 1995. *La filosofia di Aristobulo e i suoi nessi con il « De mundo » attribuito ad Aristotele*. 2nd edn. Milan: Vita e Pensiero.

Radice, Roberto. 2008. "Philo's Theology and Theory of Creation." In *Philo of Alexandria and Post-Aristotelian Philosophy*, edited by Francesca Alesse, 124–145. Leiden: Brill.

Reydams-Schils, Gretchen. 1999. *Demiurge and Providence. Stoic and Platonist Readings of Plato's* Timaeus. Turnhout: Brepols.

Reydams-Schils, Gretchen. 2008 [2002]. "Philo of Alexandria on Stoic and Platonist Psycho-Physiology: the Socratic Higher Ground." In *Philo of Alexandria and Post-Aristotelian Philosophy*, edited by Francesca Alesse, 169–195. Leiden: Brill.

Reydams-Schils, Gretchen. 2013. "The Academy, the Stoics and Cicero on Plato's *Timaeus*." In *Plato and the Stoics*, edited by Alex G. Long, 29–58. Cambridge: Cambridge University Press.

Reydams-Schils, Gretchen, ed. 2003. *Plato's* Timaeus *as Cultural Icon*. Notre Dame: University of Notre Dame Press.

Runia, David T. 1981. "Philo's *De aeternitate mundi*: the Problems of its Interpretations." *Vigiliae Christianae* 35: 105–151.

Runia, David T., ed., tr. 2001. *Philo of Alexandria. On the Creation of the Cosmos according to Moses*. Leiden: Brill.

Runia, David T. 1986. *Philo of Alexandria and the Timaeus of Plato*. Leiden: Brill.

Runia, David T. 1990. "*Polis* and *Megalopolis*. Philo and the Founding of Alexandria." In *Exegesis and Philosophy. Studies on Philo of Alexandria*, 398–412. Aldershot: Variorum.

Runia, David T. 2000. “The Idea and the Reality of the City in the Thought of Philo of Alexandria.” *Journal of the History of Ideas* 61: 361–379.

Runia, David T. 2003. “The King, the Architect, the Craftsman: a Philosophical Image in Philo of Alexandria.” In *Ancient Approaches to Plato's* Timaeus, edited by Robert W. Sharples and Anne Sheppard, 89–106. London: Institute of Classical Studies.

Runia, David T. 2008. “Philo and Hellenistic Doxography.” In *Philo of Alexandria and Post-Aristotelian Philosophy*, edited by Francesca Alesse, 13–54. Leiden: Brill.

Runia, David T. 2009 [1996]. “Atheists in Aëtius: Text, Translation and Comments on *De placitis* 1.7.1–10.” In *Aëtiana. The Method and Intellectual Context of a Doxographer*, edited by Jaap Mansfeld and David T. Runia, vol. 3, 341–373. Leiden: Brill.

Runia, David T. 2017. “From Stoicism to Platonism: the Difficult Case of Philo's *De Providentia* I.” In *From Stoicism to Platonism: the Development of Philosophy, 100 BCE to 100 CE*, edited by Troels Engberg-Pedersen, 159–178. Cambridge: Cambridge University Press.

Sacchi, Paolo, ed. 2012–2019. *La Bibbia dei Settanta*, 4 vols. Brescia: Paideia.

Scarpat, Giuseppe. 1977. *Il pensiero religioso di Seneca e l'ambiente ebraico e cristiano*. Brescia: Paideia.

Scarpat, Giuseppe. 1989. *Il libro della Sapienza*, 3 vols. Brescia: Paideia.

Schwartz, Daniel R. 2009. “Philo, His Family, and His Times.” In *The Cambridge Companion to Philo*, edited by Adam Kamesar, 14–31. Cambridge: Cambridge University Press.

Sedley, David. 2007. *Creationism and Its Critics in Antiquity*. Berkeley: University of California Press.

Sharples, Robert W., and Anne Sheppard, eds. 2003. *Ancient Approaches to Plato's* Timaeus. London: Institute of Classical Studies.

Steel, Carlos G., and Thomas Leinkauf, eds. 2005. *Plato's* Timaeus *and the Foundations of Cosmology in Late Antiquity, the Middle Ages and Renaissance*. Leuven: Leuven University Press.

Sterling, Gregory E. 1992. “*Creatio temporalis, aeterna vel continua*? An Analysis of the Thought of Philo of Alexandria.” *Studia Philonica Annual* 4: 15–41.

Trabattoni, Franco. 2009. “Philo. *De opificio mundi* 7–12.” In *The Origins of the Platonic System: Platonisms of the Early Empire and Their Philosophical Contexts*, edited by Mauro Bonazzi, and Jan Opsomer, 113–122. Leuven: Peeters.

Wendland, Paul. 1912. *Die hellenistisch-römische Kultur in ihren Beziehungen zu Judentum und Christentum*, 2nd edn. Tübingen: Mohr Siebeck.

Winston, David, tr. 1979. *The Wisdom of Solomon*. New York: Doubleday.

Wright, Benjamin G. 2015. *The Letter of Aristeas: 'Aristeas to Philocrates' or 'On the Translation of the Law of the Jews'*. Berlin: De Gruyter.

CHAPTER 5

Providence and Responsibility in Philo of Alexandria. An Analysis of Genesis 2.9

Roberto Radice

As already expressed in the title, this contribution deals with the notions of providence and responsibility in Philo of Alexandria: it offers an application of his cosmology as it appears in *On the Creation of the World* and in *On Providence* to his allegorical reading of the Garden of Eden. This approach will help both to connect his cosmological with his ethical thought as well as to set it in the contemporary philosophical debate. Therefore, in section 1 of this contribution I will introduce some coordinates on Philo's foundation of human responsibility and its place within his theory of virtues. This presentation will follow Philo's exegesis of Genesis 2.9, containing the well-known image of the "Tree of good and evil", which is explained as an allegory of human free will. In order to clarify Philo's perspective, I will focus on his *Allegories of the Laws* and *Questions and Answers on Genesis*, which provide two different, but not inconsistent explanations of the biblical verse. From section 2 onwards, then, I will set Philo's presentation of human responsibility within his understanding of divine providence. In this sense, I will introduce some coordinates on *On Providence*, showing how Philo's discussion is a reply to some Stoic challenges and an anticipation of the Middle Platonist debate as a form of compatibilism between God's and human will, and natural necessity. As will be shown, however, Philo holds a peculiar position within the Stoic-Platonist controversy of the early Imperial age, since he deals with both schools, but rearrange their material in a biblical and Jewish perspective. The result of Philo's discussion is an original picture of God's providence and human responsibility, which will influence the subsequent debates, at least in the Jewish and Christian traditions.

1 The Exegetical Tradition of the "Tree of Good and Evil" in Philo

1.1 *The Perspective in the* Allegories of the Laws

Genesis 2.9 is the first reference in the Bible to human free will. This is expressed through the image of the "Tree of good and evil", which plays a piv-

 | DOI:10.1163/9789004436381_007

otal role in Philo's presentation of the relationship between divine providence and human autonomy. However, Philo's interpretation of this allegory is made complex by a range of philosophical and theological problems arising from the biblical text. For the text of Genesis, after describing the creation of the world (in chapter 1), after stating that man was created "in the image and likeness of God" (1.26) and that the male and the female should be fruitful and multiply, having dominion over the other creatures (1.26–28), goes on to say on chapter 2 that man became a living being through the breath of life infused by God (2.7) and that he was put in the Garden of Eden, which God had planted eastwards (2.8). At this point, in Genesis 2.9, the following description of the Garden contains a controversial ambiguity, at least in the reading of the *Septuagint*. For the original Greek text reads:

> καὶ ἐξανέτειλεν ὁ Θεὸς ἔτι ἐκ τῆς γῆς πᾶν ξῦλον ὡραῖον εἰς ὅρασιν καὶ καλὸν εἰς βρῶσιν καὶ τὸ ξύλον τῆς ζωῆς ἐν μέσῳ τοῦ παραδείσου καὶ τὸ ξύλον τοῦ εἰδέναι γνωστὸν καλοῦ καὶ πονηροῦ.

This is a modern translation:

> And God made to spring up also out of the earth every tree beautiful to the eye and good for food, and the Tree of life in the midst of the garden, and the Tree of knowledge of good and evil.

"Tree of knowledge of good and evil" is the translation commonly adopted by Philonian scholars of the past century, such as Heinemann,[1] Colson and Whitaker,[2] Mondésert,[3] Triviño,[4] and Mercier,[5] who translated from the Armenian.[6] "Tree of knowledge of good and evil" is the customary name for the first tree one encounters when entering Paradise. In a way, this translation is philosophically motivated, but it is not accurate; for it does not abide by the text. It differs from the original text in that it resembles the Stoic definition of virtue, which was actually dominant in Alexandrian Judaism. The Stoic definition can be found in various passages of Hans von Arnim's *Stoicorum Veterum*

1 "Baum der Erkenntnis des Guten und des Bösen" (Heinemann, Cohn, Adler, and Theiler 1962–1964, vol. 1, 146).
2 "Tree of knowledge of good and evil" (Colson and Whitaker 1929, vol. 1, 183).
3 "Arbre de la connaissance du bien et du mal" (Mondésert 1962, 69 and 73).
4 "El árbol de la ciencia del bien y del mal" (Triviño 1975–1976, vol. 1, 146).
5 "Arbre de la connaissance du bien et du mal" (Mercier 1979, 73 ff.).
6 In Radice 2005, 135, I also translated "tree of knowledge of good and evil."

Fragmenta in which reference is made to Chrysippus, who claimed that virtue is "the science of good and evil things",[7] or, in a longer yet corresponding form, "the science of good and bad things and of that which is neither good nor evil."[8] This definition reflects indeed that of Philo's translators, who thereby attributed to him a notion of virtue as knowledge or science. But the correct version of the biblical passage is usually given by translators of the *Septuagint*, who are not influenced by Philo; in Sgiaroviello's translation,[9] for example, *gnōston* is not overlooked as often happens in other translations of Philo. The passage is best read as follows:

> And God made to spring up also out of the earth every tree beautiful to the eye and good for food, and the Tree of life in the midst of the garden, *and the Tree of learning the knowledge of good and evil.*

The second tree could be described likewise, equally faithful to the original, yet stylistically somewhat clumsy, as "the tree-virtue, which allows one to achieve (γνωστόν) the knowledge (εἰδέναι) of things good and evil".[10] Heinemann had already noted that the *Septuagint*'s text had been censored.[11] However, he had justified his own translation by citing other texts,[12] where Philo himself deleted the term *gnōston* while transposing from Greek to Greek.[13]

Philo apparently considered the biblical expression τὸ ξύλον τοῦ εἰδέναι γνωστὸν καλοῦ καὶ πονηροῦ as identical to his own ⟨τὸ ξύλον⟩ τοῦ γινώσκειν καλῶν καὶ πονηρῶν.[14] In doing so, he took the meaning of the episode to be different from the one the biblical text actually demands. Philo first of all

7 See Galen, *On the Doctrines of Hippocrates and Plato* 7.2.2 (*SVF* 3.256), 5.5.40 (*SVF* 3.257: ἐπιστήμη ἀγαθῶν καὶ κακῶν); Pseudo-Andronicus, *On Emotions* (Περὶ παθῶν), p. 19 Schuchardt (*SVF* 3.266).

8 Stobaeus 2.59.5–6 (*SVF* 3.262): ἐπιστήμη ἀγαθῶν καὶ κακῶν καὶ οὐδετέρων.

9 Sgiaroviello 2012, 119.

10 It would be much easier to understand by adding "in the practice of life." A reference to Aristotle's virtues would aid us even more. Φρόνησις (the equivalent of wisdom) refers to reason applied to practical life (that is, "to human goods and the things which can be chosen", which are not necessarily imposed by reason). It is committed to finding the right rational balance between two extremes, and for this purpose it needs a guide and a general rule that can enlighten our mind at all times.

11 At the end of the 19th century, Heinemann began a complete translation of Philo's Greek works in German.

12 Above all *Allegories of the Laws* 1.60 and *Questions and Answers on Genesis* 1.11, which, in Jean-Baptiste Aucher's translation from the Armenian (reported in Mercier 1979, 72), is introduced as follows: *Quid est lignum ad sciendum, cognoscibile boni et mali?*

13 For the critical edition used here see Cohn, Wendland, and Reiter 1962.

14 See *Allegories of the Laws* 1.56–60: the trees in the garden are the particular virtues, or the actions to which they correspond: the right actions and those that philosophers deem

wonders where the Tree of good and evil is actually located. The answer to this question helps to clarify the nature of good and evil and to explain them as (real) possibilities for human deliberation. As a reply, in the *Allegories of the Laws* Philo provides the following interpretation. The *demonstrandum* is that the Tree of knowledge is at the same time *inside* and *outside* the Garden. For this purpose, Philo uses two Aristotelian terms: δυνάμει and κατὰ τὴν οὐσίαν, in order to explain that the Tree is in the garden "in potency", while "in substance" it is outside it. Apparently, the distinction between potency and substance is introduced by Philo to distinguish between the ontological status of good and evil in the Garden and the possibility of choice for the first man. In other terms, Philo's explanation seems to move from the "physical" location of the Tree of good and evil within the Garden to the nature of the choice between the two options. In a way, the Tree can be said to be "bilocated" – both inside and outside the Garden – as long as it is given both an ontological and a psychological meaning – depending on whether it expresses good and evil as real and original entities, or as a result of human choice. This shift is possible because the ruling part of our soul is made up of both good and evil, even when it chooses evil. An example in this sense occurs in *Who is the Heir of Divine Things?*, at 82, where the relationship between soul and body is explained as follows: "Would you not say that a high priest who is not entirely pure when he celebrates the sacred rites of the fathers in the sanctuary, is at the same time *inside* and *outside*? Inside with respect to his visible body, but outside with respect to his soul, which is roaming about and wandering?"[15] Therefore, the high priest is inside the sanctuary in a physical sense with his body, but he is outside the sanctuary in a psychological sense with his soul, which is turned to God.

After discussing the theoretical and practical meanings of *aretē*,[16] Philo identifies virtue as an *ideal model* with the *psychological act* that derives from

"duties". These are the trees in the garden, since virtues are both theoretical and practical. Their beauty to the eye represents their theoretical feature, while their sweet taste is their practical and instrumental aspect.

15 ἢ οὐκ ἂν εἴποιτε, τὸν μὴ τέλειον ἀρχιερέα, ὁπότε ἐν τοῖς ἀδύτοις τὰς πατρῴους ἁγιστείας ἐπιτελεῖ, ἔνδον εἶναί τε καὶ ἔξω, ἔνδον μὲν τῷ φανερῷ σώματι, ἔξω δὲ ψυχῇ τῇ περιφοίτῳ καὶ πεπλανημένῃ; This text thus considers two levels, physical and spiritual, while the allegory of Paradise is entirely localized within the spiritual sphere.

16 *Allegories of the Laws* 1.57: "Virtue is both theoretical and practical; for it takes in theory, since the road which leads to it is philosophy [...], but it also includes action; for virtue is the *expertise of life in its entirety*, which includes all actions." Stoic influence can also be detected in the passage in italics, which resembles Seneca, *Letter* 95.56: *virtus ad totam pertinet vitam*. This line of thought, too, facilitated the transition from the model to the act that realizes the model, for, according to the Stoics, virtue in theory is meaningless, and would not exist.

virtue: he thus moves from the model towards him who made the choice and put it into practice. So in Paradise Adam saw goodness and could have acted well. In the same way, since Adam did evil, he must have "seen" evil: thus, in a sense, evil was actually present in Paradise.[17] But where, exactly? In the Tree of knowledge of good and evil? This cannot be correct, since "evil is forbidden from the divine choir" (*Allegories of the Laws* 1.61). Adam obviously pays the price for his choice, but why did the good God not prevent the man and his progeny from performing such an ill-fated deed? In God's case, would this amount to an omission to help someone in danger?

The subsequent allegorical interpretation seems somewhat confused, since Philo introduces several philosophical and theological problems without dealing with them systematically. Here I offer a list of the most relevant problems involving divine responsibility debated or at the very least touched upon by Philo, who relates these problems with his interpretation of the Tree "of good and evil":

- Why does God place the weakest ("moulded") man in Paradise, instead of the most perfect one (the image of man)?[18]
- How can evil, even if only as a hypothesis and in potency, be present in the Garden of Eden?

Or, in a more general sense:

- Is God perhaps not *responsible* for human evil, since he did not create the wicked man's soul?[19] But what about His omnipotence, then?

Evidently, one would now be forced to tackle the complicated matter of theodicy (about which Philo is quite unclear), which goes beyond the scope

17 Philo seems to imply, if a negative model had not existed within Paradise, Adam would not have sinned. This stance is also legitimized by the psychological terms derived from Stoic thought in *Allegories of the Laws* 1.61, where Philo explains why the Tree of knowledge of good and evil was simultaneously "in Paradise and also out of it" (1.60): "For the ruling part (τὸ ἡγεμονικόν) of our soul is malleable and resembles wax, which is capable of receiving every impression, whether good or bad." Therefore, if Adam has sinned, evil was already present in potency within Paradise. See further Radice 2000, 145–156.

18 The problem had already been posed in *Questions and Answers on Genesis* 1.8, regarding Genesis 2.9. The solution suggested was that the "moulded" man is the one who needs guidance in the form of above all "philosophy" because of his material constitution, whereas the man-image, on the other hand, does not. This makes Paradise seem more like a school of moral teaching, rather than a prize.

19 See *On the Change of Names* 30: "Indeed, did God not make the soul of the wicked man, for wickedness is hateful to God and the soul, which is between good and bad, he made not by himself alone, […] since that, like wax, was about to receive the different impressions of good and evil." From this point of view, the expression "man-image" [that is, good] would coincide with the idea of man made by God himself; other types of men, such as the "moulded man", would not be entirely his work.

of this paper. Here I rather stick to the fundamental issue, which, after all, is the question posed in Book 1, *Question* 11: what does the Tree of good and evil actually represent?

Heinemann undoubtedly meant well when he censored the text of Genesis in an attempt to safeguard Philo's exegesis. He must have asked himself: "If Philo himself simplifies Genesis 2.9 – what else is a commentator-translator of Philo to do?" However, one must note that due to this "hermeneutical twist", the biblical passage we are examining becomes incoherent: if it is stated that in Paradise "all plants" are good, and so is the Tree of life, why should an exception be made for the Tree "of good and evil?" Or, in other words, how could the Tree of good and evil be entirely good and present in the Garden? As we have seen, Philo's psychological reading in *AL* is not without inconsistencies or, at least, it leaves unsolved some crucial issues I have raised here above.

1.2 *The Perspective in the* Questions and Answers on Genesis

Fortunately, another interpretation exists that is less complicated and more faithful to the biblical text than the one found in the exegetical treatises (in which, as seen above, the *gnōston* is eliminated from the text of Genesis). This interpretation is adopted by Philo in book 1 of *Questions and Answers on Genesis*. Here, the allegorical projection of Genesis 2.9 is probably derived from an earlier exegetical tradition, which – as we have seen above – Philo was to rationalise at various levels in his *Allegorical Commentary to the Bible*. This tradition is preserved in the *Questions and Answers on Genesis* (1.6–11), which can be taken as a collection of all issues the Bible posed from the point of view of reason. In this section of the work there is evidence that evil does not belong to God's original plantation, which contains only virtues as universal Forms or perfect paradigms, but rather depends on human individual and concrete deliberations.

Question 6 specifies that the Garden of Eden, in its entirety, represents wisdom "as the science of the things divine and human", while from *Question* 8 we can infer that such an understanding was either invented or strongly promoted by Philo himself. Moreover, in *Questions and Answers on Genesis* 1.6 the plantation of Paradise corresponds to the "plantation of *Forms* as trees in the *hēgemonikon*" (that is in the rational or ruling part of the soul), while the Tree of life that lies at the centre of paradise represents the knowledge of both the world and the cause of the world. From *Question* 10, then, one can infer that the Tree of life represents a scientific view of reality, though understood in a religious sense (*pietas*).[20] As a whole, this representation explicitly implies

20 Cf. *On the Creation of the World* 154: "Piety towards God, through which man becomes immortal."

the fact that Paradise-Wisdom came into being after the creation of the world; for the plantation of Eden implies the actualisation of an "ethical" world in a "theonomic" perspective, i.e. as a result of God's commandments. The Tree of knowledge corresponds to prudence (*Questions and Answers on Genesis* 1.11),[21] "by which all things are known: the good and beautiful on the one hand, the bad and unseemly on the other", in an *individual-concrete* sense, contrary to the abstract and universal idea, which is captured in the image of the "plantation."[22] How would a good act or deed be recognised from a wicked one, if it were not for grace (or virtue, or talent)? Discernment is needed in its most perfect form: without it, moral virtue cannot exist. But, along with discernment, the real possibility of choice and, therefore, also of transgressing the divine order, belongs to human nature as endowed with free will. In this sense, within the Garden of Eden only virtue and whatever else is necessary for one to be virtuous exists, whereas its transgression by Adam comes only at a later stage and does not affect the goodness of God's creation. But how should God's providential plan for the created world coexist with human free will and the possibility to choose the evil? To address this question, Philo's moral psychology should be related to his cosmology, and especially to his conception of providence.

2 The Work *On Providence*

Philo's ethical exegesis of Genesis 2.9 and its relation to cosmology should be placed in the context of Greek philosophy, more specifically of Stoicism, which clearly influenced Philo even though he was openly faithful to Plato and his "second sailing."[23] This influence can be clearly noticed with regard to the notion of "providence", about which Philo wrote a separate monograph. Evidence thereof has been preserved by Eusebius of Caesarea, Jerome and the Suda.

On Providence is a complicated text both in its structure and in its transmission.[24] It is made up of two books that are different in form. The text that I use here contains various fragments that are partly in Latin, partly in Greek.[25]

21 Cf. also Plutarch, *On Stoic Self-Contradictions* 11.1037F (*SVF* 3.175).

22 As just noted, this corresponds to the implantation of Ideas as trees in the ἡγεμονικόν.

23 See the contributions in Alesse 2008 and, also, Niehoff 2018, 225–241.

24 See Runia 2017 and Ludovica De Luca's contribution to the present volume.

25 Hadas-Lebel 1973, which offers Aucher's Latin version of the Armenian translation (5th–6th century CE) published at the beginning of the 19th century, together with the *excerpta* from Eusebius' *Preparation for the Gospel* in Greek.

Moreover, it is partly a dialogue (in book 2), partly an essay. What the text lacks in originality, it makes up for coherence. It is clearly Hellenised: quotes from the Bible are rare, no obvious exegetical prompts are given; moreover, in book 2 an exalted praise of Greek poets can be found, which is rather unusual for Philo. For these reasons, some scholars have thought the text to be spurious. But Philo had a nephew, who was not only an atheist, but also an apostate and a philosopher – a rationalist, in other words – and wanted to redeem him with the help of reason. At the end of book 2, at 113, Philo reached his goal: "ALEXANDER: I repent of my previous doubts; you have countered each doubt with an abundance of arguments, which I must accept."

If *On Providence* is to be seen as a "textbook" written by a Jew, who believed in the Bible, but was also a student of philosophy, then the text can be convincingly attributed to Philo. It entirely aligns with the effort Philo made to gain respect from his nephew as an experienced and learned man, an intellectual and philosopher, yet someone who was still a believer. Philo's family had probably been experiencing what had been occurring – at a larger scale – within the Jewish community in Alexandria, where many Jews were fascinated by philosophy. Evidence for this fascination can be found all over the Mediterranean world, especially in the form of the rational explanation of allegories.[26] Of course, this rationalisation was risky in the religious sense: for religious convictions often gave way to speculative reason. In Philo's exegesis in *On Providence* most issues are resolved at a theological level. The first book deals with cosmology, while the theme of the second book is theodicy, which is in line with its apologetic goal, a typical feature of the allegorists, and which pertains more directly to the scope of this paper.[27] Therefore, we will take a closer look at it.

3 Providence and Creation

On Providence, at 2.48 in particular, gives us a glimpse of how Philo operated in relating ethics to cosmology. Here, his rearrangement of the Platonist theory of creation and the Stoic notion of providence is particularly evident. For, once Philo had introduced God and His creative act, he had to clarify the nature

26 See Ramelli and Lucchetta 2004.

27 Allegorists in the late Hellenistic period often defended the works of mythologists, thus showing that some less-than-edifying narrations about the gods had not be understood to the letter, but rather in a figurative, mainly philosophical manner, which restored the gods' role.

of this creation, whether it be demiurgic or *ex nihilo*. For Philo, the problem is not easy to solve, for, if matter originally coexist with God, the question concerns God's omnipotence as creator of the cosmos; if instead matter is created directly by God, the question concerns God's goodness and his innocence with respect to the existence of evil. "God is not responsible" (θεὸς ἀναίτιος), Plato had claimed;[28] but God is omnipotent, the Bible says.[29] How to reconcile these two statements, if it is true that, for both Plato and Moses, God is good and the evil really exists? In the Platonist tradition, the question is frequently addressed with reference to the material principle, which is credited with a negative nature, depending on its being animated by an evil soul, which Plato had apparently introduced in a passage of his *Laws*, at 10.896d–e.[30] In this sense, matter and soul, rather than God, are responsible for evil. Clearly, for Philo this assumption threatens the omnipotence of God, but not so much as to prevent him from introducing his providence into the created world. If matter is uncreated, God would operate as a sculptor-creator of the statues themselves (not of the bronze matter, which is produced by the miner or the smelter), but this does not impede the existence of a providential plan, since Philo clearly assumes the existence of Logos understood as providence preserving the universe. *Universal sympathy* and the organic structure of the cosmos prove thus the existence and triumph of providence, since they link the parts to the Whole and to its Logos as the active principle.

Clearly, Philo is here rearranging Stoic material, which he adopts in a Platonizing as well as biblical framework. In Philo, Logos is the highest power of God, his mind in its creative activity or the "glue" (κόλλα) and "chain" (δεσμός) of the universe; in this sense, it is also providence, or the divine plan of God who is full of grace for human beings.[31] The Stoic notion of Logos is here elevated to a supernatural level, whereas the Stoic and Platonist conception of providence is teleologically and graciously oriented to the good of human beings, who are created in the image and likeness of God. However, Philo does not assume Stoic organicism in full, which would have implied adherence to the doctrines of causal determinism and astral fate. Rather, human beings can escape physical necessity and are granted a margin of autonomy in their actions, as we shall see. After all, though the Stoics allowed for astrology and

28 Plato, *Timaeus* 42d3–4, *Republic* 10.617e5.

29 See, e.g., Genesis 17.1, 18.14, 28.3; for Philo, too, God's powers are infinite in number (see *On the Confusion of Tongues* 171).

30 See Plutarch, *On Isis and Osiris* 45.369A–D, Atticus, fr. 23 Des Places, Numenius, fr. 52 Des Places; for further references see Emmanuele Vimercati's contribution to this volume.

31 See, e.g., Philo, *On the Creation of the World* 20, 24–25; *On Flight and Finding* 112; *On the Cherubim* 127; *Who is the Heir of Divine Things?* 188 and 201; cf. Calabi 2008, 3–16.

divination, even they did not believe the sage to be dominated by the stars or fate. Rather, they held the doctrine that assent is "in our power", such that the sage freely assents to do those things which are fated, and in this sense does what he wants.[32] The main difference between Philo and the Stoics lies in the fact that according to Philo, God is personal, while the Stoics see the divine as an impersonal, natural and material principle.

From this point of view, the allegory of Eden as a whole (as discussed in section 1.2) would not be particularly problematic, since it focuses *on a second creation* concerning the ethical world, when Adam had already left God's hands *as a man-in-the-world* and the world had already been in existence. Therefore, all ontological and theological issues are resolved in the first cosmological creation (the one described in *On Providence*). In Eden, God gave human creatures *all the instruments they needed to be happy and virtuous*: first of all, the perfect models of virtues in their hierarchical structure and mutual relationships (the archetypal or ideal virtues); secondly – since virtues are both theoretical and practical – He endowed mankind with the *principle of discernment* of evil and good, which can respectively be ascribed to *philautia* (self-love), as embodied by Cain,[33] and *theophilia* (love of God), as embodied by Abel.

4 The Tree of Life and the Tree of Discernment

Philo was well aware of the Hellenistic ethical debate, including its Socratic and Platonist presuppositions. As has been noted, "the Platonic notion of the unity of virtue, so often taken up by the Stoics, is taken up by Philo when he

---

32 Cicero, *On Fate* 41 (= SVF 2.974): "Chrysippus, dissociating himself from the theory of necessity on the one hand, and wanting to defend the idea that nothing happens without a cause on the other, distinguishes causes in categories, so that he can escape necessity and preserve fate. 'Some causes – he states – are complete and principal, others are auxiliary and proximate. [...] If everything happens by fate, then everything happens by antecedent causes that are not complete and principal, but rather auxiliary and proximate. These are surely not in our power, but this implies that neither is desire.'" For that matter, he does not find it difficult to explain the theory of assent by antecedent causes. Even though assent only follows a perceived object, the latter is nevertheless a proximate and non-principal cause." Therefore, "assents are in our power" (Clement of Alexandria, *Miscellanies* 2.54.5 = SVF 2.992), but it is impossible for us to act upon the world, which is governed by a necessary series of causes.

33 *On the Special Laws* 1.344: "Those who only love themselves, and therefore deify reason and the senses. All these men are hastening to the same end, even though they are not all influenced by the same intentions, they ignore the Only, the true living God."

writes that to have one virtue is to have them all.[34] Similarly, the idea that virtue is both theory and practice is developed in the *Allegories of the Laws*, where Philo uses terms that correspond to those of orthodox Stoicism.[35] In the same work,[36] the exegesis of Genesis 2.10–14 on the four rivers of paradise enables him to recall the four traditional virtues: *phronēsis* (prudence), *sōphrosunē* (temperance), *andreia* (courage), *dikaiosunē* (justice)."[37] Furthermore, while rejecting the Stoic principle of *oikeiōsis* (appropriation) as incompatible with created and incorporeal souls, Philo adopts the Platonist notion of *homoiōsis* (likeness to God) as the end of human life.[38] This depends on the assumption that the intellect is common to God and man and is the principle of human agency.[39]

However, in his attachment to his Jewish culture and religion, Philo was in the end alien to intellectualism in the strict sense. He rather favoured the principle of *conscious choice in relation to indisputable ends*: here, the ends are the ideal virtues, which are embodied by the Tree of life, whereas the conscious choice is the capability of discerning good and evil, which is embodied by the Tree of discernment. On the one hand the principle of choice implies that Someone or Something endowed the human soul with the power and means to make that choice. In this sense, human agency depends first and foremost on God's initiative, that is on his grace, which is directed exclusively to humans.[40] But, on the other hand, when man possesses these features (and only then), he can choose whether he wants to gravitate towards *philautia* or *theophilia*.[41] Love for one's self, according to Philo, is a *wicked life* as represented by Cain, while love for God is the *just life* as embodied by Abel. In

34 See *On the Life of Moses* 2.7.

35 See *Allegories of the Laws* 1.57.

36 See *Allegories of the Laws* 1.63.

37 Cf. Lévy 2009, 150.

38 Cf. Radice 2008, 141–143, and Lévy 2009, 146–149 (with references).

39 See, e.g., *On the Creation of the World* 69, 71, 135; cf. Radice 2008, 148–149.

40 See Radice 2008, 143–144.

41 Philo usually interprets the adjective θεοφιλής (i.e. "friend of God") to the letter, though with a twofold meaning: that of "he who loves God" and that of "he who is loved by God", the "favourite", the "chosen one." In the latter sense, more than anyone else, θεοφιλής is Moses, who in *Allegories of the Laws* 2.88–89 is explicitly called "the man of whom God is especially friend." If all patriarchs were "friends of God", Abraham was in a peculiar way (*On Abraham* 89): in the allegorical interpretation of the Bible, it was Abraham who fully carried out a "migration" towards God, which stands as a model for every pious man. The goal of such ascent is represented by the Tree of life portrayed in Genesis 2.3 and mentioned above.

this sense, then, God would leave man with a choice for good or bad. Therefore, whereas providence has to do primarily with God's goodness, which is responsible for the creation of the Tree of life as a model for all good things,[42] responsibility is mainly related to human choice, which is rather shaped after the Tree of discernment and can be directed in either direction: good and evil. The issue of how God's goodness is harmonized by Philo with human responsibility for the evil, should now be addressed.

5 Man's Responsibility and God's Innocence

God's innocence with regard to evil can only be justified if one admits man's *responsibility*. This is how Philo approaches human freedom: through a winding road, his thought turned to God rather than to mankind. Of course, one could argue that a father who lets his son decide is a good father only if he has previously done all in his power to prevent his son from making the wrong choice.

In this regard, *On the Unchangeableness of God* contains a brief passage that is key in understanding Philo's point of view on the topic, since it encompasses many ideas that are otherwise scattered around his other writings (some are tucked away in the biblical context); in this passage the supremacy of ethical intellectualism is interrupted and replaced by the thesis that "all is necessary except intelligence." The text reads as follows:

> 47: [A] The Father who created us, judged only our *intelligence* to be *worthy of freedom* (ἐλευθερία); and, unloosing the bonds of necessity, he let it go unrestrained, bestowing on it that gift as far as it was able to receive it […] *spontaneous will* (ἑκούσιος) […] [B] Man, who has had bestowed on him a *tireless* conscience that *operates on the basis of its own deliberate purpose* (ἐθελουργός αὐτοκέλευστος); since it can operate by means of activities that are founded upon free choice (προαιρετικός), man *properly receives blame for the bad actions which he commits with foresight, and, by contrast, praise for the right actions which he performs out of his own will* (ἑκών) [i.e. responsibility, RR]. […] In other living beings, plants and animals, one cannot praise fertility or blame infertility, since *all their motions and transformations* are in one or the other direction, but without choice *and* involuntary (ἀπροαίρετος καὶ ἀκούσιος); *only the soul of man*

42 This is proved by the fact that, in the description of creation, the biblical text frequently repeats: "… and God saw that it was good."

> has received from God the power of voluntary motion, and most of all, in this respect it has been made to resemble God; it has been freed as far as possible from a grievous and severe mistress, necessity.

This passage makes clear that God gives *the power of being free*, but not *freedom* itself; human responsibility lies precisely between these two conditions, since he who chose evil would be enslaved by evil itself.[43] Notably, while the point made in section (A) of the text of *On the Unchangeableness of God* is related to the Stoic doctrine of *assent*,[44] this is not the case for the point about responsibility made in section (B). For the latter implies that the accomplished action also holds practical effect, and that the actor is also responsible for the consequences of his own deeds. But for the Stoics the ethical value of an action depends only on the inner disposition of the agent and not on the effect that the action produces.

For, in Stoic thought, events are chained together by necessity imposed by cosmic Logos: therefore, man cannot change his fate. For example, the fact that Adam's sin also caused damnation for his sons would have been unthinkable from a Stoic point of view. The issue of the inheritance of sin is obviously not at stake here: rather, the fact that the world's development as a whole follows a rational, pre-made and unchangeable journey. The Stoics consider good and evil to be largely interior matters that pertain to the sphere of intentions and concrete acts. The consequences of vice or virtue are only of a psychic (or possibly eschatological) nature, as they relate to man's happiness or sorrow and not to the development of cosmic events. For, even if humanity were entirely good or evil, its fate would not change.

6 Freedom and Determinism in Philo: Stoic Questions and Platonist Replies

These then are the results of Philo's exegetical-allegorical thought as they can be gathered from his allegorical commentary. Here I still want to deal with the special status of human beings, in comparison with other living creatures, plants and animals, that have neither responsibility nor freedom.[45]

---

43 See also Frick 1999, 162–175, and Troels Engberg-Pedersen's contribution to the present volume.

44 That is the evaluation, which the intellect (i.e. the ruling part of the soul) makes of each impression, accepting or refusing its content.

45 Some of these problems have already been highlighted in Radice 2008.

The group of allegorical works that tackle this topic make clear that Philo deemed *natural determinism* an *indisputable fact*, provided that this did not also include mankind in its higher functions. Moses himself – as Philo states in *Who is the Heir of Divine Things?*, at 300–301, – "like every philosopher", knew about the "fate and necessity (εἱμαρμένη καὶ ἀνάγκη) as the causes of all that happens." However, unlike other philosophers, "he did not think it determined the causes of what happens in the world." Of course – so Philo seems to imply – once the die has been cast, the consequences of the act are determinate and necessary, but their primary cause is different. Thus, in *On the Change of Names* 135, he sums up the issue by posing this question:

> To whom belongs the world, the destiny, the consequential or analogical order of all things, with *their indissoluble connection?* To whom [...] the thing of strong support, which wavers not, which is not moved; that is to say, admonition [...]? To whom the sceptre, the kingly power? Does it not belong to God alone?

Therefore, according to Philo, determinism in itself does not deny providence; rather, it delimits it, in compliance with an idea that was to become canonical in Roman Stoicism, as stated by Seneca's blunt expression in *On Providence* 5.8: "God obeys for ever, he commanded but once."[46] If it were not the case that Philo was a Jew who believed in biblical creation, one could probably say that this position anticipates the following Platonist debate. For Philo, like the Platonists, believes that natural necessity does not prevent, and indeed presupposes, supernatural causes that preserve God's autonomy from matter and the world He has created, and human responsibility from physical constraints. This is possible through a transcendent God who cannot be properly known nor named, and souls created by the grace of God and yet free to make their own choices.[47]

---

46 Cf. Radice 2008, 164. It should be noted that Philo's determinism – which is in line with the tradition of the Chaldeans, who were determinists and practiced astrology – is to be overcome, by undertaking an intellectual ascent to the so-called land of Haran. As Philo stated in *On the Migration of Abraham* 178, this land represents the phase in which intellect is contained within itself; from there, it proceeds towards θεοφιλία. Philo rejected Chaldean astrology, which was "used to adapting the things of heaven to those on earth", thus leading to pantheism and atheism. Rather, he suggested in *On the Migration of Abraham* 185: "Become acquainted with yourselves and your own nature, and do not prefer to dwell anywhere else, rather than in yourselves."

47 Cf. Calabi 2008, 39–56.

As for Philo's determinism, it is surely not of the Democritean (linear or mechanical) type based on atoms clashing with motion thus being transferred. Rather, it is organic-vital, founded upon the relationship between parts and whole. This is clear in *On Providence*, at 2.9–12 in particular, where one can easily find traces of an overall philosophical position that is substantially Stoic with Platonic influences. In general, the intellectual climate of Alexandria during Philo's time was quite similar to that in Cicero's writings, where in an Academic framework one would mainly find Stoic views, especially in ethics. But let us go back to Philo: as mentioned above, *providence* is consubstantial with the act *of creation*;[48] however, it is also valid *without creation*, for the specific sense of providence is not only that of creating and producing matter, but also that of preserving and governing creation. This is in line with Stoic thought, which was neither creationist regarding matter, nor oriented towards transcendent theology, yet is still as providentialist and it is this approach that Philo imitates here.[49]

7 Final Remarks

In conclusion, Philo's main contribution to the notion of providence and free will depends on the interaction between his philosophical interests and his work as an interpreter of the Bible. In this regard, we have addressed mainly the issue of *human responsibility*, which is crucial to explain both the status of the evil in the created world and the limits of divine providence. The notion of responsibility is mainly related to Philo's explanation of the biblical allegory of the Tree of knowledge of good and evil. As I have tried to demonstrate, unfortunately this allegory raises far more issues than it solves, while pre-Philonian exegesis as preserved in the *Questions* (which the author himself assembled there) is not only more faithful to the text of the *Septuagint*, but it also is more obvious. Clearly, most of Philo's problems in explaining the biblical text depend on what is commonly referred to as "exegetical constraint", that is the need to find philosophical arguments which are compatible with the revealed text.

48 Making him exist is God's greatest gift towards man, who was only created once a world had been made capable of welcoming him, so that he would have a dwelling place that befitted his status. See *On the Creation of the World* 77: "God wanted man to find everything in place in the world, as for the creature most resembling Himself."

49 On the heritage of these issues in Imperial Stoicism, see the contributions by René Brouwer, Ricardo Salles and Troels Engberg-Pedersen, in the present volume.

Philo discusses the Tree of knowledge as a symbol of discernment, which implies the liberty of those who choose. Liberty is thus essential, not just from an ethical point of view (which would have been its natural context), but also from a theological perspective, since it helps to avoid all connections between God and evil, which intervenes only later in the created world and depends only on human choice. In this sense, God is not responsible for evil. The independence of the human will is a sublime gift of divine providence (and surely not a vice), and a sign of God's predilection for mankind.

This line of argument has its background in Stoicism, with the notion of *assent* understood as a possible disruptive act towards nature. Only with regard to the sage, who accepts the will of Providence, *"nothing happens, except for what he wants."*[50] In Philo, this acceptance corresponds to the state of "love of God" as expressed by Abel and, overall accepted by the patriarchs. For the Stoics and Philo, freedom is *subjective* (that is, pertaining to the person and his assent), rather than *objective* (that is, pertaining to the act): no actions are free in and of themselves; rather, *actions carried out by men who are free* and who "determine" and "necessitate" themselves once they have joined the flow of universal events. However, contrary to Stoicism, Philo had to ground human freedom in created and incorporeal souls, as well as in the providential plan of a supernatural God. In this sense, the necessity of the physical order is surpassed (or rather preceded) by God's grace as the cosmological and ethical principle of the cosmos. Outside of Revelation, some of these aspects were inspired by Plato' s thought, and as such, remained as an inheritance to the following centuries.

Bibliography

Alesse, Francesca, ed. 2008. *Philo of Alexandria and Post-Aristotelian Philosophy*. Leiden: Brill.

Calabi, Francesca. 2008. *God's Acting, Man's Acting. Tradition and Philosophy in Philo of Alexandria*. Leiden: Brill.

Cohn, Leopold, Paul Wendland, and Siegfried Reiter, eds. 1896–1930. *Philonis Alexandrini opera quae supersunt*. Berlin: Reimer.

Colson, Francis H., and George H. Whitaker, tr. 1929. *Philo*, vol. 1. Cambridge, Mass: Harvard University Press.

Daniel, Suzanne, tr. 1975. *Philon d'Alexandrie, De specialibus legibus I–III*. Paris: Cerf.

50 For the Stoic doctrine see Augustine, *On the Happy Life* 25 (= SVF 3.572).

Frick, Peter. 1999. *Divine Providence in Philo of Alexandria*. Tübingen: Mohr Siebeck.

Gorez, Jean, tr. 1966. *Philon d'Alexandrie, De Abrahamo*. Paris: Cerf.

Hadas-Lebel, Mireille, tr. 1973. *Philon d'Alexandrie, De providentia I et II*. Paris: Cerf.

Heinemann, Isaak, Leopold Cohn, Maximilian Adler, and Willy Theiler, tr. [1909–1938] 1962–1964. *Philo von Alexandria, Die Werke in deutscher Übersetzung*. Berlin: De Gruyter.

Lévy, Carlos. 2009. *Philo's Ethics*. In *The Cambridge Companion to Philo*, edited by Adam Kamesar, 146–171. Cambridge: Cambridge University Press.

Marcus, Ralph, tr. 1971. *Philo. Supplement I*. Cambridge, Mass.: Harvard University Press.

Mercier, Charles, tr. 1979. *Philon d'Alexandrie, Quaestiones et solutiones in Genesim I et II e versione armeniaca*. Paris: Cerf.

Mondésert, Claude, tr. 1962. *Philon d'Alexandrie, Legum allegoriae I–III*. Paris: Cerf.

Niehoff, Maren R. 2018. *Philo of Alexandria. An Intellectual Biography*. New Haven: Yale University Press.

Radice, Roberto. 2000. *Allegoria e paradigmi etici in Filone di Alessandria. Commentario al "Legum allegoriae."* Milan: Vita e Pensiero.

Radice, Roberto, ed. 2005. *Filone di Alessandria, Tutti i trattati del "Commentario allegorico alla Bibbia."* In collaboration with Giovanni Reale, Clara Kraus Reggiani, and Claudio Mazzarelli. Milan: Bompiani.

Radice, Roberto. 2008. "Philo and Stoic Ethics. Reflections on the Idea of Freedom." In *Philo of Alexandria and Post-Aristotelian Philosophy*, edited by Francesca Alesse, 141–168. Leiden: Brill.

Ramelli, Ilaria, and Giulio Lucchetta. 2004. *Allegoria* 1: *L'età Classica*. Milan: Vita e Pensiero.

Runia, David. 2017. "From Stoicism to Platonism. The Difficult Case of Philo of Alexandria's *De Providentia* I." In *From Stoicism to Platonism: The Development of Philosophy, 100 BCE–100 CE*, edited by Troels Engberg-Pedersen, 159–178. Cambridge: Cambridge University Press.

Sgiarovello, Elena, tr. 2012. Genesi. In *La Bibbia dei Settanta* 1: *Pentateuco*, edited by Paolo Lucca. Brescia: Morcelliana.

Triviño, José María, tr. 1975–1976. *Obras completas de Filón de Alejandría*. Buenos Aires: Acervo Cultural Editores.

CHAPTER 6

Stoic Freedom in Paul's Letter to the Romans 6.1–8.30 and Epictetus, *Dissertation* 4.1: from Being under an Obligation to Wanting

Troels Engberg-Pedersen

1 The Issue

Fate, providence, and free will: do we find any substantial reflection in the New Testament on the set of philosophical issues raised by these terms? Were we to put the same question for Graeco-Roman philosophy that is contemporary with the New Testament, the answer would be both yes and no. Yes: in Stoicism we find an extensive reflection on fate (εἱμαρμένη, *fatum*), providence (πρόνοια, *providentia*), and the question whether human action is "up to us" (ἐφ' ἡμῖν) – what I shall henceforth speak of as "self-determination." Thus von Arnim in his *Stoicorum Veterum Fragmenta* (SVF) volume 2 has a whole chapter on fate (6: *De fato*), on providence (Cap. 8: *De providentia et natura artifice*), and an extensive section on fate and free will (6 § 10: *Fatum et liberum arbitrium*). But also no: although von Arnim spoke of *liberum arbitrium*, there is general agreement among students of Stoicism that we should not speak of "free will" in connection with the Stoics: a) there is no distinct, modern concept of "the will" in Stoicism;[1] b) they did not speak specifically of "freedom" in connection with human action in a world where everything is causally determined by fate (instead, they spoke of "self-determination"); they did speak of "freedom", but in connection with the passions;[2] c) and in any case, when one unpacks what they meant by saying that human action is "up to us", one should not invoke anything like a modern concept of a radically "free will".[3] Still, the Stoics did reflect deeply on the issues relating to fate, providence, and free will. Did the New Testament writers do the same?

The quick answer is: no! Fate lies entirely outside their horizon. Providence does not. But the issue with which the Stoics did grapple was generally not understood as a problem in the New Testament, namely, this: if God has providentially determined everything that happens in the world, including the

---

1 See, e.g., Inwood 2005.

2 This was strongly emphasized in Bobzien 1998a, followed by others, e.g. Long 2002.

3 See, e.g., Bobzien 1998a and b; Salles 2005 and 2013; Frede 2007 and 2011.

 | DOI:10.1163/9789004436381_008

understanding and behaviour of human beings, are they themselves then also "free" (or at least "morally responsible", as the Stoics would have said) in the same respect? Though the issue itself was in fact touched on at least by Paul, it appears not to have been felt as a problem. And so, the answer to our question should be this: no, there is no substantial reflection in the New Testament on fate, providence, and free will.

And yet! In this essay I shall try to show that in a fairly extensive, central section of his Letter to the Romans, Paul, the most philosophical among New Testament writers, employs the concept of freedom in a complex and initially puzzling manner that is best illuminated if understood in the light of Stoicism. Moreover, we shall see that his treatment may in fact be relevant to the issue raised under fate, providence, and free will. If so, the New Testament may not be completely silent on this topic.

2 A Warning

This essay, then, is not a general account of 'fate, providence, and free will in the New Testament'. Rather, it is a case study of a specific passage. Thus, the reader must be prepared to delve into one of the most complex and fascinating texts in the whole of Western culture. Here I am writing for readers with an expertise in ancient philosophy, but none in the New Testament. Such readers must swallow some camels (reflecting the mythological world view that was Paul's) in order to follow the text's own train of thought. At the same time, they should become able to see that Paul's handling of the concept of freedom does make interesting, philosophical sense. However, I am also writing for readers with an expertise in the New Testament, not least since I will be presenting a reading of the passage that aims to solve a puzzle in Paul's treatment of freedom from Romans 6.1–8.13 into 8.14–30. Here too readers will need to provide something in order to follow the argument, namely, a genuine interest in a philosophical approach to Paul, including the Stoic material that I will bring in for illumination. I trust, however, that the sacrifice will be worth it.

3 Some Preliminary Methodological Observations

For the benefit of both groups of readers, I list here some methodological points derived from my own work in the field of "the New Testament and Graeco-Roman philosophy".[4]

4 See, e.g., Engberg-Pedersen 2000, 2010, and 2017.

First, there are in fact connections between Graeco-Roman philosophy and the New Testament that should be explained genealogically as due to influence from the former on the latter.

Secondly, and at the same time, the New Testament writings are deeply rooted in Judaism going much further back than Alexander the Great – and of course in Jewish writings from the Hellenistic and Roman periods that were themselves influenced by Graeco-Roman philosophy.

Thirdly, while it may be correct to describe the Pauline (and in fact Johannine) writings in the New Testament as "philosophical", such "philosophy" has a somewhat different shape from what we find in Plato, Aristotle, Epicurus, the Stoics, and others.

Fourthly, when one studies the Pauline (and Johannine) writings from the perspective of "philosophy", the primary aim should be to understand *better* those writings *themselves* – as opposed to enrolling them in some overview of "Graeco-Roman philosophical texts in antiquity".

Fifthly, the comparative use of Graeco-Roman philosophical topics for studying the Pauline (and Johannine) texts should therefore be understood as being primarily heuristic. It aims to – and is vindicated by its capacity to – throw new and better light on those texts.

Sixthly, the researcher must therefore constantly "listen carefully" to the texts themselves to see whether or not they are in fact illuminated by the Graeco-Roman philosophical comparison.

Add then the following two observations for the specific issue to be addressed here:

Seventhly, it seems certain that Paul might draw on a traditional Jewish understanding of the relation between divine determinism and human responsibility as being unproblematic. Concern about that relation only came in at a later stage (but before Paul), namely, within Graeco-Roman philosophy.

Eighthly, and similarly, it is important to recall that the Stoic position on fate and self-determination itself stands in an intriguing relationship with what we may call the traditional *Greek* understanding. Here, just as in the traditional Jewish understanding, there was no sense of any intrinsic opposition between some form of determinism (divine or otherwise) and the amount of moral responsibility that is required for praise and blame. What the Stoics did was to find ways of arguing for the essential correctness of the traditional view.

We cannot know beforehand whether Paul merely relied on the traditional Jewish (and indeed also Greek) picture or whether he had in fact been in some way infiltrated by the philosophical query. That only makes the sixth observation, in particular, especially relevant: that we must listen carefully to the texts themselves to see whether or not the query is in fact there and may be illuminated by a Graeco-Roman philosophical comparison.

4 The Stoic Theory of Freedom (and Epictetus, *Dissertation* 4.1)

Whereas the Stoic theory of fate, providence, and what is 'up to us' is discussed in fragments in *SVF* vol. 2, the relevant fragments on "freedom" (ἐλευθερία) are found in vol. 3, primarily in sections 6 of chapter 6 (*De nobilitate et libertate* in a chapter *De iure et lege*) and 5 of chapter 9 (*Sapiens est dives, formosus, liber* in a chapter *De sapiente et insipiente*). In both sections, the person who is free is the wise man, in contrast to all fools, who are slaves. It is evident that the pair "slave-free" had a strongly socio-political flavour in ancient texts due to the central role of slavery in ancient society. Correspondingly, being free was highly valued, whereas being a slave was not. However, in accordance with the famous Stoic paradoxes, it is only the wise man who is in fact "rich", "handsome", "free", a "king", etc. (cf. *SVF* 3.597), no matter what his social position was. Thus even a slave might also (if he was wise) be in this sense free. What, then, is it about wisdom that makes a person free? And *from* what is the Stoic wise man free?

The first sentence of Epictetus' *Dissertation* 4.1, "Of Freedom", gives the beginning of the answer (§ 1): "He is free (ἐλεύθερος) who lives as he wishes (βούλεται), whom it is not possible either to compel (ἀναγκάσαι) or hinder (κωλῦσαι) or constrain (or force, βιάσασθαι) […]." Let us take this as a definition of freedom. To be free is to live as one wishes in such a manner that no external influence can either compel or hinder one or, more generally, make one think or do anything through the use of force. One thinks and acts as one oneself wishes.

In the rest of the diatribe, Epictetus develops a number of cases where a person is in fact either compelled, hindered, or constrained. What brings this about is primarily other people. But in his summary (§§ 51–61), which leads up to his account of how a person may then avoid being compelled, hindered, or constrained, Epictetus also notes that *behind* all these masters lies something else to which we are also slaves (§§ 59–60):

> For we have the *things* (themselves, τὰ πράγματα) as masters (κύριοι) *before* those others. And these (things) are many […]: death, exile, loss of property, prison, disfranchisement […]; wealth, a tribuneship, a praetorship, a consulship. When we love and hate and fear these things, it necessarily follows that those who have control (ἐξουσία) over them are our masters.

Other people, the things themselves – and then the passions with which we respond to either, namely, love, hate, and fear: these are the things *from* which the wise man is free and is *made* free by his wisdom. Elsewhere the passions were gathered under four rubrics: "pleasure" (ἡδονή), "pain" (λύπη), "fear" (φόβος), and "desire" (ἐπιθυμία).[5] Thus Epictetus' "love" may well cover both the pleasure of having one or the other of the valued things and also the desire to get it.

The way in which wisdom frees a person from the passions is by making the person reach the ultimate insight in Stoic ethics: that the human good does not consist in any of the supposed "goods" (the valued things in the quotation), but instead in "living in accordance with nature", that is, in accordance with the way the world has been structured by God and continuously unfolds that structure. This unfolding of the world's structure is itself "rational" in a sense that includes that of being fully causally determined and hence fated. By coming to understand that the person himself is both a bodily being that is part of the world's own flow and also, and primarily, a rational being who is capable of *understanding* both the world and himself, the person may come to see that his own good lies, not in the initially valued things, but in the overall, rational understanding which *gives* the proper value to everything. Through this rational act of understanding, the person will undergo a change from seeing the initially valued things as "good" to seeing them as basically "indifferent" (ἀδιάφορα) and at most "preferable" (προηγμένα) and hence not a worthy object of any passionate reaction. In this way, the wise man becomes free from the passions.[6]

Another way of putting this point is by saying that the wise man has come both to understand that living in accordance with the flow of the world (the facts) is what is good for him – and also to want to live in that way. He has, in a way, become "at one" with the world and with the world's ultimate causal agent, God.

Epictetus addresses this latter way of expressing the point later in *Dissertation* 4.1. From § 89 onwards he begins to spell out how he "has himself never been prevented when he wishes (θέλειν) to do something and never been compelled when he wishes (again θέλειν) *not* to do something" (§ 89). What lies behind this is, as he has just mentioned (§ 87), that he has learned to "yield up [all the ἀδιάφορα, namely,] the paltry body, its members, powers, property, reputation, offices, honours, children, brothers and friends" – "all these things (he

5 See *SVF* 3.391–394.

6 The Stoic doctrines mentioned in this paragraph are not directly addressed in Epictetus, *Dissertation* 4.1. They belong under the central Stoic notion of *oikeiōsis*, which is presupposed by Epictetus. (For *oikeiōsis*, see Engberg-Pedersen 1990 and, among more recent treatments, Klein 2016.)

has learned to) view as alien (ἀλλότρια)", as not belonging to himself. But how has he managed to do this (§ 89)? Well, he "has submitted (προσκατατεταχέναι) his impulse (ὁρμή) to God": if God wills (θέλειν) something, then Epictetus wills that too. Epictetus takes up a little later the idea of "submitting" or "attaching oneself" (προσκατατάξαι) to God (§ 99): how may that come about (§ 100)? "How else than by *observing God's impulses* (ὁρμαί) and his governance (of the world, διοίκησις)?" This is the kind of understanding of the world that we saw the wise man to have reached. What it leads to is a certain attitude towards God: attaching oneself to God, submitting one's impulses to God, in other words, willing what God wills. But note that this attitude is all through an expression of the wise man's cognition, of what he has *understood* about the world. Epictetus expresses this connection between willing and understanding by putting the following question (§ 90): "Who, then, can prevent me (κωλῦσαι) any longer against *what appears (right) to me*, or (who can) compel (ἀναγκάσαι) me? (None), no more than (anybody can prevent or compel) God." Thus, following one's own understanding of the world as a whole is also attaching oneself to God and willing what God wills.

We may summarize the Stoic theory (in Epictetus' version) of ἐλευθερία as freedom from the passions by speaking of two 'movements': from the outside in and from the inside out. The wise man is free in relation to the local input from the world (from the outside in) that would elicit passionate reactions in the fool. Here he adopts a certain epistemic withdrawal from the world. At the same time, the wise man is also characterized in epistemic terms by a total openness (from the inside out) towards the world taken globally. Here there is the opposite of a withdrawal: an active epistemic openness (an understanding) that takes the form of an attachment to the world as a whole (and God). This is the theory behind the Stoic claim that the wise man, and he alone, is free.

As presented so far, my account of Stoic ἐλευθερία as freedom from the passions will find support among most students of Stoicism. Not so with what follows.[7]

The Stoics also discussed a different topic that we ourselves might also articulate in terms of "freedom", but the Stoics themselves did not – at least, not initially. Is human decision and action free if one also takes it that all events in the world are fully causally determined? As we saw, this question falls under

7 I am drawing here on an unpublished article of mine (under review): "Freedom and Determinism in Stoic Philosophy: From Epictetus to Chrysippus" (63 pp.).

the Stoic reflection on fate, providence, and "self-determination". The Stoic answer was: yes, adult human acts are "up to us" and "self-determined." Moreover, this holds not only for the wise, but for fools and wise men alike.

It has become customary in scholarship – not least since a splendid book on the subject by Susanne Bobzien (1998a) – to explicate this positive Stoic answer as follows. Although all cases of "assent" (συγκατάθεσις) – which is what (causally) determines any given act – are themselves causally determined, nevertheless they are also, in each particular case, "up to" the assenters in the sense that they are the assenters' *own*, as reflecting the kinds of people (with the kind of insight etc.) that each person individually is. As against this understanding, I argue that although everything in the world is in fact causally determined, including human assents, nevertheless assents (whether of fools or the wise) are special as reflecting the distinctive faculty of reason(ing). When presented with external input from the world around them, both fools and wise (as opposed to animals) can *think* about the most correct way of understanding such input. They can engage with a large repertoire of *possible* ways of understanding the input before assenting to any one of them. This capacity does give adult human beings a capacity for "self-determination". But it all stays within the framework of full causal determination (fate) of everything in the world, including the assents themselves. What makes assents special is the fact that they are the result of an activity of reason as a *second*-order capacity, one that precisely enables *reflection*. There is no "free will" here, but there is a capacity for reflection which gives room for *thought* before the assent, even if such thought is in the end just as "bound" (namely, by the way the reflecting person actually sees the world) as everything else.

If this is a correct understanding of what in Stoicism makes assent "up to us", then one may take the following additional step. In the theory as described, what makes assent "up to us" is exactly the capacity which in the wise man led to freedom from the passions: the capacity to reflect on how the world immediately presents itself in relation to what it actually is. When this capacity is put to full use, it results in the full understanding of the world that gives the wise man freedom from the passions. Since this is so, we might – if we so wished – speak of a "freedom of assent", too, in addition to the freedom from the passions to be found in the wise. Such freedom of assent in a way underlies the freedom from the passions. Where the latter is only to be found in the wise and is a *result* of the kind of reflection that is open to all adult human beings, the former is found in fools and wise alike. Since it itself involves an initial freedom vis-à-vis the immediate input from the world, one might – if one so wished – speak of "freedom" in this case, too. It still is not a matter of a "free will" in a modern sense since everything is in the end causally determined, including by the way the local input *appears* to the reflecting person. But it *is* a freedom *of* reflection (thought) and assent.

I said that we *might* speak of "freedom" in this case, too. The Stoics apparently did not do so, at least, if we go back to our sources for Chrysippus.[8] The reason for that may be that the issue (namely, are human beings morally responsible if everything in the world is also fully causally determined?) did not initially present itself to philosophers in terms of "freedom". And the reason for that may be the following. In ancient society, as we noted, the question of freedom was probably one that mattered hugely. The ancients may therefore initially have reserved the 'slave-free' pair for an issue that also mattered hugely to them: how to cope with the passions. By contrast, the issue of whether human action is up to us in a fully determined world may have appeared much more of an "academic" one, which arose from within philosophy in the light of certain metaphysical doctrines that the philosophers had reached. For this reason it may not have been felt to be a matter of slavery and freedom even though the human capacity that made adult actions up to us (in fools and wise alike) was also the one that yielded freedom from the passions (in the wise only).

So, in Stoicism there is freedom from the passions in the wise man alone, derived from his insight into the world as a whole and his corresponding attachment to God. There is also something like an idea of "freedom of assent" in fools and wise alike, which is derived from the adult human capacity for reflection before assenting and which makes it the case that assent is "up to us" and "self-determined" even in a fully causally determined world. In the latter context, the Stoics apparently did not speak of "freedom", but they might well have done so since the capacity for reflection that makes assent "up to us" is also the one that may result – when it is put to proper use – in freedom from the passions.

Now we are ready to look at Paul.[9]

5 Freedom in Galatians and 1 Corinthians

Paul's Letter to the Romans contains the fullest exploration of the idea of freedom that we have in the letters. Before that, Paul had made repeated use of

8 Here I accept a basic line of thought in Bobzien 1998a and 1998b.

9 Let me emphasize here that my aim in this essay is only to follow the trajectory of Paul's talk of freedom through Romans 6–8. The topic of freedom in Paul more generally is itself much wider, even more so that of slavery in Paul. (For the latter, see, e.g., Martin 1990, Glancy 2002, and Harrill 2006. Much relevant literature is discussed in Goodrich 2013.)

the concept in two other letters: Galatians and 1 Corinthians.[10] In Galatians, the concept comes in at high points in the argument (2.4 and especially 3.28, 4.21–31, 5.1, and 5.13). There are two basic usages. The pair "slave-free" is used in its concrete, straightforwardly social sense of a slave or free person (3.28). But the pair is also used in a more metaphorical manner of freedom from the Mosaic law, e.g. at 5.1: "For freedom Christ has set us free. Stand firm, therefore, and do not submit again to a yoke of slavery"[11] – or at the introduction to the letter's hortatory section (5.13–6.10): "[13] For you were called to freedom, brothers; only do not use your freedom as an opportunity for the flesh, but through love become slaves to one another." We may note in passing that in the latter text Paul begins to play with the notion of freedom: one may be free from the Mosaic law – but then also a slave to one another.[12]

In 1 Corinthians, Paul similarly uses the concept both in its concrete, social and political sense (7.1 and 12.13) and also in relation to the (Mosaic) law (9.19, cf. 9.20–21) and in a wider, metaphorical sense, as in 7.21–22:

> [21] Were you a slave when called? Do not be concerned about it. Even if you can gain your freedom, make use of your present condition now more than ever. [22] For whoever was called in the Lord as a slave is a freed person belonging to the Lord, just as whoever was free when called is a slave of Christ.

These various usages of the "slave-free" pair are intriguing in themselves and they make excellent sense in either letter. It is only in Romans, however, that the metaphorical and wider usages are spelled fully out.

Before we come to that, we should note three passages in Romans in which the issue of human responsibility vis-à-vis divine determination is raised rather explicitly.

10 Mention should also be made of 2 Corinthians 3.17, which in a way captures it all: "[17] Now the Lord [i.e. Christ] is the Spirit, and where the Spirit of the Lord is, there is freedom." – On freedom in Paul the basic work is Vollenweider 1989, to which I wish to refer once for all. This is a mine of information on scholarship on the topic, supplemented by an intensive "theologische Interpretation." However, although Vollenweider is an expert on Epictetus, *Dissertation* 4.1 (see now also Vollenweider 2013), he does not bring Epictetus and Paul so closely together as I am doing here.

11 All translations are my own, though with heavy input from the New Revised Standard Version.

12 Special mention should also be made of Paul's handling of slavery and freedom in Galatians 4.21–31, which is too complex to be discussed here.

6 Romans 1, 3, and 9: Human Responsibility and Divine Determination

In Romans 1, 3, and 9, Paul touches on the question whether people who do not follow what God has decreed are themselves responsible for their bad behaviour when it is also a direct result of God's determination. In the two latter passages, the people in question are Jews. In the first, they are Gentiles. Let us first consider the two latter passages.[13]

In 3.1–8, Paul engages in a complex interchange with an adversary who is a non-Christ-believing Jew. He lets his adversary suggest two ideas. First, if human injustice only serves to confirm God's justice (as Paul has just claimed), will God not be *un*just if he also punishes the unjust person? Secondly, if a person's lying only means that God's truthfulness will abound all the more to his glory (as Paul has claimed, too), then why is the person himself to be judged as a sinner? In both cases, Paul himself completely rejects this reasoning: human beings are liable to punishment even if their behaviour only serves to confirm God's justice and glory. Here, then, there is absolutely no acknowledgement that a person might not be responsible (as in "why am I still being condemned as a sinner?") when God is in total command, punishing whom *he* considers deserving of punishment.

In 9.14–24, Paul similarly raises an objection to an earlier argument of his to the effect that God's "purpose of election" (κατ' ἐκλογὴν πρόθεσις, 9.11, namely, of Jacob over Esau) shows that God had made his choice even 'before they had been born or had done anything good or bad' (9.12). Does this not mean that there is "injustice on God's part" (9.14)? – "14 By no means! 15 For … 18 he [God] has mercy on whomever he chooses, and he hardens the heart of whomever he chooses" (9.14–18). – "19 Why then does he still blame (us)? For who can resist his will?" (9.19). – "20 But who indeed are you, a human being, to argue with God? Will what is molded say to the one who molds it, "Why have you made me like this?"?" Etc., etc. (9.20–24). Thus Paul firmly believed in divine determination as an intrinsic part of his whole conception of God. God's "purpose of election" stands fast, and nothing can take away his right to blame those whom he has himself molded "for destruction" (9.22).

In 1.18–21, Paul speaks of Gentiles who have failed to honour God. The message is the same as before, but Paul now makes it explicit that these people are "without excuse" (ἀναπολόγητοι) and even attempts to explain why (1.19–20):

13 Let it be stated once for all that the meaning of almost all passages in Paul is strongly contested. I will only comment on this where it is absolutely required.

> [19] For what can be known about God is plain to them, because God has shown it to them. [20] Ever since the creation of the world his eternal power and divine nature, invisible though they are, have been understood and seen through the things he has made. So they are without excuse [...]

They knew, so they are without excuse. But we also know that even if their lack of the necessary *full* understanding was of God's own making, they would remain liable to punishment.

In short, Paul is both aware of the question of responsibility and groping for some explanation for the claim that people are indeed responsible. But his understanding of God remains such that even if one cannot find an adequate explanation, human responsibility remains fully in place.

7 Freedom in Romans 6.1–8.13

Up until ch. 5 of Romans, Paul has explained why there was a need for God's direct intervention with the 'Christ event' (Jesus Christ dying and being resurrected) in order to rectify the previous period of sinning. Ch. 5 then partly celebrates (5.1–11) what has happened to "us" through the Christ event, partly explains this (5.12–21) as inaugurating a new phase of history in which the period of sin and death begun with Adam has been overcome by Christ. The celebration of 5.1–11 takes two forms. Something *has* happened to Christ believers and something *will* happen to them. They *have* been "justified" (5.1) and "the love of God *has* been poured into our hearts through the holy *pneuma* that has been given to us" (5.5).[14] But it all also stands under the sign of "hope" (ἐλπίς, 5.2 and 5), a hope that they will in the end find "salvation" (5.9–10), namely, in the form of a resurrection like Jesus'. This duality then determines the next three chapters.[15] The forward-looking state of hope is taken up in 8.14–39, which corresponds to 5.1–11. By contrast, 6.1–8.13 spells out what the new situation is like of pneumatic Christ believers with regard to their *present* behaviour. Elsewhere I have argued that this passage is through and through hortatory in form.[16] Paul's idea is to *encourage* them to behave in a manner

14 Instead of speaking of "spirit" or "Spirit", I shall just transliterate the Greek word. Paul's *pneuma*, as I have argued elsewhere (Engberg-Pedersen 2010), is a material entity like in Stoicism.

15 I have argued for this claim, which is not always recognized, in Engberg-Pedersen 1995, 479–485.

16 See Engberg-Pedersen 1995.

that matches the new situation in which they *already* find themselves: with holy *pneuma* poured into their hearts.

He begins (ch. 6) by reminding his addressees of what happened to them when they were baptized. In baptism "to Christ's death" (cf. 6.3), they have been "buried together with him ... in order that ... we ... might walk in newness of life" (6.4), more specifically, "in order that the body of sin might be destroyed, and we might no longer be enslaved to sin" (6.6). Here we have our key idea: being enslaved to sin, which – together with its matching concept of freedom – governs the whole of 6.12–23. What Paul aims to bring out here is that since his Christ-believing addressees are no longer "under the (Mosaic) law, but under a gift" (6.15, namely, the Christ event), they are free of sin and must therefore also show this in their actual behaviour. He attempts to achieve this aim by addressing them according to a pattern of what I shall call "parallel opposition": being free of sin, they are also *slaves* of justice (6.18) and later of God (6.22). Here is 6.17–18:

> [17] Thanks be to God that you, having once been slaves of sin, have become obedient from the heart to the form of teaching to which you were entrusted,
> [18] and that you, having been set free from sin, have become slaves of justice.

Paul goes immediately on to apologize for the latter way of speaking (6.19a):[17] "I am speaking in human terms because of the weakness of your flesh." But he also capitalizes on this peculiar notion of slavery (6.19b): "For just as you once presented your members as slaves to impurity and to greater and greater iniquity, so now present your members as slaves to justice for sanctification." And the parallel opposition continues: having been 'freed from sin', the Christ believers are also "enslaved to God" (6.22); and similarly (7.5–6):

> [5] While we were living in the flesh, our sinful passions, aroused by the law, were at work in our members to bear fruit for death. [6] But now we are discharged from the law, dead to that which held us captive, so that

17 This understanding of what Paul apologizes for is not generally recognized, but accepted by Vollenweider 1989, 326. See also Fitzmyer 1993, 450: "Paul means that his referring to the Christian's devotion to uprightness as "slavery" is a very human way of putting it." It matters a great deal to my argument that Paul precisely apologizes for speaking of "slavery" in connection with his Christ believers.

> we are slaves not under the old written code but in the new life of the *pneuma*.

What we have, then, is first an idea that freedom from the law and sin also means slavery to justice, God, and in the new life of the *pneuma*. But exactly what does that mean? One can understand that living "under" the law is a form of slavery in the sense that when one follows the law, one does not necessarily do what one wishes. Moreover, Paul also goes directly on to explain – in the famous section, 7.7–25, showing that "I do not do what I want [namely, what is enjoined by the law], but what I hate, that thing I do" (7.15) – why living under the law may also issue in a different form of slavery, namely, to sin and the passions *against* what the law has enjoined. But in what sense is the new life of the *pneuma* also one of slavery? This is more puzzling than it may initially appear. In doing what justice and God require, does the pneumatic Christ believer act *against* his or her own will? (Remember our earlier definition of freedom.) That, then, is the first question. What we also have in the passage (6.19) is an indication (if ever so slight) that speaking of slavery in this context may not, after all, be quite right. Then how does *that* fit into the overall picture? Thus both Paul's use of the pattern of parallel opposition and his slight qualification of its appropriateness raise a genuine question of understanding: is the new life in fact one of slavery, and if so, in what sense?

This question is not answered in the rest of 6.1–8.13. 7.7–25, which spells out 7.5 (quoted above), celebrates in 7.15 (quoted above) the split in relation to the law and sin, ending with finding a double form of "slavery" in living under the law (7.25b): "So then, with my mind I am a slave to the law of God, but with my flesh I am a slave to the law of sin."

This desperate situation is only resolved by the Christ event, as already summarized in 7.6 and spelled out in 8.1–13. Here we again meet the idea of freedom, namely, from the law, as generated by the *pneuma* (8.2): "For the law of the *pneuma* of life in Christ Jesus has set you free from the law of sin and of death."

We do not admittedly find in 8.1–13 the corresponding idea that freedom from the law also constitutes slavery in the *pneuma*. But 7.6 has already stated that; and Paul at least claims in 8.12–13 that "we are *debtors* (ὀφειλέται), not to the flesh, to live according to the flesh – [...] but if by the *pneuma* you put to death the deeds of the body, (then) you will live." Thus, at the end of 6.1–8.13 the question has not been answered of how to understand slavery to justice, to God, and in the newness of the *pneuma*. We can immediately understand that Paul's idea of freedom from sin and the passions corresponds closely with the Stoic notion of freedom from the passions. What is not yet clear is what is meant by speaking of this freedom as also a state of slavery.

8 Freedom in Romans 8.14–30

In 8.14–30 Paul again looks towards the future. He addresses the identity of Christ believers once they have received the *pneuma*. They are not, in fact, just slaves of God (8.14–15):

> 14 For all who are led by the *pneuma* of God are sons of God. 15 For you did not receive a *pneuma* of slavery to fall back into fear, but you have received a *pneuma* of adoption into sonship (υἱοθεσία), in which we cry, "Abba! Father!"

The theme here is the reception of the *pneuma* in baptism. The *pneuma* gives "sonship", a status as "children of God" (τέκνα θεοῦ, 8.16) and "heirs of God", indeed as "joint heirs with Christ" – if, that is, "we suffer with him so that we may also be glorified with him" (8.17). This last sentence gives the line for the whole of 8.18–30, in which Paul spells out how Christ believers and the whole of creation suffer now in the hope of future glory. And here we get a description of the new state in terms of slavery and freedom that may finally help us understand better the paradoxical claim of continued slavery under God.

The whole of creation, says Paul, has been subjected to "destruction" (φθορά) – but "in hope" (8.20):

> 21 For the creation itself will also be set free from its slavery to decay and will obtain the freedom of the glory of the children of God.

This is all highly "mythological". But the notion of a "freedom of the glory of the children of God" is noteworthy. It is partly a freedom from decay. "Glory" stands for eternal life (over against decay) as something that is generated by the *pneuma*. But this freedom is also one of "the children of God", which leads us directly back to 8.15. This freedom is not just a freedom *from* something. It is also a freedom *of* something (namely, the new status of sonship) and a freedom *for* something, namely this: for oneself *wanting* – *as* a "son of God" – what God wills, and just that. It is for this precise reason that this freedom is not one of "slavery to fall back into fear" (8.15). The person who by receiving the *pneuma* has become a "son of God" is no longer under a command. This person now at long last *wants* to do what God wills – and wants nothing else. That is how reception of the *pneuma*, as described in 8.1 ff, constitutes a solution to the agonized split described in 7.7–25, where the person both willed and did *not* will what God has ordained in his good law.[18] Perhaps, then, the slavery to God is not in the end a genuine slavery after all?

In 8.28–30 Paul ends his account of the state of hope in which believers now stand in a manner that – in effect – combines the idea of freedom in sonship with another idea that has played no role so far: that of divine election and pristine determination. Here is the text (8.28–30):

> [28] We know that all things work together for good for those who love God, who are called (κλητοί) according to his purpose (πρόθεσις). [29] For those whom he foreknew (προέγνω) he also predestined (προώρισεν) to be conformed to the image of his Son, in order that he might be the firstborn within a large family. [30] And those whom he predestined he also called (ἐκάλεσεν); and those whom he called he also justified (ἐδικαίωσεν); and those whom he justified he also glorified (ἐδόξασεν).

Those who "love" (ἀγαπᾶν) God are his sons and children. For these people all things will also work together for good. And why? Because God has *in advance* "foreknown" them, "predestined" them, "called" them, etc. But we also heard that when these people have finally received the *pneuma* as part of being glorified (and this, too, happens by God's own intervention), then in possessing the glory of being the children of God they are also *free*. How do these claims hang together? Did Paul want to say that these people are both "enslaved to God" (6.22) and also "free" as God's sons and children (8.15, 21) – and then also owing *everything* to God?

9 The Stoic Solution

This is where the Stoic theory of freedom provides a solution that is both striking and genuinely illuminating. Think of Paul's pneumatic Christ believers on

18 Commentators rightly take 8.15 on slavery "leading to fear" to refer back to the description in 7.7–25 of the person who is a slave both to the law and to sin (7.25). Basically, the fear must spring from the realization of not doing what God has decreed in his good law – and what one oneself (though ineffectually) wants to do. With the arrival of the *pneuma*, by contrast, the person *fulfils* the law since his willing is no longer divided. He now wills one thing alone.

the analogy of the Stoic sage. Having the proper insight into the way God has organized the world (here in terms of the Christ event), they have become free of the (Mosaic) law so as to be able to *fulfil* it (cf. 8.4). In this way their freedom from the law is also a freedom from the passions, just as the Stoic sage is completely free of the passions. Like the Stoic sage, however, Paul's Christ believers are also bound in another direction: to justice and to God. They *cannot but* do what is required by justice and by God. As Epictetus had it, the sage has "attached himself" to God and therefore wills whatever *he* wills. However again, this "slavery" is *not*, in fact, a proper slavery. For both the sage and the Christ believers only *want* to do what they are also required to do. And so their "slavery" is in fact a state of freedom: of *wanting* to do what one *sees* one *should* do. Paul's Christ believers are no longer under an *obligation*.

This Stoic reading of Paul's initially quite puzzling claims about slavery and freedom in Christ believers gives a sharp point to his handling of these concepts from 6.1 to 8.28: free from the law, but also bound by justice and God (and hence "slaves" to them) – but then also free "in" God. All through, the key lies in the idea that "He is free who lives as he wills" (Epictetus, *Dissertation* 4.1.1). Free of the law, Christ believers *want* to live justly and as required by God – and they want nothing else. And so they are in fact no longer slaves of God.

At 8.28–30, however, Paul brings in an idea that would initially seem to throw everything up in the air: it is all a matter of God's "predestination" (προόρισις)! What kind of freedom will his Christ believers *then* have? This is where the second half of the Stoic theory may possibly help us out. Were we to consider Paul's Christ believers from a Stoic perspective in this respect, too, we should say that it would be "up to" them to will and act in the proper way that they do, not in the sense that they *could* concretely will and act in any other way (for they know this to be the proper way of acting), but in the way that they *could have* willed and acted differently. This is because the whole issue is one of cognition and understanding. Previously, the person described in 7.7–25 served God's law with his νοῦς (reason) – but then there also was the flesh (7.25). Now, however, he has received the *pneuma*, which (one suspects) has given him *full* understanding, not least since there is something overwhelmingly new to understand: the Christ event. And this final insight has completely blotted out the flesh so that the person only wills one thing: what God wills in the law.[19] Since this change is ultimately one of the understanding, it would also be correct to say that whatever a Christ believer wills

19 By contrast, Paul says, the flesh is "*dead*" (νεκρόν) (8.10).

and does is "up to" that person, no matter how the new understanding has come about. An understanding is always the result of input from the outside (what we call information) and a person's internal handling of such input. It is therefore always a person's own; and the person's aims and actions are in that sense always "up to" that person. In this sense, too, – as the Stoics might have said, but probably did not – the person is *free* in relation to the world and God, namely, free to *understand* them, no matter how much the understanding is determined by the facts themselves. From this perspective, then, the fact that things in the world have been (providentially) predestined (or even "fated") by God in no way curtails or reduces the freedom of the individual person. There is freedom from passions when a person has reached the final and full understanding. There is the freedom of wanting what God wills, which is no longer a state of slavery. And there is a freedom of the understanding vis-à-vis any external determination in reaching the final and full understanding.

Or at least: that is what one should say if one were to apply a Stoic perspective to Paul's Christ believers as he describes them also in 8.28–30. But was that perspective also Paul's? Or should we recall here our methodological principle that Paul *may* not have had any such concerns?

10 Conclusion

We have been engaged in employing material from Stoicism to elucidate a conundrum in Paul's handling of slavery and freedom in Romans 6.1–8.30. The operation has been heuristic. If it has succeeded in solving what initially appeared puzzling and giving a sharp point to Paul's claims, then it has been a success. Then we may also conclude that although the New Testament does not address head-on the issues that go into fate, providence, and free will, nevertheless in Paul's use of the term "freedom" in Romans 6.1–8.30 we find an indication that the Stoic engagement with the overall topic was not unknown to him. This definitely holds for the first – and much the largest – part of his talk of slavery and freedom: from freedom from the passions to a "slavery" to justice and God that was in actual fact a genuine freedom. It is not completely clear that it also holds for the second part of the Stoic theory, which addresses the issue of self-determination vis-à-vis determination from the outside. However, let us venture the following proposal based on two facts. There is the fact that in 8.28 Paul *combines* a central feature from the first half of the theory (that of people "*loving*" God, which will make them will what God wills) with a forceful statement of God's predestination. And there is the fact that elsewhere in the letter he has himself brought up the question whether people who err as a result of God's predestination are to be blamed for their errors. These two facts suggest that Paul was in fact aware of the issue of "freedom" and determinism and that he acknowledged a close *connection* between such "freedom" and the freedom of wanting to do what God wills. If so, we have yet another indication of the close connection between earliest Christianity and philosophy.

Bibliography

Bobzien, Susanne. 1998a. *Determinism and Freedom in Stoic Philosophy*. Oxford: Clarendon.

Bobzien, Susanne. 1998b. "The Inadvertent Conception and Late Birth of the Free-Will Problem." *Phronesis* 43: 133–75.

Destrée, Pierre, Ricardo Salles and Marco Zingano, eds. 2014. *What is Up to Us? Studies on Agency and Responsibility in Ancient Philosophy.* Sankt Augustin: Academia.

Engberg-Pedersen, Troels. 1990. *The Stoic Theory of Oikeiosis: Moral Development and Social Interaction in Early Stoic Philosophy*. Aarhus: Aarhus University Press.

Engberg-Pedersen, Troels. 1995. "Galatians in Romans 5–8 and Paul's Construction of the Identity of Christ Believers." In *Texts and Contexts: Biblical Texts in Their Textual and Situational Contexts, Festschrift Lars Hartman*, edited by Tord Fornberg and David Hellholm, 479–505. Oslo: Scandinavian University Press.

Engberg-Pedersen, Troels. 2000. *Paul and the Stoics*. Edinburgh: T&T Clark.

Engberg-Pedersen, Troels. 2010. *Cosmology and Self in the Apostle Paul: The Material Spirit*. Oxford: Oxford University Press.

Engberg-Pedersen, Troels. 2017. *John and Philosophy: A New Reading of the Fourth Gospel*. Oxford: Oxford University Press.

Fitzmyer, Joseph A. 1993. *Romans* (The Anchor Bible 33). New York: Chapman.

Frede, Michael. 2011. *A Free Will: Origins of the Notion in Ancient Thought*, edited by Anthony A. Long. Berkeley: University of California Press.

Frede, Michael. 2014 [2007]. "The *eph'hêmin* in Ancient Philosophy." In *What is Up to Us? Studies on Agency and Responsibility in Ancient Philosophy*, edited by Pierre Destrée, Ricardo Salles and Marco Zingano, 351–363. Sankt Augustin: Academia. (Originally published in ΦΙΛΟΣΟΦΙΑ 37: 110–123.)

Glancy, Jennifer A. 2002. *Slavery in Early Christianity*. New York: Oxford University Press.

Goodrich, John K. 2013. "From Slaves of Sin to Slaves of God: Reconsidering the Origin of Paul's Slavery Metaphor in Romans 6." *Bulletin of Biblical Research* 23: 509–530.

Harrill, James A. 2006. *Slaves in the New Testament: Literary, Social and Moral Dimensions*. Minneapolis: Fortress Press.

Inwood, Brad. 2005. "The Will in Seneca." In his *Reading Seneca: Stoic Philosophy at Rome*, 132–156. Oxford: Oxford University Press.

Klein, Jacob. 2016. "The Stoic Argument from *Oikeiōsis*." *Oxford Studies in Ancient Philosophy* 50: 143–200.

Long, Anthony A. 2002. *Epictetus: A Stoic and Socratic Guide to Life*. Oxford: Oxford University Press.

Martin, Dale B. 1990. *Slavery as Salvation: The Metaphor of Slavery in Pauline Christianity*. New Haven, CT: Yale University Press.

Salles, Ricardo. 2005. *The Stoics on Determinism and Compatibilism*. Aldershot: Ashgate.

Salles, Ricardo. 2013. "Determinism, Fatalism, and Freedom in Stoic Philosophy." In *A Companion to the Philosophy of Time*, edited by Heather Dyke and Adrian Bardon, 59–72. Chichester: Wiley-Blackwell.

Vollenweider, Samuel. 1989. *Freiheit als neue Schöpfung: Eine Untersuchung zur Eleutheria bei Paulus und in seiner Umwelt* (Forschungen zur Religion und Literatur des Alten und Neuen Testaments 147). Göttingen: Vandenhoeck & Ruprecht.

Vollenweider, Samuel, ed. 2013. *Epiktet: Was ist wahre Freiheit? Diatribe IV 1* (SAPERE 22). Tübingen: Mohr Siebeck.

CHAPTER 7

Middle Platonists on Fate and Providence. God, Creation, and the Governance of the World

Emmanuele Vimercati

1 Introduction

Fate and providence are two cornerstones of Imperial Platonism, for two reasons. First, they regulate the relationship between the first principles – mainly god and the Ideas – and the physical world: by doing so, they also help us understand the principles' nature and their intervention in cosmic events. Second, they warrant the continuity of the ontological levels, in order to explain human conduct. Even though Plato had already introduced such themes in his dialogues,[1] it is undeniable that in the following centuries they came to be more significant: this already started in the Hellenistic period and continued among philosophers and religious thinkers in the early Imperial age.

The Middle Platonist doctrine of fate has received particular attention in recent scholarship,[2] which has enhanced our knowledge of the topic in terms of both history and theory. However, the issue of fate has been tackled mostly with respect to human agency, namely, in terms of the margins of autonomy attributable to man's conduct in the cosmos – which the ancients classified as "what is up to us" (τὸ ἐφ' ἡμῖν).[3] This approach has certainly helped to clarify the prerogatives of human action and the margins of freedom of the embodied soul. Thus, much attention has been given to anthropological and ethical interpretations of fate and physical causality, which were indeed important for Middle Platonists. However, in focussing on the aspect of human agency, the action of god or of the principles is somewhat neglected. But the action of god

1 See especially Plato, *Timaeus* 30b–c, 41d–42d; see also, *Republic* 10.617d–e (the Myth of Er), *Laws* 10.904a–906b.

2 See especially Mansfeld 1999, Boys-Stones 2007, 2016, 2018, Eliasson 2008, Algra 2014, Opsomer 2014, and Bonazzi 2014; see also Whittaker 1990, 133–135, Dillon 1993, 160–164, Reydams-Schils 1999, 204–205, 225–243, Reydams-Schils 2008, Frede 2011, 58–64, and Trabattoni 2014.

3 This also includes, among others, the concepts of free will, freedom, choice, self-determination and responsibility. The theme of fate also has important logical implications (see Mansfeld 1999), which fall outside the scope of this paper.

 | DOI:10.1163/9789004436381_009

is fundamental with respect to providence and fate: indeed, if one does not fully comprehend this aspect, it is also difficult to correctly understand human conduct. This is why I shall here deal mainly with this issue starting out from the nature and the action of god: because such action, from a Platonic point of view, is a premise to cosmic causality, and because this allows some margins of originality with respect to the analyses of contemporary scholars.

This study is divided into three parts. In the first part, some general remarks on fate and providence in Middle Platonist debate will be offered. In the second part, I will discuss these notions from the standpoint of the first principles, showing how fate and providence presuppose the Platonic theory of the generation of the world. As I shall argue, the Middle Platonist understanding of free will was ultimately based upon the nature and activity of god and its relation to matter. Finally, in the third part, I explain fate and providence as instruments of god in governing the world. The very nature of such governance will be investigated starting from the definition of fate as "law" (νόμος). In this sense, it will become clear that the Middle Platonists developed these theories by taking elements from the Stoics and Peripatetics, which were nonetheless traced back to Plato's thought. The Platonists, however, ultimately formulated a theory that would offer an alternative to that of the other two philosophical schools.[4]

Two preliminary observations regarding terminology are due at this point. First, the expression "Middle Platonism" is used here for merely conventional reasons: as the debate about the term in the last decades has made clear, the expression has its merits and limits. Just like other scholars, I believe that elements common to this tradition do, however, exist with respect to fate and providence. Second, the term "creation" is not used here in its biblical sense, but rather in the Platonic one, that is as a synonym of "generation" (γένεσις) or "production" (ποίησις) of the cosmos.

2 Some Remarks on Fate and Providence in Middle Platonism

In introducing the theme, a brief explanation on how Middle Platonists understood fate and providence might be useful. The main sources in this case are Pseudo-Plutarch's *On Fate*, chapter 26 of Alcinous' *Didaskalikos*, and Apuleius' *On Plato and His Doctrine* (1.204–207). Later works, among which Calcidius' *Commentary on the Timaeus* (esp. 143–189) and Nemesius of Emesa's *On the Nature of Man* (esp. 35–43), also seem to partially reflect Middle Platonist

4 See Opsomer 2014, 139.

sources – and are as such examined in this study.[5] A shared overall approach emerges from these works, although with certain differences. In *On Fate* 1.568B Ps.-Plutarch identifies two meanings of "fate" (εἱμαρμένη), respectively as "activity" (ἐνέργεια) and as "substance" (οὐσία).[6] "Fate as a substance appears to be the entire soul of the universe" (2.568E),[7] while fate as activity is defined as follows (1.568D):[8]

> [Fate] as described in the *Phaedrus* [248c] might be called "a divine formula" (λόγος θεῖος) which, owing to a cause from which there is no escape (ἀνεμπόδιστον), is not transgressed (ἀπαράβατος)"; as described in the *Timaeus* [41e], it would be "a law (νόμος) conforming to the nature of the universe, determining the course of everything that comes to pass"; while as described in the *Republic* [10.617d], it is "a divine law (νόμος θεῖος) determining the linking (συμπλέκεται) of future events to events past and present."

The type of law referred to here is specified in a later passage: "We meant by 'consequent of an hypothesis' that which is not laid down independently, but in some fashion is really 'subjoined' to something else, wherever there is an expression implying that if one thing is true, another follows" (4.570A).[9] In brief, one may say that fate is understood as the order or the inviolable norm of physical causality.[10] But, although physical causality affects every cosmic event, Ps.-Plutarch made the point that only general cases are under direct control of fate, whereas individual events are only virtually fated: for, "the law of nature, while dealing with universals primarily (προηγουμένως), deals secondarily (ἑπομένως) with particulars." Thus, it "embraces the particular cases potentially in its general provisions" (νόμος δυνάμει τὰ καθ' ἕκαστα τοῖς ὅλοις συμπεριλάμβανει: 4.569E).[11] This might be surprising (*On Fate* 4.570A), but – as will be shown – it reflected the Middle Platonist understanding of fate as general norm presiding over individual cases. For, this understanding of fate was

5 On these authors, see Theiler 1966, den Boeft 1970, 8–46, Sharples 1983, Dillon 1993, 160–164, Valgiglio 1993, Reydams-Schils 1999, 2008 and 2020, 99–117, Eliasson 2008, 119–167, Algra 2014.

6 See also Calcidius, *On Plato's Timaeus* 143–149.

7 Tr. by De Lacy and Einarson 1959, which I will use throughout in my paper.

8 See also Calcidius, *On Plato's Timaeus* 143.

9 ἐξ ὑποθέσεως δὴ ἔφαμεν τὸ μὴ καθ' ἑαυτὸ τιθέμενον, ἀλλά πως ἑτέρῳ τινὶ ὡς ἀληθῶς ὑποτεθέν, ὁπόσα ἀκολουθίαν σημαίνει.

10 See also Plutarch, *On the E at Delphi* 6.387B, Calcidius, *On Plato's Timaeus* 149, 152–154.

11 On these definitions see Boys-Stones 2007, 435–437, and Opsomer 2014, 144–161.

"appropriate to divine wisdom" (οἰκεῖον τῇ θείᾳ φρονήσει), which deals primarily with universals, as well as human autonomy.

In this sense, the main point of Middle Platonist compatibilism is – in Ps.-Plutarch's words – the assertion that "everything is contained in fate" (*On Fate* 5.570C), but not everything is fated. Fate is thus understood as the finite set of infinite cosmic events (3.569A),[12] ordered in a cyclical concatenation (3.569C). Other authors – such as Plutarch, Apuleius, and Calcidius – describe fate as *one* of the causes of events, alongside chance and human free will.[13] In Middle Platonism, the "potential" nature of fate takes up the attribute of conditionality, that is, of subordination to a given cause, which can be free. Accordingly, in order to reconcile free will with the constraints of the cosmos, the Middle Platonists claim that the autonomous principle of action is the soul, and that, however, the consequences of each action are necessitated. In other words, if a person *x* freely carries out action *y*, consequence *z* will necessarily follow. The example from the *Didaskalikos* is well known: "As Apollo put it to Laius: 'If you beget a son, that offspring will kill you.'"[14] This formulation is commonly defined as conditional necessity (or conditional fate), an expression derived from Ps.-Plutarch, who claims that fate "presupposes hypothetical assumptions" (ἐξ ὑποθέσεως; *On Fate* 4.569D6). In other words, only the consequences would be fated, whereas the causes of the actions can depend on the autonomy of individuals. The Middle Platonists thus compared fate to the role of law in civil society, as law 1) prescribes the universal, but does not decide the particular (namely, the behaviour of individuals), and nonetheless 2) it necessarily determines the consequences of an action (for example, a law establishes the penalty for a crime). In the same way, fate is the principle determining the consequences of the free individual agency, ordering them in an indefectible universal sequence.[15]

Finally, fate is subordinate to providence, which Apuleius and Calcidius defined as "the divine decree" (or "design", *divina sententia*).[16] In order to guaran-

---

12 See also Calcidius, *On Plato's Timaeus* 149.

13 Plutarch, *Table-Talk* 9.5.2, 740B–D; Apuleius, *On Plato and His Doctrine* 1.206; Calcidius, *On Plato's Timaeus* 145.

14 See Alcinous, *Didaskalikos* 26.2, 179.17 Hermann, quoting Euripides, *Phoenician Women* 19. For the Stoics, see Cicero, *On Fate* 30 (= *SVF* 2.956); Origen, *Against Celsus* 2.20 (= *SVF* 2.957).

15 Ps.-Plutarch, *On Fate* 4.569D, 5.570B–E, Philo, *On Providence* 2.82, Alcinous, *Didaskalikos* 26, Calcidius, *On Plato's Timaeus* 151–154, 179–180, 188–189; see also Nemesius, *On the Nature of Man* 38.

16 Apuleius, *On Plato and His Doctrine* 1.205, Calcidius, *On Plato's Timaeus* 144, 176, Nemesius, *On the Nature of Man* 42–43. Cf. Moreschini 2015, 280–281.

tee god's intervention in the cosmos and, at the same time, to defend god from the responsibility for evil, the Middle Platonists distinguished different orders of providence. Apuleius, Ps.-Plutarch, Calcidius, and Nemesius identified three orders: that of the Primal god, that of the gods in the heavens, and that of the demons responsible on earth for controlling human actions.[17] In some cases, the actions of the demons are also included in fate, so that the lowest level of divine providence coexists with the constraints of the world (see Ps.-Plutarch, *On Fate* 9.572F–573B). Thus, "whereas fate most certainly conforms to providence, providence most certainly does not conform to fate" (*On Fate* 9.573B), so that fate is subordinate to providence.[18] One must here observe that this represents a clear departure from the Stoic position, which equated the two concepts.

As a modern commentator noted, this doctrine is not without inconsistencies:

> If the (fated) consequences of (unfated) choice reach only as far as the next human choice, they may rarely have very much impact. [...] It is, on the other hand, difficult to see what the basis would be for identifying some decisions as unfated while viewing others, as they are supposed 'consequences', as fated.[19]

Some of these inconsistencies perhaps originated from the fact that the relation between fate and free will became an important topic only in the Hellenistic period, and was systematically discussed neither by Plato nor Aristotle.[20] This required projecting onto the past theories that Platonists and Aristotelians developed only at a later stage.[21] As for providence and fate as instruments of divine governance over the world, Ps.-Plutarch and Calcidius made clear that Plato had already spoken of fate "not in high tragic style, but in the language of theology" (Ps.-Plutarch, *On Fate* 1.568D; Calcidius, *On Plato's Timaeus* 143). In other words, Plato did not speak in poetical or mythologi-

17 See here above, n. 16.

18 See Opsomer 2014, 161–164, Reydams-Schils 2008, 243–247, Moreschini 2015, 284–285, Timotin 2012, 118–122, Boys-Stones 2016, 327–332.

19 See Boys-Stones 2007, 431–432, who speaks of "a terrible theory"; on the (in-)coherence of the Middle Platonist doctrine of fate, see also den Boeft 1970, 33, Dillon 1996 [1977], 325, Sharples 2003, 109, Boys-Stones 2007, 431ff. (also for a possible solution to the Middle Platonist inconsistencies), Trabattoni 2014, 103–108, Opsomer 2014, 142–143.

20 As for Aristotle, see Carlo Natali's contribution in the present volume.

21 See Bonazzi 2014, 283–285.

cal terms, but in a scientific manner, with reference to the theory of the first principles and to the divine beings in particular. That is to say that, for later Platonists, Plato, although occasionally, had already introduced fate and providence with some coherence in his own works.

3 The First Principles and the Creation of the World

To begin with, one should note that, in a theological sense, the relationship between fate and providence was developed by the Middle Platonists in debate with the Stoics and Aristotelians.[22] The Stoics in particular, more than anyone else, had examined the concepts of fate and providence, which they linked to the will or the activity of god or to god's very nature.[23] In this sense, the Stoics were monists, corporealists, and immanentists, since they understood god as a physical principle and confined his activity to the generation and the governance of the world. They thus explained the world as a solid and complex causal network,[24] for whoever claims the necessity of all events must then account for the cause-effect nexus that necessarily determines them.[25] However, this solution entailed some drawbacks.

In identifying god, providence, and fate, the Stoics were in danger of subjugating the nature and activity of god to the necessity of the world. Take Seneca's statement in his *On Providence*, at 5.8: "Although the great creator and ruler of the universe himself wrote the decrees of Fate, yet he follows them. He obeys for ever, he decreed but once."[26] For a Platonist, this Stoic account had dangerous consequences: first of all, it reduced god to a purely physical entity and subordinated him to the law of fate, which he himself had created. Secondly, if the nature of god is identified with fate and providence, the evil in the

22 Ps.-Plutarch, *On Fate* 11.574D–F, Calcidius, *On Plato's Timaeus* 174–175. On the relationship between providence in Plutarch and in the Stoics, see Algra 2014.

23 See Aëtius, *Placita* 1.27.5 (= *SVF* 1.176); Calcidius, *On Plato's Timaeus* 144 (= *SVF* 2.933); in general, *SVF* 2.928–932, 962; also, Bobzien 1998, 44–58. Some possible distinctions are introduced by Calcidius, *On Plato's Timaeus* 144, according to Cleanthes (see also Algra 2014, 122–126).

24 Cf. Sauvé Meyer 2009, Brouwer 2015.

25 See Plutarch, *On Stoic Self-Contradictions* 34.1050A–B, 37.1051D, 47.1056C–D (god as the cause of evil, and the suspension of human responsibility, in the Stoics), *To an Uneducated Ruler* 4.781F (Plutarch against Stoic materialism and immanentism), Ps.-Plutarch, *On Fate* 11.574D–F, Calcidius, *On Plato's Timaeus* 144–145, 179.

26 *ille ipse omnium conditor et rector scripsit quidem fata, sed sequitur; semper paret, semel iussit.* My translation is from Basore 1928.

cosmos would be hard to explain.[27] Thirdly, two anthropological and ethical issues accompanied these theological problems: Stoic determinism threatened human free will – which Plato had, more or less consistently, assumed in the myth of Er[28] – and the individual responsibility for human agency – which, for a Platonist, was crucial in the eschatology of the souls.[29]

In order to avoid such drawbacks, a possible solution was provided by Aristotle, who in Book 12 of the *Metaphysics* had postulated an incorporeal Prime Mover, separate and in actuality, a first intellect which thinks eternally of itself. Placed at the top of a sequence of movers, the Prime Mover was also responsible for the motion of the cosmos and the heavens. It is known that some Middle Platonists, notably Alcinous, had been influenced by Aristotle in the way they presented god.[30] However, Aristotle's solution had its own difficulties, both theological and psychological. As for the theological difficulty, Atticus accused Aristotle of atheism, since Aristotle, just like Epicurus later, was deemed to have rejected the providence of god in the world.[31] According to Atticus, Aristotle had excluded god's concern for human events and god's rule over the world, limiting his action to the heavens above the Earth. This criticism was based on Aristotle's rejection of the creation of the world and his assumption of its eternity.[32] Alongside the accusation of god's "inactivity" and lack of interest in human affairs, Atticus' second difficulty, also reported by Calcidius,[33] was directed against Aristotle's psychology. For the claim that the soul is form or "actuality" (ἐντελέχεια) of the body would imply the corruptibility of the soul itself. If, therefore, the soul is corruptible, faith in providence

27 See, e.g., Plutarch, *On the Generation of the Soul in the Timaeus* 6.1015B, *On Isis and Osiris* 45.369D; in this regard, the Platonist argument against the Stoics can be found mainly in Plutarch (*Against the Stoics on Common Conceptions* 15.1066B–21.1068E, *On the Generation of the Soul in the Timaeus* 6.1015B) and Numenius (see Calcidius, *On Plato's Timaeus* 295–299 = Numenius, fr. 52 Des Places). Cf. Algra 2014, 122–126, 131–135.

28 See Plato, *Republic* 10.617d–e.

29 See Plutarch, *On Stoic Self-Contradictions* 34.1050A–B, 37.1051D, 47.1055F–1057C, Ps.-Plutarch, *On Fate* 11.574D–F, Calcidius, *On Plato's Timaeus* 144–145, 151–152 (on the judgment *post mortem*), 179. Cf. Babut 1969, 307–317, Hershbell 1992, Moreschini 2015, 280, O'Brien 2015, 87–111, Reydams-Schils 2020, 99–117.

30 See, e.g., Alcinous, *Didaskalikos* 10.3, 164.18–34 Hermann, with reference to Aristotle, *Metaphysics* 12.6–9. Cf. Boys-Stones 2018, 151–152, Karamanolis 2006, 136–144, is sceptical about the possibility that Numenius (frs. 11, 15, 17 Des Places) is inspired by Aristotle.

31 Eusebius of Caesarea, *Preparation for the Gospel* 15.5.1–14 (= Atticus, fr. 3 Des Places); also, Plutarch, *On the Generation of the Soul in the Timaeus* 4.1013E.

32 Eusebius, *Preparation for the Gospel* 15.6.1–17 (= Atticus, fr. 4 Des Places). Cf. Boys-Stones 2016, 319–326, and Boys-Stones 2018, 323–326.

33 Calcidius, *On Plato's Timaeus* 175 (on the "inactivity" of god), 222–223 (on psychology).

would also seem affected (naturally, the Stoic attempt to reconcile the two things appeared to be inconsistent to the Platonists).

These issues take us to the solution offered by the Middle Platonists. How could free will in the world be guaranteed, without rejecting natural necessity and god's providential rule (as maintained by Aristotle)? And how could one do so without identifying these necessity and providence (as held by the Stoics)? For Platonists, the foundation of freedom in the world rests, first and foremost, on the free and voluntary nature of god's productive act and on his distinction from the role of matter. Plato had indeed affirmed that god "desired (ἐβουλήθη) that all should be, as far as possible, like unto himself (παραπλήσια ἑαυτῷ)"[34] and that "he is the best of all the causes (ἄριστος τῶν αἰτίων)",[35] so that his activity is completely autonomous. In the Platonic tradition, amongst those who had interpreted Plato's cosmogony literally, i.e. "according to time" (κατὰ τὸν χρόνον), Plutarch and Atticus note that the act of creation is the time when god places providence at the head of the world.[36] Thus, it is no coincidence that Ps.-Plutarch and Calcidius spoke of providence as "the eldest of all the things" or as the intellection and will of the supreme god.[37] Like *nous* and intelligible essence, providence imitates the goodness of god: providence thus reflects this goodness and is adorned by it. As such, providence is conceived of as a sort of second principle after the Primal god, or as an attribute of god. Fate is subject to providence thanks to the world soul, which transmits the will of god in the world and which is identified with fate itself. Furthermore, through separating god from matter, Platonists gave each of the two principles a different and opposite role in the creation of the world. While god is the cause of the providential project which reproduces the perfection of the Model (the Forms), matter is responsible for the necessity of the cosmos, that is it sets the physical constraints. Through such dualism – in line with the *Timaeus* – Middle Platonists tried to overcome reducing god to a mere physical entity, and his subordination to the laws of fate which he himself had created.[38] As we shall see below, moreover, the god-matter dualism will also be used by the Platonists in order to explain evil in the cosmos, without attributing its responsibility to god.

34 Plato, *Timaeus* 29e3.

35 Plato, *Timaeus* 29a6.

36 See, e.g., Plutarch, *On the Face in the Moon* 13.927A–B, *On the Generation of the Soul in the Timaeus* 4.1013E–F, Atticus, frs. 3–4 Des Places.

37 Ps.-Plutarch, *On Fate* 9.572F–573B, Calcidius, *On Plato's Timaeus* 176, 188.

38 See Plutarch, *To an Uneducated Ruler* 4.5781E–782A, *On Isis and Osiris* 45.369D. Cf. Babut 1969, 317, Boys-Stones 2007, 440–441, Algra 2014, 129–131, Bonazzi 2014, 289–290.

Now, through providence, the free actions of the individual souls are also conceived of as a reproduction, on a lower scale, of the free act of god. The soul is free as long as it conforms its action to that of god, who is free of all constraints.[39] This was clearly expressed in Plato's theory of the "likeness to god", which is the ultimate end in human life and the source of happiness.[40] In his *Didaskalikos*, at 2.2, 153.2–15 Hermann, Alcinous states:

> Contemplation, then, is the activity of the intellect when intelligizing the intelligibles, while action is the activity of a rational soul which takes place by way of the body. The soul engaged in contemplation of the divine and the thoughts of the divine is said to be in a good state (εὐπαθεῖν), and that state of the soul is called 'wisdom', which may be asserted to be no other than likeness to the divine. For this reason, such a state would be of priority, valuable, most desirable and most proper to us, free of (external) hindrance, *entirely within our power* (ἐφ' ἡμῖν) and cause of the end in life *which is set before us*. Action, on the other hand, and the active life, being pursued through the body, *are subject to external hindrance*, and would be engaged in when circumstances demand, by practicing the transferral to human affairs of the visions of the contemplative life.[41]

The relationship between likeness to god and the role of god in the cosmos is further explained by Alcinous: "Sometimes he (*sc.* Plato) says that the end is to liken oneself to God, but sometimes that it consists in following him, as when he says [*Laws* 4.715e]: 'God who, as old tradition has it, holds the beginning and the end', etc."[42] Likeness refers here to the celestial god, who is engaged in contemplation of the Forms, but also in practical activity – the production and governance of the world. Also with regard to the soul, the principle of likeness has a theoretical aspect – the contemplation of the intelligibles – and a practical aspect – the exercise of virtue.[43] It is worth recalling that, in Platonic terms, action is an imitation of contemplation, or an imperfect form of it. Contemplation is free since it involves only the intellect, and it is accordingly fundamental for action, which is a product of contemplation. The priority of

---

39 See, e.g., Apuleius, *On the God of Socrates* 3.123–124.

40 Ps.-Plutarch, *On Fate* 7.572E. Cf. Plato, *Theaetetus* 176a–b, the classic passage on likeness to god.

41 Tr. Dillon 1993. See also *Didaskalikos* 27.2.

42 Alcinous, *Didaskalikos* 28.3, 181.36–39 Hermann, tr. Dillon 1993.

43 Calcidius, *On Plato's Timaeus* 180.

contemplation allowed Platonists to introduce a meta-physical form of causation, on the basis of which the course of nature can be determined. In some way, insofar as the soul perfects the contemplative life, it is also able to act in autonomy on the natural order and, therefore, to escape the constraints of fate. This is possible if the soul reflects the activity of god in contemplating the Forms and producing the world. The freedom of god is thus the necessary premise of the freedom of man, who acts by imitation of his creator.[44] Since for Platonists the soul is a demon or a divine principle,[45] its free agency contributed to the perfection of the divine providence in the world, of which the soul itself is the third and final level.[46]

In order to understand god's freedom and its paradigmatic relevance for human freedom, the nature of demiurgic action is best explained.[47] In this regard, Middle Platonists seem to have provided a literal interpretation of Plato's *Timaeus*. In the dialogue, Plato had claimed that god is good and that he is the best of causes, since he looks at the eternal Model.[48] Accordingly, god's decision to produce the world as it is, is guided by god's good nature, by his perfect causality, and by the stability of the Model. In this regard, however, Plato noted that the world had been produced by "reasoning" (λογισμός), that is by a pondered calculation by the demiurge.[49] This seems to imply a choice between multiple options that are the object of god's attention. But this implication is problematic, since it presupposes the existence of alternatives that precede god and, also, god's contemplation of something that is imperfect. For, the autonomy of the material principle implies that god faces a concurrent cause, that is opposed to god himself and to the Model. The interaction of god's deliberation, on the one hand, and the pre-existence of a cause that escapes his control, on the other hand, prompts one to believe this cosmos to be but one among the many possible alternatives, in the sense that it "needs not have been this way."[50] For necessity affects the stability of god's contemplation of the perfect Model during creation. Such literal interpretation of *Timaeus*

---

44 See Babut 1969, 311–312.

45 Plato, *Timaeus* 90a, *Phaedo* 107d, *Republic* 10.617e, 620d–e; also, Apuleius, *On the God of Socrates* 15.150–154, Numenius, fr. 37 Des Places.

46 Also, Apuleius, *On the World* 30.358.

47 Though the Middle Platonist accounts of the nature and hierarchy of the different gods are clearly divergent (see, e.g., the contributions included in Calabi 2002; and also Ferrari 2005, Brenk 2005, Vorwerk 2010, O'Brien 2015, ch. 4–6), as for fate and providence I do believe some common traits can be found.

48 Plato, *Timaeus* 28a–29b.

49 Plato, *Timaeus* 30a–b.

50 See Boys-Stones 2007, 432.

left its traces in the Middle Platonist tradition. In Plutarch, for instance, god is sometimes referred to as a "prophet" (μάντις), who is capable of foretelling future events based on their causes, but is not directly nor entirely responsible for them.[51] For the existence of contingent events seems to be a remainder of the original "necessity" (ἀνάγκη), which after all introduces a margin of indeterminacy in the cosmos.[52] Elsewhere, Plutarch acknowledges that the world's perfection does not depend upon the constraint that governs each thing, but on a deliberate choice by god – the product of his *logos* – to make the better prevail over necessity.[53] One should also note that by Plotinus at least, such demiurgic causation would be challenged, the idea that providence and world order depend on pure prevision and calculation by god being rejected.[54] For this would limit the omniscience of god, who would be a mere spectator of future events, and his perfect contemplation of the Forms, which would be distracted by the production of the world.[55]

Cosmogonic dualism was useful for the Middle Platonists not only in proving the existence of events which escape necessity, since this is only one of the possible worlds, but also in explaining the relationship between providence and evil in the cosmos, a much debated issue in the Imperial era.[56] In spite of the declared beauty of the cosmos, one should understand why not everything reflects the goodness of god, which would actually seem to limit or negate the efficacy of providence.[57] Hints that may explain how god's activity related to the constraints of fate were mostly found in three passages from Plato: *Timaeus* 48a, *Timaeus* 52d–e, and *Laws* 10.896d–e.[58] The *Timaeus* passages deal with necessity as the principle that opposes the intellect and as the nurturer of the becoming, lacking equilibrium and being shaken by uneven forces (τὸ μήθ' ὁμοίων δυναμένων μήτε ἰσορρόπων ἐμπίμπλασθαι). The passage from the *Laws* contains a reference to the soul opposite to the "good" or

51 See Plutarch, *On the E at Delphi* 6.387B.

52 See Plutarch, *On the Obsolescence of Oracles* 47.435F.

53 See, e.g., Plutarch, *On the Face in the Moon* 15.928A–B, *Table-Talk* 8.2.4, 720B–C (on the role of *logos*), Calcidius, *On Plato's Timaeus* 176.

54 See, e.g., Plotinus, *Enneads* 3.2.1, 5.8.7.

55 See Chiaradonna 2015, 35–43 and Enrico Peroli's contribution in the present volume.

56 In Calcidius, *On Plato's Timaeus* 174, for example, the problem of evil serves as an introduction for the discussion about fate and providence.

57 See Calcidius, *On Plato's Timaeus* 176–189, esp. 179–180, which is the second part of his survey on fate and providence; see also Apuleius, *On Plato and His Doctrine* 1.205.

58 Cf., e.g., Plutarch, *On the Generation of the Soul in the Timaeus* 6.1014D–F.

"beneficent" one.[59] The texts were discussed by notably Plutarch, Atticus, and Numenius, who – in different ways – refer the agitated nature of matter to the activity of an evil soul.[60] Numenius' discussion is especially interesting here. In the extant remains of his writings, the existence of a counter-principle at the origin of evil is associated with the postulation of a transcendent Primal god, who is not directly involved in the production and governance of the cosmos, but only through a Second god, namely, the demiurge. Numenius states that:

> The First god, who exists in himself, is simple; for as He absolutely deals with none but himself, he is in no way divisible; however, the Second and Third god are one. When, however, this (unity) is brought together with Matter, which is Doubleness, the (one divinity) indeed unites it, but is by Matter split, inasmuch as Matter is full of desires, and in a flowing condition.[61]

The Third god, Numenius makes clear elsewhere, is the cosmos.[62] The appeal to an antagonist principle to the demiurge had the advantage of exonerating god (both Primal and Second) from being the cause of evil, which on the other hand lays entirely in the evil soul. The Middle Platonists thus projected a dualist architecture of the cosmos, which is produced by the interaction of two competing principles: god and matter. Despite the passivity and neutrality of matter as defended by Aristotle and reiterated by Alcinous (amongst others),[63] Plutarch and Numenius preferred to endow matter with an active nature that

59 "[Athenian] One soul, is it, or several (πλείους)? I will answer for you – 'several.' Anyhow, let us assume not less than two – the beneficent soul and that which is capable of effecting results of the opposite kind (τῆς τε εὐεργέτιδος καὶ τῆς τἀναντία δυναμένης)" (tr. Bury 1926).

60 See Plutarch, *On Isis and Osiris* 45.369A–D (on which, recently, O'Brien 2015, 96–105, 113–115, Petrucci 2016), Atticus, fr. 23 Des Places, Numenius, fr. 52 Des Places (on which Vimercati 2012; O'Brien 2015, 158–167; and Boys-Stones 2018, 106–109).

61 See Eusebius of Caesarea, *Preparation for the Gospel* 11.17.11–18.5 (= Numenius, fr. 11 Des Places; tr. Guthrie 1917, modified); see also Plutarch, *On the Generation of the Soul in the Timaeus* 6.1014E–1015A, and Numenius, fr. 3 Des Places.

62 See Proclus, *On Plato's Timaeus* 1.303.27–304.7 Diehl (= Numenius, fr. 21 Des Places): "Numenius, who teaches three Gods, calls the First Father; the Second Creator, and the Third Creature; for, according to his opinion, the world is the Third God. According to him, therefore, the Demiurge is double, (consisting) out of the First and the Second God; but the Third is the demiurgic product (tr. Guthrie 1917, modified)." See also Plato, *Timaeus* 34a–b.

63 See Alcinous, *Didaskalikos* 8, 162.29–163.10 Hermann.

interferes with the action of god.[64] This made it possible to bypass the difficulties of Stoic monism, but also has two serious implications: the downgrading of demiurgic activity and a threat to the perfection of the creator god. The downgrading of demiurgic activity has a parallel in *Timaeus*, at 42e5–6, where Plato states that, once the cosmos is produced, the demiurge goes back to contemplating the Forms, his typical activity. The loss of god's perfection might mean that god could not fully organise the disorder of matter – which implies that the demiurge is not omnipotent – with god being split from matter, and thus suffering a kind of reduction. But it is the Second god who is dealt with here, and not the Primal god, who remains impassible and devoted to contemplation alone. In sum, as this brief sketch has shown, Middle Platonist cosmogony offers a relevant, but provisional attempt at reconciling god's perfection and goodness, his care for the world, and the traces of evil that remain in the cosmos escaping divine control.

4 Fate, Providence, and the Governance of the World

I now move on to my third and final topic, the governance of the world through law. This topic appears in Plato's *Laws*, but also in the political and cosmological prologue of the *Timaeus*. The image of god as legislator or as king, who governs the universe is well attested in Middle Platonism,[65] as is the definition of fate as law, also with respect to the *Timaeus*.[66] In particular, I would like to answer two related questions: first, is god concerned with the world that he has produced?, and, second, has god knowledge of universal Forms only, or also of the particulars, the accidents?

As is the case with regard to creation, when it comes to the governance of the world, too, Middle Platonists remained faithful to Plato (different from Plotinus), for two kinds of reasons: exegetical and theoretical. As for the first kind, as Platonists they wanted to offer reliable explanation of what Plato had expressly or implicitly said. As for the second kind, they wanted to offer a consistent but Platonic solution of problems that had emerged after Plato. By

64 See above, nn. 58–59.

65 See Philo, *On the Creation of the World* 17–20, Alcinous, *Didaskalikos* 16.2, 172.8–13 Hermann, Plutarch, *Life of Demetrius* 42.9, Eusebius of Caesarea, *Preparation for the Gospel* 15.6.12 (= Atticus, fr. 4 Des Places: God as *pambasileus*), Ps.-Aristotle, *On the World* 6.398a–b, Ps.-Plato, *Letter* 2.312e–313a.

66 Ps.-Plutarch, *On Fate* 9.573D.

acting on a pre-existing and co-eternal matter, the Middle Platonists' god produces the world as something different from himself. They thus argued that the cosmos does not "proceed" directly from god, and contains aspects independent of him. The cosmos is therefore the result of a mixture, as Plato had maintained in the *Timaeus*, at 48a. Plutarch and Atticus insist that the protection of the world from destruction depends on god's will, namely, on god's providence.[67] The cosmos, therefore, exists and enjoys eternal life because god wants it to. This is clear especially in the case of a literal interpretation of cosmogony, which stresses the reality of god's creation (i.e. according to time). Plutarch points out:

> And it seems to me right to address to the god the words 'You are', which are most opposed to this account, and testify against it, believing that never does any vagary or transformation take place near him, but that such acts and experiences are related to some other god, or rather to some demon, whose office is concerned with Nature in dissolution and generation.[68]

Accordingly, god's attention is focused first and foremost on the contemplation of the Forms, and, once matter is organized, god is only concerned with the permanence of the world. This permanence is possible because he wants it, that is, because the eternity of the world is the object of divine providence. However, the governance of nature is delegated to subordinate deities: the gods of the heavens, the world soul, and the demons – in short, the lower steps on the "scale of nature." This delegation implies that god is not immediately interested in particulars,[69] as is clear from Apuleius' Latin translation of the (pseudo-)Aristotelian *On the World*: "If it is improper for a man or king to deal himself with each and every thing he ⟨wants to⟩ perform, then even more so it is improper for god."[70] In Apuleius' *On the World* the comparison between god and the kings Cambyses, Xerxes, and Darius is added and illustrated with the image of the world as the universal community (πολιτεία).[71] Yet, if god is

67 Plutarch, *On the E at Delphi* 21.393E–394A, *Table-Talk* 8.2.4, 720B–C, Eusebius of Caesarea, *Preparation for the Gospel* 15.5.1–14 (= Atticus, fr. 3 Des Places).

68 Plutarch, *On the E at Delphi* 21.393F–394A (tr. Babbitt 1936, modified).

69 See Boys-Stones 2007, 440–441, Opsomer 2014, 165–167. In Plato, *Timaeus* 39e, the Intellect knows the species and projects them into the cosmos.

70 Apuleius, *On the World* 25.350 (but see also 344–345). See also chapter 9 of *Didaskalikos*, where no Forms of the individuals are admitted.

71 Cf. Plato, *Timaeus* 26c–d, Plutarch, *On the Fortune or the Virtue of Alexander* 6.329A–C, 8.330D–9.330E, *To an Uneducated Ruler* 3.780C–F.

not directly involved in particulars, one might wonder how could god be called "king of all" or "universal sovereign" (παμβασιλεύς in Atticus, fr. 4 Des Places) with unlimited power in a world-state.[72] Or, one should explain how his power relates to the individuals of the universal community he governs.

The answer can be found in that god exercises his rule over the world by two means, one is direct, the other indirect: god has direct control through virtue and indirect control through the laws of nature. He governs first of all with the degrees of his providence and, secondarily, with the constraint of fate. These two orders of causality are not alternative, but subordinated to each other.[73] They reflect two different meanings of "necessity", which are both attested in the Platonic tradition: necessity as perfection, as an intrinsic orientation towards Good, and necessity as constraint, as an obstacle to free agency.[74] In his *Table-Talk* 9.14.6, 745D, Plutarch puts the contrast in the framework of a dialogue between Menephylus the Peripatetic and Ammonius the Platonist:

> "Hence, I think, the Muse 'hated intolerable Necessity' (Empedocles, fr. 116 DK) far more than does the Charm of Empedocles." "She does indeed," said Ammonius, "if you mean the Necessity of our world, a constraining cause outside the sphere of our will. But the necessity that holds sway among the gods is not intolerable nor, as I believe, resistant to persuasion either nor yet coercive, except for wicked men, just as in a city the law is for those who look to its best interests something inflexible and immutable, not because a change would be impossible, but because it would be undesirable."[75]

Elsewhere, Plutarch also made clear that "in everything, the better has control of necessity."[76] One could thus say that the autonomy of the soul makes it possible for the soul to dominate the necessity of fate. This can only happen if the soul acts according to virtue, that is according to the will of god or providence. We indeed know that both soul and virtue are "without a master" (ἀδέσποτον)[77] and that, as such, they are directly connected with god.[78] Contemplating and acting according to virtue are the best ways for the soul to imitate god and, therefore, to live a perfect and happy life. Freedom and necessity

72 Cf. Apuleius, *On the World* 24.343–25.344, 30.357.
73 Apuleius, *On the World* 25.344.
74 Plutarch, *Table-Talk* 9.5.2, 740B–D, Plotinus, *Enneads* 4.8.5.
75 Plutarch, *Table-Talk* 9.14.6, 745D (tr. Sandbach 1961).
76 Plutarch, *On the Face in the Moon* 15.928C; see Plato, *Timaeus* 48a.
77 See also *Didaskalikos* 26.2 (on the soul), 31.1 (on virtue), Plutarch, *Table-Talk* 9.5.2, 740B–D.
78 Apuleius, *On Plato and His Doctrine* 2.220 and 235–236.

are not in conflict: they are both expressions of the intrinsic and perfect order towards the Good that characterizes the action of god and of the souls who liken themselves to god. See Plutarch: "(For) we have come into this world, not to make laws for its governance, but to obey the commandments of the gods who preside over the universe, and the decrees of Fate or Providence."[79] Thus, man is not called upon to be a legislator, but to imitate the law given by god through providence. According to Plutarch, the same should be said of political law and of whoever intends to govern, especially a king. His conduct must draw inspiration from the knowledge and goodness of god. Plutarch states it in the following manner:

> But these gifts and blessings, so excellent and so great, which the gods bestow, cannot be rightly enjoyed nor used without law and justice and a ruler. Now justice is the aim and end of law, but law is the work of the ruler, and the ruler is the image of God who orders all things. Such a ruler needs no Pheidias nor Polycleitus nor Myron to model him, but by his virtue he forms himself in the likeness of God and thus creates a statue most delightful of alll to behold and most worthy of divinity.[80]

According to the Middle Platonists, the autonomy of the soul is based upon god's autonomy, which is the model for the action of individuals. In this sense, likeness to god is the condition for full access to the divine, which also presupposes a common nature between the intellect and god. An account of this hierarchy is found in a passage by Plutarch:

> We must not, therefore, violate nature by sending the bodies of good men with their souls to heaven, but implicitly believe that *their virtues and their souls, in accordance with nature and divine justice*, ascend from men to heroes, from heroes to demons, and from demons, after they have been made pure and holy (καθαρῶσι καὶ ὁσιωθῶσιν), as in the final rites of initiation, and *have freed themselves* (ἀποφυγοῦσαι) from mortality and

79 Plutarch, *Consolation to Apollonius* 16.111E (tr. Babbitt 1928).

80 Plutarch, *To an Uneducated Ruler* 3.780E (tr. Fowler 1936); see also Plutarch, *Dinner of the Seven Wise Men* 2.147D, *On the Fortune or the Virtue of Alexander* 6.329A–C, 8.330D, 11.342A, *To an Uneducated Ruler* 3.780D–4.781B, *Precepts of Statecraft* 15.811C–D, 31.823E–32.824A, *Against Colotes* 32.1126A–E, *Whether an Old Man Should Engage in Public Affairs* 4.785C, 11.790A, *Life of Lycurgus* 11.6, 28.13, 30.4, *Life of Numa* 6.2, 20.4; cf. Aalders 1982, 5–11, 33–34, 45–47.

> sense, to gods, not by civic law, *but in very truth and according to right reason*, thus achieving the fairest and most blessed consummation.[81]

Divine justice and right reason, which is what makes souls virtuous, converge here. They are capable of becoming like god, following the cosmic law, transcending civil law. According to Platonism, the ascension to god is presented here as a "flight" from the world, namely as a liberation from the constraint of the body, its passions and mortality. This ascension is "according to nature" (κατὰ φύσιν), that is pertinent to the perfection of the virtuous soul. Nature as a "cosmic constraint" is substituted here by nature as "divine perfection", in other words, as likeness to god in intellect, will, and virtue. This represents the fulfilment of god's providential action on the world, since virtue does not depend on physical norms or constraints, but on contemplation and right reason.

5 Conclusion

Middle Platonists formulated the topic of fate and providence by combining Platonic doctrine with elements they took over from Aristotelian and Stoic theology. In particular, the Platonists recognised the Stoics' efficacy in explaining physical causality, but criticised their account of divine and human action. In revising Stoic doctrine, they thus used an adapted version of the Stoic understanding of fate within the context of a correct interpretation of Plato. Boys-Stones observes:

> They [*sc.* the Platonists] standardly represent Stoicism not as a philosophy in diametrical opposition to Plato, but one that is an *inadequate reception* of Plato: a Plato without the metaphysics, in fact, and prone to all the absurdities implied in that oxymoron. Platonists of this period *want* to show that their thought includes all that is good about Stoicism – but with the crucial addition of the proper explanatory principles as well. By ignoring the metaphysical, the Stoics lost the means to appeal to a non-providential cause of the cosmos quite distinct from god, and lost with it the ability to distinguish things that are under god's general control from things for which he takes specific responsibility.[82]

---

81 Plutarch, *Life of Romulus* 28.10 (tr. Perrin 1982, modified, italics mine).

82 See Boys-Stones 2007, 445 (italics mine).

In this sense, Middle Platonists maintained that an additional step had to be taken in the direction of god's autonomy and, with that, of the autonomy of human beings. This step consisted in stressing god's transcendence with respect to physical nature, his freedom with respect to matter, and his providential care with respect to the cosmos he has created. The harmonization of necessity and freedom was effected by redefining the concept of law which now had a twofold meaning: as an indefectible norm of physical causality (that is, as fate), and as a principle of behaviour for the souls who strive to be similar to god (that is, as right reason and perfect virtue). In these terms, god is no longer subject to law: rather, he is its ruler. In this general account, however, further issues had to be developed further and more consistently, especially regarding creation and god's real ability to acknowledge and govern cosmic events. This task would be taken up by later Platonists, starting with Plotinus.

Bibliography

Aalders, Gerhard J.D. 1982. *Plutarch's Political Thought*. Amsterdam: North-Holland Publishing Company.

Algra, Keimpe. 2014. "Plutarch and the Stoic Theory of Providence." In *Fate, Providence and Moral Responsibility in Ancient, Medieval and Early Modern Thought. Studies in Honour of Carlos Steel*, edited by Pieter d'Hoine and Gerd Van Riel, 117–136. Leuven: Leuven University Press.

Babbitt, Frank C., tr. 1928. *Plutarch's Moralia*, vol. 2. Cambridge, Mass.: Harvard University Press.

Babbitt, Frank C., tr. 1936. *Plutarch's Moralia*, vol. 5. Cambridge, Mass.: Harvard University Press.

Babut, Daniel. 1969. *Plutarque et le stoïcisme*. Paris: Université de Paris, Faculté des Lettres et Sciences Humaines.

Basore, John W., tr. 1928. *Seneca, Moral Essays*, vol. 1. Cambridge, Mass.: Harvard University Press.

Bobzien, Susanne. 1998. *Determinism and Freedom in Stoic Philosophy*. Oxford: Clarendon.

Bonazzi, Mauro. 2014. "Middle Platonists on Fate and Human Autonomy: a Confrontation with the Stoics." In *What is Up to Us? Studies on Agency and Responsibility in Ancient Philosophy*, edited by Pierre Destrée, Ricardo Salles, and Marco Zingano, 283–293. Sankt Augustin: Academia.

Boys-Stones, George. 2007. "'Middle' Platonists on Fate and Human Autonomy." In *Greek and Roman Philosophy 100 BC–200 AD*, edited by Robert W. Sharples and Richard Sorabji, vol. 2, 431–447. London: Institute of Classical Studies.

Boys-Stones, George. 2016. "Providence and religion in Middle Platonism." In *Theologies of Ancient Greek Religion*, edited by Esther Eidinow, Julia Kindt, and Robin Osborne, 317–338. Cambridge: Cambridge University Press.

Boys-Stones, George. 2018. *Platonist Philosophy 80 BC to AD 250. An Introduction and Collection of Sources in Translation*. Cambridge: Cambridge University Press.

Brenk, Frederick E. 2005. "Plutarch's Middle-Platonic God: About to Enter (or Remake) the Academy." In *Gott und die Götter bei Plutarch. Götterbilder – Gottesbilder – Weltbilder*, edited by Rainer Hirsch-Luipold, 27–49. Berlin: De Gruyter.

Brouwer, René. 2015. "Stoic Sympathy." In *Sympathy. A History*, edited by Eric Schliesser, 15–35. Oxford: Oxford University Press.

Bury, Robert G., tr. 1926. *Plato, Laws*, Books 7–12. Cambridge, Mass.: Harvard University Press.

Calabi, Francesca, ed. 2002. *Arrhetos Theos. L'ineffabilità del primo principio nel medio platonismo*. Pisa: Edizioni ETS.

Chiaradonna, Riccardo 2015. "Plotinus' account of demiurgic causation and its philosophical background." In *Causation and Creation in Late Antiquity*, edited by Anna Marmodoro and Brian D. Prince, 31–50. Cambridge: Cambridge University Press.

De Lacy, Phillip H., and Benedict Einarson, eds., tr. 1959. *Plutarch. Moralia*, vol. 7. Cambridge, Mass.: Harvard University Press.

Den Boeft, Jan. 1970. *Calcidius on Fate. His Doctrine and Sources*. Leiden: Brill.

Destrée, Pierre, Ricardo Salles, and Marco Zingano, eds. 2014. *What is Up to Us? Studies on Agency and Responsibility in Ancient Philosophy*. Sankt Augustin: Academia.

D'Hoine, Pieter, and Gerd Van Riel, eds. 2014. *Fate, Providence and Moral Responsibility in Ancient, Medieval and Early Modern Thought. Studies in Honour of Carlos Steel*. Leuven: Leuven University Press.

DK: Diels, Hermann, and Walther Kranz. 1952. *Die Fragmente der Vorsokratiker*. 6th edn. Berlin: Weidmann.

Dillon, John, tr. 1993. *Alcinous, The Handbook of Platonism*. Oxford: Clarendon.

Dillon, John. 1996 [1977]. *The Middle Platonists. A Study of Platonism (80 BC to AD 220)*. London: Duckworth.

Eliasson, Erik. 2008. *The Notion of* That Which Depends On Us *in Plotinus and Its Background*. Leiden: Brill.

Ferrari, Franco. 2005. "Der Gott Plutarchs und der Gott Platons." In *Gott und die Götter bei Plutarch. Götterbilder – Gottesbilder – Weltbilder*, edited by Rainer Hirsch-Luipold, 13–25. Berlin: De Gruyter.

Fowler, Harold N., tr. 1936. *Plutarch's Moralia*, vol. 10. Cambridge, Mass.: Harvard University Press.

Frede, Michael. 2011. *A Free Will. Origins of the Notion in Ancient Thought*, edited by Anthony A. Long. Berkeley: University of California Press.

Guthrie, Kenneth S. 1917. *Numenius of Apamea: The Father of Neo-Platonism. Works, Biography, Message, Sources, and Influence*. London: George Bell and Sons.

Hershbell, Jackson P. 1992. "Plutarch and Stoicism." In *Aufstieg und Niedergang der römischen Welt*, edited by Wolfgang Haase, vol. 2.36.5, 3336–3352. Berlin: De Gruyter.

Hirsch-Luipold, Rainer, ed. 2005. *Gott und die Götter bei Plutarch. Götterbilder – Gottesbilder – Weltbilder*. Berlin: De Gruyter.

Karamanolis, George E. 2006. *Plato and Aristotle in Agreement? Platonists on Aristotle from Antiochus to Porphyry*. Oxford: Clarendon.

LM: Laks, André, and Glenn W. Most. 2016. *Early Greek Philosophy.* Cambridge, Mass.: Harvard University Press.

Mansfeld, Jaap. 1999. "*Alcinous on Fate and Providence*." In *Traditions of Platonism. Essays in Honour of John Dillon*, edited by John J. Cleary, 139–150. Aldershot: Ashgate.

Moreschini, Claudio. 2015. *Apuleius and the Metamorphoses of Platonism*. Turnhout: Brepols.

O'Brien, Carl S. 2015. *The Demiurge in Ancient Thought. Secondary Gods and Divine Mediators*. Cambridge: Cambridge University Press.

Opsomer, Jan. 2014. "The Middle Platonic Doctrine of Conditional Fate." In *Fate, Providence and Moral Responsibility in Ancient, Medieval and Early Modern Thought. Studies in Honour of Carlos Steel*, edited by Pieter d'Hoine and Gerd Van Riel, 137–168. Leuven: Leuven University Press.

Perrin, Bernadotte, tr. 1914. *Plutarch's Lives*, vol. 1. Cambridge, Mass.: Harvard University Press.

Petrucci, Federico M. 2016. "Plutarch's Theory of Cosmological Powers in the *De Iside et Osiride*." *Apeiron* 49: 329–367.

Reydams-Schils, Gretchen. 1999. *Demiurge and Providence. Stoic and Platonist Readings of Plato's* Timaeus. Turnhout: Brepols.

Reydams-Schils, Gretchen. 2008. "Calcidius on God." In *Platonic Stoicism – Stoic Platonism. The Dialogue Between Platonism and Stoicism in Antiquity*, edited by Mauro Bonazzi and Christoph Helmig, 243–258. Leuven: Leuven University Press.

Reydams-Schils, Gretchen. 2020. *Calcidius on Plato's* Timaeus*. Greek Philosophy, Latin Reception and Christian Contexts.* Cambridge: Cambridge University Press.

Sandbach, Francis H., tr. 1961. *Plutarch's Moralia*, vol. 9. Cambridge, Mass.: Harvard University Press.

Sauvé Meyer, Susan. 2009. "Chain of Causes: What is Stoic Fate?" In *God and Cosmos in Stoicism*, edited by Ricardo Salles, 71–90. Oxford: Oxford University Press.

Sharples, Robert W. 1983. "Nemesius of Emesa and Some Theories of Divine Providence." *Vigiliae Christianae* 37: 141–156.

Sharples, Robert W. 2003. "Threefold Providence: the History and the Background of a Doctrine." In *Ancient Approaches to Plato's Timaeus*, edited by Robert W. Sharples and Anne Sheppard, 107–127. London: Institute of Classical Studies.

Theiler, Willy. 1966. "Tacitus und die antike Schicksalslehre." In his *Forschungen zum Neuplatonismus*, 46–103. Berlin: De Gruyter.

Timotin, Andrei. 2012. *La démonologie platonicienne. Histoire de la notion de* daimōn *de Platon aux derniers néoplatoniciens*. Leiden: Brill.

Trabattoni, Franco. 2014. "Libertà e destino da Platone al neoplatonismo." In *Libero arbitrio. Storia di una controversia filosofica*, edited by Mario De Caro, Massimo Mori, and Emidio Spinelli, 99–113. Rome: Carocci.

Valgiglio, Ernesto, ed. 1993. [*Plutarco*], *Il fato*. Naples: D'Auria.

Vimercati, Emmanuele. 2012. "La materia e il male in Numenio di Apamea." *Filosofia e Teologia* 26: 77–92.

Vorwerk, Matthias. 2010. "Maker or Father? The Demiurge from Plutarch to Plotinus." In *One Book. The Whole Universe*, edited by Richard D. Mohr and Barbara Sattler, 79–100. Las Vegas: Parmenides.

Whittaker, John, ed., Louis, Pierre, tr. 1990. *Alcinoos, Enseignement des doctrines de Platon*. Paris: Les Belles Lettres.

CHAPTER 8

Determinism and Deliberation in Alexander of Aphrodisias

Carlo Natali

1 In this paper I defend a minority position in contemporary scholarship on Alexander of Aphrodisias with regard to the theme of determinism and his theory of what is up to us. Many modern scholars agree about the following basic points. The first point is that Aristotle did not develop a specific stance on the problem of determinism, given the fact that at the time this problem was not considered a central theme in the philosophical debate. Second, Alexander's position on indeterminism was influenced by the debate in the imperial period and was not merely a precise account of what Aristotle had maintained. In the third place, indeterminism is a slightly embarrassing position to hold; therefore, it is better to liberate the ancient philosophers from it, as far as possible. What is more, a strong tendency can be discerned to attribute some form of compatibilism to most of the ancient philosophical schools – which cannot be easily reconciled with the polemics that existed between the schools.

As for me, I think that already in Plato's Academy philosophers began to reflect upon the problem of determinism, freedom and human responsibility, starting out from certain statements in Plato's *Republic* and in book 10 of the *Laws*.[1] As far as Alexander is concerned, I think that his position can be characterised as a kind of "creative orthodoxy", which consists in trying to show the vitality of the Aristotelian viewpoint in the debate in imperial times. In order to make this clear, I will concentrate on the problem of deliberation and the Peripatetic notion of causality, particularly in relation to chapters 11–15 in Alexander's *On Fate*. Moreover, I would like to make the point that the fact that in contemporary theory of action some form of determinism prevails should not be a reason for having at least an historical interest in a different position held by ancient philosophers.[2] Few philosophers today accept the independent existence of ideas, but that does not prevent us from studying Plato's doctrine of Ideas with profit. Hence, without wanting to give even a preliminary judgment on the theoretical value of Peripatetic indeterminism, I think

1 See further Natali 2014.
2 See e.g. Davidson 2001, 96–97.

 | DOI:10.1163/9789004436381_010

that it might be interesting to offer a reconstruction of certain elements in the ancient debate on necessity and what is up to us, in order to get a better understanding of the underlying reasons for the clashes between the different schools and for their opposing views.

In this paper I will not deal with all problems relating to the sources I mentioned above. More specifically, I will not deal with the question whether the account Alexander gives of Stoic thought is reliable. Here I will restrict myself to describing the logical structure of Alexander's argument, for the simple reason, so it seems to me, that many of the objections put forward in modern scholarship against his position follow from the fact that the internal logical structure of his argumentation has not been taken into account. In this respect it would already be a step forward if one were to accept that Alexander does not contradict himself as often as some commentators are inclined to think and that his critique of determinism follows a certain logic which can be understood better if placed with an Aristotelian framework (see Natali 1994).

2 In chapter 7 of *On Fate* Alexander starts the second part of his discussion of fate, thus:

> A clearer foundation (κατασκευή) of what has been stated will be obtained if we place the absurdities (ἄτοπα) that follow for those who say that all things come in accordance with fate alongside the preceding demostration of our position (171.18–20).[3] (Tr. Sharples)

He continues with a series of refutations of the views of the determinists; he starts with an analysis of the notion of "the things that occur by luck and by accident" (τὰ ἀπο τύχης τε καὶ τοῦ αὐτομάτου); he continues with the notion "of the contingent" (τὸ ἐνδεχόμενον), and of the fact that some things happen "in whichever way" or "the possible" (τὸ δυναντόν), which cannot be saved by the determinists, unless in a Pickwickian sense;[4] the third notion, which cannot be saved by the determinists is that of βουλεύεσθαι ("to deliberate").

Here arguments are presented, which as Alexander states himself in his commentary on the *Topics* are most suitable to the theme at hand. This is the passage from Aristotle's *Topics* he quotes approvingly:

---

3 ἡ δὲ κατασκευὴ τῶν εἱμαρμέμων ἔσται φανερωτέρα παρατιθέντων ἡμῶν ταῖς προηγουμέναις τῶν κειμένων ἀποδείξεσιν τὰ ἑπόμενα ἄτοπα τοῖς πάντα καθ' εἱμαρμένην γίνεσθαι λέγουσιν. The text is Sharples 1983.

4 See 7–8, 171.18–174.28; 9, 174.30–176.13; 10, 176.14–178.8.

> Clearly, then, an argument is not open to the same criticism when taken in relation to the proposed conclusion and when taken by itself. For there is nothing to prevent the argument being open to reproach in itself, and yet commendable in relation to the problem, or again, vice versa, being commendable in itself, and yet open to reproach in relation to the problem (8.11, 161b38–162a2).[5] (Tr. Pickard-Cambridge)

Alexander maintains that several instances of this rule can be given, including that of an argument that may not be worthy of criticism in itself, but which becomes so if applied to a certain problem. For example, so Alexander adds, the argument on the basis of which it is established that praise and blame happen in vain is not bad in itself, but becomes bad if it is used to establish that not everything happens necessarily and by destiny:

> The argument that does away with the generation of all things in accordance with fate and reason on the basis the praise and blame will be in vain […] in relation to the question at issue would seem inadequate. The question at issue can be demonstrated by using more premises and more accepted, as the thesis that everything that is contingent is done away with that position as is also what depends on us, so that deliberating too is in vain (*Commentary on the Topics* 570.4–11).[6] (Tr. Sharples, modified)

Alexander appears to criticise Carneades' position on fate, while proposing a better antideterminist strategy.[7] In *On Fate* he starts with the arguments he considers to be strongest, and thereafter adds the weaker ones. He thus begins to discuss the question of the contingent, then moves on to deliberation, and finally also argues that if fate exists, praise and blame are in vain.

The argument about deliberation occupies four chapters, 11–14, with chapter 15 as an appendix, that is eight pages in Bruns' edition; on the contrary

5 φανερὸν οὖν ὅτι οὐδὲ λόγῳ ἡ αὐτὴ ἐπιτίμησις πρός τε τὸ προβληθὲν καὶ καθ' αὑτόν· οὐδὲν γὰρ κωλύει καθ' αὑτὸν μὲν εἶναι τὸν λόγον ψεκτόν, πρὸς δὲ τὸ πρόβλημα ἐπαινετόν, καὶ πάλιν ἀντεστραμμένως καθ' αὑτὸν μὲν ἐπαινετόν, πρὸς δὲ τὸ πρόβλημα ψεκτόν.

6 ὁ γὰρ ἀναιρῶν τὸ τὰ πάντα καθ' εἱμαρμένην γίνεσθαι καὶ λόγον διὰ τὸ μάτην εἶναι τούς τε ἐπαίνους καὶ τοὺς ψόγους […] οὐκ ἂν ἄξιος ἐπιτιμήσεως φαίνοιτο. εἰ δέ τις αὐτὸν ἐξετάζοι πρὸς τὸ πρόβλημα ἐνδεεστέρως ἂν ἔχειν δοκοῖ τῷ διὰ πλειόνων καὶ ἐνδοξοτέρων δύνασθαι τὸ προκείμενον δείκνυσθαι· διὰ γὰρ τοῦ ἀναιρεῖσθαι πᾶν τὸ ἐνδεχόμενον, ἀλλὰ καὶ τὸ ἐφ' ἡμῖν· οὕτω δὲ καὶ τὸ μὴ εἶναι τὴν ἀρετὴν καὶ τὴν κακίαν ἐφ' ἡμῖν ἀναιρεῖται, ὡς μάτην εἶναι καὶ τὸ βουλεύεσθαι.

7 The argument based on the inutility of praise and blame are at the core of Carneades' critique, according to Amand 1945, 143–148; Alexander uses these arguments as well, but only in a subordinate way (*On Fate* 16–21).

there are two and half pages for the first refutation and a little over three pages for the second one. It is a really long section, which shows Alexander's interest for this argument, and the importance he attributes to it.

3 Modern scholars usually contrast Alexander's position with Aristotle's in his *Nicomachean Ethics*, highlighting the differences between Alexander and his master (Long 1970, Donini 1974, Sharples 1983, Bobzien 1998), but ethics is not Alexander's starting point. It is very likely that the starting point of *On Fate* is a part of his lost commentary of Aristotle's *On Interpretation*, and that the *Nicomachean Ethics* plays a somewhat subordinate role in the treatise. In other words, Alexander also uses doctrines from the *Nicomachean Ethics*, but does not start out from the ethical-political problems, which with it deals; on the contrary: he starts out from the logical and ontological questions that lie at the core of the argument in *On Interpretation*.

In chapter 9 of *On Interpretation* Aristotle states:

> (1) These and others of the same kind are the absurdities that follow if it is necessary that of every affirmation and negation, either about universals spoken of universally, or about individuals, (2) that one of the opposites must be true and the other false, and that nothing of what happens is as chance has it, but everything is or takes place by necessity. (3) So, there would be no need to deliberate or to take trouble, thinking that if we do this, this other thing would follow, while if we did not, it will not follow [...] (4) for we see that both deliberation and action are principles of the future events, (5) and that, more generally, in those things which are not always actual there is the possibility of being and not being, and consequently of coming to be and not coming to be. (18b26–33 and 19a7–11).[8] (Tr. Ackrill)

In *On Interpretation* Aristotle moves from (2) the negation of the contingent to (3) the thesis of the uselessness of deliberation, and the same does Alexander

8 τὰ μὲν δὴ συμβαίνοντα ἄτοπα ταῦτα καὶ τοιαῦθ' ἕτερα, εἴπερ πάσης καταφάσεως καὶ ἀποφάσεως, ἢ ἐπὶ τῶν καθόλου λεγομένων ὡς καθόλου ἢ ἐπὶ τῶν καθ' ἕκαστα, ἀνάγκη τῶν ἀντικειμένων εἶναι τὴν μὲν ἀληθῆ τὴν δὲ ψευδῆ, μηδὲν δὲ ὁπότερ' ἔτυχεν εἶναι ἐν τοῖς γιγνομένοις, ἀλλὰ πάντα εἶναι καὶ γίγνεσθαι ἐξ ἀνάγκης. ὥστε οὔτε βουλεύεσθαι δέοι ἂν οὔτε πραγματεύεσθαι, ὡς ἐὰν μὲν τοδὶ ποιήσωμεν, ἔσται τοδί, ἐὰν δὲ μὴ τοδί, οὐκ ἔσται. [...] εἰ δὴ ταῦτα ἀδύνατα, ὁρῶμεν γὰρ ὅτι ἔστιν ἀρχὴ τῶν ἐσομένων καὶ ἀπὸ τοῦ βουλεύεσθαι καὶ ἀπὸ τοῦ πρᾶξαί τι, καὶ ὅτι ὅλως ἔστιν ἐν τοῖς μὴ ἀεὶ ἐνεργοῦσι τὸ δυνατὸν εἶναι καὶ μή, ἐν οἷς ἄμφω ἐνδέχεται καὶ τὸ εἶναι καὶ τὸ μὴ εἶναι, ὥστε καὶ τὸ γενέσθαι καὶ τὸ μὴ γενέσθαι.

(*On Fate* ch. 9–10: doing away with the contingent; ch. 11–15: doing away with deliberation and what is up to us).

That at the origins of the manner of argumentation that can be found in *On Fate* lies a commentary on *On Interpretation*, and that this is not a simple coincidence, is suggested by the fact that Boethius in his *Second Commentary on On Interpretation* uses material that stems from Alexander of Aphrodisias, and sticks to the same order of argumentation.[9] When he comes to commenting upon *On Interpretation* 9, 18b26–33 and 19a7–9, Boethius extends the horizon of his treatise considerably and presents a whole series of arguments against determinism, which closely resemble, even in the words chosen, those of Alexander's *On Fate*.[10] Hence the sequence I would like to propose is the following: that from Alexander's commentary on *On Interpretation* are derived a) his *On Fate*, b) Boethius' *Second Commentary*, and that the resemblances between the arguments of a) and b) make clear that the two treatises have a common source, that is the commentary on *On Interpretation*. As a matter of fact, Alexander's manner of working consisted in "recycling" parts of his commentaries in other treatises, often repeating them literally. Here are some examples: in his *On the Soul* passages from his commentary on Aristotle's *On the Soul* can be found: unfortunately the commentary is lost, but the passages survived in the work of Simplicius and others;[11] in his commentary on Aristotle's *Metaphysics* 5.2 a passage is repeated in an abbreviated manner from his commentary on *Physics* 2.3, which is also lost, but extensively quoted by Simplicius (*Commentary on the Physics* 310.25–31).[12] So we can assume that rather than a simple parallel between Alexander's and Aristotle's treatise these chapters of *On Fate* contain sentences that are derived from the commentary on the *On Interpretation* relating to 18b26–33 and reflect the same polemical spirit. In the same manner it can be inferred that chapters 9–10 probably contain material from that same commentary on *On Interpretation* that relate to other sections of the text, presumably 18b23–25, 19a27–32. This observation is not only of antiquarian interest, but provides a clearer account of some of Alexander's arguments, which are at times misunderstood.

In his discussion in chapters 11–15 Alexander does not simply use the particular theory of deliberation that can be found in book 3 of the *Nicomachean Ethics*; on the contrary: he partly modifies it, adapting it to new circumstances and to the philosophical debate of his time. In principle he uses a more general

9 Cf. Sorabji 1998, vii.
10 See 220.8, 236.16, 196.19, and 148.11 respectively.
11 Cf. Donini 1994, 5027–5099.
12 Cf. Natali 2003, 157–162.

notion of deliberation, while defending in an overall manner Aristotle's theory, for whom factual necessity deriving from the admission of a truth value for singular contingent propositions about the future eliminates both deliberation and what is up to us. Also the very polemical aspect of the *On Fate* could harken back to Aristotle's account, when he states that the determinist position is *absurd*.

4 In *On Fate*, chapter 11 Alexander gives a definition of "deliberation", which is not Peripatetic, but rather a definition which "is agreed by all" (ὁμολογεῖται δὴ πρὸς ἁπάντων, 178.17), and hence also by his adversaries:

> It is agreed by everyone that man has the advantage from nature over all living creatures that he is not forced to follow the appearances in the same way as they do, but he has reason as judge of the appearances that impinge him, about the choice of some things. Using this reason and examining the appearances, if they are indeed what they seemed at the beginning he *assents* to them and goes in pursuit of them. But if they appear different or if something else appears more deserving his choice, he follows it, leaving behind what at the beginning looked choiceworthy (178.17–24).[13] (Tr. Sharples)

He then affirms, on the basis of this definition, that "we are in control" (ὄντων κυρίων) of the deliberating and of the choice that is the result thereof (178.27–28), and hence concludes that deliberation is put into practice only when it is not done in vain (178.28–179.12).

The definition of "deliberation" is presented as a thesis about which all philosophers are in agreement, and is formulated in terms that can also be accepted by determinists.

In this definition the notion of "assent" is present (συγκατατίθεταί τε τῇ φαντασίᾳ), which surprised Verbeke and others, and has been taken especially seriously. It is true that at times Alexander uses Stoic terminology in his treatises, but in this case, they say, the use of Stoicising terms is not innocuous and makes Alexander hold a theory of choice that is rather different from that of

13 ὁμολογεῖται δὴ πρὸς ἁπάντων τὸ τῶν ἄλλων ζων τὸν ἄνθρωπον τοῦτο παρὰ τῆς φύσεως ἔχειν πλέον τὸ μὴ ὁμοίως ἐκείνοις ταῖς φαντασίαις ἕπεσθαι, ἀλλ' ἔχειν παρ' αὐτῆς κριτὴν τῶν προσπιπτουσῶν φαντασιῶν περί τινων ὡς αἱρετῶν τὸν λόγον, ᾧ χρώμενος, εἰ μὲν ἐξεταζόμενα τὰ φαντασθέντα, οἷα τὴν ἀρχὴν ἐφάνη, καὶ ἔστι, συγκατατίθεταί τε τῇ φαντασίᾳ καὶ οὕτως μέτεισιν αὐτά, εἰ δὲ ἀλλοῖα φαίνεται ἢ ἄλλο τι αὖ αἱρετώτερον, ἐκεῖνο αἱρεῖται καταλείπων τὸ τὴν ἀρχὴν ὡς αἱρετὸν αὐτῷ φανέν.

Aristotle.[14] This observation leaves one perplexed, given the fact that Alexander here wants to present a position that is acceptable for all schools, not just the Peripatetic school, and for this reason makes conscious use of a Stoicising vocabulary. This does not hinder him from stating what for him is the most important point. He posits as the central element of deliberation the fact that one can choose a thing, or something else (178.22) if that is more preferable. In choosing something, in his opinion, it is not just a matter of refusing to assent to a presentation, but to prefer one good over another.

In short, the argument from deliberation, in *On Fate* 11, is a fairly complex type of *modus tollens*. It can be found in the first lines of the chapter:

> If all things that come to be follow on some causes that have been laid down beforehand, people deliberate in vain about the things to be done. And if deliberating were in vain, people would have the power of deliberating in vain; but nature does nothing in vain, among the principal things, and it is a primary product of nature people's capacity of deliberating [...] the conclusion would be that people do not have the power of deliberating in vain (178.8–15).[15] (Tr. Sharples, modified)

This can be formalised in the following manner:

1. if p, then q
2. if q, then z
3. but w, hence non-z
4. non-z, hence non-q, non-p

(p = "all events follow from antecedent and determinant causes"; q = "all human beings deliberate in vain about the their actions"; z = "man is given the capacity to deliberate in vain"; w = "nature does nothing in vain")

The first two steps of the argument recall what Aristotle stated in *On Interpretation* 9, 18b29–33. But whereas Aristotle restricts himself by stating that

14 Verbeke 1968, 93, Long 1970, 259. The introduction at this point of assent is not causal; it can also be found in his other writings, e.g. *On the Soul* 73.10–12: "Assent that can be given to doing or not doing something, and of which the cause is reason, is up to us. In fact, it is up to us to prefer something by means of deliberation and assent to this" (ἡ δὲ ἐπὶ τοῖς πρακτέοις ἢ μὴ πρακτέοις γινομένη, ὧν συγκαταθέσεων ὁ λόγος αἴτιος, ἐφ' ἡμῖν). See also 99.3–6 and *Questions* 3.13, 107.6–37.

15 τῷ πάντα τὰ γινόμενα προκαταβεβλημέναις καὶ ὡρισμέναις καὶ προυπαρχούσαις τισὶν αἰτίαις ἔσεσθαι τὸ καὶ βουλεύεσθαι τοὺς ἀνθρώπους μάτην περὶ τῶν πρακτέων αὐτοῖς. εἰ δὲ τὸ βουλεύεσθαι μάτην, μάτην ⟨ἂν⟩ ἄνθρωπος εἴη βουλευτικός. καίτοι εἰ μηδὲν μάτην ἡ φύσις ποιεῖ τῶν προηγουμένων, τὸ δὲ βουλευτικὸν εἶναι ζῷον τὸν ἄνθρωπον προηγουμένως ὑπὸ τῆς φύσεως, ἀλλ' οὐ κατ' ἐπακολούθημά τι καὶ σύμπτωμα τοῖς προηγουμένως γινομένοις γίνοιτο, συνάγοιτο ἂν ⟨τὸ⟩ μὴ εἶναι μάτην τοὺς ἀνθρώπους βουλευτικούς.

this position entails "absurdities" (ἄτοπα), Alexander searches for a reason as to why this is so. Applying the rule of interpreting Aristotle with Aristotle, he then refers to the principle "Nature does nothing in vain", which occurs several times in the *corpus aristotelicum* (Bonitz 1870, 836b28–38).

Deliberation is not something done with a view to itself, but it is an instrumental procedure of our mind, and is aimed at the selection of an action that is both possible and dependent on us. If the future is predetermined we do not deliberate, just as we do not try to break an iron bar with a wooden hammer.

That this argument was originally formulated in Alexander's commentary on *On Interpretation* is suggested by the fact that in Boethius, after an explicit quote from Alexander (219.30), the same argument can be found:

> Nothing that is by nature is in vain, but delibrating is something that humans have naturally. But if necessity alone has mastery over all things, deliberation is for no reason. But deliberation is not in vain, therefore there cannot be full necessity in all things (220.8–15).[16]

At the end of the same chapter, 179.8–20, Alexander presents a second argument with regard to deliberation that can be captured in the form of a *modus ponens*:

1. if y, then p
2. but y
3. thus p

(y = "deliberation is not useless"; p = "not all events follow from antecedent and determinant causes")

In defending the second premiss, Alexander makes reference to the common opinion that deliberating is considered useless if it is not presupposed that it is up to us to do or not do something: "What advantage comes to us from deliberating about what we should do, as far as our action is concerned" (τί πλέον ἡμῖν εἰς τὸ πράττειν ἐκ τοῦ βουλεύσασθαι περὶ τοῦ πραχθησομένου γίνεται; 179.14). In fact, we do not deliberate in cases where the action of the result thereof appear predetermined.

The next chapters are dedicated to the notion "what is up to us". Logically this would precede the discussion of deliberation, and the fact that Alexander starts out from deliberation shows that he primarily follows the order of the

16 *omne quod natura est non frustra est; consiliari autem homines naturaliter habent; quod si necessitas in rebus sola dominabitur, sine causa est consilitatio; sed consilitatio non frustra est; non igitur potest in rebus cuncta necessitas.* Cf. also 195.10ff., 196.19–197.4, 217.23–5, 236.16ff.

arguments in *On Interpretation*, and then moving on to what is up to us, comes to a more profound understanding of Aristotle's words, going from the theme of deliberating to a more fundamental notion.

5 Chapters 12–15 of *On Fate* discuss the notion of "what is up to us", which Aristotle had introduced for the first time in his discussion of the responsibility for one's actions (*Eudemian Ethics* 2.7, 1223a6–9),[17] and which Alexander uses as a technical term.

After having defined "what is up to us" as "that over which we gave control both to do it and not to do it, not following some causes which surround us from outside or giving up to them" (180.5–7),[18] Alexander argues as follows:

> Deliberating is done away according to them, as has been shown, and so clearly what depends on us [...] Choice does not apply to the things that come to be necessarily.[19] (180.3–4 and 9–10).

The argument is a *modus tollens*.

1. if q, then n,
2. but m, thus not-n,
3. thus non-q.

(q = "human beings deliberate in vain over their actions"; n = "nothing is up to us"; m = "the choice derived from deliberation has as its object that which is up to us")

Alexander defends the second premiss in the lines 180.7–23. His thesis is the following: as Aristotle states in the *Nicomachean Ethics* 2.4, choice, which has as its object that over which "we have control both to do it and not do it" (τοῦ πραχθῆ ναι καὶ τοῦ μὴ πραχθῆναι κύριοι, 180.5–6), is "the peculiar activity of man" (ἡ προαίρεσις το ἴδιον ἔργον τῶν ἀνθρώπων, 180.7–8). In a certain sense Alexander accepts the idea that faced with a choice made necessary by events, a human being reacts according to his nature,[20] in the same way as a cylinder and a cone

17 "So it is evident that all the actions which a man controls and of which he is the origin can either happen or not happen, and that their happening or not happening – those at least for whose existence or non-existence he is authoritative – is in his power. But for what is in his power to do or not to do, he is himself responsible (ἐφ' αὐτῷ)" (tr. Barnes and Kenny).

18 οὗ ἡμεῖς μὲν καὶ τοῦ πραχθῆναι καὶ τοῦ μὴ πραχθῆναι κύριοι, οὐχ ἑπόμενοί τισιν ἔξωθεν ἡμᾶς περιστᾶσιν αἰτίοις οὐδὲ ἐνδιδόντες αὐτοῖς.

19 ἀναιρουμένου δὲ ὡς ἐδείχθη τοῦ βουλεύσασθαι κατ' αὐτοὺς ἀναιρεῖται καὶ τὸ ἐφ' ἡμῖν προδήλως [...] οὐδὲ ἐπὶ τοῖς ἀναγκαίως γινομένοις ἡ προαίρεσις.

20 Cicero, *On Fate* 39–43, LS 62C.

which, when pushed on a slope, move according to their own nature, as in the famous Stoic example. Determinists take the nature of a subject to be his actual moral disposition, either that of a sage or a fool, whereas Alexander takes it to be more profound, consisting in being in control over choosing something or its opposite; this nature precedes the moral disposition, and cannot be annulled by this disposition. In order to show this, Alexander summarizes in the remainder of chapter, at 180.9–20, Aristotle's notion of deliberation, esp. as set out in the *Nicomachean Ethics* 3.5, 1112b19–27.

Hence for Alexander the more profound nature of a human being consists in being able to choose in each situation between something and "its opposite" (τὰ ἀντικείμενα, 181.6). To establish this he relies on Aristotle, who often insists on the idea that we can do something or its opposite.[21]

According to the Peripatetics, one's moral nature is only a "second nature", and it is for this reason that the virtuous person can always choose not to follow his acquired moral disposition and do something contrary to what is expected, as Alexander states later, *On Fate* 29, 200.2–12.[22] Aristotle himself states that

> it is possible to have deliberated well either generally, or in reference to a particular end. Good deliberation in general is therefore that which is correct with reference to the end absolutely understood, good deliberation of a special kind is that which is correct with reference to a particular end (6.8, 1142b28–31).[23]

So with regard to a particular end, for example in order to show the freedom of action in the case of a fortune-teller predicting some action (see *On Fate* 200.4–7), it is possible to deliberate in order to do something which one otherwise would not have done. The different choices that can be made depend on the differences between the final causes, which however do not have a necessitating force. I will come back to this later.

By contrast, modern scholars who do not read Alexander from an Aristotelian point of view, but from a Stoicizing perspective, have difficulties at

---

21 *Nicomachean Ethics* 3.5, 1113b5–7, *Eudemian Ethics* 2.7, 1223a2. Some scholars (e.g. Bobzien 1998, 396–412) have insisted on the fact that a difference exists between the possibility of *doing* something and its opposite on the one hand and the possibility of *choosing* between something and its opposite on the other hand. This is an interesting point that I cannot deal with in this paper.

22 On this chapter see now also Zingano 2014, 207–16.

23 ἔτι ἔστιν καὶ ἁπλῶς εὖ βεβουλεῦσθαι καὶ πρός τι τέλος, ἡ μὲν δὴ ἁπλῶς ἡ πρὸς τὸ τέλος τὸ ἁπλῶς κατορθοῦσα, τὶς δὲ ἡ πρός τι τέλος.

this point. They think that being virtuous or vicious is a quality that always determines someone's conduct, rather than simply most of the time.

A final argument can be found in 184.20–185.1. Here Alexander denies the thesis that deliberation is an indispensible element of an action, like the Stoics' concept of assent. In fact we often act without having deliberated, because even deliberation is something that is up to us; it is not absolutely necessary in order to able to act.

In chapter 15 Alexander applies Aristotle's theory of the four causes against the determinist thesis, which goes like this:

> If in the same circumstances someone acts now in a way and now in another, a motion without a cause will be introduced (185.8–9).[24]

Against this thesis he makes use of the different causes, which had already been the basis of the positive treatment of fate in chapters 1–6. He distinguishes between the moving cause, which is in us and makes that something is up to us, and the final cause (σκοπόν, 185.22), which determines the moving cause with a necessity that is hypothetical only (cf. *Nicomachean Ethics* 3.1, 1110b9–12). The moving cause is examined at 185.11–21, the other at 185.21–28. With regard to the moving cause Alexander highlights the fact that it comes *first* and that human beings, unlike all other animals, are not moved by other, external moving causes. With regard to the final cause he states that the end is variable, and that it determines the judgment on the basis of which we make our choices. But for the variations in the judgment about the end, the responsibility lies with the human being, without an intervening external cause, in a single act of choosing. The discussion is somewhat simplified and not very technical.

The reference to the specific nature of human beings does not explain how the final cause can have an indeterminate origin; it can even be counterproductive, because it brings Alexander back to the Stoic example: under given circumstances each being acts according to its nature. That human nature is the origin of variation is stated, but is not developed further. This can leave the reader in doubt.

The reference to human nature offers a connection between this chapter 15 and § 25 of Cicero's *On Fate*, according to whom voluntary movement is our natural movement; it has the quality of being up to us, since this is its nature

24 εἰ δὴ τῶν αὐτῶν περιεστώτων ὁτὲ μὲν οὕτως ὁτὲ δὲ ἄλλως ἐνεργήσει τις, ἀναίτιον κίνησιν εἰσάγεσθαι.

(*motus enim voluntarius eam naturam in se ipse continet, ut sit in nostra potestate nobisque pareat, nec id sine causa; eius rei enim causa ipsa natura est*).

The only typically Aristotelian argument offering a somewhat deeper understanding can be found in the final part of chapter 15, when Alexander states that a human being does not assent to a presentation, because through deliberation he can also take as point of reference some things that take "the cause of their appearing through reason and from reasoning".[25]

The lack of typically Aristotelian arguments is due to the exoteric nature of the treatise, which is addressed to a non-specialist audience, as the dedication of *On Fate* to the emperors Severus and Antoninus makes clear. A more careful analysis can be found in *Mantissa* 23, which I discussed elsewhere (Natali 2007). Here I will restrict myself to the conclusion of my discussion of that text. In the *Mantissa* Alexander, or his pupil, maintains:

> [The human being] having in himself the power of deliberating about the circumstances, has also the ability not to make the same choice from the same things. And this is not asserted unreasonably, nor what is said is an empty presupposition. For if he had one goal to which he *referred* this decision, it would be reasonable that he should always choose the same thing, if at least he had and preserved the same position in relation to the goal set before him, towards which he *looked* in his judgement of them. But since there are several ends, *looking* towards which he makes his judgement and choice of the things he should do, for he has both the pleasant and the advantageous and the noble *before the eyes*, and these are different from each other, and not all the things surronding the agent are in the same position in relation to each of these ends, he makes his judgement between them and choice among them at one time with regard to the pleasant, at another with regard to the noble, at another with regard to the advantageous, and will not always do or choose the same things when the circumstances are the same, but in each occasion he will do those things which seem to him most conducive to the goal which he has selected (23, 174.11–24).[26] (Tr. Sharples, modified)

---

25 186.9: φαίνεται δέ τινα καὶ διὰ λόγου τε καὶ παρὰ συλλογισμοῦ.

26 ἔχων ἐν αὑτῷ τὴν ἐξουσίαν τοῦ βουλεύεσθαι περὶ τῶν περιεστώτων, ἔχει καὶ τὸ δύνασθαι ἐκ τῶν αὐτῶν μὴ τὰ αὐτὰ αἱρεῖσθαι. καὶ τοῦτο οὐκ ἀλόγως τίθεται, οὐδέ ἐστιν αἴτημα τὸ λεγόμενον. εἰ μὲν γὰρ ἦν εἷς ὁ σκοπὸς αὐτῷ, πρὸς ὃν τὴν ἀναφορὰν τῆς κρίσεως ἐποιεῖτο, εὔλογον ἦν ἀπὸ τῶν αὐτῶν ἀεὶ ταὐτὸν αὐτὸν αἱρεῖσθαι τὴν αὐτήν γε σχέσιν ἔχοντα ἀεὶ καὶ φυλάττοντα πρὸς τὸν προκείμενον αὐτῷ σκοπόν, πρὸς ὃν ὁρῶν ἐποιεῖτο τὴν κρίσιν αὐτῶν. ἐπεὶ δέ ἐστι πλείω τὰ τέλη, πρὸς ἃ βλέπων τὴν κρίσιν καὶ τὴν αἵρεσιν τῶν πρακτέων ποιεῖται (καὶ γὰρ τὸ ἡδὺ καὶ

The difference between the moving and the final cause is enough to break the necessity in the chain of causes. In this passage the relation between the goal and the means, which can be chosen, are described in a precise and complex manner. Someone who chooses has the "goal" (σκοπός, τὰ τέλη) as a given, to which he will make reference, and "looking" (ὁρῶν, βλέπων) at it, he will make his choice. The "circumstances" (τὰ περιεστῶτα) will also be given; they will be in a certain relation, a "position" (τὴν σχέσιν) with regard to the goals, which obviously can be – to put it metaphorically – either closer or further away, that is having a greater or lesser capacity to reach the goal. The circumstances are at the same time the things from which and about which the choice is made, which is a choice to act.

The goal is related to the agent, not in terms of moving cause, but in terms of being presented, coming from another faculty, and of being contemplated. It is a relation of dependency, but not one in which one is the moving cause of the other; it is rather a relation of hypothetical necessity, as described in *Physics* 2.9. With its being watched, and therefore being visible, the goal attracts: like any motionless motor, it moves as a final cause. The goal is a cause that does not precede the choice but is simultaneous with it, it is present in each of the steps made by the agent towards bringing something about. At each step the goal guides the choice and gives the reason for the choice made.

The vocabulary chosen by Alexander is significant, because it indicates that in deliberating, the goal is something that "shows itself", in the same way that the circumstances show themselves to the decision maker. The goal is thus not an external *input*, like the push that sets the cylinder and the sphere down the slope, to use Chrysippus' classic example, but it is a term in the intellectual process of decision making, functioning in the search for an answer as an unmoving motor. The end, being the goal, is thus not a moving cause.

The goal is not only something imagined; for Alexander, there are also real relations, in the world between the possible goals and the given circumstances, and these relations help to make the choice. According to Alexander the circumstances do not stand in the same relation to the goal, which could be described as a "state" (σχέσις) relative to the end: depending on the chosen end some circumstances may prove to be more useful than others. When the agent deliberates, he does not hold a single representation, an appetitive and

τὸ συμφέρον καὶ τὸ καλὸν ἔχει πρὸ ὀφθαλμῶν), ταῦτα δὲ ἀλλήλων διαφέρει, οὐ πάντα δὲ τὰ περιεστῶτα ὁμοίαν τὴν σχέσιν ἔχει πρὸς τούτων ἕκαστον, τὴν κρίσιν αὐτῶν καὶ τὴν ἐξ αὐτῶν αἵρεσιν ποιούμενος ποτὲ μὲν πρὸς τὸ ἡδύ, ποτὲ δὲ πρὸς τὸ καλόν, ἄλλοτε δὲ πρὸς τὸ συμφέρον καὶ οὐκ ἀεὶ ταὐτὰ πράξει οὐδὲ ἀεὶ ταὐτὰ αἱρήσεται τῶν αὐτῶν περιεστώτων ἁπάντων, ἀλλ' ἑκάστοτε ταῦτα τὰ πρὸς τὸν κριθέντα σκοπὸν μάλιστα συντείνειν δοκοῦντα.

immediate impression of what ought to be done, that is whether to assent or not to assent, as in the Stoic account of the mental process that leads to action. According to Alexander, the agent in his imagination has before him a more complex framework, in which the fixed points are the circumstances and the preferred goal among the possible goals. Starting out from these the agent develops his courses of action: the characteristic of the goodness and the preferability of the different possible courses will vary, in relation to the given circumstances, the courses of action, the different ends deliberated, and the effectiveness of the course of action envisaged. Circumstances may be more favourable with regard to one end than with regard to an other, but this does not exclude the possibility that the goal that is most difficult to achieve may be the best. The practicality and the goodness of the action vary from case to case, in this extremely complex model. With the help of Aristotle and the *Mantissa* one can infer that the "fruits of reasoning", that is the outcome of the practical syllogism, can be programmes of action that are contrary to what a first superficial assessment of the state of things would suggest.

In comparison with the version in the *Mantissa*, the argument in *On Fate*, chapter 15 appears simplified and abbreviated in such a manner that it looses essential elements which affect its persuasiveness and validity. The arguments have been placed in a different order,[27] and *On Fate* contains various polemical attacks against the Stoics, whereas the *Mantissa* above all offers a detailed account of the different kinds of causes involved and how they operate. For an overall evaluation of Alexander's position it is thus necessary to look into the smaller treatises, too, and not only in his *On Fate*.

Bibliography

Amand, David. 1945. *Fatalisme et liberté dans l'antiquité grecque*. Louvain: Bibliothèque de l'Université (repr. Amsterdam 1973).

Bobzien, Susanne. 1998. *Determinism and Freedom in Stoic Philosophy*. Oxford: Clarendon.

Bonitz, Hermann. 1870. *Index aristotelicus*. Berlin: Reimer.

Davidson, Donald. 2001. *Essays on Actions & Events*. 2nd edn. Oxford: Oxford University Press.

Donini, Pier Luigi. 1974. *Tre studi sull'aristotelismo del II secolo D.C.* Turin: Paravia.

27 *Mantissa* 23, 172.24–27 = *On Fate* 15, 186.4–5; 173.7 = 186.15–16; 174.3–4 = 185.8–9; 173.7–9 = 185.31; 174.13–15 = 185.21–28.

Donini, Pier Luigi. 1994. "Testi e commenti, movimenti e insegnamento." In *Aufstieg und Niedergang der römischen Welt*, vol. 2.36.7, edited by Wolfgang Haase, 5027–5099. Berlin: De Gruyter.

Long, Anthony A. 1970. "Stoic Determinism and Alexander of Aphrodisias *De fato* (I–XIV)." *Archiv für Geschichte der Philosophie* 52: 247–268.

LS = Long, Anthony A., and David N. Sedley. 1987. *The Hellenistic Philosophers*. Cambridge: Cambridge University Press.

Natali, Carlo. 1994. "Alessandro di Afrodisia, de fato II–VI, in prospettiva aristotelica." *Rivista di storia della filosofia* 49: 629–663.

Natali, Carlo. 2003. "Causa formale e causa motrice in Alessandro d'Afrodisia." In *Alessandro d'Afrodisia e la Metafisica di Aristotele*, edited by Giancarlo Movia, 153–165. Milan: Vita and Pensiero.

Natali, Carlo. 2007. "La causa dell'azione umana secondo Alessandro d'Afrodisia, *Mantissa*, 23, e *De fato*, 15." *Philosophia* [Athens] 37: 72–91.

Natali, Carlo. 2014. "Aristotele e il determinismo." In: *Libero arbitrio. Storia di una controversia filosofica*, edited by Mario De Caro, Massimo Mori, and Emidio Spinelli, 39–57. Rome: Carocci.

Sharples, Robert W. 1983, ed., tr. *Alexander of Aphrodisias. On Fate*. London: Duckworth.

Sorabji, Richard. 1998. "Introduction." In: *Ammonius, On Aristotle's On Interpretation 9*, translated by David Blank. London: Duckworth.

Verbeke, Gerard. 1968. "Aristotélisme et stoïcisme dans le 'De fato' d'Alexandre d'Aphrodise." *Archiv für Geschichte der Philosophie* 50: 73–100.

Zingano, Marco. 2014. "Alexander and Aristotle on Character and Action." In *What is Up to Us? Studies on Agency and Responsibility in Ancient Philosophy*, edited by Pierre Destrée, Ricardo Salles, and Marco Zingano, 199–220. Sankt Augustin: Academia.

CHAPTER 9

Alexander of Aphrodisias on Fate as a Problem in Epistemology and Moral Psychology

Péter Lautner

The logic and metaphysics behind Alexander's notion of fate have been much discussed in the literature about ancient views on determinism. By contrast, the ethical and epistemological aspects have received considerably less attention. In what follows I shall concentrate, first, on the way the various definitions of ἐφ'ἡμῖν, what is "up to us", culminate in the account of character states involving knowledge, and then, second, on the inner conditions that make free action possible. It will involve a discussion of the appropriate cognitive and conative states alike. My aim is to give a unitarian explanation in the sense that I shall try to show that the accounts we find in the *Mantissa* and in *On the Soul* are by no means exclusive of one another. As a consequence, I shall have much less to say about the metaphysical conditions of fate and free action or about the logic behind them.

1 Four Definitions of What Is "Up to Us"

Before dealing with that matter a few preliminary remarks need to be made. They concern the target of Alexander's critique. As is well known, nowhere in his *On Fate* Alexander mentions the Stoics, or even names his determinist opponents. In the *Mantissa* he refers to them twice, and only one is related to providence. However, most of the commentators take it for granted that the primary target of his libertarian attack were the Stoics. It is interesting that at the same time some commentators also claim that he was concerned with determinism as a philosophical thesis in itself, and not in the context of the Stoic system as a whole.[1] The assumption raises the possibility that his primary

1 See Sharples 1984, 20–21, whereas Natali 1996, takes Alexander's critique as directed straightforwardly against the Stoics. On the other hand, some of the problems discussed in *On Fate* are internal to Aristotle's ethics, such as the question if our character depends on us or not (26, 196.24–197.3). On this, see Zingano 2014, 199–220. For recent overview of the *status quaestionis*, see Fazzo 2017, 123–151, esp. 130–136.

 | DOI:10.1163/9789004436381_011

aim was not so much to attack Stoic theories for themselves, but to criticize determinism as such, which involves a critical inquiry into some Stoic theses, too. It explains an interesting feature of Alexander's approach, that he neglects some of the specific aspects of the Stoic theory such as the distinction between primary and proximate causes or the Stoic attempts to qualify the contribution of the agent to his own action.

The central notion of Alexander's account is the action that is "up to us" (ἐφ' ἡμῖν). Let us see a few definitions of what is up to us. They are sometimes vague but I believe the opacity is not a result of carelessness. Alexander gives a whole range of definitions and here it would be useful to list them in an order which gives the term an increasingly specific meaning. It gives us a perspective that is useful in assessing his contribution to the ethical and epistemological side of the theory. First of all, the term refers to an act that is not determined by antecedent and *external* constraints. According to the most common definition (1), an action is up to us if we have the power also not to do it.[2] In that case, things that happened would not have happened had we ourselves not done certain things rather than others. Alexander may not be quite content with such a broad approach since it blurs the difference between doing something and abstaining from doing it. For this reason, perhaps, he gives a more narrow definition that has a different emphasis.[3] As he says (2), there are actions which are up to us of which the opposite is also possible and up to us to do it.[4]

We have to have in mind that Alexander refers both to actions and to psychic activities such as choices.[5] On the other hand, when referring to opposite actions he uses the term *ἀντικείμενον* which might show that we should

2 *On Fate* 2, 166.10–13: κατορθοῦντες δὲ ἐν τοῖς προκειμένοις αὐτοὺς αἰτίους εἶναι τῶν κατορθωμάτων ὑπολαμβάνουσιν, ὡς οὐκ ἂν ἀπαντησάντων τῶν ἀπηντηκότων, εἰ μὴ αὐτοὶ τάδε μᾶλλον ἔπραξαν ἀντὶ τῶνδε, ὡς ἔχοντες καὶ τοῦ μὴ πράττειν αὐτὰ τὴν ἐξουσίαν. See also 5, 169.7–14; 12, 180.5–6; 20, 195.25; 28, 199.9; 33, 205.19–20; 39, 212.15; *Mantissa* 23, 173.5–6; 25, 184.8.

3 The first approach is a fair rehearsal of Aristotle's thesis (*Metaphysics* 5.1, 1129a10–16) that the one and the same ἕξις cannot give rise to contrary behaviours.

4 *Mantissa* 22, 169.39–170.2: λέγω δὲ τοιοῦτον ἐφ' ἡμῖν, οὗ καὶ τὸ ἀντικείμενον δυνατόν τέ ἐστι καὶ ἐφ'ἡμῖν, ὁποῖον ἡμεῖς εἶναι τὸ ἐφ'ἡμῖν ἀξιοῦμεν. The Greek text is quoted from Sharples 2008. For a translation, which I shall use here, see Sharples 2004. The authenticity of the *Mantissa*, entirely or of some parts of it, has been challenged, but now see Sharples' introduction. On passages with the same thesis, see also *On Fate* 12, 180.20–21; 32, 204.19–20; 38, 211.32–33; Simplicius, *Commentary on the Physics* 941.28–942.2. On the latter passage, see M. Rashed 2007, 297–298.

5 On the possibility of choosing the opposite, see also *On Fate* 12, 180.26–27, 181.5–6, *Mantissa* 23, 174.11–12. Sharples draws attention to the contradiction between this passage and *On Fate* 24, since the author of the Mantissa relates the non-deterministic account of responsibility to an account of indeterminism in the world as a whole, see Sharples 2004, 201. It leads him

not think of contrary actions by all means. As we shall show later, there is a distinct possibility that the opposition is between contradictory, and not contrary, actions. On this view, actions that depend on us are those which can be avoided for the sake of actions that are not contrary to, only different from them in a certain way. Furthermore (3), more importantly, in the *Mantissa* 22, at 171.23–27, he states that actions are up to us insofar as they are uncaused:

> ἃ οὖν ἀναιτίως καὶ μὴ προϋπαρχούσης αἰτίας προαιρούμεθα, ταῦτα ἐστιν τὰ λεγόμενα ἐφ' ἡμῖν, ὧν καὶ τὰ ἀντίκειμενά ἐστι δυνατὰ διὰ τὸ τὴν αἰτίαν μὴ προκαταβεβλῆσθαι, ἥτις προϋπάρχουσα πάντως ἂν τοῦ γενέσθαι τοῦτο τὴν ἀνάγκην παρεῖχεν. διὰ ταῦτα πολλάκις τινὲς καὶ πεφυκότες ὁμοίως καὶ ἐν τοῖς αὐτοῖς ἔθεσιν ἠγμένοι διαφέροντες ἀλλήλων γίγνονται παρὰ τὰς ἀναιτίους προαιρέσεις.
>
> So it is those things that we choose without a cause and with no cause existing beforehand that are said to depend on us; and the opposites of these, too, are possible, as that cause has not been laid down beforehand that, if it *had* existed beforehand, would certainly made it necessary that this should come to be. For this reason, it often happens that some who are similar in nature and have been brought up in the same habits come to differ from one another, as a result of the uncaused choices.[6] (Tr. Sharples)

The account supplements and specifies what is meant by actions of which the opposite is also possible. They are uncaused insofar as they do not have antecedent causes that may determine them fully.[7] If people have similar nature and have been brought up in the same habits and thus differ from one another then the difference is due to their choices that are not determined by the circumstances. It seems that the emphasis is on full-scale determination since this kind of determination of an action makes the opposite action impossible. It does not rule out that nature and upbringing are causal factors that are responsible for certain aspects of the action. Action without cause may only

to the assumption that the author of *Mantissa* 22 may not be by Alexander. The assumption does not necessarily follows, however, since we may suppose that Alexander himself revised the theory of the *On Fate*.

6 See also *On Fate* 19, 189.9–12. He makes the point that we can choose or do different things in the same circumstances twice, see *On Fate* 15, 185.7, *Mantissa* 23, 174.3. For the context, see Sorabji 2017, 49–65.

7 Sharples 2008, 225 suggests that in chapter 23 ἐφ' ἡμῖν is connected to weakness and falling short. I am not sure that it is necessarily the case. The passage quoted above contains a general thesis with no specific emphasis on this issue.

mean that it is not necessitated by one's own nature and upbringing. Unsurprisingly, Alexander's view is deeply rooted in the Aristotelian theory. There are two theses that are linked together here. The first thesis is that in nature everything happens for the most part.[8] It implies a second thesis according to which there is room for "counter-nature" and for "counter-fate", and so for human responsibility.[9] Moreover, in using a terminology reminiscent of Platonic theories Alexander assumes that there is a kind of not-being in the things that exist; it is diffused somehow among them and accompanies them (*Mantissa* 22, 170.10–12).[10] The notion is linked to the explanation of being *contingent*. Unlike mathematical entities or celestial bodies, things in the sublunary world are such that they deny full regularity; they are neither eternal nor existing always in the same way, which means that regularity is confined within limits. It is true that divine providence is active in the sublunary world insofar as it preserves the species and thus brings about the substance of the particulars. It does not mean, however, that providence fully determines all individual actions.[11] The two theses are of a general nature since they do not refer to the specific conditions of the agent. As an underlying assumption, Alexander refers to the Aristotelian doctrine according to which in living beings "impulse" (ὁρμή) or "desire" (ὄρεξις) is also among the causes for action.[12] In humans, we have a "will" (βούλησις) as an additional factor as well. Furthermore (4), assumption of a not-being in human action creates problems that call for explanation. One of them is hinted at in the *Mantissa*, at 173.2–5:

> ἔστι δὲ τὸ ἐφ' ἡμῖν ἐν τούτοις, περὶ ἃ καὶ τὸ βουλεύεσθαι. βουλευόμεθα δὲ οὔτε περὶ τῶν γεγονότων οὔτε περὶ τῶν ὄντων ἤδη, ἀλλὰ περὶ τῶν μελλόντων καὶ ἐνδεχομένων [γενέσθαι] καὶ μὴ γενέσθαι, καὶ ὧν αἰτία διάνοια.
>
> What is up to us is located in those things with which deliberation, too, is concerned. And we deliberate neither about things that have come to

8 Although I think we can agree with Sharples 1975, 247–274, esp. 252 saying that the assertion of variation is not relevant as a critique of the determinist position. All that matters is the claim it is impossible that when all circumstances are the same then sometimes things may happen in such a way, sometimes not in this way. For a critique of Sharples' claim, see White 1985, 160–162.

9 See Bonelli 2013, 83–101. She also emphasizes that fate is a productive cause, i.e., a principle that is active and external to the change it causes. She also stresses that in *On Fate*, although an internal principle of production, nature as a fate cannot be identified with individual nature, see also Bonelli 2014, 119–135.

10 It may reflect discussions among the Peripatetics as well, see Donini 1974, 167.

11 See his *On Providence* 87R in Thillet 2003, 122.

12 See, e.g., *On the Principles of the Universe* 8, in Genequand 2017, 54; *On the Soul* 22.27–23.3.

> be [already] nor about those which are already, but about those which are in the future and are able [to come to be and] to not come to be as well, and of which the cause is intelligence.[13] (Tr. Sharples, slightly modified)

Alexander insists that actions that are up to us characterize agents whose assent relies on reasonable judgement. The objects of deliberation, future actions, are caused by intelligence. The causal role of "intelligence" (διάνοια) qualifies the view that some events in the external world can be contingent since their causal factor can produce different events at the same time in the same circumstances.[14] Elsewhere he seems to argue that events are not necessitated in the sense that we cannot choose differently in the same circumstances.[15] The motivational forces within do cause us to act, but that does not mean that we opt for one such force necessarily. As we have three motivational force, appetite, spirit and will (or rational wish), it is up to us which of them to go for.[16] We may choose either the pleasant or the advantageous or the noble. The distinction between two classes of agents (those who are "wise" (φρόνιμοι) and those who are not) also serves to support the thesis according to which the appropriate use of intelligence may determine the range of those actions that are up to us. But we have to bear in mind that in his account not even the wise person is necessitated in his or her actions. In certain cases, it may seem "reasonable" (εὔλογον) to the wise person to act against what is predicted of his or her action if the manifestation of freedom is at stake.[17]

It seems, therefore, that deliberation is a necessary ingredient for actions that are rooted in us and not simply an upshot of the influence of external causes. Alexander finds a way to express it when clarifying the meaning of "contingency" (ἐνδεχόμενον). To put it into Aristotelian terminology, contingent processes occur for the most part. In discussing the meaning of the term in the

13 Sharples 2004 omits the first γενέσθαι, since it is added to one of the authoritative manuscripts by a later hand and is otherwise present in one Greek ms. only.

14 The point was reiterated by Nemesius of Emesa, *On the Nature of Man* 105–106 Morani. It also refers us to the distinction between the causal role of nature on the one hand and skill and choice on the other. The former is internal, whereas the latter are external to the change/action they give rise to (*On Fate* 4, 168.12–17).

15 See *On Fate* 11, 178.28–179.3; *Questions* 4.29, 160.5–16.

16 See *On Fate* 15, 185.21–28 and *Mantissa* 23, 174.13–24. For an analysis of the passages, see Sorabji 2017, 240–255. I shall have more to say about the issue when discussing the passages in Alexander's *On the Soul*.

17 *On Fate* 29, 199.27–200.2. Note also that gods can also perform such actions, see *On Fate* 32, 204.22–25.

commentary on the *Prior Analytics*, at 162.31–163.1, he says that it can also refer to actions that happen in accordance with "choice" (προαίρεσις):

> τὸ μὲν οὖν ἕτερον τῶν τοῦ ἐνδεχομένου σημαινομένων τοῦτο, εἴη δ᾽ ἂν ὑπὸ τοῦτο καὶ τὰ κατὰ προαίρεσιν γινόμενα τεταγμένα· καὶ γὰρ ἐπὶ τούτων τὸ ὡς ἐπὶ τὸ πλεῖστον.
>
> One of the things which contingency signifies, then, is this. Also ordered under this would be things that come about as a result of choice. For being for the most part also applies to these things. (Tr. Mueller and Gould 1999, slightly modified)

Alexander thus classifies the notion of what is up to us as a subtype of the contingent.[18] The introduction of deliberation and choice seems to answer the problem created by the assumption of not-being, for it rules out that actions that are up to us can be still random. By introducing deliberation into the account the author rules out the possibility that just because they are not fully determined by antecedent external causes such actions can be still haphazard which rules out that the agent can be responsible for them. They cannot be so, however, since they draw on previous consideration of the agent about the circumstances, for instance. Deliberation and choice are also crucial factors in actions that are up to us. This is how the problem of what is up to us leads to an investigation into internal factors such as knowledge and moral character.[19]

In order to see the connection between the theory of fate and moral psychology we have to draw attention to Alexander's distinction between what we do "voluntarily" (ἑκούσιος) and what we do by "choice" (προαίρεσις) because it is up to us, in *On Fate* 14, at 183.26–30:

> οὐ μὴν ταὐτόν τό τε ἑκούσιον καὶ τὸ ἐφ᾽ ἡμῖν, ἑκούσιον μὲν γὰρ τὸ ἐξ ἀβιάστου γινόμενον συγκαταθέσεως, ἐφ᾽ ἡμῖν δὲ τὸ γινόμενον μετὰ τῆς κατὰ λόγον τε καὶ κρίσιν συγκαταθέσεως, διὸ εἴ τι μὲν ἐφ᾽ ἡμῖν, τοῦτο καὶ ἑκούσιον, οὐ μὴν πᾶν τὸ ἑκούσιον ἐφ᾽ ἡμῖν.
>
> But the voluntary and what depends on us are not indeed the same thing. For it is what comes about from an assent that is not enforced that is voluntary; but it is what comes about with an assent that is in accordance with reason and judgement that depends on us. And for this

18 For a further analysis, see Bobzien 1998a, 397–8; she also refers to Nemesius of Emesa, *On the Nature of Man* 104.4–7.

19 On the relation between choice and action in Alexander, see Bobzien 1998b, 163 n. 54.

> reason, if something depends on us it is also voluntary, but not everything that is voluntary depends on us.[20] (Tr. Sharples)

The distinction between voluntary and what is up to us is present in Aristotle's writings as well.[21] It serves to stress, not the external conditions of free action, but the conditions within the agent's soul. Against Chrysippus and Carneades who considered the notion of what is up to us and the notion of the voluntary coextensive, Alexander makes a distinction between what we do of our own accord and what we do by choice. Moreover, he characterizes voluntary action more narrowly. It must be based on assent that is not forced.[22] In line with it, the characterization of what is up to us also sets clear limits for the use of the notion. In order to lead to genuine free action assent must draw on appropriate calculation on practical matters. It is an important point because the use of reason and judgement is thus connected with action that is up to us. They are prerequisite for such an action. It is here that Alexander's notion of freedom is connected to the liability to be blamed as well.[23] The distinction enables Alexander to attack the Stoic position by saying that they misuse the notion and put an end to "freedom" (τὸ ἐλεύθερον) and our having the "power" (ἐξουσία) for opposite actions (38, 211.32–33). Indeed, if we say with the Stoics as Alexander presents them, that the only criterion for what is up to us is nothing but a previous assent, then we will not be able to tell the difference between those actions which are compelled by inborn characteristics and those which are the result of careful consideration. The distinction has far reaching consequences for character development. It is indicated by the story of Zopyrus, the physiognomist (*On Fate* 6, 171.11 ff.); when he met Socrates, he said some strange and quite inappropriate things about him, that he was stupid and dull-witted because he did not have hollows in the neck above the collar-bone. Zopyrus was ridiculed by Socrates' associates but Socrates himself said that as a matter of fact he was right as far as Socrates' nature was concerned.[24] The reason of his failure in assessing the actual condition was that by way of practising philosophy Socrates has become better than his nature. The remark leads us towards the problem, discussed also by Aristotle in

20 See Sharples 1984. See also *On Fate* 15, 185.15–16 and *Mantissa* 23, 174.9–10.

21 *Nicomachean Ethics* 3.1, 1111b6–10.

22 Frede 2011, 95 thinks that the notion of the voluntary as based on unforced assent comes from Carneades, which means that Alexander's critique was directed towards the Academic reformulations of Stoic views as well.

23 See Sorabji 2017, 49–65.

24 The story is mentioned in Cicero as well, see his *On Fate* 10.

Nicomachean Ethics 3.5, 1113b3 ff., of the development of character. The example suggests that Alexander considered nature not a sufficient condition for character; it can only constitute a necessary condition of the effect.

2 Can the Wise Person Act in Many Ways?

Successive definitions of what is up to us then lead us into the domain of cognition and moral psychology, and we can already have got an impression on how epistemology and ethics get interconnected here. To show the details of the link we have to turn first to Alexander's *On the Soul* and then back to the *Mantissa*.

Before that, however, we also have to answer an important question which is related to the role of character and knowledge in actions that are truly up to us. To put it briefly, can the virtuous man act unjustly? It seems that even if the outer criteria for what is up to us apply, the internal criteria do not. Given that his state of character is settled in the right way he cannot act but justly. If this is the case the options of the virtuous are less extensive than the possibilities that are open to the common man. There is an interesting distinction which may be relevant to the issue. Pier Luigi Donini suggested that Alexander wavered between two notions of what is up to us: first, that we are masters of doing and not doing something, and, second, that we have the power of doing the opposite as well.[25]

The first, more cautious and general, description is to be found in *On Fate* 12, 180.4–6:

> τοῦτο γὰρ ἐφ' ἡμῖν πάντες, ὅσοι μὴ θέσει τινὶ παρίστανται, παρειλήφασιν εἶναι, οὗ ἡμεῖς μὲν καὶ τοῦ πραχθῆναι καὶ τοῦ μὴ πραχθῆναι κύριοι, οὐχ ἑπόμενοί τισιν ἔξωθεν ἡμᾶς περιστᾶσιν αἰτίοις οὐδὲ ἐνδιδόντες αὐτοῖς, ᾗ ἐκεῖνα ἄγει.
>
> For this is what all those who are not defending some position accept as depending to us – that over which we have control both to do it and not to do it, not following some causes which surround us from outside or giving in to them [and following] in the way in which they lead us. (Tr. Sharples)

25 Donini 2010, 159–176. For a new analysis, see Zingano, 2014, 205–207, distinguishing between doing otherwise and doing differently, with the first implying the second but not *vice versa*.

It is more cautious because it commits us to the quite general claim that the term ἐφ' ἡμῖν refers to a condition in which we can do good and bad alike. Nevertheless, it maintains multiple possibilities for behaviour. It is corroborated by the short description of the psychological processes that precede action. Accepting some of the Stoic theses he claims that human reason is a judge of the "representations concerning what is done" (φαντασίαι τῶν πρακτῶν) and we use it to check whether the representation in question is reliable. If it is not, then we resist and abstain from acting in accordance with the representation.[26] The second description, which seems to be more straightforward, is to be found in *On Fate* 12, 180.20–23:

> γίνεται δὲ καὶ ἡ ζήτησις αὐτῷ ὡς ἐξουσίαν ἔχοντι τοῦ πράττειν καὶ τὰ ἀντικείμενα. καθ' ἕκαστον γὰρ τῶν ὑπὸ τὴν βουλὴν ἡ ζήτησις βουλευμένῳ γίνεται, πότερον τοῦτο ἢ τὸ ἀντικείμενον αὐτῷ πρακτέον μοι, κἂν πάντα λέγῃ γίνεσθαι καθ' εἱμαρμένην.
>
> But his enquiry too is carried out on the assumption that he has the power also to do the opposite things [to what he in fact does]. For concerning each of the things that fall under the deliberator's enquiry is "whether this or its opposite should be done by me" – even if he says that all things come to be in accordance with fate. (Tr. Sharples)

Alexander offers this description when discussing the failure of a deterministic interpretation of deliberation and choice.

The difference of the descriptions has been put into the context of another division, the one between the virtuous person who is also "wise in practical matters" (φρόνιμος) and the ordinary human being who is not vicious but making progress towards virtue. Donini's suggestion is that whereas the ordinary human being can act in opposite ways, doing either the good or the bad, the virtuous person cannot act unjustly. However, that does not mean that the virtuous person is completely lacking alternatives; he may perform various actions. The only restriction is that they cannot be unjust. The distinction relies on the ambivalence of the term ἀντικείμενον, the term Alexander uses in the second description; it can refer to both contrary and contradictory qualities. His notion is much embedded in his criticism of the Stoics.[27] The use of the term "contradictory" may serve to help us explain the case of the virtuous person who can perform actions that are opposite to one another in a

26 See *On Fate* 14, 184.6–12.

27 For Alexander's critique of the Stoic view of the possibility of choosing and enacting of opposite alternatives, see *On Fate* 19, 189.9–11; for an analysis, see Sorabji 2017, 249–450.

contradictory way. To use Aristotle's example (*Categories* 10, 11b21–23), he or she can sit down or avoid sitting down. It creates a latitude which does not rule out a compatibilist reading. One could object, of course, that the difference between doing the good and doing the bad is not of the same type as the difference between sitting down and avoiding sitting down. The former is a difference between types of value or quality, if you like, while the latter is between particulars or types of another nature. One can also note that Alexander does allow for the wise person to act against predictions if it seems reasonable; in this way he or she is able to manifest freedom of action.[28] Nevertheless, it may not affect the point I am going to make here: by definition the virtuous person cannot perform the full range of actions that are possible in the situation but that does not rule out that he or she is allowed to perform many particular actions in a given situation. In order to understand the link between actions that are up to us and the various processes and events in the soul that precede them, we have to turn to Alexander's own *On the Soul*. We shall see that the Alexander gives a rich description of the psychic conditions that have to be met so that we perform actions that are truly up to us. Let us start with the cognitive side of the process that leads to human action.

3 Epistemology

Phantasia is a capacity by which we restore and sometimes transform the images coming from sense-perception. It has many forms starting from images of sensory qualities and culminating in representations of things as worthy of choice. The latter type may be a result of the creative side of the representational capacity. Interestingly enough, Alexander employs the Stoic notion of assent as a reaction to representation. However, in *On the Soul*, he also uses it in a different sense for he distinguishes two kinds of assent, at 73.8–14:

> ἔστι δὲ ἡ συγκατάθεσις ἡ μὲν ἐπὶ τοῖς ἁπλοῖς[29] καὶ ἐπὶ[30] τῷ εἶναί τι ἢ μὴ εἶναι γινομένη οὐκ ἐφ' ἡμῖν (ἕπεται γὰρ τῇ τε αἰσθήσει καὶ τῇ φαντασίᾳ ἡ τοιάδε συγκατάθεσις), ἡ δὲ ἐπὶ τοῖς πρακτέοις ἢ μὴ πρακτέοις γινομένη, ὧν συγκαταθέσεων ὁ λόγος αἴτιος, ἐφ' ἡμῖν. τὸ γὰρ διὰ τοῦ βουλεύσασθαι

28 See *On Fate* 29, 199.27–200.2, referred to in n. 16.

29 73.8 ἁπλοῖς: Bruns *non intellego*; Bergeron and Dufour: *faits simples*; Accattino and Donini: *fatti elementari*. I take καὶ as an explicative of what 'ἁπλοῖς' is meant to say.

30 ἐπὶ Accattino and Donini, Bergeron and Dufour; ἐν archetype and the Aldine translation. For an explanation of the emendation, see Accattino and Donini 1996, 254.

> προκρῖναί τι καὶ τούτῳ συγκαταθέσθαι ἐφ' ἡμῖν. ἥτις συγκατάθεσις οὐκέτ' ἂν ἐπὶ φαντασίᾳ γίνεσθαι λέγοιτο.
>
> The assent which is concerned with the simple [facts], i.e., with the issue of whether something is there or not, is not up to us (for such kind of assent follows sense-perception and *phantasia*), the one, however, which is concerned with things to be done or not to be done – an assent of which the cause is reason – is up to us. For it is up to us to prefer something through deliberation and assent to it. One may say that this assent does not follow on *phantasia* any longer.

The distinction is relevant to our purposes because it draws attention to a kind of assent that decides about courses of actions. Unlike brute animals, humans can withstand *phantasia* and act accordingly. This kind of assent is up to us because it rests on the activity of reason, which is deliberation. Interestingly, such deliberation is not about the circumstances and validity of sense-perception, rather it concerns the action to be done. Although Alexander does not acknowledge it explicitly, he seems to be following Aristotle's line of thought in *Nicomachean Ethics* (6.8, 1141b10–11) that deliberation itself is a proof against determinism. The very fact that we are endowed with the capacity for deliberating is a sign that we do have multiple choices for action. The distinction also shows that *phantasia* alone does not cause an assent that is up to us. The assent it does cause is characteristic to all sentient beings. When we are going to approve simple facts, whether something obtains or not, *phantasia* is our main guide. However, when assent has a different object by switching its focus from judging appearances to assessing various options for action, then it is no longer confined to mere appearances. This is where the notion of 'up to us' is to be applied. Approval of appearances does not depend on us, which, of course, does not rule out that we are liable to error. The switch of focus does not involve either that the causal role of *phantasia* can be done away with altogether. There is a text that denies it explicitly. As we read in *Mantissa* 23, at 173.25–31,

> τὸ μὲν γὰρ λέγειν αἰτίαν τὴν φαντασίαν τοῦ βουλεύεσθαι περὶ τοῦ φανέντος οὐδὲν ἄτοπον, τὸ δὲ καὶ τοῦ πράττειν τόδε τι μὴ τὴν βουλήν, ἀλλὰ τὴν φαντασίαν αἰτιᾶσθαι ἀναιρεῖν ἐστι τὴν βουλήν, ἥν τε ἔχομεν ὡς οὔσης τινὸς τὴν φαντασίαν αἰτίαν. ὥστ' εἰ τοῦ μὲν βουλεύεσθαι τὸ φανὲν αἴτιον, τῆς δὲ κρίσεως ἡ βουλή, τῆς δὲ ὁρμῆς ἡ κρίσις, ἡ δὲ ὁρμὴ τῶν πραττομένων, οὐδὲν ἐν τούτοις ἐστὶν ἀναίτιον.
>
> to say that the *phantasia* is the cause of [our] deliberating about what appeared is not at all absurd; but to regard not the deliberation but the

> *phantasia* as the cause also of [our] doing this particular thing is to do away with deliberation and also with the causal role of *phantasia* that we assign to it as [we hold it to be the cause] of something that is. So, if what appeared is the cause of the deliberating, the deliberation is of the judgement, the judgement of the impulse, and the impulse of what is done, nothing among these will be without a cause.[31] (Tr. Sharples, modified)

There is, then, an unbroken causal chain leading from *phantasia* to action. It is unbroken since there is no other factor that could intervene in the process. Alexander seems to respond to those who claim that *phantasia* is the single decisive factor in the arousal of action. They may have argued that just like in other animals appearances fully determine our reaction to them as well. If this were the case, he argues, we have to draw a paradoxical conclusion since the claim itself destroys the causal efficiency of *phantasia* as well. In order to save causal efficiency we have to describe the whole causal process in detail, pointing out the individual actors. We have *phantasia*, deliberation, judgement impulse and action, each in the appropriate order. One may say that on compiling the list Alexander paints with a broad brush, since he omits three or four acts or activities that are relevant here. The most striking feature of the description is the absence of assent. One may also miss πρόκρισις, referred to in *On the Soul* 73.12 (quoted at the beginning of this section), and αἵρεσις or προαίρεσις.

I think the absence of assent has a relatively easy solution. It seems that the role of "judgment" (κρίσις) and assent is quite similar. In *Mantissa* 23, 172.27–28 Alexander suggests that we can deliberate whether to assent to a particular appearance or not. After having deliberated and judged it we have an impulse towards appropriate action. As I see it, the passage offers us two possibilities for explaining the relation between judgement and assent. Either we take the two names as referring to the same act, or we think that judgement determines assent. In either case, there will be not much of a difference between judgement and assent since even if the second option prevails the functional independence of assent from judgement will be denied. We make judgements not only about the options for action but also about the appearance to which we are supposed to react.[32] The consequence is that the term κρίσις can be a fitting substitute for συγκατάθεσις in the list.

31 On the role of *phantasia* as cause of deliberation, see also *Questions* 3.13, 107.25–37, *On the Soul* 72.15–73.13 (discussed at the beginning of this section).

32 See *Mantissa* 23, 174.27: ἡ τῆς φαντασίας κρίσις.

Judgement is also related to "preference" (πρόκρισις). It seems that they are not different functions, rather they are different aspects of the same function. The explanation of πρόκρισις may start from Alexander's note that it is linked to deliberation. It is a causal link since elsewhere he says that preference comes from deliberation.[33] Furthermore, it seems that deliberation is the sole cause of preference. Since both judgement and preference are based on deliberation we may assume that they are at the same level of the causal chain. The assumption is corroborated by the passages suggesting that both are prior to "choice" (αἵρεσις) (174.1, 17–18). The parallel position of judgement and preference may indicate that preference is nothing but an expression of the fact that when, based on deliberation, we judge that a certain course of action is to be followed, we also, by the very same act, reject other options for action.

Moreover, preference is associated with αἵρεσις or προαίρεσις since we choose what is preferred (173.25).[34] The two acts are not simultaneous, which allows us to infer that there is a causal connection between preference and choice, that we do not choose what we do not prefer. If there is acratic action, its roots are not here. As a result, we have a fuller list of the factors in the causal chain from appearance to action. It is the following: [perception], appearance, deliberation, judgement/preference, assent, choice, impulse, action.[35] Thus we can see that on Alexander's account there are many factors that mediate between appearance and assent.

If *phantasia* as an appearance itself does not give rise to an assent that is up to us, then what is its causal role in the arousal of action? The key element in the answer lies in the distinction between two kinds of *phantasia*. There is a kind which is associated with perceptual appearance, and it is not up to us. It is the kind Alexander talks about in the passages quoted above. By contrast, there is another kind that is up to us; we can have a *phantasia* about things that are not around.[36] Having *phantasia* about things to be done or to be avoided is up to us since such representation belongs to the second category. As a consequence, to show that actions are up to us we have to emphasize first that some of the *phantasiai* we have when facing a situation are up to us and then to point out that the processes following *phantasia* such as deliberation, judgement, preference, choice and assent are not determined by it altogether. This

33 See also *Mantissa* 23, 172.29, 173.25.

34 My guess is that αἵρεσις or προαίρεσις mean the same thing in this context, see 174.9–10 as compared to 174.17–18.

35 Assent is mentioned separately because we are committed to the view that it is different from judgement without being independent of it functionally.

36 *On the Soul* 67.1–2, repeated in the commentary on Aristotle's *Metaphysics* 312.5–10.

is the route Alexander seems to follow. He shows that deliberation is not fully determined by appearance in *Questions* 3.13.[37] In the passage quoted above (*On the Soul* 73.8–14) he points out that the causal distance between appearance and specifically human assent is so great as to render all sorts of direct determination impossible, not to mention the multitude of intervening activities, some of them depending on us. If we also bear in mind that the *phantasia* relevant to action depends on us then the epistemology behind actions that are up to us seems to be settled.

4 Moral Psychology

However, human actions are not only rooted in cognitive states, but also in desires. We have to see, therefore, whether desires are mere products of external causes or made by us in a way that is not fully determined by such causes. If we find that some of the desires arise without being fully determined by external causes we may say that actions depending on us have a conative basis as well. In order to show that we have to return to the problem of assent. As we have seen earlier, human assent is a kind of opinion. It is a considered opinion since it must draw on deliberation; this is what makes it truly up to us. It is not just a spontaneous or random reaction to things as they appear to us. The further question is how this cognitive state can be turned into action. This much is clear, Alexander claims, that the "wise person in practical matters" (φρόνιμος) incorporates all virtues since practical wisdom concerns all practical matters and brings together all virtues (*Mantissa* 18, 156.22–23). But that only emphasizes that in order to have practical wisdom we need the ordered state of all the opinions that are about all the practical issues the practically wise person encounters. It does not lead us to the appropriate action immediately. The transition to action requires that we find a link between a cognitive state and the appropriate kind of desire.

Some of the most interesting passages in Alexander's *On the Soul* concern the phenomenon of "desire" (ὄρεξις) or "impulse" (ὁρμή). Alexander defines it as a single distinct "faculty" (δύναμις, 74.13–14, 78.2–23), different from all the cognitive capacities. It does not mean, however, that it is fully independent of them since its main task is to determine our behaviour on the basis of the cognitive capacities. He argues that just as we have a singular, common "discerning" (κριτικόν) faculty of the soul, which is comprised of the cogni-

37 We can take it as a work reflecting Alexander's views, as has been noted by Sharples 1994, 141. The work has been discussed in Sharples 1983, 140ff.

tive capacities from sense-perception to thinking and enables us to tell the difference between various sense-modalities, so animals are endowed with a common "impulsive and desiring" (ὁρμητικὸν καὶ ὀρεκτικόν) faculty, too, which is responsible for animal motion (78.22).[38] The impulsive and desiring faculty contains three capacities: "appetite" (ἐπιθυμία), "spirit" (θυμός) and "rational wish" (βούλησις) (74.1–2). Unsurprisingly, the division can be found in Aristotle as well.[39] The relevant difference lies in the relation of ὄρεξις to ὁρμή. Although the faculty containing appetite, spirit and rational wish is called impulsive and desiring part, the relation between impulse and desire is somewhat difficult to explain. Different from Aristotle, it seems as if for Alexander impulse is a more generic term, since he states explicitly that desire is an "impulse towards something" (78.23: ὁρμὴ ἐπί τι). On the other hand, desire cannot be equated with any of the kinds of impulse. There is no hint in the text suggesting the identification. It cannot be identical with appetite, spirit or rational wish. Rather, the term ὄρεξις may express, not a species, but an aspect of impulse.[40]

Usually, Alexander assumes that assent, *phantasia* and impulse are intimately linked to one another. However, the assumption does not prevent him from referring to cases where the link is broken. In criticising the Stoics he shows that. He makes two claims. First, he states that a certain kind of assent does not follow on *phantasia*. We may have a representation without feeling any urge to assent to it; for instance, it may be all too neutral. Furthermore, just because we assent that Socrates is the one who is approaching, it by no means implies that we have an impulse for anything. And even if we do have one, it does not follow that we act accordingly. He makes it clear in a highly interesting passage in his *On the Soul*, 72.26–73.2:

> ἡ γὰρ ἐπί τισι συγκατάθεσις οὐ παροῦσιν ὡς αἱρετοῖς ὁρμή, τὸ δ' αὐτὸ καὶ ὄρεξις, ἔστι δὲ ἐφ' ὧν καὶ ὁρμήσαντες οὐκ ἐπράξαμεν, μηκέτι τῆς βουλήσεως συνδραμούσης.
>
> For the assent to what are worthy of choice, although they are not present, is impulse, and the same is also desire. There are also cases in which, although we have impulse, we do not act since rational wish does not go with it any longer.

38 It is important to see that Alexander uses the expression ὁρμητικὸν καὶ ὀρεκτικόν elsewhere (76.6, 15–6), too, to refer to a single faculty of desire.

39 For Aristotle's list, see *On the Soul* 3.7. Of course, the origin of the tripartition is Plato's *Republic* 4.

40 As has been suggested by Accattino and Donini (1996, 253–4). They think that ὁρμή refers to motions of attractions and repulsions alike, whereas ὄρεξις is confined to attractions alone. Against the identification, see also Bergeron and Dufour 2008, 321.

The passage is intriguing for at least two reasons. First, impulse can be rendered inefficient if rational wish does not come up. It implies that rational wish has a crucial role in genuine human action. Because "impulse" is used as a generic term Alexander seems to claim that even if there are other kinds of impulses that support a certain course of action the lack of rational wish impedes us from performing it. As rational wish is linked to reason, which has the consequence that human action, free or not, presupposes not only choice and judgement, but also the desiderative element based on them.[41] In this way, rational wish is able to block the impulse which is another kind of desiderative force. The second reason concerns the meaning of the verb συνδραμεῖν; does it refer to an accompaniment or to a supervenient act? The latter option implies that rational wish depends on impulse in general, because it cannot arise without impulse. If it does not come about, however, we do not act, since with regard to human action impulse alone does not suffice. In the case of its being an accompaniment, there is no such dependence, which in turn implies that rational wish has other roots and is not just a capacity of the desiring part. I do not think the passage gives us an answer but this much is clear: that, if rational wish only accompanies impulse, then impulse cannot be the genus to which rational wish also belongs. At any rate, rational wish is described (74.6–8) as a desire for good things and is accompanied by judgment and deliberation. It means that it is a desiring factor primarily. True, in order to have it we need a specific kind of cognition – cognition about what is good. Along with judgment and deliberation it this kind of cognition that makes rational wish specifically human. For all that, however, it seems that it belongs to the desiring part. Alexander makes this clear at the end of *On the Soul*, at 98.29–99.3.

> ἔνθα γὰρ τὸ ὀρεκτικόν, ἐκεῖ καὶ τὸ βουλητικόν, ὄρεξις γάρ τις ἡ βούλησις. ὅπου δὲ τὸ βουλητικόν, ἐκεῖ καὶ τὸ βουλητικόν τε καὶ τὸ λογιστικόν. ἡ γάρ βούλησις ὄρεξις βουλευτική τε καὶ λογιστική.
>
> In fact, where is the desiring [part], there is also the [part of] rational wish for rational wish is some kind of desire. On the other hand, where is the [part of] rational wish, there are also the deliberative and the calculating [capacities]. For rational wish is a deliberating and calculating desire.

41 Alexander defines it as a "deliberative" (βουλευτική) and calculating desire in 99.2–3, to be discussed later. In *Mantissa* 23, 173.13–16 it is mentioned along with choice and judgement as the productive cause of action.

The passage forms a part of the argument to the effect that the guiding principle of the soul is in the heart. For desire is in the heart (77.5–15, 97.14–17) and rational wish is a kind of desire, it must be in the heart, too. Furthermore, because rational wish is tied to reason, reason must also reside around the heart.[42] The passage also shows, again, that in Alexander's account rational wish belongs to the desiring and impulsive power and therefore cannot be treated as a practical side of the intellect. This is not to deny, of course, that it involves cognitive activities necessarily.

We have already seen, in *Mantissa* 22, 173.2–5, that actions that are truly up to us are caused by "intelligence" (διάνοια). We have also seen, in *On the Soul* 72.26–73.2, that rational wish, which is connected to διάνοια, is a necessary prerequisite of human action. It shows that cognitive elements have a crucial role in human action. Rational wish, however, is only one kind of desire, whereas human activities may arise from different kinds of desire as well. The question is, first, how the desiring part in general is linked to the cognitive power and, second, how it can acquire a stable character.

To start with the first question, Alexander follows Aristotle in maintaining that there is a close link between desire and *phantasia*, the representative capacity. In short, without representations there is no desire. On the other hand, even if it furnishes us with a detailed picture – and sometimes misrepresentation – of the outside world, *phantasia* cannot move us on its own. To do that job it needs desire and impulse. Furthermore, "thinking" (νόησις) alone cannot initiate motion either, even though it is required for motion since before getting moved an animal needs a kind of affirmation or negation. Alexander speaks about animals in general, not human beings specifically, which implies that beasts must possess some kind of cognition, too, analogous to thinking (79.27–80.1). On the basis of representations they may approve or disprove certain kind of reaction. Consequently, it seems that this kind of (dis-)approval is different of human assent, since human assent is about the reliability of representations, not about the reaction to it. The reason is that unlike humans, animals may take the truth value of their representations for granted. They are endowed with a *phantasia* that is devoid of opinion and conviction. It implies that they do not have "assent" (συγκατάθεσις) in the full sense.[43] Assent is distinctively human because it is a kind of "opinion" (δόξα) and always accompanied with "conviction" (πίστις, 67.17–19). By contrast, brute animals lack

42 For an analysis of the whole argument, see Bergeron and Dufour 2008, 371.

43 In *Mantissa* 1, 105.28 assenting is said to belong to the sensitive power, which implies that brutes must have it, see also *On Fate* 14, 183.31, *Questions* 3.13, 107.8. But it cannot be the kind of assent that is called opinion.

opinion and their *phantasia* does not seem to meet Alexander's standards of being up to us. As we have already seen, their assent follows on *phantasia* blindly.[44]

Thus the link between desire and cognition can be made. In *On the Soul* 98.29–99.3, just quoted, Alexander discusses the connection between "rational wish" (τὸ βουλητικόν) on the one hand and "deliberation and calculation" (τὸ βουλευτικὸν καὶ τὸ λογιστικόν) on the other. We do not have to decide – Alexander does not do it himself either – about the precise nature of the connection. The text suggests only that there is a strong parallel between the appearance of conative and cognitive activities. If the conative is there, the cognitive is also there, but we are not told that it applies *vice versa* as well. In order to say more about the connection between cognitive and conative activities we have to have a clear picture about the emergence of rational wish. Fortunately, we have a passage that describes it clearly. It states that rational wish is a desire for the good and is accompanied by judgement and deliberation. It is a rational desire, characteristic to humans only, and it is called rational because it supervenes on the activities of the rational faculty (*On the Soul* 74.6–9). This is how it depends on the rational faculty. The dependence is expressed in terms of persuasion. It is due to such a dependence that it can be persuaded by reason (74.10–11). Furthermore, this is the reason why rational wish can be associated very closely with choice which is called deliberative desire (80.7).[45] Of course, close association ought not to mean identification, for choice seems to be an instantaneous act, whereas rational desire is a state or a lasting activity of the soul. One might guess that the way of explaining the link is to say that choice is a specific act of rational desire. At any rate, perhaps, we are in a position to see how Alexander connects conative and cognitive activities in a way to make room for actions that are up to us.

We can turn to the second question now. How does that affect the development of character? If there is a distinctively human assent which is up to us and it originates from deliberation which is also up to us, then how can we apply the thesis to a description of the character which is supported by and gives rise to a multitude of particular assents? How can we describe the process that leads from a single assent to an accumulation of assents that build up charac-

44 For a short description of the causal chain leading to animal activity, see *On the Soul* 73.20–21.

45 This is a distinctly anti-Aristotelian move, see Bergeron and Dufour 2008, 325. On the broader issue involving the intimate link between choice and rational wish, see Donini 1987, 72–89.

ter? The possibility of extrapolation is supported by a passage in *Mantissa* 23, at 175.23–29:

> ἐφ' ἡμῖν ἂν εἴη καὶ τὸ ποιοῖς γίνεσθαι τὰ ἤθη καὶ τὰς ἕξεις κτήσασθαι, ἀφ' ὧν ἢ τάδε ⟨ἢ τάδε⟩ αἱρησόμεθά τε καὶ πράξομεν.
>
> αἱ δὲ εὐφυΐαι τε πρός τινα καὶ ἀφυΐαι ἔστ' ἂν ἐν τῇ οἰκείᾳ φύσει τηρῶσιν τὸν ἄνθρωπον, πρὸς εὐκολωτέραν ἀνάληψιν τούτων συντελοῦσιν μόνον ἢ χαλεπωτέραν, πρὸς ἃ πεφύκασιν εὖ τε καὶ κακῶς, πᾶσιν γὰρ ἀνθρώποις τοῖς κατὰ φύσιν τε ἔχουσιν καὶ ἀδιαστρόφοις[46] ἐπὶ τὴν κρίσιν τε καὶ τὴν αἵρεσιν δυνατὸν ἀρετὴν κτήσασθαι καὶ δυνατὸν δι' αὑτοῦ.
>
> It will be up to us both to come to be a certain sort of character as well as to acquire the dispositions as a result of which we will choose and do these things or those.
>
> Good and bad natural endowments for certain things, as long as they preserve a person in his own proper nature, contribute only to the easier or more difficult acquisition of the things for which [people] are well or badly endowed by nature. For it is possible for all people who are in a natural state and not perverted in their judgement and choice to acquire virtue, and possible [to do so] through one's own [agency]. (Tr. Sharples, slightly modified)

Again, one may say that Alexander gets support for the claim from the *Nicomachean Ethics*, even if Aristotle's remarks are fairly terse.[47] Alexander's text gives a more detailed explanation. It states that we are responsible for our character because in every ethically important situation we are capable of deliberating about what is to be done. Here we have to remind ourselves that judgement is linked to assent and choice to rational wish. Both assent and rational wish are up to us. It implies that our actions originate in activities or acts in the soul that are up to us. Since assents lead us to actions that – cumulatively – make up our character, we may claim that as the causes of assent, deliberations are responsible for the character we acquire. However, one final distinction can be made between two sorts of deliberation concerning what to do. One sort is deliberation focusing on circumstances; its aim is to survey the actions that circumstances allow. The other sort is not just about circumstances but about the attitudes or traits of the agent as well; its aim is to reflect on such character traits and enable the agent to choose the best option

46 175.28: ἀδιαστρόφοις Rovida, Sharples: ἀστρόφοις v., Bruns.

47 7.1, 1145a15–33; 7.4, 1148b15–1149a20 and, on character development, 3.5.

to improve them. Alexander does not examine the latter type of deliberation directly, but it seems that he is aware of it; in the example of Zopyrus the physiognomist he makes it clear that Socrates had succeeded in overcoming his own nature so as to become a philosopher – his deliberations were made accordingly. The example does not suggest that deliberation is about desire, but rather, that it is about character or a character trait: Socrates aims at acquiring another character. If, however, rational wish is a deliberating and calculating desire, then what happens is that deliberation gives rise to a kind of desire. If, as a result, this desire, the rational wish, supervenes on deliberation which up to us, i.e., it is not determined by the circumstances, then we can see how certain desires are not tied to our natural set-up. In this account, then, we can do the noble thing even if our nature is against it. As mature agents, we are responsible for our dispositions for they are caused and maintained by choices, to some extent at least.[48] Moreover, when someone has reached the state of being wise, this does not mean that the wise person always necessarily acts in the right way. As Alexander notes, just like the gods, a wise person is not tied to such performance. When he has reached the state of being free he is still free to act in one way or another. He may even choose what does not seem to be reasonable.[49] It does not mean necessarily, however, that he does something quite unreasonable. Rather, it may mean only that he does something that is just a bit different from what he is expected to do.[50] He does it in order to display his freedom in action. He can do it since his nature does not bind him in the sense that it would abolish the up-to-us character of his deliberation and assent.

To sum up, my aim was to show that in Alexander's theory of "up to us" epistemology and moral psychology played a highly significant role. The physical or metaphysical conditions are only the most basic prerequisites for free actions. If we want to give a more subtle account of what is up to us we must take into consideration all the cognitive and conative elements, and their connections, that make such actions possible. I also hope to have shown that Alexander's description of the relevant cognitive and conative processes is not just a rehearsal of Aristotle's account and differs considerably from the Stoic position as well.

48 With regard to *On Fate* 27 and *Questions* 4.29, Zingano 2014, 211 pointed out that Alexander is content to show only that dispositions are brought about by some actions, at least that are performed according to a deliberation.

49 *Mantissa* 23, 174.33–35, *On Fate* 29, 199.29–200.5.

50 As has been emphasized by Zingano 2014, 213–4.

Bibliography

Accattino, Paolo, and Pierluigi Donini. 1996. *Alessandro di Afrodisia. L'anima*. Rome: Laterza.

Bergeron, Martin, and Richard Dufour, ed., tr. 2008. *Alexandre d'Aphrodise. De l'âme*. Paris: Vrin.

Bobzien, Susanne. 1998a. *Determinism and Freedom in Stoic Philosophy*. Oxford: Clarendon.

Bobzien, Susanne. 1998b. "The Inadvertent Conception and Late Birth of the Free-Will Problem." *Phronesis* 43: 133–175.

Bonelli, Maddalena. 2013. "Alexandre d'Aphrodise et le destin comme cause productrice." In *Fate, Chance, and Fortune in Ancient Thought*, edited by Francesca Masi and Stefano Maso, 83–101. Amsterdam: Hakkert.

Bonelli, Maddalena. 2014. "Alexandre d'Aphrodise et la cause ποιητική." In *Aitia II. Avec ou sans Aristote. Le débat sur les causes à l'âge hellénistique et impériale*, edited by Carlo Natali and Christina Viano, 119–135. Louvain-la-Neuve: Peeters.

Donini, Pierluigi. 1974. *Tre studi sull' aristotelismo nel secondo secolo d.C.* Turin: Paravia.

Donini, Pierluigi. 1987. "Aristotelismo e indeterminismo in Alessandro di Afrodisia." In *Aristoteles, Werk und Wirkung: Paul Moraux gewidmet*, edited by Jürgen Wiesner, 72–89. Berlin: De Gruyter.

Donini, Pierluigi. 2010. "Alexander's On Fate: Questions of Coherence." In his *Aristotle and Determinism*, 159–176. Louvain-la-Neuve: Peeters.

Fazzo, Silvia. 2017. "Alessandro di Afrodisia e il sistema aristotelico in età imperiale. Stato dell'arte e prospettive di ricerca." In *Studi su ellenismo e filosofia romana*, edited by Francesca Alesse, Arianna Fermani and Stefano Maso, 123–151. Rome: Edizioni di storia e letteratura.

Frede, Michael. 2011. *A Free Will. Origins of the Notion in Ancient Thought*, edited by Anthony A. Long. Berkeley: University of California Press.

Genequand, Charles, ed., tr. 2017. *Alexandre d'Aphrodise. Les principes du tout selon la doctrine d'Aristote*. Paris: Vrin.

Mueller, Ian, and Joshua B. Gould, tr. 1999. *Alexander of Aphrodisias: On Aristotle Prior Analytics 1.8–13*. London: Duckworth.

Natali, Carlo, tr. 1996. *Alessandro di Afrodisia. Il destino*. Milan: Rusconi.

Rashed, Marwan. 2007. *Essentialisme: Alexandre d'Aphrodise entre logique, physique et cosmologie*. Berlin: De Gruyter.

Sharples, Robert W. 1975. "Aristotelian and Stoic Conceptions of Necessity in the *De fato* of Alexander of Aphrodisias." *Phronesis* 20: 247–274.

Sharples, Robert W., ed., tr. 1984. *Alexander of Aphrodisias. On Fate*. London: Duckworth.

Sharples, Robert W., tr. 1994. *Alexander of Aphrodisias. Quaestiones 2.16–3.15*. London: Duckworth.

Sharples, Robert W., tr. 2004. *Alexander of Aphrodisias. Supplement to On the Soul*. London: Duckworth.

Sharples, Robert W., ed. 2008. *Alexandri Aphrodisiensis De anima libri mantissa*. Berlin: De Gruyter.

Sorabji, Richard. 2017. "A Neglected Strategy of the Aristotelian Alexander on Necessity and Responsibility." In *Rereading Ancient Philosophy. Old Chestnuts and Sacred Cows*, edited by Verity Harte and Raphael Woolf, 240–255. Cambridge: Cambridge University Press.

Sorabji, Richard. 2017. "Freedom and Will. Graeco-Roman Origins." In *Selfhood & the Soul. Essays on Ancient Thought and Literature in Honour of Christopher Gill*, edited by Richard Seaford, John B. Wilkins and Matthew Wright, 49–65. Oxford: Oxford University Press.

Thillet, Pierre, ed., tr. 2003. *Alexandre d'Aphrodise. Traité De la providence. Version arabe de Abū Bišr Mattā ibn Yūnus*. Lagrasse: Verdier.

White, Michael J. 1985. *Agency and Integrality. Philosophical Themes in the Ancient Discussions of Determinism and Responsibility*. Dordrecht: Reidel.

Zingano, Marco. 2014. "Alexander and Aristotle on Character and Action." In *What is Up to Us? Studies on Agency and Responsibility in Ancient Philosophy*, edited by Pierre Destrée, Ricardo Salles, and Marco Zingano, 199–220. Sankt Augustin: Academia.

CHAPTER 10

Free Will According to the Gnostics

Aldo Magris

1 A General Survey

We will find nowhere within either the primary or indirect sources related to ancient Gnosticism a systematic inquiry about human free will, such as was available in ancient Greek philosophical literature.[1] As is well known, this problem came up relatively late, at the earliest with certain developments in Greek law in the mid-fourth century and among the Sophists. Homer's characters never ask themselves whether they really are "free" to plan and act on the deeds they have decided to carry out. Also, the word "freedom" (ἐλευθερία) did not yet have that particular meaning in Greek.[2] Aristotle was the first to

1 The word "Gnosticism" is used here as a conventional "label" for the documents produced by a great number of religious groups between the first and fourth centuries which share some common features. Nevertheless, these documents do not possess a set of shared doctrines, as if they were specific variants of one single genre. I addressed the matter in Magris 2011, 13–56, and Magris 2005.

2 A lexicographical clarification may be helpful. In fifth and fourth century BCE Greek, above all in Aristotle's writings, an ἑκούσιος act is carried out "spontaneously" or, more precisely, "on one's own initiative" and is therefore "free", since it is ἐφ' ἡμῖν ("up to us"), especially if it is accompanied by a rationally pondered decision. The philosophers of the Hellenistic schools used different expressions from the ones employed by Aristotle. According to Epicurus (*Letter to Menoeceus* 133), a "free" choice is παρ' ἡμᾶς, "resulting from us" and thus not caused by necessity or chance. The very same term, next to ἐξ ἡμῶν, "on our part", is used by Chrysippus *SVF* 2.998 and 2.999 (from Diogenianus, in Eusebius, *Preparation for the Gospel* 6.8); Cicero, *On Fate* 9 and 41 uses *in nobis, in nostra potestate.* Only in later Stoicism, in Epictetus, can τὸ ἐφ' ἡμῖν be found. Along with the Stoic paradox that the wise man is always "free", even if he should find himself enslaved (*SVF* 1.219, 1.222, 3.362, 3.363, 599 and 3.603), it can be inferred that the originally political meaning of ἐλευθερία gradually extended to the domain of morality; with this meaning the word τὸ ἐλεύθερον is found once in Alexander (*On Fate* 18) and Plotinus (*Enneads* 3.1.8). From the first century CE onwards another term occurs to indicate the faculty of free choice between alternatives. It derived from ἐξουσία, "power" or "permission", "authority" to act as someone wants. In the variant αὐτεξουσία, which referred originally to the condition of an emancipated slave, it means "giving oneself permission" or "having an autonomous power by himself" (not depending on one's master): the term was thus used to designate freedom of choice by Alexander and the Neoplatonists. Its Latin translation in medieval philosophical texts was *liberum arbitrium indifferentiae.* The back-

 | DOI:10.1163/9789004436381_012

define the conditions under which agents ought to be held morally and legally responsible for their actions: it will be that way if they had taken the initiative and were thus capable (or not) of carrying them out, and if they were, of performing them in a particular manner. He also discussed the theoretical and more problematic issue of the agent who could or should *not* have done what he did, or conversely could or should have done what he did not in fact do. Aristotle plays here with a certain ambiguity of the term δύναμις, which could mean both actual operative "power" and abstract – even unrealized – "possibility". Two millennia later, the problem of free will is looked at in the same manner as Aristotle viewed it, even by those who have no familiarity with Aristotle, or never read book 3 of the *Nicomachean Ethics*, where he tackled the problem.

The remarkable absence of the problem in the available Gnostic documents (except for the Valentinians, whom we will discuss later) is due not to a lack of sources, but rather to the fact that the Gnostics had a different approach to the problem. They believed that free will could not be spoken of as an abstract faculty, permanently at the disposal of every man in every circumstance, without taking into account the concrete conditions on the basis of which human actions are performed. These conditions go with the theological and cosmological framework described by the Gnostic myth, which explains how awkward the exercise of an allegedly free Aristotelian "rational potency" – either to do or not to do something – can be.[3] Inasmuch as humans live in an imperfect or even a perverted world, constrained in their submission to nature, wicked demons, astral influences and fate, they can only be released not by their own will alone but by the intervention of an *external*, divine factor dispensing strength and awareness. This does not mean that the Gnostics deny

ground of "lordship" and "being one's own master" in ἐξουσία can also be found in its Semitic equivalents: in the Hebrew *rəšūt* (רְשׁוּת) (from the root רשה, "to allow"), which is used in the Rabbinic literature of the Tannaitic period, and in the Aramaic *ḥe'rūtā'* (from the root ḤRR, "being master"), which can be found in Bardaisan's *Book of the Laws of the Countries*. It is noteworthy that the Greek language, though including the words βούλησις, "will", and βούλευσις, "counsel", "deliberation", never employs – as we have just seen in the expressions τὸ ἐφ' ἡμῖν or τὸ αὐτεξούσιον – derivatives from βούλομαι, with the root WEL, in order to build a signifier for moral freedom analogous to the Germanic forms "freier Wille", "free will" and so on. The judicial terminology too designates a "voluntary" murder as φόνος ἑκούσιος resp. φόνος ἐκ προνοίας. By contrast, in Latin the focus is on the concept of "will": Cicero (*On Fate* 9, 11, 17 and 29) speaks of *libera voluntas* and *motus voluntarii*. In the rare instances in which the topic is addressed in Gnostic documents in either Greek or Coptic, apart from Hermetic writings, τὸ ἐφ' ἡμῖν is never attested and one finds instead τὸ αὐτεξούσιον (Coptic: ⲁⲩⲧⲉⲝⲟⲩⲥⲓⲟⲛ).

3 On the δύναμις μετὰ λόγου see *Metaphysics* 9.2, 1046b2; 9.5, 1048a5; 9.7, 1049a5.

the existence of a free will altogether; on the contrary, they explicitly accepted it in many cases and allowed for it more or less implicitly in others. However, if we look more closely at the Gnostics' account, we will recognize that, according to their point of view, free will – regardless of how we think about it theoretically – is constrained to such extent that human beings by themselves are not able to overcome these limitations.

This paper is aimed at explaining the Gnostics' position by discussing two examples taken from two otherwise different forms of Gnosticism: the first example is found in the *Corpus Hermeticum*, which is influenced by "pagan" Hellenistic philosophy; the second example comes from the *Nag Hammadi Codices*, which have a Judaic and Christian background.

2 The Hermetic Writings

In many treatises of the *Corpus Hermeticum* the philosophical (mainly Platonic and Aristotelian) terminology is recurrent. The faculty of "choosing" (αἱρεῖσθαι) good or evil is "up to us" (ἐφ' ἡμῖν): thus, human beings themselves are "responsible for evil" (αἴτιοι τῶν κακῶν), for the cause of evil in no way should be charged to God, as Plato had stated.[4] But human beings often make unwise or perverted use of this faculty. The woeful outcomes of such bad usage are well deserved on the basis of the *Wenn-Gesetz*, which formed the core of the anti-determinist position of the Middle Platonists: *if* (and only *if*) the individual autonomously chooses a specific course of action, will he then be unable to avoid the consequences established by the laws of fate.[5] In order to carry out good deeds, human beings not only need the faculty of choosing what is "up to us", they need "intelligence" (νοῦς) first of all, which is not a natural feature all possess, but rather a *prize* God grants to those who engage in the moral "struggle" for virtue.[6] However, should free will not be the prerequisite through which man decides whether he is going to act or not, and in

4 *Corpus Hermeticum* 4.4 and 8; *Stobaean Hermetics* 18.3–4. For the thesis that God is the cause of everything, but not of evil, which is caused by man instead, see Plato, *Republic* 2.379b, 380c (cf. 10.617e: αἰτία ἑλομένου θεὸς ἀναίτιος).

5 *Wenn-Gesetz* is the term used by Theiler 1966, 72. For evidence in the Hermetic corpus, see *Stobaean Hermetics* 23.39; *Asclepius* 12. For the evidence outside the Hermetic corpus see further Alcinous, *Didaskalikos* 26, Hippolytus (if he is indeed the author, see Magris 2016a, 9–12), *Refutation of All Heresies* 1.19.19, Ps.-Plutarch, *On Fate* 570A–E, Nemesius, *On the Nature of Man* 38. See also Vimercati's chapter in this volume.

6 *Corpus Hermeticum* 1.22, 4.3–4, 9.5; *Asclepius* 7–9 and 22.

which way, after having evaluated the possible alternatives? No, for the choice the soul is called upon to make is really a single one: the positive decision for "God" or for "piety" (εὐσέβεια), which implies detaching oneself from the material world and body, converting to God, and a steadfast change of life (like the *voluntaria mors* of the protagonist of Apuleius' *Metamorphoses*).[7] This process is carried out within the soul by the *nous* God has granted his chosen ones, and cannot be reduced to a neutral option between equivalent alternatives. In general, the Hermetic concept of moral action is marked by the dualism between sensible and intelligible worlds, between nature and God. Nature is ruled by "fate" (εἱμαρμένη) and nothing escapes it, even though fate – according to Platonic doctrine – is subordinate to "providence" (πρόνοια). Analogously, a human being is "twofold": in his natural dimension, he is subjected to fate, whereas in his noetic dimension alone he is clear of its rule and consequently "free."[8]

Human beings thus appear to be caught in a vicious circle. In order to escape the condition of being subjected to matter, and to the passions consequent on their being corporeal, an act of choice is simply not enough. It too would be a manifestation of the same state of subjection, a sign of mere "desire" that would be inconclusive in itself (here the "unhappy Consciousness" from Hegel's *Phenomenology of Spirit* springs to mind). Rather, what is needed is a *leap* to a different, divine dimension, from which "knowledge" (γνῶσις) is obtained. However, a prerequisite for this very goal is the divine gift of *nous*, otherwise the free will would in and by itself instinctively choose the wrong values connected to the bodily sphere. Choosing goodness, God, and *eusebeia* is the work of *nous*, which provides the soul with *gnōsis*; the choice of evil follows from being subjected to fate. Choosing the "right thing" is possible, pro-

7 *Metamorphoses* 9.21: […] *inferum claustra et salutis tutelam in deae manu posita, ipsamque traditionem ad instar voluntariae mortis et precariae salutis celebrari*. The conception of freedom as a positive and constant decision (rather than as an indifferent possible choice between various alternatives) is Stoic. See Alexander of Aphrodisias, *On Fate* 27–29; cf. Magris 2016b, 447.

8 *Corpus Hermeticum* 1.19, 12.5, 16.16, fr. 16 Nock and Festugière. For the Neoplatonists see Plotinus, *Enneads* 3.1.8, Porphyry in Stobaeus 2.8.11, Amelius in Proclus, *Commentary on Plato's Republic* 2.29 and 276 Kroll, Iamblichus in Stobaeus 1.5.18, 2.8.43, Proclus, *Commentary on Plato's Timaeus* 3.272–277 Diehl. The double nature of man, at the same time subjected to necessity as a natural being and free in his "spiritual" inner life, re-appears to some extent in Kant's distinction between an action's "sensible" and "intelligible character" (Kant 1787, 366–376, Kant 1788, 42, 95, 99). According to Kant, each action considered as a "phenomenon" is the effect of necessary causes operating in nature, while if it is considered as a "noumenon" it depends upon the individual's free will and is therefore liable for ethical evaluation.

vided that the soul gets aid from the divine *nous*; however, it is not something that someone can do at any moment.[9]

The question thus arising is the following: Is there a direct link between man's choice of "piety" and his own ethical behaviour, such that he will be pursuing virtue by exercising free will under the guidance of reason, as understood by Aristotle or Alexander of Aphrodisias? If we analyze the Hermetic texts in depth, this is apparently not the case. Of course, the demand for good conduct is strongly underlined throughout the *Corpus Hermeticum*; nevertheless, the dualistic character of the Hermetic doctrine sets some limits that make the condition of humankind in the world more complicated. *Eusebeia* only provides the soul with *gnōsis*, *i.e.* the capability of understanding what happens to it; but what actually happens is still determined by fate, which rules the whole of life in this world. Therefore, the soul is beyond fate only if it has gained the faculty of intelligence, while as long as the soul stays embodied in a physical person, it is reluctantly involved in the web of causal processes that happen in the actual world, both in nature and in human society.

Particularly interesting here is *Corpus Hermeticum* 12, in which the first part contains a discussion between *Hermes* and his "son" Tat (a Hellenistic version of the ancient Egyptian god Ḏḥoty, who had been cited already by Plato in *Phaedrus* as Theuth) about the link between fate and moral action. Once Tat has understood that everything that happens to beings in the world is due to fate, including human actions and their consequences,[10] he asks why men should undergo punishment for their wicked deeds, such as adultery or

9 A striking similarity with Manichaeism can be discerned here, although it otherwise differs from Hermeticism, both in its origin and contents. Manichaean eschatology is moralistic: salvation only occurs due to the merits a man acquires by observing the precepts of the "Religion of Light." It assumes no individual predestination, only a general predestination, according to which the luminous substance that got lost after the first battle against the forces of darkness will eventually return to its place. The carrying out of the works of Light depends upon someone's interior constitution, *viz.* the presence of a sufficient amount of light substance that allows for making the right choices. Should anyone prove weak in this respect, he will inevitably fall into sin, because the opposing forces of darkness, as they materialize inside the body, will ultimately compromise his freedom of choice (sources in Magris 2001, 153–156). Nevertheless, the slightest glimmer of light would be enough to at least convert a person to Manichaeism on earth, thus earning a better reincarnation during which one will be able to behave better, and ultimately be saved (*Kephalaia* 1.224–232 Böhlig-Polotsky). Augustine condemned the doctrine as too lenient and indulgent towards sinners (*On Two Souls* 10.12–13, *Against Fortunatus* 20, *Against Secundinus* 19). Faustus the Manichaean also included "Hermes Trismegistus" among those who had preceded Mani in offering a similar type of revelation (see Augustine, *Reply to Faustus the Manichaean* 13.1; cf. Lieu 1992, 158).

10 Fate determining both guilt and punishment is a typical Stoic view (see the anecdote Diogenes Laertius 7.23 = SVF 1.298), somehow anticipated in a verse by Aeschylus, *Libation*

homicide, since everything always happens according to fate. Hermes answers that indeed everything happens according to the planning of fate, yet he distinguishes between two groups of human beings. The first group of humans belong completely to the realm of nature: they judge matters from the perspective of the body, they act following bodily instincts or passions and thus deserve punishment. The second group includes the *ellogimoi*, humans whose the souls are endowed with *logos*, which brings them a deeper insight, beyond and independently from fate's activity, of what happens in the world. Although these men can never be wicked, since they possess a divine gift, they are living, however, inside a body that is in relationship to other bodies and to events in the world. They are not only exposed to the universal effects of fate and as such going to suffer negative effects from some external causes, they might also find themselves committing the same bad deeds. "Therefore," Tat asks, "if they are adulterous or assassins, will they not be wicked because of this?" Hermes' reply is disconcerting: "The *ellogimos*, my son, will pay for adultery not as an adulterer, but 'as if' (ὡς) he were an adulterer; he will not pay as a murder, but as if he were a murder. It is impossible to avoid the quality of change (ποιότης μεταβολῆς) or the unfolding (γένεσις) of events; nevertheless, those who possess *nous* flee from wickedness."[11]

This puzzling dialogue seems to imply that from the Hermetic point of view, not even the *ellogimos* is immune to acting badly, due to a series of causes preestablished by fate and irrespective of any criminal intention on his behalf. Guilt seems to be one of the many things that happen on earth, and which are linked to one another by a series of causes and effects that impact the *ellogimos* too.[12] He will surely undergo the consequences of the operations of fate, but this relates to his corporeal reality, not his inner capacity to understand why things happen. In this sense, he appears *as if* he were an adulterer or

Bearers 911. Chrysippus elaborates on the issue his theory of συνειμαρμένον: see Calcidius, *On Plato's Timaeus* 160 (*SVF* 2.943), Cicero, *On Fate* 30 (*SVF* 2.956), Origen, *Against Celsus* 2.20 (*SVF* 2.957).

11 *Corpus Hermeticum* 12.5–8. The final sentence combines terminology that is Stoic (the ποιότητες are the changeable features of a substance) as well as Platonic (the sensible world is γένεσις). The pairing μοιχεύειν-φονεύειν appears in many sources. It might go back to Carneades' criticism of astrological determinism: according to Carneades (see Ps.-Clement of Rome, *Homilies* 4.21 [μοιχεύειν], 10.6 [μοιχεύειν, φονεύειν], *Recognitions* 9.19 [*homicidium, adulterium*]) adultery and murder, due to the widespread frequency thereof, cannot be linked to a specific horoscopic constellation.

12 See *Corpus Hermeticum* 16.11: impiety (ἀσέβεια, cf. 12.3: ἀθεότης) is utter wickedness; men commit all other types of fault by mistake, by temerity, by fatal necessity or by ignorance. According to fr. 11 Nock and Festugière, the soul can scarcely intervene or modify material phenomena, since they are the necessary effect of causes. Thus, it must let nature run its course.

assassin (and he factually *is* such in the sphere of the natural processes that occur among bodies); however, his own consciousness (his νοῦς and/or λόγος) is incorporeal, such that fate holds no power whatsoever over him.[13]

Hermes makes his account even more challenging by citing the well-known phrase "all is one" (ἕν ἐστι τὰ πάντα), used not only by Heraclitus, but also by others.[14] He attributes the phrase to Agathadaimon, the "Good Demon" (according to Hermetic genealogy, the son of Hermes Trismegistus and father of Tat, and the alleged author of a mysterious "book" of wisdom).[15] In this context, the phrase refers to the divine view of worldly things in which human antinomies and contradictions no longer exist. God's mind does not recognize the distinction between good or evil, beautiful or ugly, just or unjust, as *we* usually do. Here another phrase by Heraclitus may be recalled: "For the god, all things are beautiful, just and good, while for human beings some are unjust, others just."[16] Therefore, "all is one" means that everything belongs to a plan that fate has arranged; fate is not a blind force, however, but the executor of divine providence, in which all things the human mind deems either good or bad, beautiful or ugly, just or unjust, have from the divine perspective but one single, positive meaning. God is beyond good or evil, at least in the sense that human beings are used to understand "good" and "evil". Ultimately, Hermetic *gnōsis* does not stand for immoralism, but rather for a sane relativization of all socially acquired values.

---

13 I am not convinced by Scott's interpretation (1925, 347). According to Scott, this passage only refers to the punishment of alleged crimes, which have not been actually committed by the ἐλλόγιμος; so it is "as if" he were an adulterer merely because public opinion deems him in such way, taking into account the sentence imposed on him. The sentence, however, was unjust, since the ἐλλόγιμος never committed any adultery, and was thus not an adulterer at all. I find Scott's amendment ὡς ⟨ὁ⟩ μοιχεύσας, "as (it would appear to be) *the* (real) adulterer (meant of course as a different person)", quite tendentious. The explanation would be trivial. If it were a simple judicial mistake that imposes a sanction on an innocent man (something that could affect anyone, not just the ἐλλόγιμος), and if he were just a rational human being accepting his own fate, since it only strikes his body, it is not clear why treatise 12 offers a cryptic argument against common sense, and also why another text (*Stobaean Hermetics* 11.5) recommends not sharing the Hermetic conception of fate with unlearned people, because they could use it as a pretext to indulge in wickedness. The source evidently alludes to the pains the righteous human being suffers due to undeserved punishment, but also to the illicit acts he could have been the author of, in a world in which each human deed is governed by fate.

14 ἕν ἐστι τὰ πάντα: 12.8. ἕν πάντα εἶναι: Hippolytus, *Refutation of All Heresies* 9.9 (= Heraclitus, fr. 50 DK, D46 LM); ἓν εἶναι τὰ πάντα: Plato, *Parmenides* 128a–b; ἓν πάντα εἶναι: Plato, *Theaetetus* 180e; ἓν τὸ πᾶν: Plato, *Sophist* 244b; ἓν τὰ πάντα: Aristotle, *Physics* 1.2, 185a22.

15 On this genealogy (not in the *Corpus Hermeticum*), see Syncellus, *Chronography* 72 (Mosshammer 1984, 41). The *agathos daimōn* receives also many other designations.

16 Fr. 102 DK, D67 LM (= Porpyhry, *Commentary on the Iliad* 4.4, 69.5–7 Schrader).

3 The Sethite-Barbeloite Writings

A similar ambivalence comes out in the Gnostic literature with a Judaic and Christian background. Here we must bear in mind that neither Judaism nor Christianity had been holding an unequivocal position on whether free will is the overall principle of actions and events, in the rare instances in which the issue is touched on, because God's omnipotence must take absolute priority. As for Gnosticism, the answer largely depends on the type of sect or on the type of document. In the first place, an emphasis on free will appears in rather popular documents aimed at a mainly Christian audience, which are thus compatible with the teachings of the Church. An example is the Acts of Thomas (second-third centuries), a treatise that claims to be Christian, but in fact contains fundamental Gnostic themes (see the *Hymn to the Pearl* in particular). Here an explanation of the problem of evil is given that could fit Christian doctrine perfectly: God has created man in his image, therefore man is free; yet, he made incorrect use of his free will and thus fell into sin. Therefore, God himself had to intervene by sending his own Son, Jesus Christ the Saviour, in order to make repentance possible for those who believe in his Word.[17] Another example is Bardaisan of Edessa (third century), a Christian author, who nevertheless gave his theological views a "mythological" form with a markedly Gnostic flavour. Fiercely arguing against astrological fatalism, he wrote a treatise in Greek, which was entitled *Against* (or *On*) *Fate*. It also survived in a Syriac version under the title *The Book of the Laws of the Countries*. Bardaisan stresses the importance of free will (*ḥeʾrūtā*', literally the "mastery ⟨of one's own actions⟩"), and challenges the "Chaldean" astrologers with well-known arguments of social and ethical relevance, which had been developed earlier by the Academic philosopher Carneades.[18]

---

17 Acts of Thomas 34. The relevant passage only appears in the Syriac version of the Acts (Wright 1871, vol. 1, 201, vol. 2, 174 ("free will"), and Klijn 2003, 98); the Greek version (Tischendorf 1903) omitted it. That God's "image" in man (Genesis 1.26) refers to his rationality and moral freedom rather than to his physical aspect (but instead, for God's nearly human appearance see Exodus 33.23 and Ezekiel 1.26) is made clear by Philo, *On the Creation of the World* 69, by the Rabbinic tradition following R. 'Aqibā' in his polemic with R. Pappus (*Bərešit rabbah* 21.5, in Freedman-Simon 1961, vol. 1, 174–175; cf. Jervell 1960, 72–92), and by the Church Fathers: Irenaeus, *Against Heresies* 4.4.3, and Tertullian, *On the Soul* 21.

18 Ramelli 2009, 140–142, 152–156. A long section (176–190) is devoted to the laws and customs of different peoples, going back to Carneades' inquiry into the νόμιμα βαρβαρικά; see further Amand 1945, 55–60. Carneades had maintained that these "legislations" (hence the Syriac title of Bardaisan's book) could not be deduced in general from astral influences, since the horoscopes of the single individuals that make up a people are simply

Secondly, in those Gnostic texts I characterised as – in a specific meaning – "Judaeo-Christian",[19] free will is implicitly presupposed everywhere the sources lay stress on the moral education in which the Gnostic is engaged,[20] or on the appeal (followed by an oath) to change one's life, to live "according to the Law", to flee, like the ancient Jews,[21] from the "land of Egypt" – metaphorically understood as the world of corporeal existence –, and to follow the example of the moral "athlete" Thomas, who fought in the "arena" of life (ἀγών) against the demonic cosmic powers.[22] In general, faith in the Gnostic sense is act of choice that in and of itself is subjective and plainly free.[23] This, however, does not mean that the Gnostics considered free will as an absolute starting point of action, as Aristotle did, or that it operated unconditionally. Rather, the vast majority of Gnostic texts (not just the Judaeo-Christian ones) make clear that free will is heavily impaired, or even paralysed, by the malicious activity of cosmic powers. These powers, called "archons", create and govern the physical world, and impose themselves upon all things, including incarnate souls, the domination of fate, from which no one can escape.[24] This conception of fate is different from that of the Stoics (with the exception of the *Corpus Hermeticum*, which conceives it, in the Stoic manner, as a web of causes and effects) or Platonists: here it has a special, astrological sense. The dwelling place of the archons is the circle of the Zodiac; from there they exercise their influence not only over bodily matter, but also over the psychic-cognitive processes

too different from one to another. See Amand 1945, 250–252, 318–325. This section is also taken up in Ps.-Clement of Rome, *Recognitions* 9.19–29. The Pseudo-Clementine works, which along with the *Recognitions* also include the *Homilies* (see Rehm 1969 and Rehm 1953), should be placed in a Judeo-Christian context. Even though they pleaded against Gnosticism (their topic was the apostle Peter's dispute vs. the chief heretic Simon the Magician), they still contain many Gnostic elements, such as dualism and the incarnation of the "Spirit of Truth" in various figures (derived from Judaic apocalyptic texts), with Jesus as the final one. They, too, accept free will: *Homilies* 2.15, 11.8, 20.3 and 10 (αὐτεξούσιον), *Recognitions* 1.27, 3.20, 4.19, 8.51 (*arbitrium*); in *Recognitions* 3.21–25 Carneades' full argumentation is set out.

19 Magris 2016a, 369.

20 Hippolytus, *Refutation of All Heresies* 6.9.6, 6.12.4 and 6.14.6 (Simonians).

21 Hippolytus, *Refutation of All Heresies* 5.7.40 (Naassenes), 5.7.27 (Justin), 9.14.1 (Elcasaites).

22 *Book of Thomas, Nag Hammadi Codices* 2.7; *Authoritative Teaching, Nag Hammadi Codices* 6.3, 26. The theme of the "athlete" belongs to Hellenistic Judaism; see Book of Wisdom 4.2.

23 *Secret Book of James, Nag Hammadi Codices* 1.2, 13–14; *Resurrection, Nag Hammadi Codices* 1.4, 46.

24 Hippolytus, *Refutation of All Heresies* 5.7.6 (Naassenes), 13.12, 16.1, and 17.6 (Perates); Origen, *Against Celsus* 6.24–28 (Ophites); *Paraphrase of Shem, Nag Hammadi Codices* 7.1, 27.

of human beings.[25] Another condition that impairs free will is the state of the mixture of the soul with matter in the world, which results in weakening the soul's capability to manage itself.[26]

This *mixture* is the very topic of the *Secret Book of John*, the most important of the Christian-oriented texts of the Nag Hammadi Library, which belongs to the kind of Gnosticism I have called "Sethite-Barbeloite" (and which should be distinguished from the Judaeo-Christian kind).[27] The *Secret Book* is a long dialogue between the Apostle John and the resurrected Jesus, who begins by outlining the protology, *i.e.* the narration of the origin of universe. Firstly, the "Father" is mentioned, who transcends all being and divinity as an infinite abyss of light. By reflecting himself in the primordial bright "waters", He emanates *Barbēlō* (the "Fourness")[28] that is the virginal "Spirit" (πνεῦμα) becoming in turn the "Mother" of the "Son" (the eternal Christ), accompanied by twelve "eons" (Seth among them), which are as many images of his spiritual properties. Jesus' exposition goes on to describe the "sin" of the twelfth eon, *Sophia*: in her vain pretense to imitate the Father's creative power she gives birth – in the darkness outside the divine sphere – to a miscarriage, a monster named *Yaltabaoth* (a negative caricature of the biblical Yahweh). The monster exploits the energy of the *pneuma* he took from his Mother in order create of the lower natural cosmos. His lordship over Nature is supported by a retinue of executives, composed of twelve dangerous powers (the zodiacal constellations) and seven malevolent "archons" (the planets), having a clear astrological function. Eventually, Yaltabaoth creates Adam and Eve and forces them to be his servants, forbidding them to eat from the tree of knowledge (an obvious allusion to the Genesis tale), so that they shall never be aware of their situation. Sophia, however, induces her wicked son to blow into Adam the *pneuma* he had earlier taken, and then gives Adam advice to eat the forbidden fruit of *gnōsis*; in this way, the primeval man is able to rise above his "creator", and mankind descended from Adam will reach salvation, chiefly through Jesus Christ's historical coming and teachings.

The protology is followed by the question that John puts to Jesus in final pages of the *Secret Book of John*. How will human souls now be able to overcome the forces of evil in this world where they find themselves embodied,

25 See *Origin of the World, Nag Hammadi Codices* 2.5, 107 and 117. In the Greek sources εἱμαρμένη is used, in the Coptic texts ϩιμαρμενη, an exact duplication of the Greek word.

26 See Hippolytus, *Refutation of All Heresies* 5.7.7 (Naassenes), 5.8.10–11 (Docetes). For the doctrine among the Manicheans: see *Kephalaia* 2.262 Böhlig-Polotsky, Augustine, *Against Secundinus* 2, and *Licht-Nous* 9 (Sundermann 1992, 63).

27 Magris 2011, 45.

28 From Hebrew *bə-'arbā' 'elōah*, "In-the-Fourness-⟨is⟩-God" (with reference to Ezekiel 1.5).

and ascend again to the spiritual realm of the Father?[29] Jesus replies that the main obstacle to salvation lies in the fact that the archons, in order not to let Adam easily escape their control by listening to the Gnostic revelation about the origin of evil (brought to him by Sophia, and later to the entire human race by Jesus Christ himself), infuses a second spirit inside him. This is the so-called "counterfeit spirit" (ἀντίμιμον πνεῦμα), consisting in sexual desire. Sexuality apparently "imitates" the spiritual generative process that had been unfolding among the eons, whereas in fact it does the very opposite. Rather than true life, sexual intercourse brings about a reiteration of death, in the sense that every sexually reproduced living being will die someday, and then he will be reincarnated in order to die again, remaining enslaved to the cosmic powers in all these ephemeral existences. The power of the "counterfeited" *pneuma* is strong enough to obstruct the development and efficacy of the true *pneuma*, and to impede any access to *gnōsis*.

In this state of affairs, the right choice aiming at salvation should not be simplified as if it were an abstract option enabled by free will, because it depends above all on the presence of true *pneuma*, the "spirit of life", and subsequently on the relative doses of both spirits – the true and the counterfeited – inside each single person. The people into whom the spirit of life has "descended" in larger amounts will surely obtain sufficient strength to abstain from wickedness and corruption, and they will maintain firmly the sole purpose of returning to the incorruptible "location", whence the spirit originated, because only there can they obtain eternal life. Those people who instead possess a preponderant "counterfeit *pneuma*" will not be saved, unless they undergo a series of reincarnations. In Gnostic thought, reincarnation is on the one hand a perverse mechanism that is managed by the archons such that the divine *pneuma* is recycled and left in their own possession and is unable to go back to the Father's realm. On the other hand, it is also a sort of "therapeutic" device, in the sense that the souls, in their successive existences, could be given the opportunity to change the balance of forces in their interior between the two opposed spirits, in favour of the good one. Thus, after a few rounds of incarnations, the soul might be able to save itself, once it has gradually obtained a sufficient dose of divine *pneuma* to allow it to join the Gnostic sect, and follow its message. The worst state will fall to those who at first belonged to the sect but then moved away from it: these defectors "from the spirit" will not be offered forgiveness and face eternal damnation.[30]

29 For the following, see the *Secret Book of John*, *Nag Hammadi Codices* 2.1, 25–28.

30 The Dead Sea Scrolls testify to a somewhat similar doctrine. In these texts, God lets two "spirits" (*rūḥōt*) operate in the world, one of truth and the other of iniquity. God has also

One can easily see that – according to the Gnostics – the decisive factor in human behavior is always the *pneuma* (whether authentic or false), which is neither human nor natural, but something received from outside. Thus, free will – apparently never mentioned – looks like a marginal factor, though not completely irrelevant (it is still needed in order to *choose* to become a Gnostic sectarian). What does seem irrelevant for salvation, however, is moral conduct.[31] Regardless of how many virtuous actions an individual carries out, this does not guarantee redemption for him, since salvation is predestined exclusively for the "Sons of Light" who received the true living spirit. This poses the problem of the relation between free will on the one hand and predestination on the other.

Some Gnostic sources actually deal with predestination; in others it does not appear to play a role at all. One might infer that in the accounts in which predestination is absent, free will should be the decisive means through which redemption can be obtained, while in the texts that deal with predestination a truly free will cannot exist. In fact, this is not the case, since free will – in general – is *not* the opposite of predestination. Let us consider for instance the Judaic sect, in which the Dead Sea Scrolls were written. In that case, as well, the basic principle is that "all things and events coming about"[32] belong to God's "plan", and therefore the actions of each human being are already "known" to Him, before he was born or before everything was created.[33] Even though nothing can happen from man's free initiative alone, the *Rule of the Covenant* nevertheless stresses the subjective "willingness" and the moral commitment to strict observance of the precepts of the Mosaic Law. Half a millennium later Augustine, a defender of divine predestination, took care not to deny the existence of free will, apart from stating that free will cannot direct itself towards the good except with the help of divine grace; left "alone", it would only make bad choices. The Gnostic texts almost never mention free will and in any case regard it as a secondary factor, whether predestination is admitted or not. And why – contrary to Aristotle's view – is free will not the *absolute beginning* of choices and actions? Because they maintain that the only fundamental

predestined each human being to be allotted to the former or the latter, see 1QS (*Discoveries in the Judean Desert* 1) 3.15–25; however, each human being is said to possess a certain "part" (*gōral*) of *both* spirits, housed within himself in a smaller or larger quantity. The quantification of someone's *gōral* was recognised by means of an astrological calculation, see 4Q186 (*Discoveries in the Judean Desert* 5) fr. 2, 2.7–8.

31 See *Pistis Sophia* 111–116 and 131–132.

32 See 1QS (*Discoveries in the Judean Desert* 1) 3.15: "All that is and happens" (*kōl hōyeh wənihyyeh*, כול הויה ונהייה), which corresponds to the Greek: τὰ ὄντα πάντα καὶ γινόμενα.

33 1QH[a]1 (*Discoveries in the Judean Desert* 1) 9.7; 1QH[a]23 20.9–11; *Cairo Damascus Document* 2.6–13; 1Q402 (*Discoveries in the Judean Desert* 11) fr. 4.12–15.

choice to be made is the choice of the Gnostic message of salvation. The very act of making that choice shows that the choosing person has *already been chosen*, since the highest God "knows his chosen ones by name."[34] But if a *definite* number of people, and clearly not mankind in its entirety, are "known" by God as predestined, there also need to be those that are "not-known" and "not-predestined". Human beings are *not* equal, even though they might appear so from the outside. They are either the "Sons of Light", the "Sons of Seth": the chosen ones who are guided by the spirit – basically, the members of the Gnostic sect – or the others, the "Devil's Sons", the "Seed of darkness", whose existence is a mere worldly phenomenon produced by nature and subject to cosmic fate.

4 Free Will in Valentinian Eschatology

The Gnostic doctrine formulated by Valentinus in the mid-second century is a unique instance among the sources, where the philosophical concept of free will intertwines with the theological concept of predestination. The Valentinian doctrine, in the version attributed to Ptolemy (one of Valentinus' pupils) was, in its general frame, similar to that of the *Secret Book of John*. However, the fall of Sophia, the last of the thirty "eons" generated by the "Abyss" of Light, who all together shape the *plērōma* (the "Fullness" of the divine world), is explained through abstract concepts rather than by a mythical tale. Sophia does not embark on a reckless adventure in darkness; rather, she fails in her attempt to fully comprehend the nature of the Father and ends up wandering outside the Pleroma. Her "wandering" without real direction (πλάνη) marks out a space, in which feelings of anguish and regret for her failings objectivize themselves into the two "entities" or substances (οὐσίαι), which make up the lower cosmos: anguish becomes the "material" (ὑλική) substance,[35] while regret generates the "psychic" (ψυχική) substance, the latter in the double sense of biological life and ethical consciousness.[36] Psychic substance as a whole is

34 *Gospel of Truth, Nag Hammadi Codices* 1.3, 21; *Tripartite Tractate, Nag Hammadi Codices* 1.15, 126–127; *Gospel of Thomas, Nag Hammadi Codices* 2.2, 32 and 36; *Gospel of Philip, Nag Hammadi Codices* 2.3, 64; *Pistis Sophia* 7; *Corpus Hermeticum* 10.15.

35 While the concept of οὐσία as an individual entity is Aristotelian, the concept of *ousia* as a general "substrate" of corporeal entities (or "matter") is Stoic (see *SVF* 2.369–404).

36 The adjective ψυχικός has nothing to do with the root of modern terms psychology, psychoanalysis, psychopathic and so on. In the early Christian and Gnostic language, it is the rendering of the Hebrew word *nefeš* which means the life energy of every living being, in

represented by, and subordinated to a personified character, that bears the Platonic name of "Demiurge": he produces the framework of the natural cosmos. The Demiurge is not a monster like Yaltabaoth, but rather a minor God with rational and moral qualities (a positive yet still imperfect caricature of Yahweh). The Demiurge then fashions in his own image the primeval man (Adam), who is both "material" (since he is made of matter) and "psychic" (since he lives and is a moral being). But Sophia supplies Adam in addition with the gift of the divine *pneuma*, by which he becomes a real member of the pleromatic "family", while the Demiurge, who is devoid of *pneuma*, has no control over him anymore.[37] However, these three elements of Adam's personality – the material, the psychic and the pneumatical – are distributed differently in his three sons. In Cain the material element prevails (even though he also obtained a "soul"); in Abel the psychic-moral element is stronger (though he still has bodily substance), whereas Seth alone is *also* the heir of the pneumatical "seed". From them three "classes" (γένη) of men are derived, each with a different "nature" (φύσις) that corresponds to whichever element prevails over the others, thus bringing about different ways of life and different eschatological destinies.[38]

In short: the lower world consists of *two* substances: bodily mass and life/consciousness. One is material, the other is psychic; or one is external and the other is internal. Yet human beings are made up of *three* elements: the first two – *to hulikon* and *to psuchikon* – correspond to the two general *ousiai* and both are managed by the Demiurge. The third – *to pneumatikon* – bears no relation to the worldly *ousiai*, since it is the spirit of the Pleroma granted by Sophia: it cannot enter all human beings, but only Seth's descendants.[39] In relation to human beings, the two worldly elements and the heterogeneous pleromatic element come into being as three different "natures" (*phuseis*). But what does "nature" mean in this context? In Valentinian doctrine *phusis* is

particular the man created by God (cf. ψυχὴ ζῶσα in the *Septuagint* at Genesis 2.7, and 1 Corinthians 15.45). In the Gnostic, mainly Valentinian, usage ψυχικός alludes also to the fitness for moral behaviour.

37 Irenaeus, *Against Heresies* 1.1–5, Hippolytus, *Refutation of All Heresies* 6.29–35, Clement of Alexandria, *Excerpts from Theodotus* 45–48. The objectivation of ⲡⲗⲁⲛⲏ is described in the *Gospel of Truth*, *Nag Hammadi Codices* 1.3, 17 and 29.

38 Irenaeus, *Against Heresies* 1.5.5, 1.7.5, 1.8.3, Clement of Alexandria, *Excerpts from Theodotus* 53–54; cf. *Tripartite Tractate*, *Nag Hammadi Codices* 1.5, 96–98; *Gospel of Philip*, *Nag Hammadi Codices* 2.3, 75. See Magris 1999 for further details and for variants in other sources not inspired by Ptolemy (Clement of Alexandria, *Excerpts from Theodotus* 50–53, Hippolytus, *Refutation of All Heresies* 7.34, together with Valentinus, fr. 2 Förster), where the heterogeneity between hylic-psychic and pneumatic elements is reaffirmed.

39 Irenaeus, *Against Heresies* 1.5.1 and 1.6.1.

spoken of only in relation to human beings; therefore, it designates neither a physical object, nor the sum of all physical objects. In general, "nature" is not some kind of *being*, but rather a *way of being*, the existential condition of an individual who is dealing with his own reality and its constitutive "elements." Other individuals similar to him can also share it: they thus become a *genos*.[40] Adam's descendants are all *hulikoi* and *psuchikoi*, but in different ways. In Cain's *genos*, the hylical element prevails, in the sense that what matters for them are the mundane needs. In Abel's line of descent, the "interior" prevails: for them, morality is important, such that the "hylical" element is only a covering (a "body") for its real "psychic" Self. The sons of Seth are on the contrary the "chosen seed": even though they are both *hulikoi* and *psuchikoi* as worldly beings, they identify their Self with the pneumatical element: they are heading towards the divine spirit, their *phusis* is pneumatical.[41]

Since eschatological destiny prescribes that everyone should return to his own "place" according to his "nature",[42] free will does not have an active role to play either in the hylic man or in the pneumatic man. Firstly, even though he exercises his own free choice concerning the objects in the sensible world, the *hulikos* man has no higher point of reference he could turn to, and therefore his freedom is only apparent and eventually useless for his redemption.

40 The Valentinian understanding of "nature" partly resembles the Stoic notion of οἰκεῖα φύσις (see Alexander of Aphrodisias, *On Fate* 13, 181.13 Bruns = *SVF* 2.979; cf. Magris 2016b, 230–235). It is however different, in the sense that the Valentinians conceive it (in the case of the hylic, or conversely of the pneumatic, *genos*) as a *fixed* matter of fact based on the prevalence of a determined element; according to the Stoics, instead, "own nature" signifies a balance of power among various impulses within the individual in its actual arrangement, that can anyway be *modified* (getting better or worse) through moral commitment and/or exercise, cf. Magris 2016b, 232–234.

41 Of course, the reference to the triad of Adam's sons is merely symbolic and cannot be intended literally in a genetic meaning. Since the deluge wiped out the entire offspring of both Cain and Abel, all existing humans up to today come from Seth, because Noah was Seth's descendant. Therefore, eight billion living humans now are equally "Sethites" and the same applies to the age, too, when the Gnostic movement was active: everyone should be, as such, consequently a *pneumatikos*, and no *psuchikos* or *hulikos* should exist in this world anymore. The inconsistency may be overcome by thinking that the Gnostic "Seth" is not the supposedly historical person mentioned in the Bible but the namesake of a pleromatic entity generated by Barbelo, in a way an *alter ego* of the pleromatic Christ. He was thought to be ideally the progenitor of all members of the Gnostic sect, who were in this sense all "Sons of Seth."

42 A recurring Gnostic theme: *Gospel of Thomas, Nag Hammadi Codices* 2.2, 41; *Origin of the World, Nag Hammadi Codices* 2.5, 127; *Revelation of Paul, Nag Hammadi Codices* 5.1, 23; *Revelation of Peter, Nag Hammadi Codices* 7.3, 75; Hippolytus, *Refutation of All Heresies* 5.8.12, 21.8; *Stobaean Hermetics* 25.5; *Pistis Sophia* 90; Clement of Alexandria, *Miscellanies* 3.1.3, 4.13.89. In Hebrew "place" (*maqōm*, מָקוֹם) is a byword for "God".

Upon his death, both his body and his soul will come back to nature and dissolve, since he was not really a Self, but only a mass of worldly components. Secondly, the *pneumatic* man is by nature reserved for the spirit's dwelling-place and has no need to make a choice regarding this. When he abandons his body at death, his soul will dwell together with Sophia in the "Ogdoade", a celestial area just below the Pleroma. With regard to the *psuchikos* human, the case is different. He does possess an efficacious "free will" (αὐτεξούσιον) through the exercise of which he can either disappear like the hylics or live again in a so-called "intermediate Region" below the Ogdoade together with his Lord, the Demiurge (who, in the meantime, has been "converted" to the Gospel by Sophia and hence "saved"). Disappearing or living again will happen according to his "inclination" (πρόσκλισις) towards either good or evil, and the subsequent "choice" (αἵρεσις) for either the good or evil.[43] On the Day of Reckoning, the Demiurge and the *psuchikoi* will be lifted up from the "intermediate Region" to the "Ogdoade" above, while the pneumatics, by abandoning in the Ogdoade their psychical component (and thus their personal human identity), will enter the Pleroma shaped as pure spiritual entities together with Sophia.[44]

Some scholars have judged the Valentinian doctrine of "salvation by nature" (as the ecclesiastical heresiologists call it) to be a falsification that would have been introduced for polemical aims. In the vision of these scholars, salvation or damnation would rather depend upon free will alone, inasmuch as human beings are *all* equally *psuchikoi* by nature, but can become *hulikoi* or *pneumatikoi* based on the choice they make.[45] As for myself, apart from the fact that the ancient sources mention *three existing natures* in Adam's sons, and not just one for all (the other two natures being merely optional),[46] I believe such an interpretation to be unsound, as it is based on a misunderstanding of the Valentinian concept of nature. Valentinian *phusis* does not refer to the objective constitution of man in general; rather, it refers, on a *subjective* level, to the result of the *proportion* of the elements, where one element can prevail

43 Irenaeus, *Against Heresies* 1.6.1, Clement of Alexandria, *Excerpts from Theodotus* 56. The term ἐκλογή for "choice" is rare. See Basilides in Clement of Alexandria, *Miscellanies* 2.10.3, who described it nevertheless as *inferior* to πίστις. More often, its meaning is that God chooses and predestines the "nature" of the chosen ones (ἔμφυτος ἐκλογή: Clement of Alexandria, *Miscellanies* 3.3.3; σπέρμα ἐκλογῆς: Irenaeus, *Against Heresies* 1.6.4, Clement of Alexandria, *Excerpts from Theodotus* 39).

44 Irenaeus, *Against Heresies* 1.7.5, Clement of Alexandria, *Excerpts from Theodotus* 63–64.

45 The thesis was upheld by L. Schottroff, a pupil of Bultmann, and accepted by B. Aland, H. Langerbeck, S. Petrément, and more recently in the USA by M.A. Williams and E. Pagels. See also Chiapparini 2012, 375–377, who offers an excellent overview of the scholarship.

46 Clement of Alexandria, *Excerpts from Theodotus* 54.

over the other. Free will actually exists in everyone, but it is not the decisive factor. In the *hulikoi*, it is already evil-oriented, mostly unfit to bring about good actions, but above all it lacks the indispensable "element" that allows men to reach, and take part in, the Pleroma. In the *pneumatikoi* it is, on the contrary, already oriented towards the Pleroma, to which the corresponding element present in them has to come back. "Nature" is what each one *is* with reference to his primary *genos*. Anyone who belongs to one of the three classes of course exercises some "choice", but his choice necessarily conforms to the basic structure, in which one element is more or less prevailing. The man's subjective – in a sense, instinctive – attachment to one of the three *phuseis*, and the presence of that single prevailing element in him are two inseparable aspects of the same thing.

The introduction of an intermediate class of *psuchikoi* between the two original classes of elected and lost humans was probably due to a need to clarify the relationship with the Great Church from which the Gnostic sect had been recruiting a major part of its followers. It was hence necessary to give "normal" Christians a higher moral status than others have, while firmly maintaining that only the chosen are predestined to achieve the highest form of salvation.[47] That in relation to the *psuchikoi* a type of free will is admitted, which enables them to make a choice between different outcomes – comparable to Aristotle's "rational potency" – should not be overestimated in any case. After all, the *psuchikoi* have the same constitution as the *hulikoi* (two worldly "substances" and two "elements"), but whereas in the *hulikoi* the material element prevails, rather than the psychic, in the *psuchikoi* the psychic prevails and also switches to its "moral" side. Therefore, in both classes, choices "tend" to the element that is predominant, thus determining the nature of the class. In some *psuchikoi* (but not in the *hulikoi*) the two elements are almost equal, so that they will be able to "incline" indifferently towards either bodily/material or ethical values. This does not mean that – in the former case – the *psuchikoi* can change class and become "material human beings", viz. *hulikoi*. The sources clearly state that even though they are different due to the amount of the hylical, or conversely of the psychic, "element" they have, the ugly *psuchikoi* get only *associated* with the fate of the other class as a consequence of their materialistic choices. Such an option would be theoretically "unnatural" for them (although not impossible), but quite normal or even inevitable for the real *hulikoi*. On the other hand, the *psuchikoi* can never tend

47 For the *psuchikoi* as the "normal" Christians see Irenaeus, *Against Heresies* 1.6.2. Hippolytus, *Refutation of All Heresies* 5.6.7, attributes the threefold division also to the Naassenes.

towards the pneumatical element, for the simple reason that they do not possess it, nor can they bring it about through an act of good will. Hence, they by no means *become* "spiritual human beings", except perhaps in the case of a Christian joining the Gnostic sect, but even then, this only shows that behind the Christian's appearance as "psychic" he already was endowed with a pneumatic nature.

The destruction of the *hulikoi* is somewhat automatic and inevitable, whereas salvation is never so for the other two classes; not for the *psuchikoi*, who must always persevere in their commitment to morality, and not for the *pneumatikoi*, whose nature will not allow them to enter the Pleroma automatically, even if they were doing nothing. Just like fate as understood by the Stoics, so predestination in a Gnostic sense is not affected by the *argos logos*.[48] On the contrary, those who already have *pneuma* nevertheless need a "formation" (*morphōsis*) during their life on earth, so that the moral element they possess can be strengthened, and the contents of revelation enhanced. In view of this goal, they will gladly live among the *psuchikoi* in the Church, and attend public worship together with them.[49] Clearly, the willingness to undergo such a formation and to exhibit exemplary moral conduct presupposes in the agent some exercise of free choice.

At any rate, the Valentinian doctrine of three separate and inflexible "natures" shows beyond the shadow of a doubt that those who belong to the three classes face *different* eschatological ends. In the case of damnation, the end is the same for the inferior two classes, not because all *psuchikoi* who have "inclined" towards evil now change into *hulikoi*, but because they have come to share the fate of the latter, even though remaining different. On the other hand, in the case of salvation for the *psuchikoi* and *pneumatikoi*, different levels of blessedness are distinguished, which have no other explanation than the heterogeneity of the classes involved. If the level of blessedness were due only to free will – in fact to a choice for conversion – why should not the Demiurge and the good *psuchikoi*, insofar they have converted to the Gospel, be found worthy to enter the Pleroma like the "spiritual" Gnostics and remain there forever, not in the Ogdoade? After all, they were just meant to *become* pneumatic themselves! Yet this does not happen anyway. Moreover, assuming that in all human beings the free capacity exists to opt indifferently for one or another alternative, why do the sources never so much as hint at the possibility that

48 Cicero, *On Fate* 12–13.

49 Clement of Alexandria, *Excerpts from Theodotus* 21; *Gospel of Philip*, *Nag Hammadi Codices* 2.3, 76; Heracleon in Origen, *Commentary on the Gospel of John* 13.20; cf. Thomassen 1997, 260–262.

a *hulikos* – possessing psychic consciousness himself – could freely abandon his materialistic way of life, and adopt moral behaviour instead? Alternatively, why could not a *pneumatikos* – out of bad use of his own freedom – descend to a lower class?[50]

This moralistic interpretation of Valentinian eschatology defended by a group of distinguished scholars must be rejected. I deem that there is at the root of the problem a misguided understanding of the eschatology, bound, as it were, to an opposition between "determinism" and free will. Thus, in order to get rid of determinism, these scholars stress the universal relevance of free will. Indeed, the Gnostic conception never rules out the performative function of the free will. All human beings have it; even the eons, according to the Valentinians, are possessed of an *autexousion* that makes them responsible for their behaviour, for example Sophia's sin.[51] Nevertheless, the idea of a predestined salvation or destruction according to one's "nature" (which has nothing to do with a "determinism" grounded on the physical principle of causality) remains central, since it refers to a higher order of things, which is for Gnostic thought a matter of revelation rather than of philosophical inquiry. Only from the point of view of this higher order, can one understand why a human being is what he is, and why he possesses the specific nature explaining the manner and purpose of his free choices.

By the way, it is important to note in this context that we have to distinguish clearly between the *philosophical debate* over free will and fate, and the *theological debate* over free will and predestination. In philosophy, the discussion is about the flow of worldly events and their causal nexus; in theology, the discussion is eschatological, which implies, in Gnostic thought, the image of "returning" to one's naturally assigned otherworldly "location." Moreover, we can discern a certain parallel between the two different issues, i.e. about fate and about predestination. Like the Stoics, who considered *chance*, rather than free will, to be the opposite of fate, so the Gnostics considered a pretended self-redemption by one's own means alone, rather than the function of free will as such, to be the opposite of predestination.

---

50 In Manichaeism the Elects can degenerate if they do not constantly observe the precepts: this means that salvation does depend on free will.

51 *Tripartite Tractate, Nag Hammadi Codices* 1.5, 75–77 (where the protagonist is named *Logos*, rather than *Sophia*), cf. Norelli 1992, 18. The original "accident" that happened in the divine world, as described *e.g.* in the *Secret Book of John*, is in some way an irregular indeterministic event that upsets a pre-existing pleromatic order. Nevertheless, some sources attributed it to a higher πρόνοια, for instance the same *Tripartite Tractate* 107, where it occurs in accordance with a plan of the Father aimed at setting in train the process of redemption.

Bibliography

Sources

Acts of the Apostles: Wright, William, ed. 1871. *Apocryphal Acts of the Apostles*. London: Williams and Norgate; and Tischendorf, Constantin, Richard A. Lipsius and Maximilian Bonnet, eds. 1891–1903. *Acta apostolorum apocrypha*, 2nd edn. Leipzig: Hermann Mendelssohn.

Alcinous, *Didaskalikos*: Whittaker, John, ed. 1990. *Alcinoos. Enseignement des doctrines de Platon*. Paris: Les Belles Lettres; and Dillon, John, tr. 1993. *Alcinous. The Handbook of Platonism*. Oxford: Clarendon.

Alexander of Aphrodisias, *On Fate*: Bruns, Ivo, ed. 1892. *Alexandri Aphrodisiensis praeter commentaria scripta minora: Quaestiones, De fato, De mixtione* (*Supplementum aristotelicum* 2.2). Berlin: Weidmann.

Augustine: see www.augustinus.it.

Bardaisan of Edessa, *Against Fate*: Ramelli, Ilaria, ed. 2009. *Bardesanes, Contro il destino*. Bologna: Studio Domenicano.

Cicero, *On Fate*: Yon, Albert, ed. 1950. *Cicéron. Traité du destin*. Paris: Les Belles Lettres.

Clement of Alexandria, *Excerpts from Theodotus*: Sagnard, François M.M., ed. 1970. *Clément d'Alexandrie. Extraits de Théodote*. 2nd edn. Paris: Cerf.

Clement of Alexandria, *Miscellanies*: Stählin, Otto, Ludwig Früchtel, and Ursula Treu, eds. 1985. *Clemens Alexandrinus 2:* Stromata *Buch 1–6*. 4th edn. Berlin: Akademie.

Corpus Hermeticum: Festugière, André-Jean, and Arthur D. Nock, eds. 1949. *La révélation d'Hermès Trismégiste*. Paris: Les Belles Lettres.

DK: Diels, Hermann, and Walther Kranz, eds. 1952. *Die Fragmente der Vorsokratiker*. 6th edn. Berlin: Weidmann.

Epicurus: Arrighetti, Graziano, ed. 1969. *Epicuro. Opere*. 2nd edn. Turin: Einaudi.

Hippolytus [?], *Refutation of All Haeresies*: Wendland, Paul, ed. 1916. *Hippolytus. Refutatio omnium haeresium*. Leipzig: Hinrichs.

Irenaeus, *Against Heresies*: Rousseau, Adelin, and Louis Doutrelau, eds. 1979. *Irenée. Contre les hérésies*. Paris: Cerf.

Kant, Immanuel. 1904. *Kritik der reinen Vernunft*. 2nd edn [1787]. Akademie-Ausgabe, vol. 3. Berlin: Reimer.

Kant, Immanuel. 1908. *Kritik der praktischen Vernunft* [1788]. Akademie-Ausgabe, vol. 5. Berlin: Reimer.

Kephalaia I: Polotsky, Hans J., and Alexander Böhlig, eds. 1940. *Kephalaia* I. Stuttgart: Kohlhammer.

Licht-Nous: Sundermann, Werner, ed. 1992. *Der Sermon vom Licht-Nous*. Berlin: Akademie.

LM: Laks, André, and Glenn W. Most. 2016. *Early Greek Philosophy*. Cambridge (Mass.): Harvard University Press.

Nag Hammadi Codices: Robinson, James M., ed. 2000. *The Coptic Gnostic Library*. Leiden: Brill.

Nemesius, *On the Nature of Man*: Morani, Moreno, ed. 1987. *Nemesii Emeseni de natura hominis*. Leipzig: Teubner.

Origen, *Against Celsus*: Koetschau, Paul, ed. 1899. *Origenes. Gegen Celsus*. Leipzig: Hinrichs.

Origen, *Commentary on the Gospel of John*: Preuschen, Ernst, ed. 1903. *Origenes. Der Johanneskommentar*. Leipzig: Hinrichs.

Pistis Sophia: Schmidt, Carl, ed. 1959. *Pistis Sophia, die beiden Bücher des Jeu, unbekanntes altgnostisches Werk*. Berlin: Akademie.

Plotinus, *Enneads*: Harder, Richard, Rudolf Beutler, and Willy Theiler, eds. 1956–1971. Plotins Schriften. 2nd edn. Hamburg: Meiner.

Proclus, *Commentary on Plato's Republic*: Kroll, Wilhelm, ed. 1899–1901. *Procli Diadochi in Platonis Rem publicam commentarii*. Leipzig: Teubner.

Proclus, *Commentary on Plato's Timaeus*: Diehl, Ernest, ed. 1903–1905. *Procli Diadochi in Platonis* Timaeum *commentaria*. Leipzig: Teubner.

Ps.-Clement of Rome, *Homilies*: Rehm, Berhard, ed. 1953. Ps.-Clemens Romanus, *Homiliae*. Berlin: Weidmann.

Ps.-Clement of Rome, *Recognitions*: Rehm, Berhard, ed. 1969. Ps.-Clemens Romanus, *Recognitiones*. 2nd edn. Berlin: Weidmann.

Ps.-Plutarch, *On Fate*: De Lacy, Phillip H., and Benedict Einarson, eds. 1959. *Plutarch's Moralia*, vol. 7. Cambridge (Mass.): Harvard University Press.

Q: Qumran Texts (Dead Sea Scrolls): in *Discoveries in the Judaean Desert*. Oxford: Clarendon 1955–2009.

Stobaeus: Wachsmuth, Curth, and Otto Hense, eds. 1884–1923. *Stobaeus. Anthologiae*. Berlin: Weidmann.

SVF: von Arnim, Hans. 1903–1905. *Stoicorum Veterum Fragmenta*. Leipzig: Teubner.

Syncellus, *Chronography*: Mosshammer, Alden A., ed. *Syncellus. Ecloga chronographica*. Leipzig: Teubner 1984.

Tertullian, *On the Soul*: Waszink, Jan Hendrik, ed. *Quinti Septimi Florentis Tertulliani De anima*. Brill: Leiden 1947.

Valentinus: Förster, Werner. 1928. *Von Valentin zu Herakleon*. Giessen: Töpelmann.

Literature

Chiapparini, Giuliano. 2012. *Valentino gnostico e platonico*. Milan: Vita e Pensiero.

Freedman-Simon: *Midrash Rabbah*, edited by Harry Freedman and Maurice Simon. 3rd edn. Austin: Hertford 1961.

Jervell, Jacob. 1960. *Imago Dei*. Göttingen: Vandenhoeck und Ruprecht.

Klijn, Albertus F.J. 2003. *The Acts of Thomas, Introduction, English Translation, and Commentary*. 2nd edn. Leiden: Brill.

Lieu, Samuel N.C. 1992. *Manichaeism in the Later Roman Empire and Medieval China*. 2nd edn. Tübingen: Mohr.

Litwa, M. David, ed., tr. 2016. *Refutation of All Heresies*. Atlanta: SBL Press.

Magris, Aldo. 1999. "L'escatologia valentiniana." In *Annali di storia dell'esegesi* 16: 133–139.

Magris, Aldo. 2001. "Augustins Prädestinationslehre und die manichäischen Quellen." In *Augustine and Manichaeism in the Latin West*, edited by Johannes van Oort, Otto Wermelinger, and Gregor Wurst, 148–160. Leiden: Brill.

Magris, Aldo. 2005. "Gnosticism (further considerations)." In *Encyclopedia of Religion*. 2nd edn. 3515–3522. New York: Macmillan.

Magris, Aldo. 2011. *La logica del pensiero gnostico*. 2nd edn. Brescia: Morcelliana.

Magris, Aldo. 2016a. "Gli altri gnosticismi di Ippolito." In *'Ippolito,' Confutazione di tutte le eresie*, edited by Aldo Magris, 359–379. 2nd edn. Brescia: Morcelliana.

Magris, Aldo. 2016b. *Destino, provvidenza, predestinazione*. 2nd edn. Brescia: Morcelliana.

Norelli, Enrico. 1992. "Marcione e gli gnostici sul libero arbitrio." In *Il cuore indurito del Faraone. Origene e il problema del libero arbitrio*, edited by Luigi Perrone, 1–30. Genoa: Marietti.

Scott, Walter, ed. 1925. *Hermetica*, vol. 2. Oxford: Clarendon.

Theiler, Willy. 1966. *Forschungen zum Neuplatonismus*. Berlin: De Gruyter.

Thomassen, Einar. 1997. "How Valentinian is the Gospel of Philip?" In *The Nag Hammadi Library after Fifty Years*, edited by John D. Turner and Anne McGuire, 251–79. Leiden: Brill.

CHAPTER 11

Providence, Fate and Freedom of the Hermetic Sage

Claudio Moreschini

1 Introduction

Until the 18th century, Hermes Trismegistus' "secret revelation"[1] has been considered a foreshadowing of the Christian revelation; thereafter, from the 19th until the mid 20th century, scholars became interested in looking at parallels between hermetic doctrine on the one hand and Greek thought of the imperial age on the other hand, using the now abandoned distinction between "technical" and "philosophical" texts.[2] In the last decades, the hermeneutical paradigm changed: scholars became convinced that hermetical texts should not be interpreted as philosophical works, but rather as religious texts of which the origins are unclear. For, though written in Ptolemaic Egypt (and thus in Greek), they often recalled various earlier traditions, namely those of pharaonic Egypt. Also, the distinction between "technical" texts (about magic, astrology, alchemy etc.) and "philosophical" texts is no longer considered to be useful,[3] since the same text might contain elements that are both technical and philosophical.[4] Hence these days scholars are more interested in non-literary Greek texts (magical papyri, for example), which supposedly contain elements of the Egyptian religion;[5] now, in the slipstream of a suggestion from Dodd,[6] the Hermetic texts are compared with Biblical books rather than Greek philosophical texts.[7] The philosophical aspect – which I believe to be

1 This is the title of the recent edition by Scarpi 2009–2011. This edition is the source for the translation of the texts (i.e. the *Stobaean Hermetica*) that are not found in Copenhaver's edition (1992), which I follow for the *Corpus Hermeticum* and the *Asclepius*.

2 For instance, Bousset 1914; at the time, an interpretation that moved away from this distinction – and hence even more important and relevant – was that of Reitzenstein 1900.

3 It had already been rejected by Festugière 2014 [1950–1954] and 1967.

4 Giving a full bibliography on Hermeticism is impossible here, even if it were limited to the 21st century. Instead, I refer to van den Broek (2005a, 2005b) and Bull (2015, 2018a, a general study).

5 Did Hermeticism derive from the cult of Isis? The suggestion is offered by Scarpi 2017, but he does not develop it further.

6 Dodd 1935.

7 See Camplani 1993.

 | DOI:10.1163/9789004436381_013

still existent – is generally neglected, as often happens to "borderline" texts that have no clear classification.[8] In my opinion this happens for no good reason: surely, "philosophical" conceptions had to be born for some specific reason.

The problem suggested by the title of this essay is therefore, in many ways, a "philosophical" one that might seem alien to current scholarship on Hermeticism. It belongs to what German scholars used to term as "Popularphilosophie", a term that has nowadays been unjustly abandoned. The surely philosophical problem of providence, fate and freedom, therefore, will need to be discussed from a philosophical point of view, rather than as an issue in the history of religion. Yet in the Hermetic texts philosophical issues are not dealt with in a purely rational manner: the methods the hermetical authors followed are not those of Greek philosophy; rather, the problems are "discussed" by means of revelatory affirmations that complied with Hermes Trismegistus' "révélation." The present discussion will not lead us into Egyptian religion (for which I am not sufficiently competent), but rather into the (Greek) culture of Hellenistic Egypt, when the hermetical texts were written by re-modelling Pharaonic documents in a way that is difficult for us to reconstruct. These texts include the *Corpus Hermeticum*, the *Logos teleios* in a Latin translation, which is called the *Asclepius*,[9] and the *Stobaean Hermetics*.[10]

Another issue that should be taken into account is that the doctrines found in the *Stobaean Hermetics*, which are usually thought to be closer to the Egyptian tradition, consider the power of fate to be much more all-absorbing than those in the treatises of the *Corpus Hermeticum*, which are more Hellenised and more philosophical in content. Thus, in the *Excerpts*, the doctrines that

8 The bibliography on this topic is also vast; here also a recent overview should suffice: Bull (2018b), who speaks of a "ritual tradition" in Hermeticism and "adherents to the way of Hermes" (209). However, the fact that it is possible to speak about "philosophical Hermetica" is also defended by van den Broek, who writes: "Therefore, the term 'philosophical Hermetica' is acceptable for almost all the works that are usually covered by that name, since they are strongly influenced by Greek philosophical ideas, especially those of Platonism and Stoicism. It would be wrong, however, to consider them as primarily philosophical works" (2005b, 488).

9 Paolo Scarpi calls it "a complete treatise" – and indeed, the *Asclepius* offers a general synthesis of Hermetical doctrines aimed at a Latin-speaking audience.

10 Since I am not an Egyptologist, I restrict myself to a couple of important features, such as the presence of names of Egyptian divinities (*Stobaean Hermetics* 23.6: Imuthes and Ptha – Ephaestus), or a statement that underlines the importance of Egyptian magic: "So that *philosophy and magic nourish the soul* and medicine heal the body should someone suffer illness" (*Stobaean Hermetics* 23.68). The reference to "*our* crocodiles" at *Stobaean Hermetics* 25.6 is also telling.

providence can also play a positive role, and that next to the power of fate free will also has its place (both of Greek origin), are less prominent: on the contrary, fate is understood as an oppressive and inescapable force.[11]

A final, preliminary issue is that, due to the origin and nature of hermetical texts, the problem here at stake – like many others – is not discussed in a systematic and consistent manner, for the treatises in the *Corpus Hermeticum* (and presumably those from which the *Stobaean Excerpts* were drawn) are not the product of a specific school, but that of various religious brotherhoods. Therefore, some treatises and fragments contradict one another: in this instance, too, it is clear that one unitary hermetical doctrine did not exist. It is thus inevitable that the issue of free will, too, is treated in a non-systematic way, and that thus my discussion of the problem will have to contain these inconsistencies.

2 A Cosmogonic Myth: the *Kore Kosmou*

The tale recounted in the *Kore Kosmou* (*Stobaean Hermetics* 23) holds the typical features of the cosmogonic myth. It is narrated by Isis to her son Thoth in a solemn and oracular tone. In the different stages of the myth elements are brought up from which a particular conception of fate can be derived as an overall disposition of the world, which has come about as a consequence of its creation. The way in which fate depends on cosmic forces has no parallel in Greek philosophy, but seems to be in line with a theosophical conception that is presumably Egyptian in origin.

Just as in other Hermetic texts (e.g. *Corpus Hermeticum* 1.15), this myth is dominated by the notion of original guilt and the subsequent fall of souls, whose dwelling inside the human body is therefore dualistically seen as a "prison" and "punishment."[12] Inspired by Hermes' teachings, Isis explains to Thoth that celestial spheres tower over the whole nature of the inferior world, hence "necessity demands that everything be ordained by the superior world, and that the nature of the inferior world has been completely filled" (*Stobaean Hermetics* 23.2).[13] The creation of the world by the god includes the various – surely material – "spirits" (πνεύματα) (*Stobaean Hermetics* 23.12–15),

11 Scarpi (2009–2011, vol. 1, lxix–lxxi) links the hermetic conception of fate too easily with the Stoic one. For the Stoics, *heimarmenē* has a positive value, since it is the manifestation of divine *pronoia*: fate realises the divine plan (see Sfameni Gasparro 2013, 157–158).

12 Sfameni Gasparro 2013, 71.

13 πεπληρῶσθαι, that is "filled" with the forces of the superior world.

from which god then created another material substance, called Psychosis, which is the cosmic soul. From it the individual souls are derived, all of which are placed within a pre-ordained hierarchy; most of all, "the god harmonized the movements of the soul to the movements of the zodiac" (the movements of the soul are hence influenced by the stars). The god addresses the souls and demands that they follow his words faithfully, as his laws. Should the souls be able to obey, the heaven and the constellation they have been given will wait for them. If, on the contrary, they act against the god's will, the god swears by his sacred *pneuma* that he will forge chains and torments for them (*Stobaean Hermetics* 23.17). But, having taken the matter mixed with the *pneuma*, the souls tried to understand what *pneuma* was, and therefore created living beings. Convinced that they had made something exceptional, the souls acquired an arrogant "audacity" (τόλμα),[14] and no longer obeyed the orders they had received (*Stobaean Hermetics* 23.24). This was an abhorrent spectacle: when the god witnessed it, he ordered the gods to create human beings, to which each of them offered a feature of its own: these gods are the various planets that exerted their influence on human beings (*Stobaean Hermetics* 23.27–29). This pattern of the *Kore Kosmou* corresponds to that of the first treatise in the *Corpus Hermeticum*. The god then ordered that the human race be born and that the souls, who had been disobedient, be enclosed into the bodies (*Stobaean Hermetics* 23.29–30). Because of this decision the souls saddened (*Stobaean Hermetics* 23.31–33) and wept (*Stobaean Hermetics* 23.34–37). The god addressed them, and told them that Eros would dominate them together with Ananke (*Stobaean Hermetics* 23.38): whereas the meaning of Ananke is clear ("constraint", clearly connected to fate), that of Eros is less so: it might mean "the subjugation of souls to the impulses of sensations and senses". As long as they remain innocent, the souls will inhabit the heavens; should they be guilty, they would then be forced to once again be enclosed within mortal bodies: if they make minor mistakes, they will be allowed to return to the heavens, but if they make serious ones, they will keep on moving from one body to the next obeying to the law of reincarnation (*Stobaean Hermetics* 23.39). Adrastea, the god with sharp eyesight, will be in charge of overseeing the arrangement of the world; for this, the god will make a secret instrument by which all things on earth, from their birth until ultimate destruction, will be enslaved; it is an instrument that is "endowed with the stability of what has been accomplished" and cannot change (*Stobaean Hermetics* 23.48). This secret instrument is the astral system, by which fate operates, well known from other hermetical texts.

14 The term has a religious meaning in some Late-Antique texts, beginning with Plotinus, Origen and the Gnostics.

Such myths are not completely alien to Greek thought. The Hermetic author, by underlining the importance of astrology (something that had been done since Plato's *Timaeus*) maintains that the planets affect the world and mankind in a restricting manner. Also, in the first treatise of the *Corpus Hermeticum*, at 9, it is stated that "*Nous*, the second demiurge, who is the god of fire and *pneuma*, created seven governors, who in their circles embrace the sensible world. Their government is called fate (ἡ διοίκησις αὐτῶν εἱμαρμένη καλεῖται)",[15] therefore mankind, "though immortal and completely dominant over all things, is affected by mortality, since it is subject to fate (ὑποκείμενος τῇ εἱμαρμένῃ). Even though it is above the cosmic framework, it has become enslaved within it" (*Corpus Hermeticum* 1.15).[16] A fragment by Stobaeus reiterates that fate, which governs all activities in the universe, is an unescapable metaphysical entity: "In the service of fate are the stars. Nobody can escape fate, nor shield himself from the momentous force of the stars" (*Stobaean Hermetics* 12.2). *Stobaean Hermetics* 14, too, restates the fact that providence firmly guides the whole cosmos, while necessity maintains and encloses it; fate propels and moves everything in a circular motion, and by operating within the world through constraint (since the nature of fate lies in constraining), it is the cause of generation and corruption. The world is thus the first to experience providence (for it is the first to be influenced by it); providence, in turn, spreads out in the sky,[17] since the gods (i.e., the stars) turn and move within the sky by a continuous and tireless motion, while fate operates through the stars and their motion according to necessity. In sum, providence foresees, and fate is the "cause of the arrangement of the stars" (αἰτία ἐστὶ τῆς τῶν ἄστρων διαθέσεως). This is the inevitable "law according to which all things have been ordered" (νόμος ἄφυκτος, καθ᾽ὃν πάντα τέτακται).

3 Fate and Providence

A theme that is clearly connected to philosophy, in this case that of the Stoics, which was widespread in Graeco-Roman culture of the Imperial era, is that fate is not only a constraint created by the influence of the stars, but is also

15 According to Sfameni (2013, 159, n. 57), this idea of "government" (διοίκησις) is Stoic, but the fact that fate is understood as a constraint seems more important to me.

16 Tr. by Copenhaver 1992, here and below.

17 "Providence" (πρόνοια) is not that different from fate; it belongs to the same set of concepts. It should not understood in the modern sense of "caring for human beings." In *Stobaean Hermetics* 23.6, too, πρόνοια is described as the "queen of all things", just like fate.

identified with providence, a metaphysical entity.[18] This connection between providence and fate is asserted in the *Asclepius* in the "optimistic" context of chapter 19,[19] where it is stated that providence is part of the activities carried out by both the supreme god and the inferior and cosmic deities.[20] The author of the *Asclepius* begins by explaining the existence of various classes of gods, some of which are intelligible, some sensible, and distinguishes them according to their kind and function: above each cosmic god there is a οὐσιάρχης, a "head of substance", that is the hyper-cosmic and intelligible god. In the universe the following "scale" can be found: god (this god includes numerous lower gods) – the world – human beings. Scarpi rightly notes that "one could almost say that Hermeticism, since it is not an exclusivist monotheism, is both a relative monotheism and a relative polytheism at the same time, since it features a "superior" god and numerous deities who carry out his will."[21]

18 On providence in Imperial Stoicism, see René Brouwer's contribution in the present volume.

19 Even though the distinction between "optimistic" and "pessimistic" Hermetical treatises (as proposed by Bousset 1914) has now been abandoned as too rigid, it nevertheless holds some truth. Instances of texts that offer an optimistic view of the world, which can be contemplated in order to arrive at god, include the *Asclepius* and *Corpus Hermeticum* 1, 4, 6, 7, 12, 13. See e.g. *Corpus Hermeticum* 12.15: "This entire cosmos – a great god and an image of a greater, united with god and helping preserve the father's will and order – is a plenitude of life (πλήρωμά ἐστι τῆς ζωῆς)." Therefore, the world is god (*Corpus Hermeticum* 12.15–16). One can grasp god by contemplating the world, its perfect order and the fullness of life. God is the whole and the whole is god; the whole contains nothing that is not god: he is the whole and the whole crosses and surrounds all things (12.23, cf. 5.9). Instances of texts that offer a pessimistic view can also be found: they consider the world a wicked place since it was not created by god, who remains infinitely above matter. Therefore, god can only be reached by fleeing the world and feeling extraneous to it. See *Stobaean Hermetics* 11.2.18: "Nothing is good on earth, nothing is wicked in heaven"; *Stobaean Hermetics* 11.2.25: "All that is in the sky is immutable, all that is on earth is fickle"; *Stobaean Hermetics* 11.2.26: "There is not slavery in the heavens, there is no freedom on earth." These two contrasting views are well expressed by Sfameni Gasparro (1995, 19; 2013, 68–73) and explained – in a way that is much more fitting for the Hermetical religious context, rather than for Greek philosophy – by Fowden (1993, 101–104). He suggests that there are two different paths to the knowledge of god, a more simple one (which consists of admiring the beauties of the world) for the beginners, and another that is reserved for the chosen ones, who are able to detach themselves from the sensation and appearance; see also Copenhaver 1992, xxxix.

20 It may be helpful to recall a few chronological details here. As is well known, *Asclepius* is the Latin translation of *Logos teleios*, cited by Lactantius in his *Divine Institutions* (310–320 CE). The *Logos teleios*, therefore, can be dated back to the 3rd century: in the 2nd and 3rd centuries the majority of the Greek hermetical texts were composed.

21 Scarpi 2009–2011, vol. 1, liv.

The "heads of substance" (οὐσιάρχαι) are the hyper-cosmic and intelligible gods; they are lords of the sensible and cosmic gods. There are five gods of such superior kind: Jupiter, Light, *Pantomorphos*, Fate or *Heimarmenē*, and yet another Jupiter.[22] To these five superior gods correspond five inferior divinities, who depend upon the superior ones: the sky, the sun, thirty-six "horoscopes", the seven celestial spheres and air. In the *Asclepius*, at 19, and also in the *Poimandres*, it reads that *Heimarmenē* uses the celestial spheres as a means of exercising its power over mankind and the cosmos.[23] The seven planetary spheres operate so that "all things change according to nature's law and a steadfast stability that stirs in everlasting variation." Next to unavoidable Fate, which is governed by the planetary spheres, lies Providence, which apparently does not obstruct Fate: Providence is the work of the celestial gods, who dwell high in the sky, in such a manner that they connect all mortal things with immortal realities.[24] In a later passage, at 38, *Asclepius* explains that the care for human deeds is entrusted to the gods, both the terrestrial and celestial ones, each according to their own prerogative:

> Do not suppose that these earthly gods act aimlessly,[25] Asclepius. Heavenly gods inhabit heaven's heights, each one heading up the order assigned to him and watching over it. But here below our gods render aid to humans as if through loving kinship, looking after some things individually, foretelling some things through lots and divination, and planning ahead to give help by other means, each in his own way.[26]

22 In Moreschini 1991, 19, 58.15 I supply *deus*.

23 *caeli vel quicquid est, quod eo nomine comprehenditur,* οὐσιάρχης *est Iuppiter: per caelum enim Iuppiter omnibus praebet vitam. solis* οὐσιάρχης *lumen est: bonum enim luminis per orbem nobis solis infunditur.* 36, *quorum vocabulum est Horoscopi, id est eodem loco semper defixorum siderum, horum* οὐσιάρχης *vel princeps est, quem* Παντόμορφον *vel omniformem vocant, qui diversis speciebus diversas formas facit. septem sphaerae quae vocantur habent* οὐσιάρχας, *id est sui principes, quam fortunam dicunt aut* εἱμαρμένην, *quibus immutantur omnia lege naturae stabilitateque firmissima, sempiterna agitatione variata. aër vero organum est vel machina omnium, per quam omnia fiunt; est autem* οὐσιάρχης *huius secundus* ⟨…⟩ *mortalibus mortalia et his similia* (38, 58.1–16 Moreschini 1991).

24 This, too, is an optimistic overtone.

25 Therefore, god is not the cause of evil (*Corpus Hermeticum* 4.8), a typical formulation of Greek philosophy, see Plato, *Republic* 10.621a: θεὸς ἀναίτιος.

26 *et ne putassis fortuitos effectus esse terrenorum deorum, o Asclepi, Dii caelestes inhabitant summa caelestia, unusquique ordinem, quem accepit, complens atque custodiens, hi nostri vero singillatim quaedam curantes, quaedam sortibus et divinatione praedicentes, quaedam providentes hisque pro modo subvenientes, humanis amica quasi cognatione auxiliantur* (83.8–14 Moreschini 1991).

This, therefore, means that just as in Middle Platonism,[27] the *Asclepius* affirms the existence of several providences that depend upon the god and the demons.

The close connection between fate and providence is discussed further in *Asclepius* (chs. 39–40), always in line with Stoic doctrine:

> 39. Then what part of the plan belongs to *Heimarmenē* or the Fates, Trismegistus? The heavenly gods rule universals, but singulars belong to the earthly gods – correct?
>
> What we call *Heimarmenē*, Asclepius, is the necessity in all events, which are always bound to one another by links that form a chain. She is the maker of everything, the, or else, the supreme god, or the second god made by the supreme god, or the ordering of all things in heaven and earth made steadfast by divine laws. Therefore, this *Heimarmenē* and Necessity are bound to one another by an unbreakable glue, and, of the two, *Heimarmenē* comes first, begetting the sources of all things, but the things that depend on her beginning them are forced into activity by Necessity. What follows them both is Order, the structure and temporal arrangement of the things that must be brought about. For without the fitting together of an order, there is nothing, and in everything the world's order is complete. Order is the vehicle of the world itself, and the whole consists of order. 40. These three, then – *Heimarmenē*, Necessity and Order – are in the very fullest sense the products of god's assent, who governs the world by his own law and divine plan, and god has barred them altogether from every act of willing or willing-not. Not disturbed by anger nor swayed by kindness, they subject themselves to the necessity of the eternal plan. And the plan is eternity itself: irresistible, immovable, indestructible. First comes *Heimarmenē*, then, who provides progeny enough for all to come with the seed she has sawn, as it were, and Necessity follows, forcing them all into activity by compulsion. Order comes third to preserve the structure of the things that *Heimarmenē* and Necessity arrange.[28]

27 The Middle Platonists who wrote about providence (Ps.-Plutarch *On Fate*, Alcinous, *Didaskalikos*, Apuleius, *On Plato and His Doctrine*) lived during the 2nd century, but the issue was debated again in the 4th century by Calcidius (see Moreschini 2015, 279–286, and Emmanuele Vimercati's contribution in the present volume). These themes, too, can thus be useful in dating the Greek source of *Asclepius*, the *Logos teleios*, to the 2nd or 3rd century.

28 *quam ergo rationis partem* εἱμαρμένη *vel fata incolunt, o Trismegiste? anne caelestes dii catholicorum dominantur, terreni incolunt singula? quam* εἱμαρμένην *nuncupamus, o As-*

The scheme proposed by the author of *Asclepius* is clear, and is in line with the Stoic position. Everything depends upon the law that god has firmly established, with rationality not alien to such inescapable necessity. In the philosophical literature that deals with the opposition between necessity on the one hand and providence and/or divine rationality on the other hand, sometimes more weight is given to necessity, sometimes to providence: sometimes fate is identified with god's providence, sometimes it is considered to be something that is superior to human beings and unavoidable. The gradation providence-necessity (which is included in providence)-chance is stated as follows in *Stobaean Hermetics* 11.2.46–47: "Providence is divine order (τάξις), necessity is submitted to providence. Chance (τύχη) is a disorderly motion, a semblance of force, a mendacious illusion."[29]

In other *Stobaean Excerpts* a similar opposition between providence and chance can be found. Sometimes the rational (or irrational) aspect of the cosmic events is emphasized: "The *logos* depends upon providence, the irrational depends upon necessity, the accidental features that qualify the body (τὰ περὶ τὸ σῶμα συμβεβηκότα) upon fate" (*Stobaean Hermetics* 8.7). All is made in accordance with nature and fate, and there is no sphere in which providence does not operate. Providence is the perfect – and thus positive – plan of the celestial god. Two powers originate from it: necessity and fate. Fate is subject to necessity and – on a superior level – to providence (*Stobaean Hermetics* 12.2). This leads to the sequence providence-necessity-fate. For the relation between providence and necessity see *Stobaean Hermetics* 13: "Necessity is an unshakable decision (κρίσις βεβαία) and inflexible power (ἀμετάτρεπτος δύναμις) of providence."

---

clepi, ea est necessitas omnium quae geruntur, semper sibi catenatis nexibus vincta; haec itaque est aut effectrix rerum aut deus summus aut ab ipso deo qui secundus effectus est deus aut omnium caelestium terrenarumque rerum firmata divinis legibus disciplina. haec itaque εἱμαρμένη *et necessitas ambae sibi invicem individuo conexae sunt glutino, quarum prior* εἱμαρμένη *rerum omnium initia parit;, necessitas vero cogit ad effectum quae ex illius primordiis pendent. has ordo consequitur, id est textus et dispositio temporis rerum perficiendarum. nihil est enim sine ordinis conpositione; in omnibus mundus iste perfectus est; ipse enim mundus ordine gestatur vel totus constat ex ordine.* 40 *haec ergo tria:* εἱμαρμένη, *necessitas, ordo, vel maxime dei nutu sunt effecta, qui mundum gubernat sua lege et ratione divina. ab his ergo omne velle aut nolle divinitus aversum est totum. nec ira etenim commoventur nec flectuntur gratia, sed serviunt necessitati rationis aeternae, quae aeternitas inaversibilis, inmobilis, insolubilis est. prima ergo* εἱμαρμένη *est, quae iacto velut semine futurorum omnium sufficit prolem. sequitur necessitas, qua ad effectum vi coguntur omnia. tertius ordo, textum servans earum rerum, quas* εἱμαρμένη *necessitasque disponit* (83.15–84.20 Moreschini 1991).

29 For the Stoics on luck see Brouwer 2019, 36–37.

Sometimes, however, providence has the greater power: "Providence is the divine order, and necessity is subjected (ὑπηρέτις) to providence" (*Stobaean Hermetics* 11.2.46); "providence is the queen of all things" (*Stobaean Hermetics* 23.6). In a fragment where the beauty of the world is emphasized (this beauty offers human beings the possibility to join god), reference is made, at *Corpus Hermeticum* 12.21, to god as present in everything that happens, past or present. Necessity and providence, therefore, depend upon him.

4 Fate and Free Will

One inescapable dilemma remains, according to the Greek mind. Tat asks Hermes:

> In that case, father, the discourse about fate that I heard finished earlier would seem to be contradicted. If it is absolutely fated for some individual to commit adultery or sacrilege or to do some other evil, how is such a person still to be punished when he has acted under the compulsion of fate? Everything is an act of fate, my child, and outside of it nothing exists among bodily entities, neither good nor evil comes to be by chance. Even one who has done something fine is fated to be affected by it, and this is why he does it: in order to be affected by what affects him because he has done it. … But all people are subject to fate and also to birth and change, which are the beginning and the end of fate (*Corpus Hermeticum* 12.5–6).

This text is mirrored in the *Corpus Hermeticum*, at 11.3:

> And if this being will understand that the world had a beginning, and that everything depends upon providence and necessity, since fate governs all things (πάντα κατὰ πρόνοιαν καὶ ἀνάγκην γίνεται, εἱμαρμένης πάντων ἀρχούσης), will he not grow more wicked? By despising all things, since they had a beginning, and by blaming fate for the cause of evil (τὰς δὲ αἰτίας τοῦ κακοῦ τῇ εἱμαρμένῃ ἀναφέρων), this being will never refrain from any wickedness.

The freedom of a human being, therefore, consists in being freed from all moral obligations, as is explained in the 12th treatise of the *Corpus*, at 7:

> And what is fated affects all people. Yet those who possess reason (ἐλλόγιμοι), whom (as we have said) mind (νοῦς) commands, are not affected as the others are. Since they have been freed from vice (ἀπηλλαγμένοι), they are not affected as a consequence of being evil. [...] it is not possible to escape the quality of change any more than of birth, though it is possible for one who has mind to escape vice.

Hermes explains this concept by referring to Agathodaimon ("the Good Demon"), who unfortunately did not put his thoughts into writing. According to Hermes, Agathodaimon ended his teachings by stating that "since mind rules all and is the soul of god, mind can do as it wishes" (*Corpus Hermeticum* 12.8). Therefore, Thot must solve the problem of fate based on this statement by Agathodaimon:

> For if you carefully avoid contentious discourse, my child, you will find that mind, the soul of god, truly prevails over all, over fate and law and all else. And nothing is impossible for mind, neither setting a human soul above fate nor, if it happens that a soul is careless, setting it beneath fate. These were the finest things that the good demon said about such matters (12.9).

But who is it that possesses mind? It is the human being, who has received it as a gift from god: therefore, the human being who possesses mind is superior to fate (*Corpus Hermeticum* 4.1–2); such superiority has been granted to him by god.[30] These few "chosen ones" stand out from the vast majority of human beings (*Corpus Hermeticum* 9.4), who are but material (*Corpus Hermeticum* 11.5) and are not capable of contemplating the true reality of the whole (*Stobaean Hermetics* 7.3); they only possess the logos and do not know the real aim of their existence (*Corpus Hermeticum* 4.4).

Therefore, the chosen man is not subject to fate: this is not possible thanks to the exercise of virtue, but rather due to the νοῦς he possesses. And since the νοῦς is god's soul and was given as a gift by god to chosen men, the latter are free from fate thanks to god, rather than due to their merits. This statement can have positive or negative consequences, as in the case where a human being feels free from all guilt and responsibility, as we have seen above: the νοῦς, as a matter of fact, does not imply moral perfection in itself.

30 The argument continues with a surprising doctrine: since it dwells in the body, mind too is an affection, a statement that Scarpi (2009–2011, vol. 1, 485) connects with Stoicism, with reference to esp. Stobaeus 2.88.6–89.3 (*SVF* 3.378).

5 Those Who Can Escape Fate

The statement from the 12th treatise in the *Corpus Hermeticum*, which frees νοῦς-equipped human beings from all responsibility, is a singular instance. In many other Hermetical texts the connection between freedom and gnosis is made. That the sage is free can be found in two passages by Zosimus (fr. 20–21 Nock and Festugière):[31]

> Hermes and Zoroaster stated that philosophers are superior to fate so that they would not rejoice in the delights that it brings (they are, in fact, stronger than pleasure). Moreover, they are not affected by the diseases fate sends upon them, since their life is always carried out in immateriality and they do not accept fate's pleasant gifts [...] In his treatise on immateriality, therefore, Hermes also condemns magic, deeming that spiritual men, who know themselves, must not benefit from magic even though they find it useful; nor must they force necessity, rather letting it operate according to its nature and judgement. They only proceed through the quest of themselves, and after acknowledging god, they possess in themselves the ineffable trinity, and let fate do whatever it pleases with their clay, that is – their body.

Two interesting passages by Didymus the Blind show how widespread this hermetical doctrine was. The author obviously underlines the Christian features of it, that is, the need for men to be superior to worldly things by detaching themselves from them:

> And that famous Egyptian they talk about, Trismegistus, states that the sage destroys the εἱμαρμένη: the sage is not subjected by constriction, nor is he subdued by the world. Rather, his thoughts have ascended above the sky and visible realities. Thus, they say that the men in the flock are under fate. Then he who has ascended above and beyond human life, can say "I do not see apparent things, but those that are not seen", since the things we can see are fleeting, while the ones we cannot see are eternal (*Commentaries on Ecclesiastes* 167.15–23).[32]

31 See Moreschini 2011, 18.

32 See 2 Corinthians 4.17b. According to Bull (2018b, 239), on the other hand, Didymus recalls *Corpus Hermeticum* 12.11 and 13; see Kramer 1970, 50–51.

> And even the Egyptians, among which Hermes Trismegistus, state that the wise man is no longer subjected to fate[33] and is outside the world, just as the Saviour says that it is possible to be in the world, but not of the world, when someone has his intellect way up and leads a celestial life. Therefore, these men [the Hermetics] murmur drawing on our doctrines,[34] and say that the wise man dissolves the εἱμαρμένη (*Commentary on the Psalms* 88.12–16).[35]

In holding this doctrine of the superiority of the perfect human being over fate, the Hermetics are similar to other Gnostics of the same era: those who are perfect are immune from fate's traps and dominance, just like those who have received Baptism and have thus been redeemed from a miserable and wicked state. This is how it is formulated in the *Excerpts from Theodotus* 78.1–2, preserved in the writings of Clement of Alexandria:

> Therefore, until Baptism, they [*sc.* the Valentinians] say that fate is real; but after Baptism the astrologers are no longer truthful. It is not just Baptism that frees us, but also gnosis: who we are, who we have become; where we are, where we have been thrown; what we are seeking, what has purified us; what generation and what regeneration are.[36]

Theodotus, a Valentinian Gnostic, here brings up a series of themes that correspond with the ones in Hermeticism. Hermetical texts naturally do not refer

---

33 οὐκέτι: before he became wise, he was subject to fate, as is stated in the continuation of the passage.

34 This is the Christian interpretation of Hermes Trismegistus' revelation.

35 The text can be found in Gronewald, ed. 1968, 134–137. Such superiority of the perfect human being also includes the possession of "piety" (εὐσέβεια). "Piety in conjunction with *gnosis*" (which is the knowledge of god) "protects" the perfect human being. However, this protection seems to be alien to the proud self-confidence that is characteristic for the hermetic sage, within whom lives the *nous*. As *nous* dwells in him, it frees him from the responsibility of evil, as is stated in *Corpus Hermeticum* 13. It is εὐσέβεια that protects the perfect human being from the wicked demons and, most of all, from εἱμαρμένη. See Lactantius, *Divine Institutions* 2.15.6–7, fr. 10 Nock and Festugière: *denique adfirmat Hermes eos qui cognoverint deum non tantum ab incursibus daemonum tutos esse, verum etiam ne fato quidem teneri.* μία, *inquit*, φυλακή, εὐσέβεια. εὐσεβοῦς γὰρ ἀνθρώπου οὔτε δαίμων κακὸς οὔτε εἱμαρμένη κρατεῖ· θεὸς γὰρ ῥύεται τὸν εὐσεβῆ ἐκ παντὸς κακοῦ. τὸ γὰρ ἓν καὶ μόνον ἐν ἀνθρώποις ἐστὶν ἀγαθὸν εὐσέβεια. *quid sit autem* εὐσέβεια, *ostendit alio loco his verbis*: ἡ γὰρ εὐσέβεια γνῶσις ἐστι τοῦ θεοῦ. *Asclepius quoque auditor eius eandem sententiam latius explicavit in illo sermone perfecto quem scripsit ad regem.*

36 Adapted from the translation by Simonetti 1993, 390–393; on this passage, see also Sfameni Gasparro 2013, 145–152.

to Baptism: yet, they make clear that an instrument of freedom and salvation must exist. Man's salvation can be reached in various ways: first and foremost, by knowing one's self and one's best part, and in that state also by exercising piety. God saves the human race through the preaching of Hermes, who in turn had been instructed by the vision Poimander had brought up (*Corpus Hermeticum* 1.26). Salvation is not transcendent: rather, it is something that is in fact concrete, and consists in defending oneself against demons, not only in this life but also in future ones.

6 Conclusion

In conclusion, just like other philosophies and theosophies at the time, Hermeticism is strongly affected by the threat of fate, from which it somehow tries to liberate itself. Such "freedom from fate" is conceived as a characteristic of the sage in the *Corpus Hermeticum*, much more than it is in the *Stobaean Excerpts*, which are of decidedly Egyptian origin. This freedom is achieved by detaching oneself from terrestrial deeds; it does not imply that the world is wicked (as would be taught by Christianity), which is another typical trait of Hellenising treatises. The separation of the world is left in the hands of the sage, who detaches himself from the mass of ignorant men: it is thus operated by free will and ends in "piety" (εὐσέβεια), upon which salvation ultimately depends. Such salvation happens in both this and in our future life.

Bibliography

Bousset, Wilhelm. 1914. "Review of Joseph Kroll, *Die Lehren des Hermes Trismegistos*." *Göttingische Gelehrte Anzeigen* 76: 697–755.

van den Broek, Roelof. 2005a. "Hermes Trismegistus I: Antiquity." In *Dictionary of Gnosis & Western Esotericism*, edited by Wouter J. Hanegraaff, Antoine Faivre, Roelof van den Broek, and Jean-Pierre Brach, vol. 1: 474–478. Leiden: Brill.

van den Broek, Roelof. 2005b. "Hermetic Literature I: Antiquity." In *Dictionary of Gnosis & Western Esotericism*, edited by Wouter J. Hanegraaff, Antoine Faivre, Roelof van den Broek, and Jean-Pierre Brach, vol. 1: 487–499. Leiden: Brill.

Brouwer, René. 2019. "The Stoics on Luck." In *The Routledge Handbook on the Philosophy and Psychology of Luck*, edited by Ian M. Church and Robert Hartman, 34–43. London: Routledge.

Bull, Christian. H. 2015. "Ancient Hermetism and Esotericism", *Aries* 15: 109–135.

Bull, Christian. H. 2018a. *The Tradition of Hermes Trismegistus. The Egyptian Priestly Figure as a Teacher of Hellenized Wisdom*. Leiden: Brill.

Bull, Christian. H. 2018b. "Hermes between Pagans and Christians: The Nag Hammadi Hermetica in Context." In *The Nag Hammadi Codices and Late Antique Egypt*, edited by Hugo Lundhaug and Lance Jenott, 207–260. Tübingen: Mohr Siebeck.

Camplani, Alberto. 1993. "Riferimenti biblici nella letteratura ermetica." *Annali di storia dell'esegesi* 10: 375–425.

Copenhaver, Brian P., ed. 1992. *Hermetica*. Cambridge: Cambridge University Press.

Dodd, Charles. H. 1935. *The Bible and the Greeks*. London: Hodder & Stoughton.

Festugière, André-Jean. 1967. *Hermétisme et mystique païenne*. Paris: Aubier Montaigne.

Festugière, André-Jean. 2014 [1950–1954]. *Révélation d'Hermès Trismégiste*. Paris: Les Belles Lettres.

Fowden, Garth. 1993. *The Egyptian Hermes. A Historical Approach to the Late Pagan Mind*. Princeton: Princeton University Press.

Gronewald, Michael, ed. 1968, *Didymus der Blinde. Psalmenkommentar* (*Tura-Papyrus*), vol. 2. Bonn: Habelt.

Hanegraaff, Wouter J., Antoine Faivre, Roelof van den Broek, and Jean-Pierre Brach, eds. 2005. *Dictionary of Gnosis & Western Esotericism*, vol. 1. Leiden: Brill.

Kramer, Johannes, ed. 1970. *Didymus der Blinde, Kommentar zum Ecclesiastes* (*Tura-Papyrus*), vol. 3. Bonn: Habelt.

Moreschini, Claudio, ed. 1991. *Apulei Platonici Madaurensis opera quae supersunt 3: Opera philosophica*. Stuttgart: Teubner.

Moreschini, Claudio. 2011. *Hermes Christianus. The Intermingling of Hermetic Piety and Christian Thought*. Turnhout: Brepols.

Moreschini, Claudio. 2015. *Apuleius and the Metamorphoses of Platonism*. Turnhout: Brepols.

Reitzenstein, Richard. 1900. *Poimandres*. Leipzig: Teubner.

Scarpi, Paolo. 2017. "Conflitti religiosi e filologia: *heur et malheur* dell'emetismo. Isacco Casaubon contro Ermete Trismegisto." *Studi e materiali di storia delle religioni*, 83: 10–36 [within a conference organised by Alberto Camplani].

Scarpi, Paolo, ed. 2009–2011. *La rivelazione segreta di Ermete Trismegisto*. Milan: Mondadori (2 vols.).

Sfameni Gasparro, Giulia. 1995. "Chaos e dualismo: la dialettica chaos-kosmos nell'ermetismo." *Cassiodorus* 1: 11–28.

Sfameni Gasparro, Giulia. 2013. *La conoscenza che salva*. Soveria Mannelli: Rubbettino.

Simonetti, Manlio, ed., 1993. *Testi gnostici cristiani*. Milan: Mondadori.

CHAPTER 12

Early Christian Philosophers on Free Will

George Karamanolis

1 Introduction

The notions of free will, human responsibility, and divine providence are as central in the thought of early Christian philosophers as they are for their pagan contemporaries, Epictetus, Alexander, and Plotinus. Already Justin Martyr, the first Christian philosopher, exhibits a strong interest in this network of issues.[1] This interest remains unfailing and gradually increases among the following generation of Christian intellectuals, Irenaeus, Tertullian, Clement, and it reaches a peak in the work of Origen. And the question is what triggered this interest and made it so dominant in the thought of early Christians.

This question allows for many different answers. One possible answer is the following: the question of human free will is crucial for deciding how man relates to God and to the world and also how God relates to man and the world. Was God free to make the world as he wished, or was he constrained by external exigencies, such as those that matter sets, as is the case in the *Timaeus*, for instance? God's freedom of choice was important especially because man is created in the image of God according to Scripture (Genesis 1.26), which means that if God's freedom of will is limited, man's also is. The issue of God's freedom of will cannot be settled, though, merely by ruling out matter as a cosmic principle, as some Christian thinkers did. The problem persists, since there remains the question of how evil or badness can be explained in the world if God is the only principle. There was a particular kind of evil, namely human vice, which occurs in various degrees, from occasional wrongdoing to deliberate and systematic vicious action, which requires special explanation given that man is created in the image of God. These issues were highly debated by early Christians and pagans alike. Both had to face the challenge of two main contemporary currents of thought, that of the astral determinists and the Gnostics.

1 This is a revised version of part of chapter 4 ("Free Will and Divine Providence") of my book *The Philosophy of Early Christianity* (see Karamanolis 2013). I would like to thank the editors for their extremely valuable feedback and Anthony Kroytor for improving my style.

 | DOI:10.1163/9789004436381_014

Astral determinism goes back to the Hellenistic age and was still popular in the second century CE, as we can tell from the many contemporary criticisms directed against it.[2] Sextus Empiricus writes against the views of the astrologists and about a century later Plotinus dedicates an entire treatise to this issue.[3] Astral determinists defended the view that our choices, our characters and our lives are essentially determined by the movements of the stars. In such a view, God would clearly have allowed for that or even wanted it. On the other hand, according to the Gnostics, especially Valentinian Gnostics, God, that is, the God of the Old Testament, created the world without goodness, that is, with no regard for his creatures. In their view, God determined people's characters and lives, privileging some and not others. Valentinians actually speak of three classes of human people that God created, those who are destined to enjoy salvation, those destined to perish, and those in between who have the power to go either way and are the only ones who have the power to choose.[4] The choices of those in the first two classes cannot make any difference with regard to their happiness and salvation, since for them everything is predetermined.

Early Christian thinkers were concerned with refuting both views, those of astral determinists and those of the Gnostics, who were fellow Christians. The reason for their concern was mainly that such views severely distorted the way God relates to man and the world. The argument of early Christian thinkers was beset with great difficulties for two main reasons. First, because Scripture does not contain a discussion of those issues but several important hints, such as Jesus' saying that man's spirit is willing but the body is weak (Matthew 26.41; Mark 14.38) or, famously, Paul's remarks in his Letter to the Romans such as the statement that he observes a law in his members unlike the one in his mind (Romans 7.19–24). Scripture not only lacks a discussion of all the important issues in this area but also lacks the relevant terminology, which early Christians employ in their writings. In particular I have in mind the terms τὸ ἐφ' ἡμῖν, προαίρεσις, and αὐτεξούσιον.

2 See Cumont 1912 and Long 1982. As Long observes, we need to distinguish between a hard astral determinism and a soft, semiotic, astrology. The former maintains that the stars determine cosmic events, while the latter that they only foreshadow them (ποιεῖν *vs* σημαίνειν, in the ancient terminology; e.g. Plotinus, *Enneads* 3.1.5.41). Plotinus, *Enneads* 2.3.1 and 3.1.5–6 rejects the former but accepts the latter. Similar is the attitude of Origen, *On Genesis*, in Eusebius, *Preparation for the Gospel* 6.11.54–72 (= *Philokalia*, ch. 23; SC 266: 258–268). For a discussion of the early Christian polemics against the astrologists see Hegedus 2007.

3 Sextus Empiricus, *Against the Astrologers* [= *Against the Professors* 5], Plotinus, *Enneads* 2.3 (*On Whether the Stars Create*); cf. Ps.-Plutarch, *On Fate* 11.574D, Nemesius, *On the Nature of Man*, chs. 35–37.

4 On the Valentinians and their views on free will, see Dihle 1982, 152–157, Thomassen 2006, Magris in this volume, 186–192, and below.

All three terms are of Stoic provenance. The term τὸ ἐφ' ἡμῖν indicates what depends on us, that is, man's unconstrained capacity of assessing and choosing.[5] The Stoic idea here is that humans have the capacity to assess their impressions and decide how to deal with them, while non-rational animals lack such an ability and impulsive impressions fully determine their actions. The term προαίρεσις on the other hand, which Aristotle uses in the sense "choice" in the *Nicomachean Ethics* (3.1), is used in a special sense by Epictetus. For him προαίρεσις is a critical disposition or power to deal with our impressions, namely the power to choose whether we would assent or not to them. For Epictetus then προαίρεσις is not a choice, as in Aristotle, but rather a willingness or ability to choose rationally; in this sense it is closer to what we would call "will."[6] For Epictetus this ability or disposition is the only thing we can actually choose and he suggests that this is man's real self.[7] Finally, the term αὐτεξούσιον is also a Stoic term that signifies the agent's power or authority (ἐξουσία) to make choices and eventually the authority over oneself. In this sense the term signifies what we would call "autonomy" today.[8]

The second difficulty that beset the theoretical work of early Christians was the need to go beyond a mere criticism of determinist theories, such as those of the astral determinists or the Gnostics, and to articulate an alternative Christian theory of human agency that would be plausible and sufficiently sophisticated. This kind of theory would need, for instance, to address the question of theodicy, namely how God as the sole principle of the world is just, given the considerable differences between individuals in terms of talents, temperaments, and propensities.

Early Christians move slowly towards the articulation of a complete alternative theory. This is finally achieved with Origen and further elaborated with Nemesius and the Cappadocians, who fall outside the scope of my paper. Both Origen and Nemesius have received quite some attention in this respect in the recent years and with good reason.[9] Much less attention has been paid to earlier Christians, however, who are my focus here. I shall argue that in the period from Justin to Clement one important step is made: while early

---

5 On the term ἐφ' ἡμῖν see Bobzien 1998a, 276–290, 334 and also Gourinat 2014. Cf. Epictetus, *Dissertations* 1.1, Marcus Aurelius 6.32, Alexander of Aphrodisias, *On Fate* 11, 181.14, Plutarch, *On Stoic Self-Contradictions* 47.1056D.

6 On the term προαίρεσις see Bobzien 1998a, 402–406, Frede 2011, 44–48, and Brouwer's chapter in this volume.

7 See Long 2002, 207–220 and Sorabji 2007.

8 The term αὐτεξούσιον occurs in Epictetus, *Dissertations* 4.1.62, 68, 100, in Alexander, *On Fate* 14, 182.22–24; cf. *SVF* 2.975 (associated with Chrysippus). See Bobzien 1998a, 332–336, 353–355 and Frede 2011, 74–75, 102–104.

9 See, for instance, Layton 2000, Sorabji 2000, 343–356, Boys-Stones 2007 and the recent book on Origen's notion of will by Hengstermann 2016. See also Edward's chapter in this volume.

Christians before Clement operate with the essentially Stoic notion of "freedom of choice" (τὸ ἐφ' ἡμῖν), which they defend as an essential feature of human nature, with the notion of the ability to make "choices" (προαίρεσις), and with the notion of "autonomy" (αὐτεξούσιον), that is the ability of human beings to deal with their impressions freely and assent to one course of action, Clement is the first, I shall suggest, who speaks of a faculty of will in the human mind. For Clement the ability to make choices and thus to have power over our impressions is a central faculty of the human mind. And as I shall show, this faculty is responsible not only for everyday choices but more importantly for the choice of a kind of life, such as Christian or pagan. Clement then paves the way for Origen's theory of will. My outline below aims to illustrate this development.

2 The First Traces of a Christian Theory of Free Will: Justin, Tatian, and Theophilus

Justin is the first Christian philosopher who seriously engages with the issues of free choice and human responsibility. In his first *Apology* he sets out to address the view that everything that happens in the world is predetermined on the grounds that God knows everything in advance and has set up the world in a certain way.[10] Justin addresses that view in the context of his discussion of the prophesies of the Old Testament about Jesus, which on the one hand point to the divinity of Jesus yet on the other raise the question of whether divine foreknowledge only predicts or also determines the future (1 *Apology* 43.1). If the latter is the case, as many Gnostics maintained, then God determines future events and especially events in our own lives regardless of our choices. If this thesis is valid, Justin argues, then nothing is "up to us" (ἐφ' ἡμῖν); and if this is the case and one person is destined to be good and another bad, then there is no justification whatsoever for any judgement, for blame or praise (43.2). In addition Justin puts forth the argument that I cite below:

> If mankind does not have the power to avoid the evils (τὰ αἰσχρά) and choose the goods in virtue of free will (προαιρέσει ἐλευθέρᾳ), then all actions whatsoever are without cause (ἀναίτιον). But that it is by free will that we act rightly or wrongly we demonstrate in the following way. We see that the same man does opposite things. If it were fated (εἵμαρτο)

10 For a discussion of Justin's view on free will, see Amand 1945, 201–207.

> that a man were either wicked or virtuous, he would not be capable (δεκτικός) of opposites nor would he have changed his mind so many times. Neither would some be virtuous and some wicked, since we would then be making fate (εἱμαρμένη) the cause of evil and exhibit her as acting in opposition to herself, unless what has been said above is true, namely that there is no virtue and vice but that good and evil things are only matters of opinion. And this, as the true account (λόγος) shows, is the greatest impiety and injustice. We claim, though, that the inevitable fate (εἱμαρμένην ἀπαράβατον) consists in the reward of those who choose the good and similarly in the fair punishment of those who choose the opposite (1 *Apology* 43.3–7).

Justin comes to the conclusion that man, unlike all other living creatures, plants or animals, is created by God equipped with the "ability to choose" (προαίρεσις), and this is why he is worthy of praise or blame (1 *Apology* 43.8). This is a point that Justin repeats in many other passages of his work.[11] In these passages Justin uses the term προαίρεσις not in the sense of "choice", as Aristotle, but in the sense of "an ability that enables free choice", as Epictetus does. In the passage cited above Justin puts forth an argument for the existence of ἐλευθέρα προαίρεσις which rests on the claim that the choices of the same agent often vary and can be even opposed to each other, since we often change our minds and opt for a course of action we had previously rejected.[12] Sometimes, for instance, the same man withholds his anger while at other times he lets it burst out, or he may abandon one choice of action in favour of its opposite. Phenomena of this kind show, according to Justin, that one and the same man is capable of different and often opposing choices and actions, and this in his view suggests that one can do otherwise, which in turn means, Justin claims, that one's choices and actions are not fated, because fate cannot determine opposites courses of action and in a sense act, as Justin says, in opposition to herself.[13] Justin goes on to suggest that it is virtue and vice that determine

11 1 *Apology* 28.3–4; *Dialogue with Trypho* 88.5, 102.4, 141.1.

12 Justin's phrase πλειστάκις μετετίθετο (1 *Apology* 43.6) is noticeable in this context. The verb μετατιθέναι can mean "change one's mind" (see LSJ, *s.v.*). Clement later uses the term μεταπῖπτον and μεταπτωτικός to indicate what is subject to change in our mind (*Miscellanies* 2.16.76.1).

13 This must have been a stock argument against necessity, that is, things that admit the opposite are not governed by necessity. Cf. Alexander of Aphrodisias, *On Fate* 9, 174.29–176.17. See Bobzien 1998a, 137–139.

the agent's choice and action, and he appeals to passages both from the Old Testament and from Plato in support of this view.[14]

The question, however, is how Justin disarms the claim that some kind of fate is operating in human decisions including, as he mentions, one's changes of mind. One could argue that every human choice may vary from time to time, as Justin claims, but that human choice remains nevertheless determined by a number of factors and it is these factors that eventually necessitate one's final choice. Justin does not address this view. All that he is concerned with refuting is the claim that the determination of human choices is solely external; and he does this by arguing, as the Stoics did, that any human choice essentially includes the contribution of a human agent to the overall causal network. The evidence from people's changes of behaviour or changes of mind, which may range from decisions to do otherwise than initially planned to changes of long-lived habits and dispositions, shows, according to Justin, that man has the capacity of choosing his own actions. And this is all that matters for Justin. If fate is not only an external network of factors but also includes human character, the human factor that is, Justin would not deny that in this sense everything we do is fated. But he is not concerned with such a view or with such a conception of fate. The view of fate that he criticizes, holds that external factors critically determine our choices, and Justin sets out to refute this. The thesis he adopts is, so to speak, an indeterminist one. Justin supports this thesis further by pointing out that if everything were fated in the sense specified above, this amounts to abolishing virtue and vice and thus the grounds for praise and blame.

In his second *Apology* Justin now argues explicitly against the Stoics, who held that "everything comes to be by necessity of fate" (2 *Apology* 6.4), that if this were the case, God would then be responsible for evils too (6.9). But this is impossible by the Stoics' own admission. Justin adds an argument similar to that of the passage cited above, namely that God made men similar to angels in being free to make their own decisions, in being able to turn toward the good or the evil (ἐπ' ἀμφότερα τρέπεσθαι), and for this reason, he claims, both men and angels are accountable for their actions (2 *Apology* 7.4–6).

Justin's claims against the Stoics are somewhat misplaced, since they distinguished between necessary and fated actions, although some sources conflate the two, as Justin does.[15] They clearly acknowledged, however, the decisive

14 1 *Apology* 44.1–8, invoking Deuteronomy 30.15 and 19, Isaiah 1.16–20, Plato, *Republic* 10.617e.

15 Compare Cicero, *On Fate* 39–43 (SVF 2.974; LS 62B) with Gellius, *Attic Nights* 7.2.6–13 (SVF 1000, LS 62D). The latter speaks of *necessitas fati*, as Justin does.

role of the human factor in the shaping of one's final choice in such a way that a distinction between causal determinism and necessity becomes clear.[16] The Stoic example of the cylinder and the cone was meant to suggest that the outcome of rolling or spinning, like the agent's action x or z, is causally determined and thus fated (in their terminology) given the external factors on the one hand as well as the agent's character on the other; yet whatever the outcome is, it is not necessary, because according to the Stoics the agent's mind, like the cylinder in their analogy, contributes the primary or the decisive cause to the causal network, namely his beliefs and his critical disposition towards them.[17] The analogy is meant to illustrate the Stoic compatibilism, that is, the view that one's mind or nature plays the critical or decisive causal role in the quality of the effect.

Justin's criticism of the Stoics may have been inspired by Plutarch and Alexander of Aphrodisias, who criticized the Stoic thesis that man's freedom consists in choosing only what is good, instead arguing that human free choice amounts to being able to choose between two possible or even opposing courses of action, X or Y.[18] Justin makes it evident that he subscribes to this view in the passage cited above, in which he says that "by free will" (προαιρέσει ἐλευθέρᾳ) we act rightly or wrongly. A wrong action, then, can count according to Justin as a perfectly free action. He employs this notion of free will because he wants to emphasize that God is not responsible for anything wrong, only man is. As a Platonist, Justin agrees with Plato in this regard (*Republic* 2.379c, 10.617e; *Theaetetus* 176a). According to Justin, man exercises his free will and makes a free choice when he chooses either to comply with God's will and act virtuously or to oppose it and act viciously, even acting against one's own interests. For the Stoics, by contrast, a choice of something vicious or evil is not a free one but one enslaved to mistaken beliefs; the choice of course remains up to us for the Stoics but our choice may be free or enslaved depending on how we choose, while for Justin the choice we make is always free no matter how we choose.

Justin's younger contemporaries, Tatian (*ca.* 120–170) and Theophilus (*ca.* 150–220) appear to oscillate between the Stoic notion of free will and the modified version that we find in contemporary Platonists and Peripatetics such as

16 The Stoics also use the argument that praise and blame require free will; cf. – again – Gellius, *Attic Nights* 7.2.

17 For a discussion of the Stoic example, see Bobzien 1998a, 259–271 and Bobzien 1998b.

18 This is the view of Alexander of Aphrodisias and of Plutarch. See Boys-Stones 2007 and Frede 2011, 89–101. Further affinities between Justin and Alexander are noted by Minnis 2010, 268.

Plutarch and Alexander. Like Justin, Tatian claims that human actions are not the work of "fate" (εἱμαρμένη) but of human "freedom of will" (ἐλευθερία τῆς προαιρέσεως), and this has to do with the fact that God endowed both men and angels with the "power of deciding freely" (αὐτεξούσιον; *Against the Greeks* 7.1). Tatian then makes an interesting claim: he suggests that originally man was free but sin made us slaves to wickedness, and that this happened because of our ability to choose on our own (ἀπώλεσεν ἡμᾶς τὸ αὐτεξούσιον; *ibid.* 11.2). In Tatian's view, we lost our freedom because of a wrong use of our autonomy,[19] and he further suggests that this had as a consequence the loss of immortality that man's soul originally possessed (7.2–3, 11.2). Nevertheless, Tatian adds, we are still capable of rejecting wickedness and regaining our ability to choose freely (11.2), although he does not tell us how this is possible. In what follows, however, Tatian implies that a life in harmony with God and creation would make that possible.

Tatian's position is close to the Stoic thesis that we cease to be free once we make the wrong, wicked choice, but he also holds that we nonetheless retain the power to choose and we can regain our freedom of choice if we change our habits and our life. Tatian does not distance himself much from the Stoic view, because his main target is not the Stoics but rather the astrologists who maintained that the stars determine the course of human lives and the events in our lives. Tatian is the first of a series of Christian thinkers who set out to specifically discredit astral determinism. Tatian's argument against it is a version of the Stoic "lazy argument", according to which if it is fated that someone remain poor, then there is no reason for one to work and save money. We clearly do not believe that, Tatian says, and for this reason we daily continue our efforts (*Against the Greeks* 11).

The same line of thought can also be found in Theophilus. He argues that God made man "free and autonomous" (ἐλεύθερον καὶ αὐτεξούσιον), but through neglect and disobedience to God man earned death for himself, while through obedience to God he can regain immortality (*To Autolycus* 2.27). The fact that Theophilus puts "freedom" (ἐλεύθερον) and "autonomy" (αὐτεξούσιον) together suggests that the latter now comes close to meaning "the ability to choose freely", not just "having power over ourselves". It is noteworthy that Theophilus agrees with Tatian in associating freedom of choice with the immortality of the soul. Theophilus, however, sets out to show that man was created neither mortal nor immortal but only "capable" (δεκτικός) of mortality and immortality, depending on whether he complies with God's commands or

19 δοῦλοι γεγόναμεν οἱ ἐλεύθεροι, διὰ τὴν ἁμαρτίαν ἐπράθημεν (*Against the Greeks* 11.2).

not – a point we can already find in Philo.[20] It is in the course of the discussion about the immortality of the soul that Theophilus introduces the notion of free choice.

Theophilus brings together two lines of thought that we find separated in Justin, namely that God has made us capable of virtue and vice, that is, endowed us with the ability to choose freely (1 *Apology* 43.3–6), and that the human soul is not immortal by nature but that its immortality is rather conferred onto it by God (*Dialogue with Trypho* 5.4–6). In so doing, Theophilus fleshes out the notion of grace that Justin only sketched out. Theophilus suggests that God grants man immortality, yet God does not do so arbitrarily but in accordance with man's own use of freedom of choice and autonomy. As Tatian claims, we lost our immortality because of a misuse of our will. Such misuse carries severe consequences, while one's proper use of will is rewarded. In doing so, God does not favour some people over others, as the Gnostics claimed, but he does reward the good use of their will by granting them immortality. This is what divine grace is: on the one hand it transcends natural necessity, while on the other it respects man's freedom of choice.

3 Irenaeus and Tertullian

Irenaeus of Lyon pays a great deal of attention to the issue of free will in his anti-Gnostic critique in his *Against Heresies*.[21] Valentinus and his supporters maintained a firm position on this issue. He distinguished three class of people; those made in the image of God, those made in God's "likeness" (ὁμοίωσιν), and those who are neither made in the image nor in the likeness of God (*Against Heresies* 5.6.1). Accordingly, Valentinus and the Valentinians distinguished three categories of people: the pneumatic, perfect men; the psychic, imperfect men; and the earthly, who are, in their view, only partly human beings. They further argued that salvation is certain only for the first category of people (*Against Heresies* 1.6.1–3). The third category of people, the earthly, are in their view by nature prone to wickedness and do not have any hope of salvation no matter what they do. The people of the second category are capable of either good or bad decisions and salvation is up to them. They are the only ones who have "autonomy" or freedom of choice (αὐτεξούσιον). For the Valen-

20 Philo, *On the Creation of the World* 135.

21 On Irenaeus' views on free will and his anti-Gnostic critique, see Amand 1945, 212–223, Fantino 1985, and Osborne 2001.

tinians, however, this is a disadvantage compared with the people of the first category, those who are destined by God to be good.[22]

Irenaeus criticizes Valentinus' doctrine of predestination as both inconsistent and unreasonable and in this context gives his own view on the question of free will. Irenaeus first argues that it is difficult to imagine on what grounds God could have divided people into distinct classes, privileging some over others and how he could have justified such as division. He further suggests that those who take such a view ultimately abolish the value and disvalue of goodness and badness, and virtue and vice, respectively, as well as the justification for either praise or blame (4.37.2). Irenaeus instead claims that God created all people equal; as a result of the divine act of the creation of man, all human beings are endowed with the same nature, that is, all are made in the image and the likeness of God. This in turn means, he says, that all human beings are "free to choose" (*liber in arbitrio et suae potestatis*) and all can be saved.[23] Irenaeus summarizes his thesis as follows:

> Man is endowed with reason and in that respect he is similar to God, being made by his creator so that he is free in judging and in deciding. The cause is placed on man, such that it depends on man alone whether he will become corn or pollen. This is why man is rightly condemned, since as a rational being he has lost true reason and he led a life without reason opposing God's justice (*Against Heresies* 4.4.3).[24]

In this dense passage Irenaeus makes three claims: (a) that man is similar to God, which means that there are no variations of similarity to God among human beings; (b) that the similarity to God consists in the fact that man is endowed with the freedom to judge and to choose, that is to comply with God's justice or not; and (c) that it is man himself who determines his success or happiness in life. Like earlier Christian thinkers, Irenaeus often stresses that "freedom of choice and judgement" (*liber in arbitrio*) is an essential feature of human beings that was given to them by God so that they can freely choose

22 On Valentinus' theory of will see further Dihle 1982, 150–157, and Magris' contribution in this volume, 186–192. Valentinus relies partly on Paul's distinction between earthly and spiritual men in the Letter to the Romans 8.5.

23 Cf. Irenaeus, *Against Heresies* 4.4.3, 4.37.1, 4; *Demonstration* 11, SC 406: 98. See further Fantino 1985, 5–8, 68–75 and Osborn 2001, 211–216, who discuss the concepts of the image and likeness of God in Irenaeus and their difference.

24 *homo vero rationabilis, et secundum hoc similis Deo, liber in arbitrio factus et suae potestatis, ipse sibi causa est ut aliquando quidem frumentum, aliquando autem palea fiat. quapropter et iuste condemnabitur, quoniam rationabilis factus amisit veram rationem, et irrationabiliter adversatus est iustitiae Dei.*

whether they want to follow the commands of God or to neglect them, that is, they can choose good or evil.[25] Irenaeus also emphasizes in this connection that in such a case all human beings are equal and it is their choice to become good or bad (*Against Heresies* 4.37.2–4). Irenaeus further claims that the good use of our freedom of choice would bring us the divine gift of immortality as a reward (*ibid.* 5.29.1). This is a point we found in Theophilus and also in some form in Justin. Irenaeus offers a stronger version of that point: he suggests that the purpose of the capacity of free choice (*arbitrium*, αὐτεξούσιον) has as an aim leading man to immortality, but this happens only if this ability is used well (5.29.1). The main aim of this human feature is not merely to enable us to choose as we please, but rather to help us lead a perfect Christian life and to thus gain salvation.

Tertullian is, like Irenaeus, also seriously concerned with arguing against the Gnostics that God is not responsible for the evil in the world, while maintaining that God is the only principle of the world; he rather suggests that evils have their origin in man alone (*Against Marcion* 2.6.1). One could, of course, argue that God is ultimately responsible for the evils that man causes on the grounds that God created man and indeed created man in his image and his likeness. Tertullian argues against such a view claiming, like many of his predecessors, that man is created by God endowed with the ability to choose freely. Like Justin and Irenaeus, Tertullian operates with a notion of free will according to which freedom consists in choosing either the good or the bad, not a notion based on siding with the good, as the Stoics had. Tertullian advances a series of arguments against the objection that God is ultimately responsible for man's misuse of his will. The first of these arguments develops a line of thought that we first encounter in Theophilus and Irenaeus.

> Freedom of will (*libertas arbitrii*) cannot discharge its own blame upon him by whom it was bestowed, but on him by whom it was not made to function as it ought. Of what wrong, then, can you accuse the creator? If of man's sin, I answer that what is man's cannot be God's, nor can he be judged the author of sin who is seen to have forbidden it, even to have condemned it. If death is an evil, not even death can bring odium upon him who threatened it but upon him who disregarded it. This one is its author: he created it by disregarding it, for it would not have come

25 *veterem legem libertatis hominis manifestavit, quia liberum eum Deus fecit, ab initio habentem suam potestatem sicut et suam animam, ad utendum sententia Dei voluntarie, et non coactum ab eo. vis enim a Deo non fit, sed bona sententia adest illi semper* (*Against Heresies* 4.37.1; cf. *ibid.* 4.37.4).

> into existence except for his disregard. (*Against Marcion* 2.9.9, tr. Evans, modified)

Tertullian adopts the position of earlier Christian thinkers in maintaining that we alone are responsible for our fortune and he relates the use of the will to the possible immortality of human beings. He claims that sin amounts to a bad use of free will that brings death with it. Tertullian sustains the claim that the author of death is not God, who linked the two, sin and death, but rather man who disregarded their necessary link between the two and continues to make bad use of the divine gift of will, ignoring God's commands.[26] Tertullian introduces an analogy here: in the same way that God's authorship of the law of gravity does not make him responsible for someone's death if that person disregards gravity by falling from a window, similarly, he claims, it is man who is entirely responsible for his death on account of disregarding the necessary link that God established between sin and death. Nor can one thrust out to God responsibility for the human misuse of free will by conveniently appealing to the existence of the devil, for instance, because, Tertullian argues, he is not God's creation either, since God made all angels originally good and it was the devil's own misuse of free will that accounts for his corruption.[27] Similarly, he contends, man was created in God's likeness but he has fallen away from the creator and original human nature (*On Spectacles* 2.11–12). Tertullian foreshadows the position later adopted by Origen, that God created a variety of intellects engaged in thinking and as a result of their good or bad use of their thinking did they determine their future lives as angels or demons, or human beings, that is, primarily their characters and inclinations.

Tertullian addresses another question, which will also be tackled by Origen, namely that of why God endowed man with free will since he knew that this would result in damaging effects, such as not only bringing vice into the world, but being self-destructive for the agent as well. Tertullian suggests that man could not exhibit goodness at all unless he were able to choose it by himself, and this ability is a divine gift, because it allows man to do the good and to have goodness.

> So that the man could have a goodness of his own, bestowed upon him by God, and that henceforth goodness can be proper to man and a natural

26 Further on this see Osborn 1997, 167–170.

27 I try to stay close to Tertullian's own language, which speaks of man *sua sponte corruptum*, that is, "corrupted of his own act" (*Against Marcion* 2.10.1).

> attribute, there was granted and assigned to him freedom (*libertas*) and the ability to choose (*potestas arbitrii*), as a kind of transfer of the good bestowed on him by God (*Against Marcion* 2.6.5).

Tertullian goes on the assumption that, given human rationality, there is no way that man can achieve goodness without reason. Following the Stoics, he holds that rational beings cannot do the good unless they make a rational choice to this effect. And like Justin and Tatian, Tertullian appears to think that the choice between good or bad, virtue or vice, are equal expressions of freedom and that having a free will amounts to choosing between opposites, between right and wrong, virtue or vice, a view defended by Alexander against the Stoic conception of freedom (according to which we achieve freedom only when we choose the good).[28] Like earlier Christians, Tertullian finds the Peripatetic view of freedom fitting to his purposes because he wants to argue against the Gnostics by maintaining that God is neither responsible for any evil nor culpable of favouritism.

One could here object, however, that not all humans are endowed with the same degree of rationality: some people have very strong non-rational desires due to their particular bodily constitution or their temperaments, while others do not. One could further argue in this vein that God may not be directly responsible for vice or evil but that he is nevertheless responsible for a certain lack of equality among men. This lack of equality raises an issue that neither Tertullian nor Irenaeus addressed. They were mainly concerned with arguing against Gnostic determinism and defending the equality of all men only in terms of their power to choose. Clement goes beyond this kind of polemic against the Gnostics and appears to draw on a fully-fledged Christian theory of free will, although he does not systematically lay such a theory out.

4 Clement of Alexandria

Clement often repeats in his work that man is equipped with the power to make choices freely, which he calls αὐτεξούσιον or τὸ ἐφ' ἡμῖν. The following passage is indicative of the centrality of this topic in Clement's thought:

28 On Alexander's notion of free will, see Frede 2011, 95–101, and the contributions of Natali and Lautner in this volume. On the impact of Alexander's notion of free will on early Christians, see Edwards in this volume, 300–301.

> Virtue, however, is not up to others but entirely up to us (ἐφ' ἡμῖν). One can prevent us from other things by opposing us, but this does not apply to our capacity of choosing (τὸ ἐφ' ἡμῖν) in any way, even if one threatens as much as he can, because this is a divine gift that belongs to nobody else but to us. As a result, licentiousness is not believed to be a vice of someone else but of the licentious one, while temperance is a good of the one who can be temperate (*Miscellanies* 4.19.124.2–3).

The above passage makes two main points: first, that the unconstrained capacity of choice is given to us by God, it is a divine gift; second, that this capacity is a characteristic feature of human beings that makes them accountable for virtue and vice. Both points are quite common to most earlier Christian thinkers. Clement, however, distinguishes himself from his predecessors by claiming that the capacity to choose freely is the most essential function of the human mind or of the ruling part of the soul, the ἡγεμονικόν, which is the reasoning part. Clement makes that clear in several passages. In his work *The Rich Man's Salvation* discussing the role of riches in human life, he makes the following claim, at 14.2–4:

> We must not therefore put the responsibility on that which, having in itself neither good nor evil, is not responsible, but on that which has the power of using things either well or badly according to its choice. And this is the mind of man, which has in itself both free judgement (κριτήριον ἐλεύθερον) and freedom of choice (αὐτεξούσιον) to deal with what is given to it.[29] (Tr. Butterworth, modified)

The above passage is important not only for clearly stating that it is the human choice that turns something into good or bad, a claim reminiscent of Socrates' argument in the *Euthydemus* (278e–281e) and the *Meno* (78b–79e), but also the view that the "mind" (νοῦς) is equipped with freedom of choice. Elsewhere Clement suggests that this is actually a "faculty of the mind" (ἡγεμονικόν) and indeed the principal one, to which all other faculties are meant to be servants:

> What we do not do either we do not do it because we cannot or because we do not want, or because of both… The will (τὸ βούλεσθαι) then has

---

29 οὐ χρὴ τοίνυν τὸ ἐξ ἑαυτοῦ μὴ ἔχον μήτε τὸ ἀγαθὸν μήτε τὸ κακόν, ἀναίτιον ὄν, αἰτιᾶσθαι, ἀλλὰ τὸ δυνάμενον καὶ καλῶς τούτοις χρῆσθαι καὶ κακῶς, ἀφ' ὧν ἂν ἕληται, κατ' αὐτὸ ⟨τοῦτο αἴτιον ὄν⟩. τοῦτο δ' ἔστι νοῦς ἀνθρώπου, καὶ κριτήριον ἐλεύθερον ἔχων ἐν ἑαυτῷ καὶ τὸ αὐτεξούσιον τῆς μεταχειρίσεως τῶν δοθέντων.

> always the first role. For the other faculties of the mind are meant to be its servants.[30] (*Miscellanies* 2.16.77.2–5.)

In this passage τὸ βούλεσθαι is clearly more than a capacity to choose; it is a faculty of the human mind and indeed one that dominates over all other faculties. And one relevant question here is what role this feature of the human mind plays to justify such centrality.

It is important to note from the start that Clement brings up the issue of free will in the context of discussing Christian faith. Clement distinguishes between religion based "on necessity" (κατ᾽ ἀνάγκην) and "on choice" (κατὰ προαίρεσιν; *Paedagogus* 1.87.2)[31] and he maintains that the *Logos* enables man to choose his commitment to the Christian faith (*ibid.* 1.30.3–31.1). Clement actually suggests that the human capacity to choose "freely" (τὸ ἑκούσιον) essentially exists so that man can accept or deny the guidance of the *Logos* (*Paedagogus* 1.87.1–2) This is a "choice" (προαίρεσις, ἐκλογή) that man can make with his "mind" (ἡγεμονικόν), given his endowment with a "deliberative faculty" (προαιρετικὴ δύναμις; *Miscellanies* 6.16.135.2–4). This choice is, of course, an act of will, but is not one of the ordinary choices we make in everyday life; it is rather a specific kind of choice, namely the choice of assenting to Christian faith, as the following passage suggests.

> Now what is in our power (ἐφ᾽ ἡμῖν) is that of which we are masters (κύριοι) equally as we are of its opposite, like for instance whether we do philosophy or not, whether we believe or disbelieve (πιστεῖν ἢ ἀπιστεῖν). Since we are equally masters of each of the opposites, it becomes manifest that we have the capacity to choose freely (τὸ ἐφ᾽ ἡμῖν) (*Miscellanies* 4.24.153.1).

The terms "believe" and "disbelieve" in this context are used in the special sense of commitment (or a lack thereof) to Christian doctrine. In the above passage Clement suggests that our freedom consists in our ability to choose either of them, to believe or disbelieve, and, more generally in the ability to choose between "opposite options" (τὰ ἀντικείμενα). Justin also makes this point, but he refers to any opposite courses of actions, while Clement refers specifically to the choice of following the Christian faith. Like all previous

30 ἃ δὲ μὴ ποιοῦμεν, ἤτοι διὰ τὸ μὴ δύνασθαι οὐ ποιοῦμεν ἢ διὰ τὸ μὴ βούλεσθαι ἢ δι᾽ ἀμφότερα … προηγεῖται τοίνυν παντων τὸ βούλεσθαι. αἱ γὰρ λογικαὶ δυνάμεις τοῦ βούλεσθαι διάκονοι πεφύκασι.

31 Cf. *Miscellanies* 7.12.73.5. On this issue see Havrda 2011.

Christian thinkers but unlike the Stoics, Clement takes the view that our freedom is expressed even when we make the wrong choice, even if we opt for the vicious or the wicked course of action. He points out, though, that such a choice can be avoided with the guidance or the exhortation we receive from God, the *Logos*.

Clement elaborates on this idea particularly in his *Paedagogus* and his *Protrepticus*. He claims that man is not left alone to choose between following or not following God, between believing or disbelieving; rather, Clement suggests, the *Logos* stirs in men the desire to follow God and become like God (*Protrepticus* 117.2). God's angels, Clement suggests, operate like the daemons of Lachesis in the myth of Er in *Republic* 10, in that they are sent to human souls to help people commit to their choice of life and fulfil it (*Miscellanies* 5.13.90.5–91.5; cf. 6.17.161.2). Clement actually suggests that Socrates' *daimon* was something like an angel, helping him to commit to the good (5.13.91.5). Clement claims, however, that there is no reason to think that there is a contradiction between God's callings and the choices we humans make, since it remains completely in our power to be convinced or not, to commit to the good and follow God's commands or not.[32] Wickedness arises in us because of ignorance or weakness, which drag us into directions where we do not actually want to go.[33] Clement adds that God appeals to everyone, although he knows that not everyone would follow him. Divine exhortations are merely a calling; their acceptance and final endorsement depends on us. As with the Stoic cognitive impressions, they cannot make us do anything but rather require our assent.[34]

There is a difference, however, between the Stoic theory regarding assent to cognitive impressions and Clement's theory of divine exhortation towards the aim of living a fully Christian life. According to the Stoic theory, assent is completely within our power, while the goal of living a perfect Christian life is not entirely within human reach. Clement suggests that the fulfilment of this aim requires both our choice and God's assistance, God's grace (*Miscella-*

32 ὁ θεῖος λόγος κέκραγεν πάντας συλλήβδην καλῶν, εἰδὼς μὲν καὶ μάλιστα τοὺς μὴ πεισθησομένους, ὅμως δ'οὖν, ἐφ' ἡμῖν τὸ πείθεσθαι· τε καὶ μή, ὡς μὴ ἔχειν ἄγνοιαν προφασίσασθαί τινας, δικαίαν τὴν κλῆσιν πεποίηται, τὸ κατὰ δύναμιν δὲ ἑκάστου ἀπαιτεῖ (*Miscellanies* 2.5.26.3).

33 ὅτι τὸ πιστεύειν τε καὶ πείθεσθαι ἐφ' ἡμῖν. κακῶν δὲ αἰτίαν καὶ ὕλης ἄν τις ἀσθένειαν ὑπολάβοι καὶ τὰς ἀβουλήτους τῆς ἀγνοίας ὁρμὰς τάς τε ἀλόγους δι' ἀμαθίαν ἀνάγκας (*Miscellanies* 6.3.16.2; cf. 6.2.9.4).

34 Sextus Empiricus, *Against the Professors* 7.247–252 (LS 40E).

nies 5.1.7.1–2).[35] In other words, for Clement the realization of the human end to live a perfect Christian life, that is, to become like God, requires collaboration between man and God. Perfection cannot be achieved by man alone, but rather requires God's assistance.[36] Man's contribution in the project of reaching perfection lies in the assent to follow divine guidance and do what he can to achieve that goal.[37] God responds to that human effort and intervenes to assist and eventually to save man. Clement makes the following remark by addressing the question of who can be saved (τίς δύναται σωθῆναι), given the various powerful passions that trouble us, such as the passion for wealth.

> But the Lord answers: "that which is impossible with men is possible for God." (Mark 10.27) This again is full of great wisdom, because when practicing and striving after the passionless state by himself man achieves nothing, but if he makes it clear that he is eagerly pursuing this aim and is in deep earnest, he prevails by the addition of the power that comes from God. For God breathes his own power into souls when they desire, but if they ever desist from their eagerness, then too the spirit given from God is withdrawn; for to save men against their will is an act of force, but to save them when they choose is an act of grace. (*The Rich Man's Salvation* 21.1–2, tr. Butterworth.)

Quite importantly, then, for Clement the main task of human free will is to choose a specific kind of life and not merely to choose a certain course of action, as earlier Christians had thought. It is for this reason that Clement draws on Plato's myth of Er in this context. For Clement, as for Plato, it is this choice of life, the kind of βίος, that matters most, because it is this choice that largely

---

35 See also *Miscellanies* 5.12.83.1, where Clement says that "when our freedom of choice (τὸ ἐν ἡμῖν αὐτεξούσιον) approaches the good it jumps and leaps over the trench, as athletes say. But it is not without special grace that the soul is … raised." For a discussion see Havrda 2011.

36 The following passage from *The Rich Man Salvation*, at 10, is important in this regard: "ἐὶ θέλεις τέλειος γενέσθαι." οὐκ ἄρα πω τέλειος ἦν. οὐδὲν γὰρ τελείου τελειότερον. καὶ θείως τὸ "εἰ θέλεις" τὸ αὐτεξούσιον τῆς προσδιαλεγομένης αὐτῷ ψυχῆς ἐδήλωσεν. ἐπὶ τῷ ἀνθρώπῳ γὰρ ἦν ἡ αἵρεσις ὡς ἐλευθέρῳ, ἐπὶ θεῷ δὲ ἡ δόσις ὡς κυρίῳ. δίδωσι δὲ βουλομένοις καὶ ὑπερεσπουδακόσι καὶ δεομένοις, ἵν' οὕτως ἴδιον αὐτῶν ἡ σωτηρία γένηται: "If thou will become perfect" (Matthew 19.21). So he was not yet perfect; for there are no degrees of perfection. And the "if thou will" was a divine declaration of the freedom of choice of the soul that was talking with Him. For the choice lay with the man as a free being, though the gift was with God as Lord. And He gives to those who desire and are in deep earnest and beg, that in this way salvation may become their own (tr. Butterworth, modified).

37 *Miscellanies* 2.5.26.3, 7.2.9.4, 7.2.12.1–5.

determines all other subsequent choices. Given the importance of this choice, Clement tries to reconcile our freedom to make this choice with some kind of divine assistance that does not violate human freedom but rather strengthens it. Quite clearly, with Clement there is a clear shift in the argument of Christian thinkers regarding our ability to choose freely. The question is not so much whether we have such a capacity, but rather whether this capacity alone suffices to bring us to Christian perfection and salvation. We can now understand why the human will is so important for Clement, namely because through this we shape our characters, our lives, and decide what kind of persons we will be. This is actually what distinguishes the Christian "wise man" (γνωστικός) from the others, that his "will" (τὸ βούλεσθαι) determines his judgement and his actions (*Miscellanies* 2.16.77.5–6). This is a step that paves the way for Origen's more complex theory of free will, which aims to show that we are responsible for our characters and constitutions; according to Clement the choice of life that our will makes also determines our future choices and our inclinations and thus critically shapes our lives.

5 Conclusion

From the above outline it becomes clear, I hope, that early Christian philosophers were strongly preoccupied with the question of free will and human responsibility. A close look at their arguments explains the reasons for this preoccupation. They wished to defend the view against those who argued that our choices are determined in this or the other way, that we have the power and the authority to choose and that nothing can force our assent. Yet while early Christian philosophers from Justin onward defend the human capacity of free choice and human autonomy, Clement takes the further step of making this capacity a faculty of the human mind (τὸ βούλεσθαι) and indeed one that has the primary role in our mental life. This faculty is responsible not only for our individual choices in everyday life but more importantly for our choice of life. For Clement this is the main choice we have to make, since this determines our lives in general. This implication is that this choice shapes all further choices, and also our temperaments and characters. For Clement this choice is important also as an indication of our commitment to God. God's assistance for salvation respects that choice and further rewards it. Clement is an important link in the development of a theory of free will in early Christianity, as he paves the way for Origen's theory of free will, according to which we are responsibly for our constitutions, characters and inclinations.

Bibliography

Amand, David. 1945. *Fatalisme et liberté dans l'Antiquité grecque*. Louvain: Bibliothèque de l'Université.

Bobzien, Susanne. 1998a. *Determinism and Freedom in Stoic Philosophy*. Oxford: Clarendon.

Bobzien, Susanne. 1998b. "The Inadvertent Conception and Late Birth of the Free-Will Problem." *Phronesis* 43: 133–175.

Boys-Stones, George. 2007. "'Middle' Platonists on Fate and Human Autonomy." In *Greek and Roman Philosophy 100 BC–200 AD*, edited by Robert W. Sharples and Richard Sorabji, vol. 2, 431–447. London: Institute of Classical Studies.

Boys-Stones, George. 2007. "Human Autonomy and Divine Revelation in Origen." In *Severan Culture*, edited by Simon C.R. Swain, Stephen J. Harrison, and Jas Elsner, 488–499. Cambridge: Cambridge University Press.

Cumont, Franz. 1912. *Astrology and Religion among the Greeks and Romans*. New York: G.P. Putnam's Sons.

Dihle, Albrecht. 1982. *The Theory of Will in Classical Antiquity*. Berkeley: University of California Press.

Fantino, Jacques. 1985. *L'homme image de Dieu chez saint Irénée de Lyon*. Paris: Cerf.

Frede, Michael. 2011. *A Free Will. Origins of the Notion in Ancient Thought*, edited by Anthony A. Long. Berkeley: University of California Press.

Gourinat, Jean-Baptiste. 2014. "*Adsensio in nostra potestate*: 'From Us' and 'Up to Us' in Ancient Stoicism – a Plea for Reassessment." In *What is Up to Us? Studies on Agency and Responsibility in Ancient Philosophy*, edited by Pierre Destrée, Ricardo Salles, and Marco Zingano, 141–150. Sankt Augustin: Academia.

Havrda, Matyáš. 2011. "Grace and Free Will According to Clement of Alexandria." *Journal of Early Christian Studies* 19: 21–48.

Hegedus, Tim. 2007. *Early Christianity and Ancient Astrology*. New York: Peter Lang.

Hengstermann, Christian. 2016. *Origenes und der Ursprung der Freiheitsmetaphysik*. Münster: Aschendorff.

Karamanolis, George. 2013. *The Philosophy of Early Christianity*. Durham: Acumen.

Layton, Richard A. 2000. "*Propatheia*: Origen and Didymus on the Origin of the Passions." *Vigiliae Christianae* 54: 262–282.

Long, Anthony A. 1982. "Astrology: Arguments Pro and Contra." In *Science and Speculation: Studies in Hellenistic Theory and Practice*, edited by Jonathan Barnes, 165–192. Cambridge: Cambridge University Press.

Long, Anthony A. 2002. *Epictetus: A Stoic and Socratic Guide to Life*. Oxford: Oxford University Press.

LS: Long, Anthony A., and David N. Sedley. 1987. *The Hellenistic Philosophers*, 2 vols. Cambridge: Cambridge University Press.

Minnis, Denis. 2010. "Justin Martyr." In *The Cambridge History of Philosophy in Late Antiquity*, edited by Lloyd P. Gerson, vol. 1, 258–269. Cambridge: Cambridge University Press.

Osborn, Eric. 1997. *Tertullian: First Theologian of the West*. Cambridge: Cambridge University Press.

Osborn, Eric. 2001. *Irenaeus of Lyons*. Cambridge: Cambridge University Press.

SC: *Sources chrétiennes*. Paris: Cerf, 1942–.

Sorabji, Richard. 2000. *Emotion and Peace of Mind: From Stoic Agitation to Christian Temptation*. Oxford: Oxford University Press.

Sorabji, Richard. 2007. "Epictetus on *Prohairesis* and Self." In *The Philosophy of Epictetus*, edited by Theodore Scaltsas and Andrew S. Mason, 87–98: Oxford: Oxford University Press.

SVF: von Arnim, Hans. 1903–1905. *Stoicorum veterum fragmenta*. Leipzig: Teubner.

Taormina, Daniela. 2014. "Choice (*hairesis*), Self-Determination (*to autexousion*) and What Is in Our power (*to eph' hêmin*) in Porphyry's Interpretation of the Myth of Er." In *What is Up to Us? Studies on Agency and Responsibility in Ancient Philosophy*, edited by Pierre Destrée, Ricardo Salles, and Marco Zingano, 265–282. Sankt Augustin: Academia.

Thomassen, Einar. 2006. *The Spiritual Seed: The Church of the Valentinians*. Leiden: Brill.

CHAPTER 13

Divine Causality. Demiurge and Providence in Plotinus

Enrico Peroli

1 Introduction

In the last years of his life, Plotinus wrote a single, long work *On Providence*, which Porphyry divided in two treatises, number 47 and 48 in the chronological order. As Emile Bréhier already remarked many years ago, in this work – "the finest of all Greek contributions to theodicy"[1] –, Plotinus discusses the classical theme of providence following a traditional framework; it included three main topics: 1) proofs of the existence of providence; 2) the way in which providence acts; and 3) the theodicy in the proper sense of the word.[2]

In the first chapters of his work, however, Plotinus presents a thesis, which is, in some important aspects, wholly un-traditional. Plotinus begins by explaining that his main purpose is to rebut the claim that our cosmos is not arranged in the best possible way. This claim is put in the mouths of Epicureans and Gnostics; the former "say that providence does not exist at all, the other that the universe has been made by an evil maker" (3.2.1.7–10). Against this claim, Plotinus asserts, at the very beginning of his discussion, that "universal providence" (ἡ τοῦ παντὸς πρόνοια) exists and that this "universal providence" has brought about the best physical cosmos. In this context, the term *pronoia* needs to be applied to Nous, since the divine Intellect is the cause of the sensible world and of its rational order (3.2.1.24–26). Immediately after that, however, Plotinus explains that this cosmic order does not reflect any rational design made by its cause. On the one hand, Plotinus makes clear that the term *pronoia*, when applied to Nous as the cause of the cosmos, designates the fact that "the universe comes from Intellect and Intellect is prior in nature", or, as Plotinus puts it in his own definition of *pronoia*, "providence for the All

1 Armstrong 1966–88, vol. 3, 38. All translations of Plotinus are taken from Armstrong's Loeb edition of the *Enneads*, with some slight changes. References to the Greek text follow Henry and Schwyzer 1964–1982.

2 Bréhier 1924–38, vol. 3, 17–23.

 | DOI:10.1163/9789004436381_015

[for the physical cosmos] is its being according to Intellect" (3.2.1.22–23). On the other hand, Plotinus denies that ἡ τοῦ παντὸς πρόνοια could be understood in the sense that the good and rational order of the physical world is the result of "a fore-seeing and a calculation of God (προόρασίν τινα καὶ λογισμὸν θεοῦ) about how this All might come into existence and how things might be as good as possible" (3.2.1.18–19).

This view is common in Plotinus, who generally claims that true and intelligible principles act on the physical cosmos without being engaged in reasoning, deliberating, planning and fore-seeing. In order to explain how divine causality determines and guarantees an optimal world order, Plotinus develops a new and alternative theory about God's creative activity. And he maintains that his new theory can deliver a more coherent and defendable story about "universal providence" than the traditional Platonic theories that appeal to a demiurgic account of the making of the world in order to support the same claims.

The purpose of my chapter is to discuss some aspects of Plotinus' dissenting story about divine causality and providence, by making three points. First, I will discuss Plotinus' criticism of the view that the cosmos is the product of God's causality based on reasoning, planning and deliberating. Second, I will deal with Plotinus' own theory on providence and divine causality, and, third, I will highlight what I believe to be the philosophical meaning and relevance of Plotinian theory. Before doing so, I will start with some introductory remarks about the historical background of Plotinus' theory. It can help us to come to a better understanding of Plotinus' theory, its origin and motivation.

2 Historical Background

First of all, the Plotinian theory about providence and divine causality is rather different from the one presented in Plato's *Timaeus*. According to *Timaeus*, our world is constituted and arranged in the best possible way by a divine craftsman or demiurge. Plato represents the demiurge as guided by his own planning or calculation (λογισμός: 30b, 34a–b) in order to bring about a well ordered cosmos. Indeed, it seems that the demiurge's causal power is labeled *pronoia* (*Timaeus* 30b–c) to reflect precisely the claim that benevolent divine planning is explanatory of various features of the physical world (44c, 45a–b).

Plotinus, however, does not accept that the divine thought responsible for cosmic order could possess any of these Platonic features; instead, he proposes a metaphorical reading of the demiurgic model of causation set out in

Plato's *Timaeus*;[3] he regards Plato's words as a metaphor suggesting that our sensible world is ordered as if it were produced by the rational plan of a provident craftsman; but, according to Plotinus, this is not what happens in reality. One of the reasons why Plotinus departs from a literal reading of Plato's demiurgic causation is to be found in his polemic against the Gnostics and their use of Platonic texts. Plotinus rejects the Gnostic account of cosmogony as a misinterpretation of Plato's demiurge. In fact, according to Plotinus, such an account emphasizes the arbitrary and anthropomorphic aspects of demiurge's activity.[4]

As many scholars already remarked, the direct confrontation with Gnosticism played an important role in Plotinus' attempt to develop a non-demiurgic account of the making of the world. However, as Dominic O'Meara already pointed out some years ago, in developing his own theory Plotinus was not inspired only by his polemics with Gnosticism.[5] Some important aspects of the Plotinian view can be found in treatises which predate the explicit polemic with Gnosticism (contained in the so-called anti-Gnostic "Großschrift", consisting in treatises 30, 31 and 32): in treatises number 4 and 5, for example, Plotinus accepts the Aristotelian position that nature, unlike craftsmen, does not deliberate when producing things and for this reason it achieves a perfection far surpassing what is attainable by craftsmanly process;[6] moreover, Plotinus rejects any anthropomorphic view of the demiurge and uses some arguments that had already been emphasized by Epicureans, for example in Cicero's *On the Nature of the Gods*, at 1.18–20.[7] In his treatises Plotinus shows a familiarity with the debate in the philosophical schools concerning demiurgic accounts of the constitution of the world. Plotinus' theory of divine causality and providence must be interpreted in light of this debate; it represents an attempt to formulate, from a Platonic point of view, an answer to the problems that came up in this debate – and which are traditionally associated with the interpretation of Plato's *Timaeus*.

Within this frame, Plotinus' theory of divine causality and providence can be plausibly understood as motivated by his desire to resolve tensions within the Platonic tradition. One approach which Plotinus could find in a variety of forms in his Platonic predecessors was to distinguish between the highest

3 Cf., for example, 3.2.14.1–6, 5.8.7.36–44, 6.7.1.28–32, 6.8.7.1–4; see Chiaradonna 2014b, 203–205.

4 Cf. 2.9.6 and Narbonne 2011, 118–121.

5 See O'Meara 1981.

6 Cf. Aristotle, *Metaphysics* 7.7, 1032a12–28; *Physics* 2.8, 199b28 (quoted by Plotinus, *Enneads* 4.8.8.15–16); *On the Heavens* 2.4, 287b.

7 Cf. *Enneads* 5.9.6.20–24; 4.8.2.20–38; 4.8.8.11–16; 5.7.3.7–12.

God and a lower principle, to which the functions of the demiurge were attributed. This approach clearly frees the highest God from implications in the demiurgic processes, but it does not eliminate them. They are merely attributed to another cosmological principle. Therefore, Middle-Platonist authors widely resorted to the demiurgic image in describing the production of the world and argued that the natural order reflects the reasonings of the demiurge and his "administrative care" of the world, in Alcinous' words (*Didaskalikos* 12, 167.13–14 Hermann).[8] Plotinus dissents from earlier Platonists on this point. He rejects the traditional Platonist conception of the demiurge based on Plato's *Timaeus*, and argues that this conception is incompatible with some important commitments that he deems all Platonists should share. Plotinus maintains that, if the fundamental principles of Platonic philosophy are taken properly into account, then it is necessary to offer an alternative theory of divine providence, which excludes any demiurgic account of the constitution of the world.

Such an alternative theory, however, had been already offered within the Peripatetic tradition, by Alexander of Aphrodisias. This Peripatetic background is plausibly another important aspect to be taken into account in order to understand Plotinus' theory and its origin.[9] In his work *On Providence*, preserved in two Arabic versions, Alexander accepts the existence of providence, which is exercised over the sublunary region from the heavens, but rejects Plato's view on demiurgic causation. Alexander defends the existence of order in nature, claiming that rational structures and regularities exist in the sublunary region. This refers in particular to natural species, which exist in virtue of their hylomorphic forms; the eternal and regular character of these immanent, specific forms is connected to the cyclical motions of celestial bodies.[10] Alexander however rejects the Platonic view that such rational structures should be seen as depending on a demiurgic and reasoning cause, that produces cosmic order contemplating an external paradigm, the Platonic transcendent Forms.

As Paul Thillet already remarked, Alexander's criticism of the demiurgic view of causality is, in some aspects, similar to that of Plotinus: although there is no clear textual parallel between them,[11] we know that Plotinus was familiar

8 See also Apuleius, *On Plato and his Doctrine* 1.8.1.10, Atticus, fr. 6.6–9 Des Places, Plutarch, *On the Generation of the Soul in the Timaeus* 26.1025E–F, 1027A; cf. Opsomer 2005.

9 See Chiaradonna 2014b, 203–207, esp. 206: "It is plausible that Alexander's rejection of demiurgic causality played a role in the genesis of Plotinus' theory."

10 See *On Providence* 33.1–8, 87.5–10 Ruland, *Questions* 1.25, 41.4–19, 2.19, 63.10–28 Bruns.

11 See Thillet 2003, 46–54; see also Adamson 2008, who has pointed out the parallels between Alexander's *On Providence* and Plotinus' discussion of astrology.

with Alexander's work.[12] Plotinus however, rejects a "horizontal", cosmological account of natural teleology, based only on the theory of immanent specific forms. From his Platonic point of view, Plotinus maintains that the good and rational order of the sensible world and of the natural ends internal to that world derives from suprasensible principles and, in particular, from a divine Nous that contains in itself the Platonic Forms. This leaves Plotinus with the challenge to develop a new theory of the casual relationship between the divine Nous and the world that could represent a coherent and plausible alternative to the traditional Platonic model of a demiurgic account of the making of the world.

3 Plotinus' Criticism

I turn to my first point: the reasons why Plotinus maintains that a demiurgic account of the making of the world is untenable. Here I cannot examine all of the Plotinian arguments; I will deal with what I consider to be the most important.

For that we need to return to the work *On Providence*. In the first chapter, Plotinus explains that "universal providence" (ἡ τοῦ παντὸς πρόνοια), that we have to attribute to *Nous* as the cause of the world, cannot be understood as the *pronoia*, "which belongs to the individual and which is a calculation before action how something should happen, or not happen in the case of things which ought not to be done, or how we may have something, or not have it" (3.2.1.11–13). This kind of description accords with the usual meaning of the concept of *pro-noia*, that, in Greek, designates the thinking (*noein*) ahead (*pro*). In this sense, *pronoia* indicates that kind of pondering that aims to reach a goal, and thus thinks ahead (*pro*) about the course of events in order to plan and arrange the necessary means to achieve it. Understood as such, the term *pronoia* occurs in Aristotle in the ethical and legal meaning of "pre-meditation" and it is connected with the concepts of deliberation and intention.[13]

Plotinus makes clear that this kind of *pro-noia* cannot be applied to Nous; the divine Intellect cannot be regarded as a practical agent engaged in

12 See Porphyry, *Life of Plotinus* 14.10–13; cf. D'Ancona 2012, 973–975.

13 See Aristotle, *Nicomachean Ethics* 5.8, 1135b25–26, *Magna Moralia* 1.16, 1188b35–37. According to its ethical and juridical meaning, Aristotle also uses the term *pronoia* to distinguish between the most serious and least serious crimes: cf. *Politics* 4.16, 1300b26, *Eudemian Ethics* 2.10, 1266b38.

reasoning, deliberating, planning and fore-seeing. He argues that these modes of thought are incompatible with, first, the perfect actuality of Nous' thought, and, second, with the eternity of its nature. Let us deal with them in turn. First, Aristotle had argued that any form of reasoning and deliberation concerns only contingent things (see *Nicomachean Ethics* 6.1, 1139a12 ff.). The perfect actuality of Nous' thought, however, excludes that any form of contingency could be in it, since all the beings of which divine Nous can be aware are wholly and simultaneously present to it.[14] Therefore, divine Nous cannot act by deliberate choice. For the same reason, given the perfect actuality of Nous' thought, also "the future" is already present in it, as Plotinus says (6.7.1.48–50); so, there are for Nous no prospective states of affairs to be for-seen or pre-planned (6.7.1.38–40). Second, the eternal nature of divine Nous excludes the notion that the world had a beginning.[15] As is well-known, according to Plato's *Timaeus*, the cosmos had a beginning, and there was a controversy among ancient Platonists as to whether this claim is to be interpreted literally or not.[16] According to Plotinus, a beginning of the world would imply a change on God's part, a turning of God from not-creating to creating the world, but this is incompatible with the immutability of his nature. In *Enneads* 2.9.8.4–5, Plotinus formulates it in the following manner: "People who assume a beginning of the world think that the cause of the making of the world was a being who turned from a thing to another and changed." This view, however, would imply another unacceptable consequence: if God is the Good, to suppose a changing in God would involve that the maker of our world was not good, according to the thesis attributed by Plotinus to the Gnostics.[17] For the same reason, as the creation has no beginning in time, therefore any new action in the world on God's part must be excluded. Should God make "new" things in the world, such a "novum" could be explained only by the fact that God has to remedy preexisting deficiencies in the cosmos, or that he wants to improve his creation. But neither of these alternatives is acceptable: in the first alternative, God would then be regarded as imperfect, in the second we would be unable to explain the reason why this improvable cosmos had not been previously improved, since there had been a beneficent cause of good already present to it.[18] In the first chapter of his work *On Providence*, at 3.2.1.15–26, Plotinus refers

14 See *Enneads* 6.7.1.45–48; see Hadot 1988, 197–199. Cf. also 4.3.18.1–10, 3.9.1.35–37.

15 See 2.9.8.3–8, 4.4.9.11–18, 5.1.6.19–27; see also 3.7.6.50–57, and Beierwaltes' commentary (1981, 211–213).

16 On this debate cf. Baltes 1976–8, Sorabji 1983, 268–83, and O'Brien 2015, 28–35.

17 See 2.9.4.12–32, 5.14–37. This aspect of Plotinus' criticism of the Gnostics has been aptly dealt with by Parma 1971, 30–38.

18 In 6.7.3.1–10 Plotinus explains that the passages in the *Timaeus*, esp. 27d–28a, in which Plato speaks of deliberation and reasoning in God must be understood as a "hypothe-

to the thesis that the physical cosmos had no beginning in time, but is rather the eternal product of Nous' activity, as sufficient to establish the claim that the sensible world is not the result of divine reasoning and planning: since the cosmos has always existed, there is no time before it existed when it could have been planned out in advance.

The fundamental objection towards a demiurgic account of the making of the world is however another one; it clearly appears in a passage of the great anti-Gnostic work, in the seventh chapter of the *Ennead* 5.8. Plotinus starts by briefly presenting the Platonic conception according to which the sensible world derives from a suprasensible principle; he then asks himself whether this causality of the intelligible is to be intended according to a deliberative and demiurgic model: "This All, if we agree that its being, and how it is, is due to something else, are we to think that its maker conceived earth in his own mind, with its necessary place in the center, and then water and its place upon earth, and then the other things in their order up to heaven, then all living things, each with the sort of shapes which they have now, and their particular internal organs and outward parts, and then when he had them all arranged in his mind proceeded to his work? – Planning of this sort is quite impossible" (5.8.7.1–9).

Immediately thereafter, Plotinus explains that, from the point of view of our discursive reason, this kind of interpretation can be regarded as something spontaneous and, so to speak, natural: we observe that the sensible world and the species within it are optimally constituted, therefore we deem the cosmos as something planned by a divine Intellect, which reasoned about the things here and arranged them in the best possible way. According to Plotinus, however, in this way we take human rationality as a paradigm for divine activity. This would imply that God is in the position of acting as a practical agent, who must have resorted to deliberation and that God's creative activity is determined by a reason that is external to him. In this way we would eliminate the absoluteness of the divine principle, namely its very nature as principle. Plotinus rejects such an account and at the end of the chapter, at 5.8.7.36–40,

sis" due to the form of discourse, to the assumption that things "had come into being." According to Plotinus, however, Plato made it clear that it was only a way of speaking by adding that things "always come to being": "Deliberation and reasoning are due to [Plato's] assumption: for he assumed that things had come into being. And this is why there is deliberation and reasoning; but by saying 'always coming into being' he also abolishes the idea that God reasons. For it is not possible to reason in what is always; for to do so would belong to someone who had forgotten how it was before. And then if things were better afterwards, they would not have been beautiful before; but if they were beautiful, they keep the same. But they are beautiful because they are with their cause." The same argument is in 5.8.12.16–26.

states: "To return to our main theme: you can explain the reason why (αἰτίαν) the earth is in the middle and round, and why (διὰ τί) the ecliptic slants as it does [...] but it is not the case that because the things must be so arranged this is why they had been so planned, but that it [the intelligible] is as it is, is why things are well arranged." In the last few lines of this chapter, 5.8.7.45–46, Plotinus refers to Aristotle's *Physics* (1.5, 188a27–30) in order to highlight that the divine principle is such inasmuch as it is the union between *archē* and *telos*: "In this sense, it is well said [by Aristotle] that we should not enquire into the reason why (αἰτίας) of a principle and of a principle like this, the perfect one, which is the same as the goal." So, the creative activity of God cannot be motivated by any reason, cause or *telos* whatsoever which is outside the nature of the divine principle. For this reason, according to a view of divine causality that will be systematically adopted by the following Neoplatonic tradition, the divine principles create only from themselves, that is "by their very being" (αὐτῷ τῷ εἶναι), *per esse suum tantum*, in the words of the *Liber de causis*.[19]

I will return to this conception of the divine causality in a moment. First, I would like to give an account how Plotinus' criticisms relate to the earlier Platonic tradition, esp. as set out in the eighth chapter of *Ennead* 6.7. In the earlier chapters, Plotinus described his own views about the causal relationship between the divine Intellect and the world. In the eighth chapter, at 6.7.8.3–4, Plotinus introduces a question that hypothesizes another possible way of conceiving the demiurgic activity of the Divine Intellect: "Wouldn't it be possible to suppose that God discovered the thought of horse in order that a horse (or some other animal) might come into being here below?" This question indirectly raises the problem of the relationship between Divine Intellect and Plato's theory of Forms. This is one of the fundamental problems in Plotinus' thought, which had already been extensively discussed by the Middle-Platonists. Plotinus accepts the common Middle-Platonist doctrine that the intelligible cosmos is not outside the demiurgic Nous, but is internal to it, and that the Forms are therefore "the thoughts of God". According to Plotinus, however, the Forms cannot be regarded as the thoughts that God conceived in his own mind in order to create the sensible world: "It is not possible – this is Plotinus' answer – for God to think the horse in order to make it [...] but the horse existed before its generation and was not thought of that it might be generated" (6.7.8.6–9). According to Plotinus, the Middle-Platonist doctrine would

19 Syrianus, *Commentary on Aristotle's Metaphysics* 163.27–34 Kroll; Proclus, *Elements of Theology* 18.20.3–22, 120.106.7–8 Dodds; *Liber de causis* 19, 181.25–26 Bardenhewer = 19.101–102 Pattin, on which see D'Ancona 1996, 366.

lead to the same conclusion that we examined in the anti-Gnostic treatise. For, if divine Intellect conceived the Forms in order to have a model on the basis of which to make the sensible things, then we should conclude that the Form of horse, for example, was thought for the sake of the sensible horse. In this case, however, what is superior and first, namely the Form, would depend – to some extent – on what is inferior, that is to say on the sensible object.

4 Plotinus' Theory

The topics I hitherto addressed are also dealt with by Plotinus in *Ennead* 6.7. In the first part of this treatise, moreover, Plotinus introduces his own theory about the causal relationship between the divine Intellect and the world. The point of departure in *Ennead* 6.7 is once again Plato's *Timaeus*. In the first chapter, Plotinus refers to a passage in the *Timaeus* on the creation of man by the demiurge (45b), which reads: "And of the organs the gods first contrived the eyes to give light, and the reason why they were inserted was as follows." The *aitia* that would have inspired the creative action of the demiurge is inherent in the fact that the eyes are the instruments through which a man can preserve himself in the sensible world (cf. *Timaeus* 33a, 45d–e, 72e–74e).

This account of the *Timaeus* passage has a clear implication: the divine reason determined that animals are to have features such as eyes because it foresaw the circumstances of their sensible life and took in consideration which feature would be useful to animals in negotiating their physical surroundings. Once again, Plotinus rejects the idea that God created sense-organs or any other feature of sensible cosmos on the basis of *prohorasis* and *logismos*, and excludes the notion that God's creative activity can involve anything like means-ends reasoning about the sensible cosmos. The arguments offered by Plotinus are those I have previously discussed, and also in this case Plotinus makes clear that the *Timaeus* needs to be interpreted metaphorically.

As discussed by Pierre Hadot, the initial chapters of 6.7 are once again directed against the Gnostics and their use of Platonic texts.[20] Plotinus, however, does not refer to the Gnostics alone. From the second chapter on, Plotinus addresses Aristotle's hylomorphic doctrines. This discussion is particularly significant for our theme, since it must be conceivably seen as part of Plotinus' argumentative strategy. As I have already mentioned, criticism of the Platonic

20 Hadot 1988, 26–30; see also Wallis 1992, 464: "The first part of VI 7 forms an anti-Gnostic interpretation of the *Timaeus*", and Corrigan 2000, 160, 176–77.

demiurgic understanding of causality is largely present in the Peripatetic tradition; Alexander of Aphrodisias had developed it in his work *On Providence*, with arguments partially similar to those of Plotinus. As with other subjects, Plotinus adopts some of Alexander's criticisms, but he believes that the right solutions can only be found beyond the Aristotelian perspective, within Platonism, or rather within that form of Platonism he himself develops.[21]

The discussion with Aristotle in chapters 2–7 is somewhat complex and can hence only be presented in outline here.[22] In the second chapter, at 6.7.2.12, after having qualified the nature of Intellect as "cause", Plotinus introduces the typical Peripatetic distinction between *hoti* and *dioti* (cf. *Posterior Analytics* 2.2, 90a15, and *Metaphysics* 8.4, 1044b14) and he refers to Aristotelian example of the eclipsis. According to Aristotle, we actually know a thing when we grasp its *dioti*, that is its essence or form, so that we can give a formal determination or a definition of it (cf. *Posterior Analytics* 2.2, 90a31). Plotinus wants to show that this Aristotelian doctrine needs to be combined with a Platonist account of reality. In the fourth chapter Plotinus presents the definition of man as "rational animal" as a classical example for an Aristotelian definition through *genus* and *differentiae*. This example often occurs in Plotinus, in order to criticize Aristotle's logical doctrine, according to which the specific differences, which determinate and qualify a genus, must come from outside of it (see *Categories* 5, 2b20). In his work *On the Kinds of Being*, for instance, Plotinus maintains that a specific difference like "rational", which makes the man a man, comes from the genus "animal", and therefore it is an activity (*energeia*) coming from the substance.[23] In treatise 6.7, at 4.22–28, Plotinus remarks that the Peripatetic definition "rational animal" does not show at all what man here below really is (that is his *dioti*, his essence or nature), but simply describes the factual structure of concrete beings composed by body and soul. In order to have an explanatory effectiveness, a definition should be able to show how in the essence or form of the thing all the features that contribute to its nature are contained, all the features that are "constituent parts" of a sensible substance, making it the kind of entity which it is,[24] or all the "completing qualities", as Plotinus states using a *terminus technicus* of the Peripatetic tradition.[25] But, according to Plotinus, this is precisely what Aristotle's understanding of definition cannot provide, since Aristotle's doctrine of *ousia* cannot provide an

21 For Plotinus' use of this argumentative strategy in other contexts, see Peroli 2013.

22 For a further analysis of 6.7.2–7, see Schiaparelli 2010, Thaler 2011, Chiaradonna 2014a.

23 See 6.2.14.14–22; cf. Lloyd 1990, 90–94.

24 See 3. 2.2.18–26, 4.4.16.4–9, 6.2.14.14–22.

25 On this topic see Peroli 2003, 84–86.

adequate ground for the thesis of the priority of substance with respect to what depends on it.[26] In his criticism of Aristotle in 6.7 Plotinus thus aims to show that the only way of solving the problems of Peripatetic view of definition and essence points to a different meaning of Form as the source of the sensible things and of all what is a "constituent" part of the nature of the things that participate of it. For this reason, as Plotinus shows in the second section of 6.7, we must go beyond Peripatetic hylomorphism and examine the nature of the divine Intellect.

What is more, the intelligible Forms can have such a structure only as objects of Nous' thought, only because they are "the thoughts of God", who knows himself in each of his objects of thought. For, as Aristotle had already argued, the divine Nous must be regarded as a fully actual self-thinking Intellect. But, if the Forms are the objects of divine thought, then Intellect thinks itself in each of its immanent Forms. Thus, in virtue of Nous' thought, in each individual Form the whole intelligible world is present, that each Form contains according to its proper nature.[27] In this way, in each of its immanent Forms the divine Intellect sees all the other Forms, each time in a different way, that is, according to the perspective of each individual Form, and so it fully knows itself in each of its objects of thought:[28] "It thinks itself as whole with the whole of itself", in Plotinus' own words (5.3.6.7).

For this reason, each Form, as object of Nous' thought, is "complete" and "self-sufficient", as Plotinus states in 6.7.3. This means that it already contains in itself everything it communicates to the sensible things. As Plotinus states in the first chapter, "it is not permitted to suppose that anything which is of God is other than whole and all" (6.7.1.46). If in each individual Form the divine Nous thinks itself in a complete and comprehensive way ("as whole with the whole of itself", as we have just seen), and if, therefore, each Form contains in itself the whole intelligible world, then there is nothing that could be added to the Forms when the sensible things are generated: therefore, all the features that characterize the sensible things are already contained in the intelligible Forms, even if according their intelligible nature; conversely, all that is present in the sensible things is nothing but an unfolding of what is "pre-contained" in the intelligible, although this unfolding takes place at a lower level, that is, according to the mode of being that is proper to the sensible.

---

26 See 6.1.2.7–18; for further details and references on this topic see Chiaradonna 2002, 64–66 and 108–110.

27 See, for example, 1.8.2.17–19, 3.8.8.40–48, 4.9.5.28–29, 5.8.4.11.22–24, 5.9.8.2–4; cf. Emilsson 2007, 199–207.

28 On this structure of the Intellect, see Peroli 2003, 51–104 and Halfwassen 1994, 24–33.

This interpretation of intelligible causality is for Plotinus the answer to the initial question of treatise 6.7. The sensible eye sight was not "added" to man at the time of his birth, nor it is due to the providential care of God, who would have given the man sight because of its usefulness: the sense-perception is rather the manifestation of what has always been inside the Form of man, in an immaterial and transcendental way (see 6.7.3.22–24: "Having senses, and senses of this kind, is contained in the Form by eternal necessity and the perfection of Intellect, which, if it is perfect, possesses the causes in itself"). At the end of this discussion, Plotinus brings up his famous distinction between the three men, and argues again that those features that characterize the human being "here below" are nothing but lower manifestations of the intelligible man: "These sense-perceptions here are dim intellections, but the intellections there are clear sense-perceptions" (6.7.7.30–33).

The main tenets of the Plotinian theory of the intelligible causality played an important role in the subsequent tradition. There is a point, however, on which the later tradition will neither be willing to follow Plotinus, nor the Neoplatonic tradition. As we have seen, according to Plotinus, the sensible world must be conceived as a "manifestation" or "unfolding" of what has always been contained in the divine Intellect. According to Plotinus, however, there can be no act of will by the divine intellect at the basis of this manifestation or unfolding, there can be no intentions or concerns whatsoever regarding the sensible world and the ends internal to it. In chapter 8, at 13, Plotinus explains that living beings and all other sensible things were generated as an ἐπακολούθησις, as a necessary consequence of what is contained in the divine Intellect. This corresponds to Plotinus' standard doctrine, according to which sensible things derive immediately from the intelligible world, as an image or a reflection of the Forms. The same rational order of the cosmos is nothing but a lower reflection of the intelligible order, without Nous having any concern or desire to produce it. Basil of Caesarea, in his *In Hexameron*, summarized Plotinus' conception in this way: "There are those who recognize that God is the cause of the world, but an involuntary cause (αἴτιον ἀπροαιρέτως), as the body is the cause of the shadow or the luminous body of light" (1.7.4).

5 The Sovereignty of Good

If Plotinus' theory of the causal relationship between divine Nous and the physical world is meant to constitute an account of divine providence, then Plotinus seems to tell an unclear story. Plotinus maintains: (1) that the sensible cosmos and the species within it are optimally constituted; (2) in contrast with any natural teleology, he claims that the rational structure of the world derives from a superior nature; in particular, he maintains that the good order of the cosmos as whole and the features of the sensible beings within it are fully determined by the contents of a divine Mind; (3) at the same time, however, he also maintains that this Mind cannot take into consideration the natural world or ends internal to this world. It is unclear how these three theses can be conciliated: Nous works out in detail structures, that will turn out to have utility here, without taking into consideration the conditions and the ends here with reference to which these structures have utility. As Noble and Powers pointed out, it is unclear "how can Plotinus explain the fact that Nous possesses those very thoughts that ensure a well-ordered physical cosmos and well-adapted organisms, given that it cannot give any thought to the sensible cosmos and the conditions of embodied life."[29]

In my last point I would like to propose an argument to support Plotinus' view. I would like to designate this argument "the sovereignty of Good", according to the title of a well-known book by Iris Murdoch.[30]

Let us briefly return to the first chapters of *Treatise* 6.7. As we have seen, Plotinus explains that all the features of the living beings of our world derive from the divine Intellect and must be understood as an unfolding of the characters that are incorporeally contained in the corresponding Forms. Plotinus, however, explains that the Forms have those features, not because they are aimed at creating the sensible world and at guaranteeing well adapted organisms. Let us take the example of the ox, which Plotinus introduces in the tenth chapter: in the Form of ox are contained those features which, then, appear in the sensible ox, such as "horns". In our experience, we observe that horns are needed by oxen to be able to defend themselves, hence we believe that the divine Intellect has conceived and designed the horns for the sake of this function. According to Plotinus, however, this is not the case: the Form of ox, like any other Form, possesses those particular features because those features are what allows that Form to best represent the divine Intellect, according to the specific nature which is proper to that Form. Due to this reason, each Form, as it is identical to the divine Intellect, contains the reason of all its features in itself rather than outside of itself. In this sense, Plotinus is able to state that in

29 Noble and Powers 2015, 65.

30 Murdoch 1970; at p. 128 Murdoch writes: "The good has nothing to do with purpose, indeed it excludes the idea of purpose. The only way to be good is to be good 'for nothing'. That 'for nothing' is indeed the experienced correlate of the invisibility of the idea of Good itself." I would like to show that Plotinus wants to build this "sovereignty of Good" into creation itself.

the divine Intellect the Forms "are in possession of their causes in themselves and with themselves", so that we can also say that they "have no cause of their being, but are self-sufficient and independent of cause" (6.7.2.40–42).

This argument can be explained in the following way. The intelligible Forms have a role as causes of the sensible things. At the beginning of his long work *On Providence*, Plotinus claims that the term *pronoia* refers to the fact that the contents and features of this world are causally determined by the Forms that Nous contemplates. The value of the Forms, however, does not depend on their use for causation and explanation.[31] The Forms are of intrinsic value as objects of spiritual vision of Intellect. For each individual Form is a manifestation of divine Nous, or is the same Nous expressed according to its own nature, or to the perspective which is proper to the single Form. Plotinus criticizes any demiurgic account of the making of the world because it eclipses the intrinsic value of the Form, to the extent that the Form is viewed only from the horizon of the particular whose existence it is invoked to explain. For this reason, Plotinus excludes that the world was planned by a divine Intellect and maintains that God's creative activity cannot involve anything like means-ends reasoning about the sensible cosmos. For in this case intelligible Forms would be only the model or the instrument planned by divine Intellect for the constitution of the physical reality, as if the intelligible world were a blueprint for creation drafted by God. It is for the same reason that Plotinus describes the productive activity of intelligible Principles in non-intentional terms and illustrates it through examples that want to exclude any intentions or concerns whatsoever regarding the sensible cosmos.[32]

Plotinus, however, does not want only to assert and to preserve the sovereignty of the Form; he wishes to build the intrinsic value of the Form into the very structure of divine causality. According to Plotinus, the sensible world is utterly dependent upon the intelligible world for its existence. The Form, however, does not derive its value from being a pattern on the basis of which other things are made. According to Plotinus, the opposite is true. The function of Form as cause depends on its intrinsic value. The eidetic causality is an *epakolouthēsis*, as we have seen in the previous section: it is a necessary consequence or a reflection of the nature of the Form, that is it is derived from its intrinsic value. For this reason, it is by being what it is in its intrinsic nature that the Form creates all that proceeds from it. Plotinus extends this model of eidetic causality to all divine principles: in the case of suprasensible causes, "to produce" coincides with "to be itself".[33] Therefore, the suprasensible principles

31 Cf. Schroeder 1992, 3–23.

32 Cf. Noble and Powers 2015, 53 n. 6.

33 Cf. 3.2.1.38–45, 3.2.2.15–17, 5.8.7.24–31, 6.5.8.20–22.

have no need to 'do' something in order to be the cause of their effects. What is required is that they "abide" (μένειν) in their nature. The verb "abide" can appropriately describe the base of every "procession" (πρόοδος), according to the typical formula of Neoplatonic causation.[34] For the μένειν is not a supplementary feature of divine principle, but the very nature of their causality: in order to create, they have only to abide what they are in their intrinsic value.

If my interpretation is correct, if Plotinus wishes to build the sovereignty of Good into the structure of creation itself, then his theory of the divine causality transforms our way of looking at the world. Let us to return for the moment to the example of the ox. We say that the ox in the sensible world has horns for defense. But, if the ox has horns only to defend itself against other animals, or vision only to keep it from bumping into things, then the attributes of horn and vision are regarded only in relation to these external purposes and to their functions. This way of looking at things is proper to our discursive reasoning, to which every form of *praxis* and *poiēsis* is connected. I can however consider and appreciate the living beings also in a different way. In the intelligible world, the Form of ox has horns for the sake of perfection and completeness (6.7.10.1 ff.). If I focus on the particular in its relation to the Form, and if I understand that the role of the Form as cause is a reflection of its intrinsic value, then I may see that a living being has those attributes in order to be itself. This is precisely what Plotinus says of the Form.

This way of looking at the things irrespective of their functions and their uses could also be regarded as an aspect of what Plotinus considers as our freedom. For in his treatise *On Fate*, at 3.1.8.9–11, Plotinus maintains that we are free when we are outside the cosmic web of causation, which involves all the phenomenal realities. This kind of freedom is the very one of intellect, which is the sole human faculty that allows us to transcend our world without abandoning it. According to Plotinus, intellect always refers to intelligible Forms and therefore thanks to it we can open ourselves to the manifestation of the single beings in their intrinsic value. By doing so, we are able to stay outside of that heteronomous web of causation, in which the sensible things are considered only in relation of their uses, functions and purposes. Such a human freedom would not represent a way of flying from the world, but a different way of staying in it: a way of looking at the singular beings in their intrinsic value, that is from the point of view of the "sovereignty of Good", or from the same point of view as God.

34 Cf., for example, *Enneads* 1.7.1.13–19, 1.7.1.23–24, 5.3.10.16–17, 5.3.12.33–38, 5.4.2.19–22, 6.4.7.22–29, 6.5.10.8–11.

Bibliography

Adamson, Peter. 2008. "Plotinus on Astrology." *Oxford Studies in Ancient Philosophy* 35: 265–291.

Armstrong, Arthur H., tr. 1966–1988. *Plotinus. Enneads. Text and Translations with Notes*. 7 vols. Cambridge, Mass: Harvard University Press.

Baltes, Matthias. 1976–1978. *Die Weltentstehung des platonischen Timaios nach den antiken Interpreten*. 2 vols. Leiden: Brill.

Beierwaltes, Werner, tr. 1981. *Plotin. Über Ewigkeit und Zeit (Enneade III 7)*. Frankfurt am Main: Vittorio Klostermann.

Bréhier, Émile, ed., tr. 1924–1938. *Plotin. Ennéades*. 7 vols. Paris: Les Belles Lettres.

Charles, David, ed. 2010. *Definition in Greek Philosophy*. Oxford: Clarendon.

Chiaradonna, Riccardo. 2002. *Sostanza, movimento, analogia: Plotino critico di Aristotele*. Naples: Bibliopolis.

Chiaradonna, Riccardo. 2014a. "Intelligibles as Causes in Plotinus' Metaphysics: *Enn.* 6.7 (38)." In *Aitia II. Avec ou sans Aristote. Le débat sur les causes à l'âge hellénistique et impérial*, edited by Carlo Natali and Cristina Viano, 185–213. Leuven: Peeters.

Chiaradonna, Riccardo. 2014b. "Plotinus' Metaphorical Reading of the *Timaeus*: Soul, Mathematics, Providence." In *Fate, Providence and Moral Responsibility in Ancient, Medieval and Early Modern Thought. Studies in Honour of Carlos Steel*, edited by Pieter d'Hoine and Gert Van Riel, 187–210. Leuven: Leuven University Press.

Corrigan, Kevin. 2000. "Platonism and Gnosticism: The Anonymus Commentary on the Parmenides: Middle or Neoplatonic?" In *Gnosticism and Later Platonism: Themes, Figures and Texts*, edited by John D. Turner and Ruth Majercik, 141–177. Atlanta: Society of Biblical Literature.

D'Ancona, Cristina. 1996. "Plotinus and Later Platonic Philosophers on the Causality of the First Principle." In *The Cambridge Companion to Plotinus*, edited by Lloyd P. Gerson, 356–385. Cambridge: Cambridge University Press.

D'Ancona, Cristina. 2012 [1989]. "Plotin." In *Dictionnaire des philosophes antiques*, edited by Richard Goulet, vol. 5a, 885–1070. Paris: CNRS Éditions.

D'Hoine, Pieter, and Geert van Riel, eds. 2014. *Fate, Providence, and Moral Responsibility in Ancient, Medieval and Early Modern Thought: Collected Studies in Honour of Carlos Steel*. Leuven: Leuven University Press.

Emilsson, Eyjólfur K. 2007. *Plotinus on Intellect*. Oxford: Clarendon.

Gerson, Lloyd P., ed. 1996. *The Cambridge Companion to Plotinus*. Cambridge: Cambridge University Press.

Goulet, Richard, ed. 2012 [1989]. *Dictionnaire des philosophes antiques*, vol. 5a. Paris: CNRS Éditions.

Hadot, Pierre. 1989. *Plotin. Traité 38 (VI, 7). Introduction, traduction, commentaire et notes*. Paris: Cerf.

Halfwassen, Jens. 1994. *Geist und Selbsbewusstsein: Studien zu Plotin und Numenios*. Stuttgart: Franz Steiner.

Henry, Paul, and Hans-Rudolf Schwyzer, ed. 1964–1982. *Plotini Opera*, 3 vols. Oxford: Clarendon.

Layton, Bentley, ed. 1980. *The Rediscovery of Gnosticism*, vol. 1: *The School of Valentinus*. Leiden: Brill.

Leinkauf, Thomas, and Carlos Steel, eds. 2005. *Plato's Timaeus and the Foundations of Cosmology in Late Antiquity, the Middle Ages and Renaissance*. Leuven: Leuven University Press.

Majercik, Ruth, and John D. Turner, eds. 2000. *Gnosticism and Later Platonism: Themes, Figures and Texts*. Atlanta: Society of Biblical Literature.

Marmodoro, Anna, and Brian D. Prince, eds. 2015. *Causation and Creation in Late Antiquity*. Cambridge: Cambridge University Press.

Murdoch, Iris. 1970. *The Sovereignty of Good*. London: Routledge & Kegan Paul.

Narbonne, Jean-Marc. 2011. *Plotinus in Dialogue with the Gnostics*. Leiden: Brill.

Natali, Carlo, and Cristina Viano, eds. 2014. *Aitia II. Avec ou sans Aristote. Le débat sur les causes à l'âge hellénistique et impérial*. Leuven: Peeters.

Noble, Christopher I., and Nathan M. Powers. 2015. "Creation and Divine Providence in Plotinus." In *Causation and Creation in Late Antiquity*, edited by Anna Marmodoro and Brian D. Prince, 51–70. Cambridge: Cambridge University Press.

O'Brien, Carl S. 2015. *The Demiurge in Ancient Thought. Secondary Gods and Divine Mediators*. Cambridge: Cambridge University Press.

O'Meara, Dominic J. 1981. "Gnosticism and the Making of the World in Plotinus." In *The Rediscovery of Gnosticism*, edited by Bentley Layton, vol. 1: *The School of Valentinus*, 365–378. Leiden: Brill.

Opsomer, Jan. 2005. "A Craftsman and his Handmaiden: Demiurgy According to Plotinus." In *Plato's Timaeus and the Foundations of Cosmology in Late Antiquity, the Middle Ages and Renaissance*, edited by Thomas Leinkauf and Carlos Steel, 67–102. Leuven: Leuven University Press.

Parma, Christian. 1971. *Pronoia und Providentia. Der Vorsehungsbegriff Plotins und Augustins*. Leiden: Brill.

Peroli, Enrico. 2003. *Dio, uomo e mondo. La tradizione etico-metafisica del Platonismo*. Milan: Vita e Pensiero.

Peroli, Enrico. 2013. "Organisme et réflexion. Plotin et la nature de l'être vivant." *Revue de Philosophie Ancienne* 2: 179–209.

Schiaparelli, Annamaria. 2010. "Essence and Cause in Plotinus' *Ennead* VI.7 [38] 2: An Outline of Some Problems." In *Definition in Greek Philosophy*, edited by David Charles, 467–492. Oxford: Clarendon.

Schroeder, Frederic. M. 1992. *Form und Transformation. A Study in the Philosophy of Plotinus*. Montreal: McGill-Queen's University Press.

Sorabji, Richard. 1983. *Time, Creation, and the Continuum*. London: Duckworth.

Thaler, Naly. 2011. "Traces of Good in Plotinus's Philosophy of Nature: *Ennead* VI.7.1–14." *Journal of the History of Philosophy* 49: 61–80.

Thillet, Pierre. 2003. *Alexandre d'Aphrodise. Traité de la Providence*. Paris: Verdier.

Wallis, Richard. T., ed. 1992. *Neoplatonism and Gnosticism*. Albany: State University of New York Press.

Wallis, Richard. T. 1992. "Soul and Nous in Plotinus, Numenius and Gnosticism." In *Neoplatonism and Gnosticism*, edited by Richard T. Wallis, 661–482. Albany: State University of New York Press.

CHAPTER 14

Lithoi Pheromenoi. Fate, Soul and Self-Determination in *Enneads* 3.1

Maria Luisa Gatti

1 Introduction

From a chronological perspective, *Enneads* 3.1, *On Fate* (Περὶ εἱμαρμένης), is Plotinus' third treatise;[1] Porphyry gave it its title or, rather, adopted this title which was already current in the school.[2] The title, however, is not wholly appropriate to the content of the treatise, since causality is in fact its main topic. Nevertheless, in the treatise Plotinus also deals with the problem of fate (especially from a Stoic perspective), next to astrological theories, principles and the soul.[3]

Plotinus starts by analysing causes and first principles, taking his lead from the Platonic tradition, and then continues with self-determination and the freedom of the sage. As already Bréhier stressed, the defence of human freedom, in opposition to Stoic conceptions of fate and astrology, is a common theme among second and third centuries thinkers.[4] Plotinus and other philosophers dealt with this issue so similarly and impersonally as to suggest these kinds of demonstrations and texts were current and shared among schools.[5]

---

1 Porphyry, *Life of Plotinus* 4; see further Reale 1990, 303–304, Brisson and others 1982–1992, vol. 1, 187–367.

2 Porphyry, *Life of Plotinus* 4, 24; see further Brisson and others 1982–1992, vol. 1, 283–287, Radice and Reale 2002, xiii, Casaglia, Guidelli, Linguiti, and Moriani 1997, 18.

3 See Radice and Reale 2002, 488.

4 See Bréhier 1936–1993, vol. 3, 3–5, Pompeo Faracovi 1996, 51–79, 143–168.

5 Bréhier 1936–1993, vol. 3, 3 mentions the Cynic Oenomaus, Alexander of Aphrodisias' *On Fate*, Diogenianus' criticism of Chrysippus, Bardaisan, and Origen. See also Bobzien 1998a, 2–15, Ioppolo 2013, 17–116, Radice 2009, 20–21, Brancacci 2001, 71–110. Eliasson (2009, 407 and 415–416) also notes, in relation to Middle Platonism: "Nous voudrions ici nous intéresser à la relation de l'analyse plotinienne du destin à celle du médio-platonisme (…). Nous tenterons de montrer en particulier comment Plotin propose une version de la théorie médioplatonicienne du destin et de 'ce qui dépend de nous' (…). Examinons maintenant la théorie médioplatonicienne 'standard' (…). Le destin, comme les lois de la cité, englobe (…) tout les choses, parmi lesquelles les actions des hommes, mais il détermine uniquement les conséquences des actions. Des actions, précisément, nous sommes nous-mêmes

 | DOI:10.1163/9789004436381_016

Plotinus' writings present a line of thought that, though in itself coherent, is expressed in a compressed and unsystematic manner. Accordingly, it is helpful to reconstruct and reorder all the steps of the arguments. Moreover, Plotinus often comments on authors whom he does not explicitly mention.[6] This further complicates our understanding of this treatise, and indeed all the other texts of Plotinus.

In this paper I will set out Plotinus' main arguments on *heimarmenē* and on the soul's freedom, starting with the structure of the treatise and an analysis of the meaning of some particularly relevant words.[7]

A large part of 3.1 is dedicated to the causes of becoming and being according to the interpretations of different philosophical schools. In the overall structure, the themes of fate, the soul and freedom are set out in ten chapters. In the first and second chapter, Plotinus deals with causation; in the third chapter, he criticizes the Atomists; in the fourth (and tenth) chapter, he discusses the actions that derive from us. In the fifth and the sixth chapter, he criticizes astrological theories; in chapter seven, he argues against Stoic monism. In chapters eight, nine and ten, the topic is the soul's self-determination, especially that of the pure soul.

According to Chappuis, the treatise consists of three parts and outlines a progressive ascent towards the principles of aetiological, ethical, ontological and ascetic-contemplative nature.[8] The three parts are: an introduction on the problem of causality,[9] a critical section concerning various hypotheses for solving this issue,[10] and a third part, which contains Plotinus' answer and conclusions.[11]

2 The Problem of Causality

The first two chapters focus on the issue of cause, the very issue on which the solution to both the problem of fate and the soul's self-determination

les agents productifs, ce qui constitue 'ce qui dépend de nous' (…). Au lieu du principe stoïcien que tout ce qui arrive serait soumis au destin – 'ce qui dépend de nous' inclus –, les médioplatoniciennes proposaient que ce qui est ἐφ'ἡμῖν soit inclus dans le destin sans être soumis au destin, évitant ainsi les conséquences déterministes les plus problématiques de la théorie stoïcienne." See further n. 166.

6 See Porphyry, *Life of Plotinus* 14; cf. Brisson and others 1982–1992, vol. 1, 257–280. Regarding the sources in 3.1, see Henry and Schwyzer 1964, 234–245, Isnardi Parente 1984, 70–73.

7 See Sleeman and Pollet 1980, Radice and Bombacigno 2004.

8 See Chappuis 2006, 21 and 35–37.

9 3.1.1.1–8.

10 3.1.1.8–7.21.

11 3.1.7.21–3.1.10.15.

depends.[12] At the beginning, referring to the *Timaeus*,[13] Plotinus offers a dichotomous scheme with alternatives on causality,[14] which modern scholars have understood in different ways.[15] In the scheme, the opening question is whether both things that exist and things that come into being have a cause. Using Plato's dichotomy between being and becoming, and considering the presence or the absence of a cause, Plotinus develops a complex classification of the doctrines of the different philosophical schools; he starts his analysis with the Atomists.

According to standard Plotinian doctrine, among the eternal realities the One is uncaused, whereas the *Nous* and the Soul are derived from the First Hypostasis.[16] All things that come into being have a cause; Plotinus does not admit an absence of causes in becoming, which would leave room for chance.[17] Human souls too are part of "the becoming beings", as they are uncaused and eternal in themselves, but have activities that are subjected to change.

12 See Graeser 1972, 101–111. Ioppolo (2013, 19) notes: "Il concetto di causa è fortemente coinvolto nel problema del determinismo e della responsabilità morale, che è stato uno dei nodi centrali intorno a cui gli Stoici e gli oppositori libertari hanno più lungamente dibattuto in età ellenistica." On causality in Plotinus see further Chiaradonna 2009, 38–48, D'Ancona 2009, 361–385, Chiaradonna 2017, 90–93. Dessì (2012, 31–33) notes: "Plotino aveva cercato di risolvere il problema, centrale nella filosofia platonica, del rapporto fra l'unità e la molteplicità, indicando nell'Uno il principio ineffabile, causa immobile di tutto ciò che è. In questo processo di generazione dall'Uno, attraverso le sue ipostasi, cioè le altre due sostanze principali del mondo intelligibile, l'intelligenza e l'Anima, tutte le realtà si susseguono secondo un ordine che va dal migliore, ciò che è più vicino all'Uno, al peggiore, ciò che è più lontano da lui, ciò che è più disperso. Questo accade perché ciò che causa deve essere migliore di ciò che è causato finché, in questa successiva degradazione delle cause, si arriva alla materia, completa assenza di unità e pura passività. Il rapporto tra le parti e il tutto spiega i rapporti di causa ed effetto. È il tutto che causa, nel senso che dà ragione delle parti: 'quando parli di cause, tu dici il tutto. Perché gli occhi? In funzione del tutto. Perché le sopracciglia? In funzione del tutto' (cf. *Enneadi*, VI 7, 3, 13–15). Anche per Plotino tutto ciò che esiste e accade deve avere una causa che non è soltanto causa efficiente, ma anche capace di dare ragione di ciò che c'è o accade (…). Trovare le cause prossime degli avvenimenti è relativamente facile (…). Sarebbe (…) indizio di pigrizia fermarsi alle cause prossime; per questa ragione molti filosofi hanno cercato di risalire alle cause prime. Come già aveva fatto Aristotele nella *Metafisica*, anche Plotino si occupa delle dottrine formulate dai filosofi che l'hanno preceduto, mettendone in luce pregi e difetti. Vengono accomunati nella critica epicurei, stoici e astrologi."

13 *Timaeus* 27d–28a; cf. Henry and Schwyzer 1964, 234.

14 3.1.1.1–8; Chappuis 2006, 60–63.

15 See Chappuis 2006, 59–81 with further references; cf. Radice 2009, 21, Kalligas 2014, 420. On Plotinus' position in the treatises on fate, with reference to the limits of its causal power mainly in relation to the Peripatetics, see Russi 2004, 86–92 and 95–98.

16 3.1.1.8–11; Casaglia, Guidelli, Linguiti, and Moriani 1997, 359 n. 3.

17 3.1.1.13–19.

Plotinus, thereafter, indicates that there is a broad consensus on the proximate causes of what becomes, since they are "easy" to grasp; he presents several examples of these causes, such as intentional action, "arts" (τέχναι), and "nature" (φύσις).[18] However, proximate causes do not offer an adequate explanation: according to Plotinus, they are not true causes.

In the first chapter, Plotinus already mentions the importance of going back to the essences of physical phenomena.[19] At the beginning of the second chapter, he stresses the urgency of reaching the first principles, referring to the condition of the lazy,[20] inert, people who stop looking for causes and fail to reach a higher perspective,[21] with the following words: "If someone gives up after going only so far and is unwilling to go higher, it is probably a sign that he is lazy (ῥᾳθύμου ἴσως), and paying no attention to those who ascend to the primary and transcendent causes (ἐπὶ τὰ πρῶτα καὶ ἐπὶ τὰ ἐπέκεινα αἴτια)."[22]

Plotinus argues that we cannot stop at the proximate causes of events (since the same phenomena, such as the moon, the environment, the activities, produce different effects on different men), but we need to go back to higher, incorporeal causes, as wise men do.

In this regard, Plotinus outlines some "topics"[23] with regard to the problem of causation, summarizing various positions on what constitutes primary causes. Among them there are: a) the material principles, i.e. atoms or other corporeal entities;[24] b) the principle that animates the universe, which runs through all things as fate;[25] c) the motion of the planets and fixed stars, which allows the predictions of the astrologers;[26] d) the chain of causes.[27] Plotinus rejects these doctrines, beginning with the doctrine of Atomism; the other doctrines are dealt with in succession, in a systematic way, up until the seventh chapter.

18 3.1.1.24–36.

19 3.1.11–12.

20 See "the lazy argument" in Cicero, *On Fate* 28–29; cf. Bobzien 1998a, 180–233, Ioppolo 2007, 103–119, Maso 2014, 143–147, Spinelli and Verde 2014, 79–80.

21 See Wagner 1982, 51–72. Russi 2004, 95 stresses that the vertical perspective guides the criticism in polemical chapters and leads to the arrival of the highest, pure and impassive Soul, which self-determines and is free from cosmic necessity.

22 3.1.2.1–4. The quoted translations from *Enneads* are by Gerson 2018. See also Alexander of Aphrodisias, *On Fate* 16; cf. Russi 2004, 93.

23 See Bréhier 1936–1993, vol. 3, 8 n. 2, Chappuis 2006, 71–73.

24 3.1.2.9–17.

25 3.1.2.17–25.

26 3.1.2.26–30.

27 3.1.2.30–35.

It should be noted that in the second chapter the term *heimarmenē* appears for the first time,[28] with reference to those who talk about something that "permeates everything as a cause which not only moves but also produces each thing"; they claim "that it is fate and the principal cause" (εἱμαρμένην ταύτην καὶ κυριωτάτην αἰτίαν), and is itself "all things" (τὰ πάντα).[29] The word *heimarmenē* further appears in this chapter in relation to the chain of causes.[30] Here Plotinus anticipates the analysis of two conceptions of fate, one as a series of causes in a subsequent concatenation, the other as the Soul understood as a causing-principle. With regard to the doctrine of the astrologers, Plotinus competently distinguishes between planets and fixed stars, remembering their positions and the constellations.[31]

The third chapter focuses on those who identify the ultimate causes with physical elements, especially the atoms. According to Plotinus, this conception involves a serious error: the body is used to explain something that belongs to a higher level. In this way, the order would be derived from disorder: how could "order, reason and the ruling Soul" (τάξιν καὶ λόγον καὶ ψυχὴν τὴν ἡγουμένην) through the disorderly motion be born?[32] Prediction and divination,[33] the various psychic activities,[34] the resistance of the Soul to physical affections, the choices,[35] the distinctions between living and inanimate beings, they all are irreconcilable with Atomism and disorder, since the Soul is considered to be only a set of material atoms.[36] In particular he observes – anticipating the metaphor of the rolling stones – that, if we were "dragged" (φερόμενοι) as inanimate bodies, these casual collisions would not explain the actions that have caused the collisions. In this case we would not be active but passive subjects; there would be no room for cognitive and contemplative activities.

3 The Problem of *Heimarmenē*

After having examined the material principle-causes – the elements and, above all, the atoms –, Plotinus continues with two further theories on causal-

28 3.1.2.21.
29 3.1.2.19–22. The passage is in *SVF* at 2.946. Cf. Natali and Tetamo 2009, 11–25, Sauvé Meyer 2009, 79–80.
30 3.1.2.35; cf. Russi 2004, 80 n. 15.
31 See Chappuis 2006, 76–78; see further below section 4.
32 3.1.3.2–4.
33 3.1.3.9–17.
34 3.1.3.17–23.
35 3.1.3.23–27.
36 3.1.3.27–29.

ity in his search for causes, namely, first, the soul as single cause and, second, the causal chain.

3.1 *The Issue of the One Soul*

The theme of the one Soul was already mentioned in the second chapter with reference to a single cause called *heimarmenē*, which penetrates everything, moving and producing everything.[37] In the fourth chapter it is analysed by focusing on the hypothesis of a Soul-Principle of the universe: Plotinus wonders whether this is a tenable idea. He poses the question whether it is possible that everything is accomplished by a single Soul that pervades the universe in its every part and if the ordered interweaving of successive causes constitutes a *heimarmenē*.[38]

As Radice already pointed out,[39] von Arnim correctly included this passage among the fragments of Chrysippus. Given the continuity of Stoic thought on this topic, it could also be attributed to other heads of the school, such as Diogenes of Babylon, or to imperial Stoics, such as Cornutus and Marcus Aurelius. Radice suggests that in this critique of the Soul of the Cosmos Plotinus targets the Stoic doctrine of *pneuma*, on which the Stoics based the homogeneity of the psychic nature.[40] In this context, Plotinus introduces the metaphor of the plant.[41] Invisible roots govern the whole from the bottom, through a continuous interweaving of actions and reactions that propagate to the parts, connecting them in a unitary plot, which constitutes a *heimarmenē* of the plant itself.

With this single Soul of the Universe, which is conceptualised as an intertwining of parts which ultimately constitute fate, one would have an absolute, necessary cause that would account for everything. Plotinus focuses his criticism on this: the Stoic error consists, above all, in an "extreme form of necessity or of fate" (σφοδρὸν τῆς ἀνάγκης καὶ τῆς τοιαύτης εἱμαρμένης).[42] According to Plotinus, there would be no possibility of distinguishing between causes or between cause and effect, as shown by way of an example with kicking; in this framework, the hegemonic principle and the feet would immediately

37 See 3.1.2.18–22.

38 3.1.4.1–5; cf. Chappuis 2006, 90–92.

39 See Radice 2009, 27–28.

40 See Radice 2009, 30; cf. Graeser 1972, 105.

41 3.1.4.5–9, 3.8.10. Radice and Reale 2002, 498 n. 16, note that the metaphor of the plant should be read in a Stoic rather than Plotinian perspective, even though Plotinus frequently uses this metaphor elsewhere (see Radice 2002, 685).

42 3.1.4.9–10; cf. Chappuis 2006, 81 and 92–93, Radice 2009, 31.

coincide.[43] The subject who directs must differentiate himself from what he directs, while instead for these philosophers "everything will be one" (ἓν ἔσται τὰ πάντα).[44]

Therefore we would not engage in "the process of going back" (ἀναγωγή) from one similar cause to another.[45] Additionally, from the point of view of fate, this excess of necessity and fate would end up eliminating fate itself, if it is intended as the interweaving of causes.[46]

The reference to action in 3.1.4.12–16 marks the beginning of Plotinus' discussion of self-determination as a characteristic of human beings. Plotinus' most important objection to the one Soul-Principle is that our nature as human beings would not be respected, because our autonomy would be removed.[47]

Plotinus anticipates the subsequent discussion by noticing poignantly that if we were to accept Stoic doctrine "neither will we be ourselves" (ὥστε οὔτε ἡμεῖς ἡμεῖς),[48] nor would our actions be ours. And we would not "engage in calculative reasoning ourselves; rather, our considered views are the acts of calculative reasoning belonging to something else" (οὐδὲ λογιζόμεθα αὐτοί, ἀλλ'ἑτέρου λογισμοὶ τὰ ἡμέτερα βουλεύματα),[49] nor would we be able to act. With an effective Platonic metaphor, he objects that, from the point of view of the subject of the action, it is not our feet which are kicking, but we are kicking through them. "But the truth is that each thing must be separate and our own actions and acts of thinking must exist" (ἀλλὰ γὰρ δεῖ καὶ ἕκαστον ἕκαστον εἶναι καὶ πράξεις ἡμετέρας καὶ διανοίας ὑπάρχειν).

According to Plotinus, reflections, will and actions belong to the soul of the individual: the responsibility for our actions is our own.[50] If we were identified with the single cause of the Stoics we would be beings deprived of responsibility. Finally, Plotinus objects that Stoic thought would ultimately attribute to the universe the responsibility for bad actions.[51]

The Stoic doctrines are unacceptable for Plotinus. As Radice pointed out, the overly rigid and homogeneous conception of the Stoics should be corrected by a non-homogeneous structure, according to which the psychic real-

43 3.1.4.12–16.
44 3.1.4.20.
45 3.1.4.18–19.
46 3.1.4.9–11; cf. Radice 2009, 31–32.
47 See Chappuis 2006, 93–94.
48 3.1.4.20–21, cf. Magris 1986, 127–138, Magris 2016, 453–455.
49 3.1.4.21–22.
50 3.1.4.22–27.
51 3.1.4.27–28.

ities depend on the Soul as hypostasis, while physical events are founded in matter unified by the logos as a causal chain.[52]

3.2 *The Causal Chain*

Plotinus only introduces the causal chain in the seventh chapter of the treatise.[53] However, since he closely links the causal chain or *heimarmenē* to the problem of the one Soul,[54] it is appropriate to discuss the two together. The causal chain, already mentioned above[55] as the fourth kind of causal explanation, is presented in the seventh chapter as a single principle[56] that makes thing come into being through the seminal reasons, thus qualifying matter.[57]

According to Plotinus, this causal chain, which determines everything, implies overall necessity.[58] It does not allow the independence of any particular event, because the seminal reasons are in fact actions of the one principle.

In order to get a better grasp of the Plotinian conception of *heimarmenē* a closer look at its occurrences in the *Enneads* is helpful.[59] The term occurs only in the first four *Enneads*, above all in 3.1. In 3.1 the term is used to refer to the cause that penetrates all things, moving them, as "fate" and as a dominating cause,[60] to the bond that weaves together all things,[61] to "necessity" (ἀνάγκη),[62] and to "fate" according to the Atomists,[63] to the ordered intertwining of causes that follow from the one Soul,[64] to the "fate" of plants.[65] Furthermore, it refers to the excess of "necessity" (ἀνάγκη) and "fate" that eliminates the "fate" in the case of the one Soul,[66] to the causes coinciding with the "fate" that nothing can hinder according to Stoic monism,[67] and to "fate" meant as external cause.[68]

---

52 See Radice 2009, 32.

53 3.1.7.1–21.

54 3.1.7.4–8. In the "topics" presented above it was the fourth kind of causal explanation: see above n. 27.

55 3.1.2.35.

56 3.1.7.1–4.

57 See Chappuis 2006, 113. Regarding the link between principle and seminal reasons, see Radice and Reale 2002, 504 n. 22 (with reference to *SVF* 1.102 and 2.1027).

58 3.1.7.8–10; cf. Eliasson 2009, 417–418.

59 See Sleeman and Pollet 1980, 303.

60 3.1.2.21.

61 3.1.2.35.

62 For *anankē* see Graeser 1972, 106, O'Brien 1997, 4–49, Adamson 2011, 9–30.

63 3.1.3.8.

64 3.1.4.5.

65 3.1.4.8.

66 3.1.4.10 and 13.

67 3.1.7.11–12.

68 3.1.10.8–9.

Outside the treatise, it is used with reference to, first, the Soul linked to the body and subject to "fate";[69] second, the one *pronoia*, which in the lower things is "fate", in the upper ones just *pronoia*;[70] third, the Souls who have come out from the sensible world and have overcome the "fate" of reincarnation;[71] fourth, the "fate" of all men;[72] fifth, the "fate" of an individual;[73] sixth, the fate of the *nous* that transcends the world to remain separate from matter and "up there";[74] seventh, the Souls descended into bodies, subordinate to the "fatality" of here below.[75] In relation to the fate of *nous*, *heimarmenē* specifically refers to the suprasensible level.

In the seventh chapter, in his criticism of Stoic monism, Plotinus brings up the metaphor of the rolling stones again and observes that there would be nothing left "to be dragged" (φέρεσθαι) from these causes, if they are identified with fate.[76] Plotinus reiterates that this doctrine of seminal reasons does not leave room for human autonomy. For an individual principle that allows us to do something "of our own" (παρ' ἡμῶν)[77] should distinguish our responsibility from fate that could not be hindered by anything.[78] Our representations and impulses would be determined by antecedent factors;[79] "and something being 'up to us' will be just words" (ὄνομά τε μόνον τὸ ἐφ' ἡμῖν ἔσται).[80] We would be passive, in the grip of impulses not directed by us, like children and fools or like fire; or rather we would be people living without reason, even if we have impulses of motion (φέρεται)[81] in our own internal structure. Plotinus con-

69 2.3.9.28.

70 3.3.5.15; cf. Graeser 1972, 107–111, Radice 2009, 35, Magris 2016, 482–491, Nagy 2017, 109–130. *Treatises* 3.2 and 3.3. focus on providence (see further Peroli's contribution in this volume).

71 3.4.6.32.

72 3.4.6.60.

73 4.3.13.21.

74 4.3.13.22.

75 4.3.15.11.

76 3.1.7.11–13.

77 3.1.7.7–8.

78 3.1.7.8–12; see Chappuis 2006, 115–116.

79 3.1.7.13–15; Trabattoni 2009, 193–195.

80 3.1.7.15; 4.3.2. Casaglia, Guidelli, Linguiti, and Moriani 1997, 368 n. 37 refer to Alexander of Aphrodisias, *On Fate* 14, 182.23: οὐκ ὄνομα μόνον τοῦ ἐφ' ἡμῖν. See further Romano 1999, 172–173, Chappuis 2006, 117.

81 See 3.1.7.15–21. Eliasson 2009, 418–419 notes: "Ce qui gêne Plotin est simplement que cette théorie contredit un certain nombre d'intuitions que nous voudrions au contraire pouvoir intégrer dans une théorie du destin: selon la conception commune, partagée d'ailleurs par Plotin, chaque théorie du destin devrait non seulement être compatible

cludes that all this leads us to "look for other causes" (ἄλλας αἰτίας ζητοῦντες),[82] underlining the need to continue ascending in the search for the principle, without stopping at this level.

4 The Doctrines of the Astrologers

The astrological problem, the third of the "topics" already mentioned in section 2 above,[83] is analysed in the fifth and sixth chapters; it is explored in accordance with the overall aim of 3.1, which is the search for causes. Excluding the one cosmic Soul, Plotinus wonders whether each event is determined by the "movement" (φορά) of the sky and the stars, understood as the principle that governs everything.[84] This is a deterministic conception, linked to Plotinus' sympathetic vision of the cosmos.[85]

As Spinelli already pointed out, the problem is examined in detail in 2.3, *On the Influence of the Stars*, one of the last treatises written by Plotinus. Plotinus tries to overcome the determinism of "*hard*" astrology; that is to say he tries to overcome in particular the risk that stars, by "a suffocating *heimarmenē*", completely determine our characters. He does this by adopting "the very strong dogma of the full self-determination of the pure Soul".[86] This is an original and unique attempt, especially in relation to genethlialogy or natal astrology.

With regard to Plotinus' interest in astrology, a direct testimony in Porphyry's *Life of Plotinus* is illuminating: "Plotinus dealt with astronomical tables

avec certains aspects de l'action humain, mais devrait explicitement démontrer comment un certain nombre d'intuitions, d'origine éthique plutôt que physique, pourraient trouver une place dans cette théorie (…). Les défenseurs de la théorie utilisaient alors la notion d'impulsion afin d'indiquer en quel sens la théorie serait compatible avec la notion de 'ce qui dépend de nous', mais, pour Plotin, la notion d'impulsion est en soi beaucoup trop vague."

82 3.1.7.23.

83 See n. 27; cf. 3.1.2.26–30.

84 See 3.1.5.2, 3.1.5.15, 2.3.1 (treatise 2.3 is explicitly dedicated to the influence of the stars).

85 See 4.5.3; cf. Spinelli 2002, 284, Emilsson 2015, 37–60. Spinelli 2002, 280 on Plotinus as a source of astrological theories, notes that, in the openly polemical writings, the philosopher does not explain in detail the adversaries' theses, but inserts them in the plot of his arguments, in a complex and continuous exchange of questions and answers.

86 See Spinelli 2002, 297–298, cf. 281–284, 288. On 288–293 Spinelli identifies the key arguments in 2.3 as the research on animated or inanimate stars, the observations of scientific-astronomical nature and the doctrine of the rational Soul, not descent, subtracted from the laws of fate, capable of exercising "the virtue that has no master".

(προσεῖχη δὲ τοῖς μὲν περὶ τῶν ἀστέρων κανόσιν), though not in great technical detail. He addressed the efficacy of horoscopes more closely (τοῖς δὲ τῶν γενεθλιαλόγων ἀποτελεσματικοῖς ἀκριβέστερον), and in the many places where he saw something unwarranted in what the treatises claimed he did not hold back from refutation."[87] Predictions about the universe and about an individual person could be obtained from the position of the stars, correlating to the movements of stars the growth of both living beings and plants, as well as the differences between various regions and the men living in them.[88] The "small catalogue" of the methods of observation outlined in this chapter[89] shows that Plotinus had detailed knowledge of astrology, although more from a philosophical than from a technical point of view.[90]

There is also a reference to Plotinus' concept of universal sympathy and to the link between all elements, according to which nothing happens without anything else being involved.[91] Plotinus opposes this kind of astral determinism, since it implies that limitations and vices can be attributed to the divine, and would subtract from "us" – he says – "what is ours" (τὰ ἡμέτερα).[92] In a famous passage about astral determinism, he states: "In answer to this, it has first to be said that the one who claims this, too, though in a different way, attributes to these principles what belongs to us, our wishes, affections, vices and impulses, and by allowing us nothing leaves us to be stones that are rolled along (ἡμῖν δὲ οὐδὲν διδοὺς λίθοις φερομένοις καταλείπει εἶναι), rather than human beings whose function has its source in themselves and their own nature (οὐκ ἀνθρώποις ἔχουσι παρ' αὐτῶν καὶ ἐκ τῆς αὐτῶν φύσεως ἔργον)."[93] On the one

87 Porphyry, *Life of Plotinus*, 15.21–26. According to Porphyry, Plotinus wanted to talk neither about his origins (1.2–4) nor about his birth (2.37–39), which can be understood as a reference to his aversion to horoscopes. See Brisson and others 1982–1992, vol. 2, 189–192 and 271–272 (with further references), and also Edwards' contribution in this volume.

88 3.1.5.4–17.

89 3.1.5.1–15, 3.1.2.26–30; cf. Bouché-Leclerq 1899, 599–604, Ioppolo 1984, 73–91, Chappuis 2006, 97.

90 See Maggi 2007, 355.

91 3.1.5.8; cf. Maggi 2007, 353–354 and 361–362, and also Gurtler 1984, 396–398, Pompeo Faracovi 1996, 156, Radice 2009, 20–21, Emilsson 2015, 40–60.

92 3.1.5.17.

93 3.1.5.15–20. For the Stoic evidence see further *SVF* 2.979 and 2.1000. Cf. Magris 2016, 232–237, and further Pompeo Faracovi 1996, 67–69, 153–158, Bobzien 1998a, 258–271, Frede 2003, 193–200, Salles 2005, 9–16, Maggi 2007, 364–367, Radice 2009, 26, Spinelli and Verde 2014, 81–83. Chrysippus, using the example of the cylindrical stone that, once moved, starts to roll, distinguishes the external cause of motion (the thrust), from its rotation along the slope, which depends on its cylindrical nature. See also Alexander of Aphrodisias, *On Fate* 13, 181.15–182.20; cf. Natali 2009, 25–35 and 219–222.

hand, the divine astral world would be interpreted anthropomorphically; on the other hand, there would no longer be any distinction between inanimate things and men. According to Plotinus, we would not be privileged creatures in any way, and we would not be different from stones which passively roll away.

Different occurrences of "being dragged" (φέρεσθαι) in treatise 3.1 are significant: they are used with regard to the different theories rejected by Plotinus. This verb is used in the critique of astral determinism, which would reduce men to "dragged" things; in the critique of the collisions between atoms, which would assimilate men to "dragged" inanimate entities;[94] and also in the critique of the monistic interweaving of causes, which would "drag" us under the impulse of a single principle.[95]

According to Plotinus, "we must grant to ourselves what is ours" (ἀλλὰ χρὴ διδόναι μὲν τὸ ἡμέτερον ἡμῖν),[96] distinguished from what we undergo "by necessity" (ἐξ ἀνάγκης), without attributing anything to the stars.[97] There are certainly influences from our environment and from our parents; however, these only influence our appearance and the irrational parts of the Soul.[98] Instead, our character and our thoughts come from a different principle, the Soul.[99]

Our capacity to oppose bodily passions is yet another objection to astral determinism,[100] as well as to determinism more broadly. Moreover, there may also be sources of prediction different from the stars, such as the birds' flight and other types of divination.[101]

Genethlialogy, which provides prophecies on the basis of the stars' position at the time of birth, is the central point of Plotinus' critique.[102] According to Plotinus, the stars' position at birth can just "signal" (σημαίνειν), but cannot "produce" (ποιεῖν) events;[103] signs cannot be considered as if they were principles or causes.[104] For example, a child's nobility depends on the parents, rather than the position of the stars.[105] It is irrational to seek information

94 3.1.3.21, 28.
95 3.1.7.13 and 21, 3.1.1.21.
96 3.1.5.20–21.
97 3.1.5.22–24.
98 Radice and Reale 2002, 500–502 n. 19 (with reference to *SVF* 1.518).
99 3.1.5.24–31.
100 3.1.5.31–33.
101 3.1.5.33–37, 2.3.7.
102 3.1.5.37–59.
103 3.1.5.36, 40–41.
104 See Chappuis 2006, 102–103, cf. Pompeo Faracovi 1996, 158–160, Magris 2016, 398–424.
105 3.1.5.41–45.

on the father's fate from his child's horoscope or vice versa, or that of brothers, husbands and wives, thus joining together the fate of the individual and that of the group.[106] If genethlialogy were correct, those who were born under the same astral configuration should have identical characters, against all evidence. Also, the birth of men and living beings of other species under the same astral configurations could not be explained.[107]

In the sixth chapter, Plotinus deepens his observations on the semantic value of stars and reiterates that the error consists in not distinguishing the causes adequately, making everything derive from the stars. Above all, he points out, as Aristotle already did,[108] that living beings are born "according to their own natures" (κατὰ τὰς αὐτῶν φύσεις): from horse comes horse, from man comes man.[109] Plotinus admits that the motion of the sky and the stars can exert an influence, but he considers this action to be "synergistic" (συνεργός): there is a collaboration in the corporeal field, involving the stars as well as the parents.[110] On the other hand, the character, habit and above all the personal choices of an individual – such as, for example, becoming a grammarian, surveyor, dice player[111] or inventor – require something else, a poietic cause.[112] Accordingly, bad choices and evil do not depend on the stars, which are divine beings and remain unchangeable.[113]

In other words, according to Plotinus, the role of astrology is related to the function of the stars: they deal with the "preservation of the universe" (σωτηρία τῶν ὅλων)[114] and are signs for the future.[115] Using an incisive metaphor, Plotinus observes that the stars are like letters for grammarians.[116] Those who know the relative grammar of the stars, namely the order and the structure of the sky, find meaning in them, analogously to how grammarians look for the meaning of a written text.

---

106 3.1.5.45–53.

107 3.1.5.53–59.

108 Henry and Schwyzer 1964, 241, refer to Aristotle, *Metaphysics* 7.7, 1032a25–26; Radice and Reale 2002, 502 n. 20 refer to 9.8, 1049b25–26.

109 3.1.6.1–3, 2.3.12.

110 3.1.6.3–9. Maggi 2007, 369 refers to *Physics* 2.2, 194b13.

111 Henry and Schwyzer 1964, 241 refer to Plato, *Republic* 2.374c. Cf. 3.1.3.26–27.

112 3.1.6.7–10.

113 3.1.6.10–15.

114 3.1.6.19; 4.4.38. Casaglia, Guidelli, Linguiti, and Moriani 1997, 368 n. 33 refer to Plato, *Laws* 10.903b5.

115 3.1.6.20–24; 2.3.7–9 and 14; cf. Spinelli 2002, 281 and 296–297, Maggi 2007, 363.

116 Radice and Reale 2002, 504 n. 21 refer to 2.3.7.4–5 and 3.3.6.18–19. In 5.8.6, Plotinus favours hieroglyphs over letters. Regarding the image of the sky as a book, see Chappuis 2006, 110, with reference to Origen, *On the Free Will* 23.15.31–46 (Junod 1976, 180–183).

The language used in this discussion suggests a connection with a central problem in Plotinus' philosophy.[117] In these passages, there are occurrences of verbs pertaining to the semantic field of seeing, which invite a comparison with the problem of "productive contemplation" in the *Enneads*.[118] In the sixth chapter, the verb "to see" (ὁρᾶν) occurs in a specific sense in the astrological context.[119] It is used in relation to the god-star who looks over another god-star and over people;[120] his seeing does not influence the nature of these people for better or worse. The verb "to look at" (βλέπειν) then appears concerning the astrologers who look at the stars "like letters" (ὥσπερ γράμματα).[121] Knowing this grammar, the experts can read "the future" (τὰ μέλλοντα) in the astral figures,[122] and "trace what they signify by analogy" (κατὰ τὸ ἀνάλογον μεθοδεύοντας τὸ σεμαινόμενον).[123] Likewise, one could say that a bird flying high means high actions.[124] Those who look neither interfere with the stars, nor are they influenced by them. The seeing in this case has no connection with "productive contemplation", that is to say, with the metaphysics of participation emblematically expressed in 3.8. There is only the possibility to look at natural, unconventional signs, readable by experts.[125]

5 The Doctrine of the Self-Determination of the Soul and of the Wise

The third part of this treatise constitutes a turning point. We enter the crucial phase of the discussion about causes and fate,[126] in which Plotinus offers the "other cause" (ἄλλη αἰτία)[127] he is looking for. Its characteristics are: a) it leaves "nothing uncaused" (ἀναίτιόν τε οὐδέν); b) it maintains "consequence and order" (ἀκολουθίαν τε … καὶ τάξιν) of the events;[128] c) it allows "us to be some-

117 See Gatti 1996a, 23–89, Gatti 2012, 5–8.
118 See Gatti 1996a, 91–133, Gatti 1996b, 29–34 and 36–37, Gatti 2012, 69–77, cf. Reale 1990, 396–398.
119 See Sleeman and Pollet 1980, 748–754.
120 See 3.1.6.16, cf. 2.3.1, 2.3.4, 2.3.6 (here θέα and θεᾶσθαι recur); cf. Pompeo Faracovi 1996, 154–155, Maggi 2007, 356–357.
121 3.1.6.20–21. On the verb βλέπειν see Sleeman and Pollet 1980, 190–191; for θεωρεῖν see their 501–502.
122 3.1.6.19–24.
123 3.1.6.22–23.
124 3.1.6.23–24.
125 See Chappuis 2006, 112.
126 3.1.7.21–3.1.10.15.
127 3.1.7.21–24.
128 3.1.8.1–2.

thing" (ἡμᾶς τέ τι εἶναι); d) it does not eliminate "prophecies and divinations" (προρρήσεις τε καὶ μαντείας).[129]

First of all, in the eighth chapter, Plotinus maintains that the difficulties of determinism are overcome by rendering the Soul a "principle" (ἀρχή).[130] The Soul is a cause in which all the listed characteristics are present, both in the case of the Soul of the Universe,[131] and in the case of the Souls of individuals. It is a principle, "of no small importance" (οὐ σμικρά),[132] and one "which weaves everything together."[133] It does not derive from seminal reasons, but it is "a cause that acts in a primary way" (πρωτουργὸς αἰτία).[134] It intertwines everything inasmuch as it is a unifying principle removed from Becoming.

Since the third characteristic listed above concerns human beings, the final part of the treatise is more closely concerned with human Souls than with the Soul of the Universe. The Soul of man is presented from two different perspectives. When it is without a body the Soul is "most in control of itself (κυριωτάτη τε αὐτῆς), free (ἐλευθέρα), and outside the influence of cosmic causality (κοσμικῆς αἰτίας ἔξω)"[135] as well as of time; it is stable. When it is immersed in the body "it is no longer in control of everything" (ουκέτι πάντα κυρία),[136] and it has an unstable equilibrium. In 3.8, the treatise dedicated to *theōria*, it is similarly stated that when the Soul contemplates what is external to it, it is no longer in control of itself.[137] If its lower part prevails, the Soul surrenders to the body and is inserted in a different order.[138] The best Soul "dominates" (κρατεῖ) more, the worse one dominates less.[139] The superior Soul, "naturally good" (ἀγαθὴ τὴν φύσιν),[140] resists the passions and modifies them rather than being modified by them.[141]

In the ninth chapter Plotinus further explores the problem of the Soul and its freedom. The things constituted by the combination of "choice" (προαίρεσις) and "chance" (τύχη) are "necessary" (ἀναγκαῖα)[142] as a set of fortuitous exterior

129 3.1.8.3–4.
130 3.1.8.5.
131 3.1.8.5.
132 3.1.8.6.
133 3.1.8.7.
134 3.1.8.8; cf. Plato, *Laws* 10.896e–897b; see further Henry and Schwyzer 1964, 243.
135 3.1.8.9–10.
136 3.1.8.10–11, 4.3.9.
137 3.8.5; cf. Gatti 1996a, 106–109, Chappuis 2006, 125, Maggi 2007, 367–368.
138 3.1.8.10–11.
139 3.1.8.14–15.
140 3.1.8.18.
141 3.1.8.19.
142 3.1.9.1.

circumstances.[143] Given all the causes, everything happens inexorably. According to Plotinus, universal motion can also be included among the external causes.[144]

The Soul has two possible motions. On the one hand, it can be directed to what is external; in this case it is passive and dependent, it functions "in a kind of blind motion" (τυφλῇ τῇ φορᾷ), which is "involuntary" (οὐχὶ ἑκούσιον), without action and impulses that are "correct and guided by reason", that is without contemplation.[145]

On the other hand, it can be addressed toward interiority, to itself and to the *nous*, "when its impulses are due to its having as its own a controlling principle that is pure and unaffected" (λόγον δὲ ὅταν ἡγεμόνα καθαρὸν καὶ ἀπαθῆ).[146] Thus the impulse that comes from this pure reason "is up to us and voluntary" (ἐφ' ἡμῖν καὶ ἑκούσιον).[147] This is "our own action" (τὸ ἡμέτερον ἔργον), "one that does not come from any other source but from within" (ὃ μὴ ἄλλοθεν ἦλθεν, ἀλλ' ἔνδοθεν), "from a soul that is pure, from a principle that plays a primary, controlling, and authoritative role" (ἀπὸ καθαρᾶς τῆς ψυχῆς, ἀπ' ἀρχῆς πρώτης ἡγουμένης καὶ κυρίας).[148] The guide of the *logos katharos*, linked to *theōria*, involves here actions that are truly free.[149] According to Plotinus, if we and what we do depend wholly on a universal principle, on the interweaving of events and on the mere acceptance or declining of them, the Stoic "what depends on us" is nothing but an empty word.[150]

In the tenth chapter Plotinus concludes.[151] Firstly, Plotinus deals with the causes of events. "The conclusion of this account tells us that everything is presaged and comes about through causes but that these are twofold" (πάντα μὲν σημαίνεσθαι καὶ γίγνεσθαι κατ' αἰτίας μὲν πάντα, διττὰς δὲ ταύτας):[152] the Soul

143 3.1.9.1–2.

144 3.1.9.2–4.

145 3.1.9.4–9, 14–16; cf. Gerson 2014, 260–264.

146 3.1.9.9–10.

147 3.1.9.10–11; cf. Andolfo 1996, 321–327, Leroux 1996, 305–314, Romano 1999, 173, Trabattoni 2009, 195–196.

148 3.1.9.11–14; cf. Graeser 1972, 112–125, Remes 2007, 181–185.

149 See Andolfo 1996, 321–323 (with reference to 3.1 and 6.8, where the different specific Plotinian terms are listed); see also 2.3.9.

150 3.1.7.11–15; cf. Chappuis 2006, 130–131, Eliasson 2009, 418–419.

151 Some scholars, such as Bréhier (1936–1993, vol. 1, xxiii–xxiv, vol. 3, 16 n. 1), speculated that this is an appendix written by Porphyry. But it should be noted that similar expressions are found not only at the end of the book, but also in the body of the text. See also Harder 1961, 419, Radice and Reale 2002, 510 n. 25.

152 3.1.10.1–2.

and the "other causes", which refers to the influences from the outside, the cosmic cycle.[153] Secondly, Plotinus deals with the Souls' actions and passions in relation to reason and fate.[154] He points out that the Souls act "of themselves" (παρ' αὐτῶν) in case they act "in accordance to right reason" (κατὰ λόγον ὀρθόν). The real cause is linked to interiority.[155]

In all other actions the Souls are hindered and "are passive rather than active" (πάσχειν τε μᾶλλον ἢ πράττειν):[156] they are lacking in thought. Those who believe that fate is an external cause believe that these actions without reason or interiority are guided by fate.[157] What we do in this way is not the best we can do. "The best actions come from us" (τὰ δὲ ἄριστα παρ' ἡμῶν),[158] "when we are alone" (ὅταν μόνοι ὦμεν),[159] collected in ourselves, in the pure and free part of the Soul, committed to contemplating the Good and not oriented towards physical multiplicity.[160] In this contemplative condition,[161] human beings find themselves linked to the Soul of the Universe, from which they have been separated, wanting to belong to themselves.

The last lines of the treatise are dedicated to the "sages" (σπουδαῖοι).[162] The Souls who live according to their own nature perform "beautiful deeds", acting "up to them" (ἐπ' αὐτοῖς). The sages do not operate according to fate as an external cause, but by self-determination.[163] In light of other texts where the sages are linked to contemplation,[164] one could say that their self-determination occurs because they contemplate the intelligible. We have this kind of nature, Plotinus says, when we are "alone" (μόνοι); namely, it is then that we are deeply ourselves. In this regard, Chappuis has pointed out that Plotinus does not speak of a single wise person, but of a group of sages; he does not speak of different natures, but of our human nature as pure reason, capable of knowing and acting in the right way.[165] Different from the sages, those who are not wise

153 3.1.10.1–3.
154 3.1.10.4–15.
155 3.1.10.4–5.
156 3.1.10.5–7.
157 3.1.10.8–10.
158 3.1.10.10.
159 3.1.10.11.
160 4.7.10, 2.3.18.
161 See Gatti 1996a, 136–144, cf. Andolfo 1996, 321, Eliasson 2009, 425–428, Trabattoni 2009, 206–211.
162 See Schniewind 2003, 89–90, Dillon 1969, 315–335.
163 3.1.10.11–12; cf. Chappuis 2006, 135.
164 See Gatti 1996a, 221–229, cf. Leroux 1996, 312, Chiaradonna 2009, 164–167, Schniewind 2003, 182–185 and 189–191, Linguiti 2009, 216–220, Trabattoni 2014, 108–112.
165 See Chappuis 2006, 136; see also 3.2.15.

perform beautiful actions only "when they have a breathing space" (καθ' ὅσον ἂν ἀναπνεύσωσι) and begin a path of ascent; freeing themselves from bodily obstacles, they follow reason, "when they do think."[166]

6 Concluding Remarks

To conclude, the analysis of the argumentative structure of 3.1 has offered us Plotinus' analysis of *fate*, the Soul and its self-determination. The term *heimarmenē* is used in different manners in the treatise: 1) in the Stoic sense as a chain of causes; 2) in relation to the one Principle-Soul; 3) in relation to Atomism; 4) as a cause that influences human actions from outside.[167]

Outside 3.1, two cases of its occurrence in the first four *Enneads* are also significant: first, *heimarmenē* related to Providence, which "down here" is fate and "up there" is Providence; and, second, as the fate of the *Nous* to stay up there and influence the next world. *Heimarmenē* refers first of all to the interweaving of causes in the sensible world, also associated with Providence in 3.3.5.15.[168] In short, according to Plotinus, *heimarmenē* is predominantly placed at an ontological level that involves what is external to the Soul and the Hypostases.

With regard to the Soul, the argument in 3.1 focuses above all on the human soul and its freedom, after the refutation of the deterministic theses that deny its freedom. Rejecting Stoic doctrine, Plotinus highlights the elevated nature of the Soul, which is part of the Hypostases. In 3.1 the processional connections related to the *theōria* are not made explicit, since the treatise only deals with the elements that are strictly indispensable for the argumentation. The pure human Soul, "not descended",[169] connected with the Hypostasis which it

166 3.1.10.12–14. Eliasson 2009, 428 notes: "Plotin donc, tout en suivant certains élémens de la théorie médioplatonicienne 'standard', propose une solution qui suit la réception des intuitions platoniciennes que l'on trouve au chapitre 2 du *Didaskalikos*. Selon la solution qui propose Plotin, les actions réalisées par les sages (…) dépendent entièrement d'eux (…), tandis que les autres réalisent seulement des actions vertueuses qui dépendent d'eux dans l'absence totale des contraintes qui accompagnent normalement la vie incarnée. Plotin propose ainsi une solution au problème du destin et surtout à celui de sa compatibilité avec la notion de 'ce qui dépend de nous' (…), selon laquelle agir 'selon le destin' désigne plutôt l'action normale des non-sages, cette quasi-activité où l'âme aveugle à cause de son ignorance (…), devient plutôt l'objet des hasards extérieurs."

167 3.1.10.8–9.

168 The term *pronoia* is absent in 3.1; it is introduced later, after the presentation of the Soul in the first treatise.

169 See Linguiti 2001, 213–236, Chiaradonna 2009, 81–115.

contemplates, is briefly analysed. In this Soul the functions are in balance even though it is still linked with the body.

Among other scholars, Linguiti emphasized the difficulty for contemporary scholars to understand the issue of freedom, choice and self-determination in ancient authors.[170] The first difficulty is presented by the complex and different constellation of the terms used to refer to these concepts; there are many lexical problems, even within the same author and within the same work. This is linked to the issues related to understanding and translating ancient texts. Many scholars, accordingly, have pointed out that we cannot be sure that we have the same conception of freedom and responsibility as the Ancients.

In 3.1, Plotinus highlights several elements concerning what depends on us, our autonomy and self-determination. Rationality, contemplation and interiority are the main features that characterise mankind, therefore self-determination and freedom are to be found at this level, detached from what is external.[171] The Soul, free of body, is master of itself; when it is embodied, it is inserted in an order of different causes that limit its autonomy.[172]

In relation to fate and self-determination, various difficulties emerge in Plotinus' theory, and are held together in a complex equilibrium. Plotinus only partially succeeds in the refutation of Stoic monism, according to which everything necessarily ultimately derives from a single principle. For Plotinus, in fact, everything comes from the first Hypostasis by a way of procession, and the procession is "a necessity that follows an act of freedom."[173]

In this derivative procession there does not seem to be a sufficient margin for a truly free choice on behalf of the Souls. At all levels following the One, there is a necessary progression, even with the profound corrections in hierarchical succession that the doctrine of contemplation implies.[174] Even the

170 See Rist 1967, 130–138, Graeser 1972, 115–125, Williams 1993, 66–68, 130–167, 207–218, Bobzien 1998b, 133–175, Frede 2003, 200, Eliasson 2008, 1–16, 217–222, Chiaradonna 2009, 168–172, Linguiti 2009, 213–215, Linguiti 2014, 211–212, Trabattoni 2009, 196–205, Gerson 2014, 251–263, Spinelli and Verde 2014, 59–61, 64, 71, Vimercati 2014, 151–167.

171 See Linguiti 2009, 216–218, the most significant text here are: 3.1, 6.8, 3.2 and 3.3.

172 3.1.8.

173 See Reale 1990, 395, Radice and Reale 2002, 489.

174 See Gatti 1996a, 47–65, 112–121, cf. Andolfo 1996, 326–327, Romano 1999, 189–191, Maggi 2007, 370–371. See also Dessì 2012, 33: "Se vogliamo continuare a essere responsabili delle nostre azioni dobbiamo essere noi a compiere le nostre azioni, quelle buone come quelle cattive, e quindi dobbiamo ammettere che ciascuno di noi possiede un'anima individuale capace di sottrarsi alla concatenazione delle cause e di autodeterminarsi. La necessità di riconoscere all'uomo la responsabilità delle proprie azioni e con essa la possibilità di quel cammino a ritroso verso il ricongiungimento con l'Uno, attraverso il dominio che

Nous, as we have seen, is subjected to *heimarmenē*, which mainly coincides with the chain of external causes. Since Plotinus considers the birth of the realities that depend on the One not only as a natural and necessary consequence of the free self-volition of the One, but also as a *tolma*, a "rashness",[175] the genesis and descent of beings can also be seen as a departure from unity, a negative though blameless fact.[176] Similarly, the Soul of the Universe, itself deriving from the necessary procession, qua *phusis* is the cause that produces the physical world and its laws, which are in turn an expression of the interweaving of *heimarmenē*.

In a context in which necessity and freedom are intermingled, the self-determination of the individual Soul, free from the body, seems only partial, although it is clearly different from the Stoic conception, where merely assent is possible.[177]

The last lines of the treatise focus on the perspective of freedom linked to contemplation. The sages, who follow reason and interiority, are, according to Plotinus, "alone" (μόνοι), when they address themselves to themselves and their principles thanks to *theōria*. They follow a path of liberation and ascent to the One-Good, in which freedom and will coincide, accomplishing the good for their own self-determination and thus realizing, alone, the famous "escape in solitude to the solitary" (φυγὴ μόνου πρὸς μόνον).[178]

l'anima può esercitare sulle passioni del corpo, obbliga dunque Plotino a negare qualsiasi determinismo. Ma l'aver posto l'Uno come causa prima di tutto lo costringe anche a fare i conti con la presenza del male nel mondo."

175 See Sleeman and Pollet 1980, 1026, Torchia 1993, 71–108, Andolfo 1996, 343–348, Gatti 1996a, 108–112, Gerson 2014, 259–261.

176 Andolfo 1996, 349.

177 4.3.13; cf. O'Brien 1993, 5–18, Andolfo 1996, 326–327 and 349–350, Radice and Reale 2002, 489, Linguiti 2009, 224. Here it should be added that there are oscillations and differentiations in the Plotinian conception of necessity and freedom, although linked and justified by the connection with procession and contemplation. Necessity can be understood in Plotinus both as positive uniformity in the order of the Universe (in the world of Hypostases arising from the freedom of the One and in the Soul linked to the *theōria*), as well as a negative constraint (linked to the procession and to what is external in the case of events caused by causes independent of the Soul). The freedom of the individual can be both the Soul's positive conforming to the order of the Universe (thanks to the *theōria*, realized in different gradations), and negative will to self-belong (as a false freedom, subject to external events, to the fate of this world, without reflection).

178 6.9.11.51; cf. Gatti 1996a, 230–236.

Bibliography

Adamson, Peter. 2011. "Making a Virtue of Necessity. *Anangkê* in Plato and Plotinus." *Études Platoniciennes* 8: 9–30.

Andolfo, Matteo. 1996. *L'ipostasi della "Psyche" in Plotino. Struttura e fondamenti*. Milan: Vita e Pensiero.

Armstrong, Arthur H., tr. 1966–1988. *Plotinus. Enneads*. 7 vols. Cambridge, Mass: Harvard University Press.

Bobzien, Susanne. 1998a. *Determinism and Freedom in Stoic Philosophy*. Oxford: Clarendon.

Bobzien, Susanne. 1998b. "The Inadvertent Conception and Late Birth of the Free-Will Problem." *Phronesis* 43: 133–175.

Bouché-Leclercq, Auguste. 1899. *L'astrologie grecque*. Paris: Leroux.

Brancacci, Aldo. 2001. *La polemica antifatalistica di Enomao di Gadara*, in *Antichi e moderni nella filosofia di età imperiale, Atti del II Colloquio Internazionale, Roma 21–23 settembre 2000*, 71–110. Naples: Bibliopolis.

Bréhier, Émile, ed., tr. 1924–1993. *Plotin. Ennéades*. 7 vols. Paris: Les Belles Lettres.

Brisson, Luc, and others, eds. 1982–1992. *Porphyre, "La vie de Plotin"*. 2 vols. Paris: Vrin.

Casaglia, Mario, Chiara Guidelli, Alessandro Linguiti and Fausto Moriani, eds. 1997. Enneadi *di Plotino*, vol. 1. Turin: UTET.

Chappuis, Marguerite, ed., tr. 2006. *Plotin, Traité 3, III 1*. Paris: Cerf.

Chiaradonna, Riccardo. 2009. *Plotino*. Rome: Carocci.

Chiaradonna, Riccardo. 2017. *Platonismo*. Bologna: Il Mulino.

D'Ancona, Cristina. 2009. "Modèles de causalité chez Plotin." *Les Études Philosophiques* 90: 361–385.

De Caro, Mario, Massimo Mori, and Emidio Spinelli, eds. 2014. *Libero arbitrio. Storia di una controversia filosofica*. Rome: Carocci.

Dessì, Paola. 2012. *Causa/effetto*. Bologna: Il Mulino.

Destrée, Pierre, Ricardo Salles, and Marco Zingano, eds. 2014. *What is Up to Us? Studies on Agency and Responsibility in Ancient Philosophy*. Sankt Augustin: Academia.

Di Pasquale Barbanti, Maria, and Daniele Iozzia, eds. 2009. *Anima e libertà in Plotino, Atti del Convegno Nazionale, Catania, 29–30 gennaio 2009*. Catania: CUECM.

Dillon, John M. 1996. "An Ethic for the Late Antique Sage." In *The Cambridge Companion to Plotinus*, edited by Lloyd P. Gerson, 315–335. Cambridge: Cambridge University Press.

Eliasson, Erik. 2008. *The Notion of* That Which Depends On Us *in Plotinus and Its Background*. Leiden: Brill.

Eliasson, Erik. 2009. "Sur la conception plotinienne du destin dans le 'Traité 3'." *Les Études Philosophiques* 90: 407–430.

Emilsson, Eyjólfur K. 2015. *Plotinus on* sympatheia." In *Sympathy*, edited by Eric Schliesser, 36–60. New York: Oxford University Press.

Faggin, Giuseppe, ed., tr. 1992. *Plotino, "Enneadi"; Porfirio, "Vita di Plotino."* Milan: Rusconi.

Frede, Dorothea. 2003. "Stoic Determinism." In *The Cambridge Companion to the Stoics*, edited by Brad Inwood, 179–205. Cambridge: Cambridge University Press.

Gatti, Maria Luisa. 1996a. *Plotino e la metafisica della contemplazione*. Milan: Vita e Pensiero.

Gatti, Maria Luisa. 1996b. "Plotinus. The Platonic tradition and the Foundation of Neoplatonism." In *The Cambridge Companion to Plotinus*, edited by Lloyd P. Gerson, 10–37. Cambridge: Cambridge University Press.

Gatti, Maria Luisa. 2012. *"Theoria" e filosofia. Interpretazioni della dottrina di Plotino sulla contemplazione a partire dagli anni Cinquanta del Novecento*. Milan: Educatt.

Gerson, Lloyd P., ed. 1996. *The Cambridge Companion to Plotinus*. Cambridge: Cambridge University Press.

Gerson, Lloyd P. 2014. "Moral Responsibility and What is "Up to Us" in Plotinus." In *What is Up to Us? Studies on Agency and Responsibility in Ancient Philosophy*, edited by Pierre Destrée, Ricardo Salles, and Marco Zingano, 251–263. Sankt Augustin: Academia.

Gerson, Lloyd P., ed. 2018. *Plotinus, The Enneads*. Cambridge: Cambridge University Press.

Graeser, Andreas. 1972. *Plotinus and the Stoics. A Preliminary Study*. Leiden: Brill.

Gurtler, Gary M. 1984. "Sympathy in Plotinus." *International Philosophical Quarterly* 96: 395–406.

Harder, Richard, ed. 1961. *Plotins Schriften*. Hamburg: Meiner.

Henry, Paul, and Hans-Rudolf Schwyzer, ed. 1964. *Plotini Opera*, vol. 1. Oxford: Clarendon.

Ioppolo, Anna Maria. 1984. "L'astrologia nello Stoicismo antico." In *La scienza ellenistica. Atti delle tre giornate di studio tenutesi a Pavia dal 14 al 16 aprile 1982*, edited by Gabriele Giannantoni and Mario Vegetti, 73–91. Naples: Bibliopolis.

Ioppolo, Anna Maria. 2007. "La critica di Carneade al concetto stoico di causa in Cic. *'De fato'* 31–37." In *Lexis* 25: 103–119.

Ioppolo, Anna Maria. 2013. "Il concetto di causa nella filosofia ellenistica e romana." In *Dibattiti filosofici ellenistici. Dottrina delle cause, Stoicismo, Accademia scettica*, edited by Riccardo Chiaradonna, Diana Quarantotto, and Emidio Spinelli, 17–68. Sankt Augustin: Academia.

Isnardi Parente, Margherita. 1984. *Introduzione a Plotino*. Rome: Laterza.

Junod, Éric, ed., tr. 1976. *Origène, Philocalie 21–27, Sur le libre arbitre*. Paris: Cerf.

Kalligas, Paul. 2014. *The "Enneads" of Plotinus, A Commentary*, vol. 1. Translated by Elizabeth K. Fowden and Nicolas Pilavachi. Princeton: Princeton University Press.

Leroux, Georges. 1996. "Human Freedom in the Thought of Plotinus." In *The Cambridge Companion to Plotinus*, edited by Lloyd P. Gerson, 292–314. Cambridge: Cambridge University Press.

Linguiti, Alessandro. 2001. "Plotino sulla felicità dell'anima non discesa." In *Antichi e moderni nella filosofia di età imperiale, Atti del II Colloquio Internazionale, Roma 21–23 settembre 2000*, edited by Aldo Brancacci, 213–236. Naples: Bibliopolis.

Linguiti, Alessandro. 2009. "Plotino e i Platonici sull'autodeterminazione e la possibilità di scelta." In *Anima e libertà in Plotino. Atti del Convegno Nazionale, Catania, 29–30 gennaio 2009*, edited by Maria Di Pasquale Barbanti and Daniele Iozzia, 213–226. Catania: CUECM.

Linguiti, Alessandro. 2011. "Sui fondamenti dell'etica plotiniana." In *"Dignum laude virum." Studi di cultura classica e musica offerti a F. Sterpa*, edited by Francesca Bottari, Laura Casarsa, Lucio Cristante, and Marco Fernandelli, 119–135. Trieste: Edizioni Università di Trieste.

Linguiti, Alessandro. 2014. "Choice, Self-determination and Assimilation to God in Plotinus." In *Fate, Providence and Moral Responsibility in Ancient, Medieval and Early Modern Thought. Studies in Honour of Carlos Steel*, edited by Pieter d'Hoine and Gerd Van Riel, 211–223. Leuven: Leuven University Press.

Maggi, Claudia. 2007. "La concezione plotiniana dell'uomo tra fascino e autodominio. La questione degli influssi astrali." *Études Platoniciennes* 4: 353–371.

Magris, Aldo. 1986. *Invito al pensiero di Plotino*. Milan: Mursia.

Magris, Aldo. 2016. *Destino, provvidenza, predestinazione*. 2nd edn. Brescia: Morcelliana.

Maso, Stefano, ed., tr. 2014. *Cicerone. Il fato*. Rome: Carocci.

Nagy, Anna. 2017. "Author and Actor. Plotinus and the Stoics on the Autonomy of Action." *Rivista di Filosofia Neo-Scolastica* 109: 109–130.

Natali, Carlo, and Stefano Maso, eds. 2005. *La catena delle cause. Determinismo e antideterminismo nel pensiero antico e contemporaneo*. Amsterdam: Hakkert.

Natali, Carlo, and Elisa Tetamo, tr. 2009. *Alessandro d'Afrodisia (Tito Aurelio Alessandro), Il destino. Trattato sul destino e su ciò che dipende da noi. Dedicato agli imperatori*. 2nd edition. Sankt Augustin: Academia.

O'Brien, Denis. 1993. *Théodicée plotinienne, théodicée gnostique*. Leiden: Brill.

O'Brien, Denis. 1997. "Immortal and Necessary Being in Plato and Plotinus." In *The Perennial Tradition of Neoplatonism*, edited by John J. Cleary, 39–103. Leuven: Leuven University Press.

Pompeo Faracovi, Ornella. 1996. *Scritto negli astri. L'astrologia nella cultura dell'Occidente*. Venice: Marsilio.

Radice, Roberto, tr. 2002. *Stoici antichi. Tutti i frammenti raccolti da H. von Arnim*. Milan: Bompiani.

Radice, Roberto. 2009. "*Libertà tra Stoicismo e Plotino*." In *Anima e libertà in Plotino, Atti del Convegno Nazionale, Catania, 29–30 gennaio 2009*, edited by Maria Di Pasquale Barbanti and Daniele Iozzia, 15–39. Catania: CUECM.

Radice, Roberto, and Roberto Bombacigno, eds. 2004. *Lexicon II. Plotinus*. Milan: Biblia.

Radice, Roberto, and Giovanni Reale, tr. 2002. *Plotino, "Enneadi."* Milan: Mondadori.

Reale, Giovanni. 1990. *A History of Ancient Philosophy*, vol. 4: *The Schools of the Imperial Age*, tr. John R. Catan. New York: State University of New York Press.

Remes, Paulina. 2007. *Plotinus on Self. The Philosophy of the "We."* Cambridge: Cambridge University Press.

Rist, John M. 1967. *Plotinus. The Road to Reality*. Cambridge: Cambridge University Press.

Romano, Francesco. 1999. *Azione morale e libero arbitrio in Plotino. "La virtù non ha padrone" ("arete adespoton") (Plat. "Rep." X, 617 e 3)*. In *La "Repubblica" di Platone nella tradizione antica*, edited by Mario Vegetti and Michele Abbate, 151–191. Naples: Bibliopolis.

Russi, Chiara. 2004. "Le cause prossime plotiniane nell'esordio di "enn". III 1 [3]. Convergenze e dissonanze con la tradizione aristotelica." In *Elenchos* 25: 73–98.

Salles, Ricardo. 2005. *The Stoics on Determinism and Compatibilism*. Aldershot: Ashgate.

Sauvé Meyer, Susan. 2009. *Chain of Causes. What is Stoic Fate?"* In *God and Cosmos in Stoicism*, edited by Ricardo Salles, 71–90. Oxford: Oxford University Press.

Schniewind, Alexandrine. 2003. *L'éthique du sage chez Plotin. Le paradigme du "spoudaios."* Paris: Vrin.

Sleeman, John H., and Gilbert Pollet. 1980. *Lexicon Plotinianum*. Leiden and Leuven: Brill and Leuven University Press.

Spinelli, Emidio. 2002. "La semiologia del cielo: astrologia e anti-astrologia in Sesto Empirico e Plotino." In *Homo Mathematicus, Actas del Congreso Internacional sobre Astrólogos Griegos y Romanos celebrado en Benalmádena (Málaga), 8–10 octubre 2001*, edited by Aurelio Pérez Jiménez and Raúl Caballero, 275–300. Málaga: Charta Antiqua.

Spinelli, Emidio, and Francesco Verde. 2014. "Alle radici del libero arbitrio? Aporie e soluzioni nelle filosofie ellenistiche." In *Libero arbitrio. Storia di una controversia filosofica*, edited by Mario De Caro, Massimo Mori, and Emidio Spinelli, 59–98. Rome: Carocci.

SVF: von Arnim, Hans. 1903–1905. *Stoicorum veterum fragmenta*. Leipzig: Teubner.

Torchia, N. Joseph. 1993. *Plotinus, "tolma" and the Ascent of Being. An Exposition and Analysis*. Frankfurt am Main: Lang.

Trabattoni, Franco. 2009. "Libertà e autodeterminazione dell'essere umano in Plotino." In *Anima e libertà in Plotino, Atti del Convegno Nazionale, Catania, 29–30 gennaio*

2009, edited by Maria Di Pasquale Barbanti and Daniele Iozzia, 189–211. Catania: CUECM.

Trabattoni, Franco. 2014. “Libertà e destino da Platone al neoplatonismo.” In *Libero arbitrio. Storia di una controversia filosofica*, edited by Mario De Caro, Massimo Mori, and Emidio Spinelli, 99–113. Rome: Carocci.

Valgiglio, Ernesto. 1967. “Il fato nel pensiero classico antico.” *Rivista di studi classici* 15: 305–330.

Vimercati, Emmanuele. 2014. *Panaetius on Self-Knowledge and Moral Responsibility*. In *What is Up to Us? Studies on Agency and Responsibility in Ancient Philosophy*, edited by Pierre Destrée, Ricardo Salles, and Marco Zingano, 151–167. Sankt Augustin: Academia.

Wagner, Michael F. 1982. “Vertical Causation in Plotinus.” In *The Structure of Being. A Neoplatonic Approach*, edited by R. Baine Harris, 51–72. Albany: State University of New York Press.

Williams, Bernard. 1993. *Shame and Necessity*. Berkeley: University of California Press.

CHAPTER 15

"Both Sun and Night Are Servants for Mortals"? Providence in Celsus' *True Account*

Pia De Simone

The notion of "providence" (πρόνοια) plays a crucial role in the second-century Celsus' *True Account* and consequently in Origen's *Against Celsus*, written in the following century as a response and our sole source for Celsus' writings. Before introducing Celsus' own conception of providence, which is the object of this chapter,[1] some preliminary remarks might be useful. For the Greek term *pronoia* has a much wider range of meaning than the English providence, since it includes "foresight" and notions related to "think before", "foresee", "take care", "premeditate". The use of the term *pronoia* in the context of ancient Greek philosophy comprises both the conception of physical causality and religious cosmology.[2] *Pronoia*, in the full spectrum of its different meanings, can encompass issues such as the divine action in the cosmos, divine prescience, predetermination and the problem of evil, and can have not only physical and metaphysical, but also ethical and anthropological implications.

In Plato's account, *pronoia* is impersonal and is not related to care for individuals; rather, in a broader perspective, it looks after the harmony and the beauty of the universe. In Aristotle's writings – at least as they were understood in the Imperial age, since Aristotle did not address this issue extensively – *pronoia* is the cause of order and harmony in the cosmos but it is operative only in the heavens, namely from the sphere of the fixed stars down to the sphere in which the moon moves around the earth. Therefore, in sublunary reality it is at work only indirectly.[3]

Between the second century BCE and the second century CE, many philosophers were interested in providence. There was indeed an intense debate between the Stoics, the staunchest proponents of *pronoia*, on the one hand, and the Epicureans, on the other hand, as attested in the writings of Cicero,

1 On Origen's notion of providence, see Mark Edwards' contribution to the present volume.

2 On *pronoia* in ancient philosophical thought see Sharples 1987, esp. 1216–1218; Dragona-Monachou 1994, 4418–4487, Ferrari 1999, 63–77.

3 Cf. here below.

 | DOI:10.1163/9789004436381_017

Seneca, Apuleius, Philo of Alexandria, Ps.-Plutarch, Boethus of Sidon and in the pseudo-Aristotelian treatise *On the World*.[4]

As I will show, Celsus' account of providence should be understood in light of this debate from the writings of Origen, who transmitted it to us, between the pagan anti-Christian polemic on the one hand and the Christian response to it on the other. This chapter is structured in four sections. Section one offers an examination of providence in the *True Account* according to Origen's *Against Celsus*; this section deals with Origen accusing Celsus of Epicureanism and with the issues on omnipotence and anthropocentrism that Celsus' understanding of providence implies. Section two focuses on the Platonic influence on Celsus' ideas on providence, whereas section three examines some authors of the second century CE who wrote on providence and share a similar view on it, in order to place Celsus' thought in its historical settings. In the final section I will characterise Celsus' thought on providence as occupying a "middle ground" between Epicureanism and Stoicism.

1 Providence in Celsus' *True Account* According to Origen. Divine Power and Anthropocentrism

The notion of providence presupposes the existence of a divine power, which relates to the world and to the human beings in it. In his *Against Celsus*, Origen clarifies that there are three main views concerning God and providence: first, the Epicurean view, that rejects a divine interest in human affairs and therefore the existence of providence; second, the Aristotelian view, according to which providence is limited to the heavens, whereas it is absent in the sublunary world; and finally the Stoic one, in which God's providential and finalistic plan is grounded in its being the living, good and normative principle of the cosmos, immanent in all things (1.21). According to Origen, all these positions are wrong, but in different manners: the Epicureans are wrong in denying providence altogether; the Aristotelians are wrong in restricting the role of providence to the heavens, that is to a limited portion of reality excluding humans; the Stoics err in their corporeal conception of God.

In the first four books of *Against Celsus*, the Epicureans are Origen's main polemical target. He repeatedly identifies them as those who reject divine providence and accuse of superstition those who believe in it and place a

4 For a survey on these positions see Dragona-Monachou 1994, 4418–4487 and Dillon 1977, 44–45.

God above all things.[5] In this context, he also "accuses" Celsus of being an Epicurean.[6] According to Origen, since Celsus' interlocutors believe in the existence of divine providence, Celsus cannot be explicit about his Epicureanism fearing that his statements would be dismissed, therefore:

> he *pretends* that there is something in man superior to the earthly part, which is related to God. He says that those in whom this part is healthy (that is, the soul) always long for him to whom it is related (he means God), and they desire to hear something of him and to be reminded about him.[7] (Tr. Chadwick 1953; my italics)

Origen explicitly links Epicurus and Celsus in their claims that providence does not exist; he declares that "some [...] have too hastily concluded that providence does not exist, and have adopted the opinion of Epicurus and Celsus."[8] In the debates on providence in the 2nd and 3rd century, in attacking opponents Epicurean doctrine was often invoked in a disparaging manner, as e.g. by Plotinus against the Gnostics, by Atticus against Aristotle, and by Alexander of Aphrodisias against the Stoics.[9] In line with this approach, Origen introduces the Peripatetics as thinkers who, too, deny that providence takes care of human beings and that there is a relationship between God and man.[10] From these sketchy references, therefore, Celsus' thought is also assimilated to Epicureanism as a rejection of any divine care for the world and, as such, it is criticized by Origen.

In *Against Celsus*, though, the debate on providence is more complex, since it should be placed within Origen's general account of Celsus' thought, which is presented as a firm and scornful rejection of Christianity. Celsus' position is thus best explained in light of his understanding of God and, specifically, of his contempt of Jesus. Since providence presupposes God and Jesus was proclaimed by the Christians to be Son of God and God Himself, clearly the

5 See Origen, *Against Celsus* 1.8, 1.10, 1.13, 1.21, 2.13, 2.42, 3.75.

6 Starting from Book 5, Origen considers Celsus as a Platonist. On Celsus as an Epicurean, see De Simone 2018, 245–258, Bergjan 2001, 179–204.

7 Origen, *Against Celsus* 1.8: προσποιεῖται κρεῖττόν τι τοῦ γηΐνου εἶναι ἐν ἀνθρώπῳ συγγενὲς θεοῦ καί φησιν ὅτι οἷς τοῦτο εὖ ἔχει, τουτέστιν ἡ ψυχή, πάντῃ ἐφίενται τοῦ συγγενοῦς, λέγει δὲ τοῦ θεοῦ, καὶ ἀκούειν ἀεί τι καὶ ἀναμιμνήσκεσθαι περὶ ἐκείνου ποθοῦσιν.

8 Origen, *Against Celsus* 1.10: καὶ τινὲς [...] συγκατέθεντο τῷ μηδαμῶς εἶναι πρόνοιαν καὶ τὸν Ἐπικούρου καὶ Κέλσου εἵλοντο λόγον.

9 See Longo 2016, 81–108.

10 See Origen, *Against Celsus* 3.75. Atticus, too, connects the Peripatetic and the Epicurean positions on providence (see Eusebius of Caesarea, *Preparation for the Gospel* 15.5.1–14 = Atticus, fr. 3 Des Places).

discussion on the nature and the actions of Jesus was related to the Christian (or Celsian, for that matter) understanding of providence.[11] In fact, for Christians the incarnation of God was the clearest evidence of God's providence and grace towards human beings. Now, since the notion of providence presupposes the existence of a divine power, according to Celsus the Scriptures showed precisely that Jesus did not have exceptional powers and that in any case the expectations that Christians associated with Jesus were based on false assumptions. He thus combines the issue of divine power with the debate on providence in order to deny Jesus' divinity. In *Against Celsus* 1.57, he asks: "If you [Jesus] say that every man has become a son of God by divine providence (κατὰ θείαν πρόνοιαν), what is the difference between you and anyone else?"[12] If God takes care of all human beings, as Christians claim, they must explain Jesus' peculiarity as God's Son, the uniqueness of his sonship. In various passages, Jesus is blamed by Celsus for being a magician and an imposter, whose miracles were only the effect of deception.[13] In other passages, Jesus' practices were described as of Egyptian origin and thus unoriginal, even as a product of illusion.[14] Therefore, since other peoples, too, had performed wonders,[15] according to Celsus Jesus should have best demonstrated his divinity by disappearing from the cross (2.68). To these objections, Origen replies by distinguishing the nature of Jesus' miracles, which reflected the will of God and were part of a doctrine of salvation for all men, from Aristea's wonders, which did not present a purpose useful for the entire mankind (3.28).

Celsus' alleged Epicureanism is challenged by his belief in spirits, miracles, apparitions of gods, soothsayers, magicians, as well as by his support for the providence of God, the creation of the world, and the immortality of souls.[16] But also his adherence to the so-called *palaios logos*, or "ancient doctrine", might be regarded as evidence for his belief in divine providence. For, according to this doctrine, a universal form of wisdom can be found among all people in the world, sharing some common philosophical and religious beliefs, including the existence of one divine *logos* leading human events.[17] Clearly, from this universal wisdom Jews and Christians were excluded by Celsus, who

---

11 Clearly, at the time of Celsus, as well as of Origen, the relation between God the Father and the Son was matter of discussion, but this is not relevant for this paper.

12 Origen, *Against Celsus* 1.57: εἰ τοῦτο λέγεις, ὅτι πᾶς ἄνθρωπος κατὰ θείαν πρόνοιαν γεγονὼς υἱός ἐστι θεοῦ, τί ἂν σὺ ἄλλου διαφέροις; The translation used here is Chadwick 1953.

13 See *Against Celsus* 1.6, 2.48–49.

14 See *Against Celsus* 1.22, 1.28, 1.66, 1.68, and 3.7.

15 See *Against Celsus* 2.55 and 3.26, but also 1.14b.

16 See Berjan 2001, 180.

17 See *Against Celsus* 1.14–16; cf. Boys-Stones 2001, 106–122.

presents them as different from all other people (or most of them). In this sense, the final chapters of Book 4 of *Against Celsus* contain Celsus' attempts to refute the claim of the Christians that they occupy a privileged position in the divine creation and with regard to providence.[18] He rather argues that the notion of providence does not necessarily implies that God takes care of individuals, not even human beings.

After assimilating Jesus to other men, Celsus tries to downplay the anthropocentric view of the world by means of arguments rooted in his critique of Stoicism. He claims that the universe was made as God's perfect work and that it was not made for human beings any more than it was for lions or eagles or dolphins:

> This is why everything was measured out: not each part for the other – except incidentally –, but *each for the whole* (οὐκ ἀλλήλων, ἀλλ' εἰ μὴ πάρεργον, ἀλλὰ τοῦ ὅλου). And God cares for the whole, and his providence never leaves it (καὶ μέλει τῷ θεῷ τοῦ ὅλου, καὶ τοῦτ' οὔ ποτ' ἀπολείπει πρόνοια), [...] nor does he get angry with it on account of men, any more than he does on account of monkeys or mice; (οὐδ' ἀνθρώπων ἕνεκα ὀργίζεται, ὥσπερ οὐδὲ πιθήκων οὐδὲ μυῶν) and he does not threaten them. Each of them has its allotted role as a part (οὐδὲ τούτοις ἀπειλεῖ, ὧν ἕκαστον ἐν τῷ μέρει τὴν αὐτοῦ μοῖραν εἴληφε).[19] (Tr. Boys-Stones 2018; my italics)

If God cares for the whole, it is also difficult to prove the existence of evil, since, even if human beings are not aware of it, each part of the whole should benefit someone else or the universe.[20] Origen stresses that God is not responsible for evil through the image of the carpenter who also produces shavings and sawdust in the processing of his product (6.55). The actions of providence are aimed at the good; evil is a secondary and unintentional product, such as shavings and sawdust.[21]

---

18 Cataudella (1937, 186–193) claims that the sophist Antiphon, author of the treatise *On Truth*, influenced Celsus in arguing against the privileged role of Jews and Christians compared to other living beings on the basis of their devotion to God.

19 Origen, *Against Celsus* 4.99.

20 Origen, *Against Celsus* 4.70: κἂν σοί τι δοκῇ κακόν, οὔπω δῆλον εἰ κακόν ἐστιν· οὐ γὰρ οἶσθα ὅ τι ἢ σοὶ ἢ ἄλλῳ ἢ τῷ ὅλῳ συμφέρει ("Even if something should strike you as evil, it is not thereby clear whether is evil: you do not know what is of benefit to you, or someone else, or the universe." Tr. Boys-Stones 2018). Origen replies to Celsus that in the Christian perspective, even if something evil could contribute to the good of the whole, it is still something evil (see *Against Celsus* 4.70).

21 This doctrine is attributed to the Stoics (see e.g. *SVF* 2.1170; Marcus Aurelius, *Meditations* 8.50) and is taken up in Maximus of Tyre, *Orations* 41.4.

Celsus does not only stress that everything was made for humans as much as it was made for irrational animals,[22] but also that, different from humans, animals do not need to sow and plow,[23] and struggle and persevere in order to sustain themselves.[24] He claims that thunder, lightning and rain are not produced by God and, even if they were, they were not made for nourishing humans any more than they were for nourishing plants, trees, grass, and thorns.[25] Quoting Euripides' verse "Both sun and night are servants for mortals,"[26] he stresses that sun and night have the same purpose also for ants and flies: just like human beings, they also rest at night, see and act during daytime.[27] Origen replies that, although providence cares mainly for rational beings, also irrational beings benefit from things created for men (4.74). He also reiterates that if events like thunder and lightning are not the work of providence, they are then the result of a casual encounter of atoms, as the Epicureans claim (4.75). If ants and flies work during the day and rest at night, it is because they reap the fruits of the things generated for men (4.77).

With regard to the superiority of humans to animals, Celsus rejects the claim according to which, since men hunt and eat irrational animals, these latter have been created for men. In fact, it is easier for animals to hunt men, because nature has given them everything they need; men instead need nets, weapons, and the help of other men and dogs.[28] As evidence for this, before the formation of societies, cities and the invention of arts that gave men the necessary tools, men were not able to capture and eat wild beasts, or at best very rarely.[29] Origen argues that God created man deficient in order for him to discover the arts and exercise his intelligence.[30]

Celsus brings up many other examples as evidence for the claim that human beings are not superior to animals. One of these is that the establishment of cities, laws, and leaders is not a human prerogative, since also bees

---

22 See Origen, *Against Celsus* 4.74.

23 See Homer, *Odyssey* 9.109, Lucretius, *On the Nature of Things* 5.195–234.

24 See Origen, *Against Celsus* 4.76.

25 See Origen, *Against Celsus* 4.75. Origen replies to Celsus that God created all things, and that Christians should feel grateful to God, not only for having been created by Him, but also for the animals which are subject to them.

26 See Euripides, *Phoenician Women* 546.

27 Origen, *Against Celsus* 4.77.

28 See Origen, *Against Celsus* 4.78.

29 See Origen, *Against Celsus* 4.79. Cf. 4.80: ὥστε ταύτῃ γε ὁ θεὸς τοὺς ἀνθρώπους μᾶλλον τοῖς θηρίοις ὑπέβαλεν ("Therefore in this respect at least it is truer to say that God subjected men to the wild beasts." Tr. Chadwick 1953).

30 According to Cataudella (1937, 189–193), Origen would have used the myth of Protagoras, in Plato, *Protagoras* 320d–322d, as his source here.

> have a leader; they have attendants and servants, wars and victories and the annihilation of the defeated, cities and suburbs and lines of succession for their jobs, and judgements against the lazy and worthless – anyway they expel the drones and punish them.[31] (Tr. Boys-Stones 2018)

Furthermore, ants, like men, prepare for food in winter, help other ants when they see them in difficulty, select a special place for the dead which then functions as a sort of cemetery,[32] and converse and have common concepts of certain universals.[33] According to Origen, though, ants and bees must not be admired for the actions they perform as they perform them without reflection. Instead, we must praise the divine nature which has extended the imitation of rational beings to the irrational ones (4.81).

Equality between humans and animals might appear Epicurean (Epicureanism rejected anthropocentrism), but this similarity is only superficial, since, according to Celsus, the equality also applies to the notion of God, which would be innate and common to all animals. For also birds have the divine power of knowing and foretelling the future, a kind of knowledge which can come only from God; also elephants can keep oaths more faithfully than any other animals, because they have a notion of God.[34] This list of similarities between human and animal behaviour ends with two examples of filial piety and dutiful regard towards parents: the storks that return affection and bring food to their parents and "the Arabian bird, the Phoenix, which after many years

---

31 Origen, *Against Celsus* 4.81: μελίσσαις γοῦν ἐστιν ἡγεμών, ἔστι δ' ἀκολουθία τε καὶ θεραπεία καὶ πόλεμοι καὶ νῖκαι καὶ τῶν ἡττημένων ἀναιρέσεις καὶ πόλεις καὶ προπόλεις γε καὶ ἔργων διαδοχὴ καὶ δίκαι κατὰ τῶν ἀργῶν τε καὶ πονηρῶν· τοὺς γοῦν κηφῆνας ἀπελαύνουσί τε καὶ κολάζουσιν.

32 See Origen, *Against Celsus* 4.83–84. Ants and bees are similarly associated in another text regarding providence written in Alexandria in the first century: Philo, *On Providence* 1.25. On Philo's *On Providence* 1, see Runia 2017, 159–178. In Philo of Alexandria we can find not only the same kind of examples, but also other doctrines held by Celsus, such as that God's prescience, goodness, and perfection, so that he cannot be the origin of the evil that is inside the human soul. Human freedom has to observe divine laws and only God can save men. The existence of divine mediators allows to protect the transcendence and omnipotence of God that can act into the world without contaminating himself with matter. See further Opsomer 2014, 137–139.

33 Origen, *Against Celsus* 4.84: καὶ μὲν δὴ καὶ ἀπαντῶντες ἀλλήλοις διαλέγονται, ὅθεν οὐδὲ τῶν ὁδῶν ἁμαρτάνουσιν· οὐκοῦν καὶ λόγου συμπλήρωσίς ἐστι παρ' αὐτοῖς καὶ κοιναὶ ἔννοιαι καθολικῶν τινων καὶ φωνὴ καὶ τυγχάνοντα καὶ σημαινόμενα. ("Also, when they encounter each other, they converse, so that they never go wrong on the roads. So a sufficiency of reason is found among them, and common concepts of certain universals, and voice; things are achieved, things are signified." Tr. Boys-Stones 2018).

34 See Origen, *Against Celsus* 4.88.

visits Egypt, and brings its dead father, buried in a ball of myrrh, and puts him in the shrine of the sun."[35] (Tr. Chadwick 1953) Against Celsus, Origen reiterates that there is a difference between performing actions by nature on the one hand or with the use of reason on the other hand. With these examples, divine providence rather wanted to show that men are not animals (4.98).

In sum: although our knowledge of Celsus' text is limited to Origen's testimony, it is, however, sufficient to prove that Celsus deals with the entire semantic spectrum of the term *pronoia*, including God's prescience and care for the world he has created. As was common in Middle Platonism, then, Celsus accepted the existence of a universal providence, through which God takes care of the entire cosmos, but not of every single individual nor, according to Celsus, of human beings more than other animals. In this framework, his criticism of Jesus should be placed, which is aimed at proving that he is neither God nor the Son of God, that his miracles were actually deceptions, and that he is no sign of God's care for men.

2 Celsus' View in a Diachronic Perspective: the References to Plato on Providence

Before moving on to examine what Celsus' contemporaries wrote on providence in the next section, it is useful to discuss the references to earlier philosophical accounts of providence in Celsus' thought. Despite Origen's accusation of Epicureanism, Celsus is commonly regarded as a Middle Platonist, whose cosmology basically rests on Plato's *Timaeus*.[36] For, in discussing the origin of the cosmos,[37] Celsus introduces demons as mediating entities between the divine and the human world,[38] and presents God as a transcendental being. In this sense, despite some Stoic and Epicurean influences, Plato is surely Celsus' main reference for his notion of providence.[39]

According to Platonic doctrine, the universe is constituted by the ordering god and ordered matter. Therefore, God precedes the world, but his providence includes all things.[40] In his famous passage from *Timaeus*, Plato asserts:

35 Origen, *Against Celsus* 4.98: τὸ ἀράβιον ζῷον, τὸν φοίνικα, διὰ πολλῶν ἐτῶν ἐπιδημοῦν Αἰγύπτῳ καὶ φέρον ἀποθανόντα τὸν πατέρα καὶ ταφέντα ἐν σφαίρᾳ σμύρνης καὶ ἐπιτιθὲν ὅπου τὸ τοῦ ἡλίου τέμενος.

36 See Vimercati 2015, 1163.

37 See Origen, *Against Celsus* 6.52.

38 See Origen, *Against Celsus* 2.17, 5.2, 6.30, 7.62.

39 See De Simone 2018, 257.

40 See Valgiglio 1964, xxvi.

> Guided by this reasoning, he put intelligence in soul, and soul in body, and so he constructed the universe. He wanted to produce a piece of work that would be as excellent and supreme as its nature would allow. This, then, in keeping with our likely account, is how we must say *divine providence* brought our world into being as a truly living thing, endowed with soul and intelligence.[41] (Tr. Zeyl 1997, my emphasis)

So, according to Plato, this cosmos was generated owing to divine providence.

In his chapter on the capacity of humans to do the good as something derived from the "beneficent agency" of God, Boys-Stones translates "providence" as "beneficent agency".[42] If God, the creator, is provident, he should have some kinds of personal features – basically, intellect and will – and take care of things created and placed in time. In order "to exempt the Demiurge from responsibility for any evil the souls might afterwards do",[43] Plato claims that God, who is good and the best of the causes (29d–30a), assigns souls to the stars and proclaims to them *the laws of fate*.[44] In line with Plato, then, in Middle Platonism fate is a divine causal principle active in the world, in harmony with, but subordinated to providence.[45] Atticus thus criticised Aristotle, who had claimed that providence only reaches as far as the moon and that god does not care for human beings. Whereas the craftsman-god of the *Timaeus* is benevolent, the first principle of Aristotle's *Metaphysics* thinks only of himself, without a teleological care for sublunary world.[46]

In this sense, the debate on determinism in Plato could be trenchantly summarised with the phrase θεὸς ἀναίτιος, a God without responsibility, from a passage of the *Republic* 10, at 617e, about the choice of life that souls have to make before reincarnation.[47] In this passage, reference is also made to God as responsible neither for evil, nor, as we have just seen, for the malice of which certain beings are guilty.[48] Another passage from the *Republic* (2.379b–c) clarifies Plato's view further:

---

41 Plato, *Timaeus* 30b3–c1: διὰ δὴ τὸν λογισμὸν τόνδε νοῦν μὲν ἐν ψυχῇ, ψυχὴν δ' ἐν σώματι συνιστὰς τὸ πᾶν συνετεκταίνετο, ὅπως ὅτι κάλλιστον εἴη κατὰ φύσιν ἄριστόν τε ἔργον ἀπειργασμένος. οὕτως οὖν δὴ κατὰ λόγον τὸν εἰκότα δεῖ λέγειν τόνδε τὸν κόσμον ζῷον ἔμψυχον ἔννουν τε τῇ ἀληθείᾳ διὰ τὴν τοῦ θεοῦ γενέσθαι πρόνοιαν.

42 See Boys-Stones 2018, 323–343.

43 Plato, *Timaeus* 42d3–4: ἵνα τῆς ἔπειτα εἴη κακίας ἑκάστων ἀναίτιος. The translation is taken from Zeyl 1997.

44 Plato, *Timaeus* 41e2–3: νόμους … τοὺς εἱμαρμένους.

45 See Opsomer 2014, 139–140.

46 See Boys-Stones 2018, 323–326.

47 αἰτία ἑλομένου: θεὸς ἀναίτιος ("The responsibility lies with the one who makes the choice; the god has none"; tr. Grube 1997).

48 Plato, *Timaeus* 42d3–4. Cf. Lanzi 2000.

> And surely nothing good is harmful, is it? I suppose not. And can what isn't harmful do harm? Never. Or can what does no harm do anything bad? No. And can what does nothing bad be the cause of anything bad? How could it? Moreover, the good is beneficial? Yes. It is the cause of doing well? Yes. The good isn't the cause of all things, then, but only of good ones; it isn't the cause of bad ones. I agree entirely. Therefore, since a god is good, he is not – as most people claim – the cause of everything that happens to human beings but of only a few things, for good things are fewer than bad ones in our lives. He alone is responsible for the good things, but we must find some other cause for the bad ones, not a god. That's very true, and I believe it.[49] (Tr. Grube 1997)

So, God is not responsible for evil and in Plato we already find the principal ramifications of this: divine goodness, the origin of evil, human responsibility, final retribution.

Fate is good, but human beings are responsible, as Plato formulates it in the *Phaedrus*, at 248c: "Besides, the law of Adrastea is this: If any soul becomes a companion to a god and catches sight of any true thing, it will be unharmed until the next circuit; and if it is able to do this every time, it will always be safe."[50] (Tr. Nehamas and Woodruff 1997, modified) In fact, according to the *Timaeus*, the Demiurge generates only divine realities; other demons generate mortal men and their mortal soul. The mortal soul in fact is the venue of the passions and the passions lure to evil. Plato states at 69c–d:

> All these things, rather, the god first gave order to, and then out of them he proceeded to construct this universe, a single living thing that contains within itself all living things, mortal or immortal. He himself fashioned those that were divine, but assigned his own progeny the task of fashioning the generation of those that were mortal. They imitated him:

49 Plato, *Republic* 2.379b–c: οὐκοῦν ἀγαθὸς ὅ γε θεὸς τῷ ὄντι τε καὶ λεκτέον οὕτω; τί μήν; ἀλλὰ μὴν οὐδέν γε τῶν ἀγαθῶν βλαβερόν: ἦ γάρ; οὔ μοι δοκεῖ. ἆρ᾽οὖν ὃ μὴ βλαβερὸν βλάπτει; οὐδαμῶς. ὃ δὲ μὴ βλάπτει κακόν τι ποιεῖ; οὐδὲ τοῦτο. ὃ δέ γε μηδὲν κακὸν ποιεῖ οὐδ᾽ἄν τινος εἴη κακοῦ αἴτιον; πῶς γάρ; τί δέ; ὠφέλιμον τὸ ἀγαθόν; ναί. αἴτιον ἄρα εὐπραγίας; ναί. παντελῶς γ᾽, ἔφη. οὐδ᾽ ἄρα, ἦν δ᾽ ἐγώ, ὁ θεός, ἐπειδὴ ἀγαθός, πάντων ἂν εἴη αἴτιος, ὡς οἱ πολλοὶ λέγουσιν, ἀλλὰ ὀλίγων μὲν τοῖς ἀνθρώποις αἴτιος, πολλῶν δὲ ἀναίτιος: πολὺ γὰρ ἐλάττω τἀγαθὰ τῶν κακῶν ἡμῖν, καὶ τῶν μὲν ἀγαθῶν οὐδένα ἄλλον αἰτιατέον, τῶν δὲ κακῶν ἄλλ᾽ ἄττα δεῖ ζητεῖν τὰ αἴτια, ἀλλ᾽ οὐ τὸν θεόν. ἀληθέστατα, ἔφη, δοκεῖς μοι λέγειν.

50 Θεσμός τε Ἀδραστείας ὅδε. ἥτις ἂν ψυχὴ θεῷ συνοπαδὸς γενομένη κατίδῃ τι τῶν ἀληθῶν, μέχρι τε τῆς ἑτέρας περιόδου εἶναι ἀπήμονα, κἂν ἀεὶ τοῦτο δύνηται ποιεῖν, ἀεὶ ἀβλαβῆ εἶναι. Adrastea is "she from whom one cannot run away", therefore Plato is talking about unavoidable fate.

> having taken the immortal origin of the soul, they proceeded next to encase it within a round mortal body [the head], and to give it the entire body as its vehicle. And within the body they built another kind of soul as well, the mortal kind, which contains within it those dreadful but necessary disturbances: pleasure, first of all, evil's most powerful lure; then pains, that make us run away from what is good; besides these, boldness also and fear, foolish counsellors both; then also the spirit of anger hard to assuage, and expectation easily led astray.[51] (Tr. Zeyl 1997)

Starting from Plato's perspective, it is now easier to understand why Celsus' providence is related to divine power and to the whole (and not to the individual as such). Celsus follows Plato's cosmological and ethical concerns. These two concerns, cosmological and ethical, can be found linked together not only in a diachronic perspective, looking back to Plato, but also in a synchronic one, in Celsus' contemporaries, to which I will now turn.

3 Celsus' View in a Synchronic Perspective: the Debate on Providence in the Second Century CE

The debate on providence was widespread in the second century CE, and it focused precisely on the relation between universality and individuality.[52] The question as to whether providence is directed towards individuals can be traced back to the Stoic school. The Stoics connected providence and fate in their monistic and pantheistic system of thought: they understood providence and fate as aspects of the divine rational force that pervades the universe. If God pervades the world, how can evil be explained? A partial answer is the doctrine ascribed to the Stoics that gods are not interested in small things or

51 πρῶτον διεκόσμησεν, ἔπειτ᾽ ἐκ τούτων πᾶν τόδε συνεστήσατο, ζῷον ἓν ζῷα ἔχον τὰ πάντα ἐν ἑαυτῷ θνητὰ ἀθάνατά τε. καὶ τῶν μὲν θείων αὐτὸς γίγνεται δημιουργός, τῶν δὲ θνητῶν τὴν γένεσιν τοῖς ἑαυτοῦ γεννήμασιν δημιουργεῖν προσέταξεν. οἱ δὲ μιμούμενοι, παραλαβόντες ἀρχὴν ψυχῆς ἀθάνατον, τὸ μετὰ τοῦτο θνητὸν σῶμα αὐτῇ περιετόρνευσαν ὄχημά τε πᾶν τὸ σῶμα ἔδοσαν ἄλλο τε εἶδος ἐν αὐτῷ ψυχῆς προσῳκοδόμουν τὸ θνητόν, δεινὰ καὶ ἀναγκαῖα ἐν ἑαυτῷ παθήματα ἔχον, πρῶτον μὲν ἡδονήν, μέγιστον κακοῦ δέλεαρ, ἔπειτα λύπας, ἀγαθῶν φυγάς, ἔτι δ᾽ αὖ θάρρος καὶ φόβον, ἄφρονε συμβούλω, θυμὸν δὲ δυσπαραμύθητον, ἐλπίδα δ᾽ εὐπαράγωγον: αἰσθήσει δὲ ἀλόγῳ καὶ ἐπιχειρητῇ παντὸς ἔρωτι συγκερασάμενοι ταῦτα, ἀναγκαίως τὸ θνητὸν γένος συνέθεσαν.

52 The problems highlighted in this section are further developed in the contributions by René Brouwer, Péter Lautner, Carlo Natali, and Emmanuele Vimercati, in the present volume.

in the fate of individual humans, as reported by Cicero: "Providence does not care for individual human beings."[53] It might seem that the Stoics and Celsus agree here. Rather, whereas for the Stoics the assertion that individuals may be neglected by providence is related to the question of evil and individual misfortunes, in *True Account*,[54] as we have seen in the first section, for Celsus' the neglect by providence is connected with his criticism of Christian anthropocentrism. According to Celsus, since God does not care for humans more than any other living being, His care for individuals is rejected in favour of a providential care for the entire universe, rather than its parts. Instead of anthropocentrism, Celsus seems thus to claim some kind of universalism.

Middle Platonists, such as Apuleius, in his *On Plato and His Doctrine*, and Ps.-Plutarch, in *On Fate*, explain the connection between universality and individuality in terms of *pronoia* and *heimarmenē*, i.e. providence and fate. According to them, fate is subordinate to divine providence. In order to explain that, they propose a hierarchical tripartition according to which firstly there are the *nous* and will of the first god, then there are the second gods, i.e. the stars (that live in the heaven and have the task to shape the bodies for the souls created by the first god and to provide for the government of mortals), and at the end there are *daimones* executors of divine order on earth, custodians and overseers of human actions.[55] At all three of these levels providential action can be located, while fate is only an accessory aspect of the second and third levels. In fact, the stars determine the rhythm of the universe but not the actions of men, and, regarding the influence exerted by the demons, man is free to undergo it or not. In his *On Socrates' God*, at 6.132–133, Apuleius lets Plato say that

> 'I deny' – for Plato will now respond for his view in my voice – 'I deny', he says, 'that the gods are so distant and disconnected from us that not even our prayers can reach them. There are certain intermediate divine powers between the highest aether and lowest regions of the earth, in

53 Cicero, *On the Nature of the Gods* 3.93: *non curat singulos homines*.

54 Origen, *Against Celsus* 5.3.

55 See Ps.-Plutarch, *On Fate* 9.572F–573A: "The highest and primary providence is an act of intellection by the first god, which is also an act of will beneficial to all things. Thanks especially to it, everything divine is arranged throughout as is best and most beautiful. Secondary providence belongs to the gods who move through the heavens: thanks to it, what is mortal comes to be in an orderly fashion, as do those things that ensure the survival and permanence of the various species. The forethought of those daemons that are set in order over the earth to guard and oversee human activities might reasonably be called tertiary providence" (tr. Boys-Stones 2018). See further Valgiglio 1964, xx–xxi, Opsomer 2014, 161–162.

> that space which is filled by the intervening air; through them our desires and our deserts reach them [the celestial gods]'.[56] (Tr. Boys-Stones 2018)

Ps.-Plutarch also identifies *heimarmenē* as both the universal soul of the world and the divine law. Concerning single events, the laws of fate operate just like human civic law: they are directed not towards the single person but towards every person that could be in the situation foreseen and ruled by the law.[57] Therefore, law is characterised by universality and conditionality: a universal principle that is subject to the occurrence of a condition and the concrete cases are implicitly part of the universal law. To clarify this further, in chapter 5, Ps.-Plutarch claims that fate embraces everything but not everything occurs according to fate, such as Providence. Thus, first-level providence includes also the fate that is *kata pronoian*; providence instead is never *kath' heimarmenēn*. The first god indirectly provides for men through the laws and the second and third providences, thus rejecting all responsibility for human wickedness. In brief, the aim of Ps.-Plutarch is to save the coexistence of fate and human freedom, and to set providence free from fate, in opposition to the Stoics, who identified providence with fate.[58]

Alexander of Aphrodias' *On Providence* is also a useful point of comparison for Celsus' *True Account*. Both Celsus and Alexander construct their arguments against a conception of divine providence that is concerned with the individual by placing emphasis on the omnipotence of God and argue against an anthropocentric view. Alexander discusses the divine and the notion of *pronoia* in the context of physics and cosmology.[59] He does not agree with the Stoics' understanding of god as something physical and their assimilation of providence and fate. Alexander, like Ps.-Plutarch, subordinates fate to providence,

56 *non usque adeo responderit enim Plato pro sententia sua mea voce non usque adeo, inquit, seiunctos et alienatos a nobis deos praedico, ut ne vota quidem nostra ad illos arbitrer pervenire. neque enim illos a cura rerum humanarum, sed contrectatione sola removi. Ceterum sunt quaedam divinae mediae potestates inter summum aethera et infimas terras in isto intersitae aeris spatio, per quas et desideria nostra et merita ad eos commeant.*

57 See Valgiglio 1964, ix–x.

58 See Valgiglio 1964, xxiv–xxv. The author of this text on Providence admires and imitates Plutarch, as can be seen, for example, by the predilection for the quotations from Plato's writings, in particular from the *Timaeus*, the doctrine of good and bad demons, certain linguistic and stylistic elements, and the fact that Plutarch has an analogous concept of fate (see Plutarch, *How to Study Poetry* 6.23D–E), common also to the Neoplatonists. This author is therefore best understood as a Middle Platonist and is perhaps to be identified with one of the commentators of the myth of Er in Plato's *Republic* as reported by Proclus: Numenius, Albinus, Gaius, Maximus of Nicea, Harpocration, Euclid, or Porphyry. See Valgiglio 1964, xxxv–xxxvi.

59 See Fazzo 1999, 21.

and associates himself to some Middle Platonic authors that assert that providence is the cause of fate.[60]

He explains that providence acts on universals rather than on individuals by bringing up the examples of Socrates and Xanto: *pronoia* does not act directly on Socrates and Xanto, Achilles' horse, but on the species "man" and on the species "horse".[61] Providence is real but "universal" in character:

> Providence over things here that would work [at the individual level] would not be in agreement with the things that actually happen, as is clear from how these things are. Epidemics and the blights that affect crops, as well as fire and cold, and the misfortune that befalls the good people and happiness that comes to the bad, and the like, are sufficient evidence for the falsehood of this belief.[62] (Tr. Adamson 2018)

So, according to Alexander, epidemics, blights and misfortunes that befall good people are adequate evidence to attest that providence does not act on individual human beings. Just like Celsus, therefore, Alexander too seems to reject anthropocentrism. However, by distinguishing the fate of good people from that of the bad, he links providence with divine justice, which is based on merit and retribution. Alexander's argument concerning the existence and the nature of providence moves from the assumption that the creator preserves his creation by taking care of it. *Pronoia*, therefore, is here given the meaning of God's "interest" or "concern" for what He is responsible for. According to Alexander, then, providence is linked with that which is subject to coming into being and to perishing. Hence the celestial world is not the object of providence, but rather its subject, in the sense that providence is an effect of the motion of the heavens on the earthly world. Alexander is not able to reconcile the theory of providence with the First Unmoved Mover, since this Unmoved Mover has only itself, the best of beings, as the exclusive object of thought, while providence must be a deliberate or voluntary activity. Aristotle thus speaks of rational deliberation and not of *pronoia*, while Alexander speaks of divine providence in the sublunar world, without clarifying if such providence is essential or accidental, deliberative or involuntary.[63] So, issues such as fate and providence are also related to the conceptions of physical causality and religion. Alexander tries to take both into consideration.

60 See Torrijos-Castrillejos 2017, 9.

61 Alexander of Aphrodisias, *On Providence* 89; see further Fazzo 1999, 53.

62 Alexander of Aphrodisias, *On Providence* 29.19–31.4.

63 See Fazzo 1999, 23, 30–31.

In his chapter on Alexander's *On Fate* and *Mantissa* (in this volume), Carlo Natali has argued that Alexander tries to adapt Aristotle's thinking to his own times, instead of bringing Stoic beliefs into Aristotelianism; he accomplishes a sort of "creative orthodoxy". Here it can be added that also regarding providence Alexander offers a form of "creative orthodoxy". In *On Fate* and *On Providence*, Alexander is not opposed in general to the deterministic Stoic position (a popular position in his 2nd century CE), but he argues against the manner in which Stoic doctrine has incorporated it into its overall philosophical system.[64]

As Peter Adamson has argued,[65] Alexander's *On Providence* has an aporetic structure; criticism of the Stoic and the Epicurean extreme views about providence is presented together with Aristotle's ideas about the influence of the heavenly bodies on our lower world. Alexander's purpose is to find a kind of compromise between these two opposite perspective, that is to say, as Sharples called it, "a via media",[66] making providence responsible for all things, but only at the universal and general level.[67] As Alexander himself explains, otherwise the risk will be: "If [God] abstains from Providence, this can only be because he is incapable of it and does not incline towards it, or because he is capable but does not want it, or because he wants it but is incapable of it."[68]

In sum, Celsus, Ps.-Plutarch and Alexander fit into the more general debate on providence between the Stoics and the Epicureans. They start out from different philosophical perspectives (Celsus and Ps.-Plutarch from a Platonic perspective and Alexander from an Aristotelian one) and do so for different aims (Celsus opposes the Christian view on providence; Ps.-Plutarch argues in favour of the coexistence of fate and human freedom and against the Stoic assimilation of providence and fate; Alexander aims at reconciling providence and Aristotle's First Unmoved Mover), but, in the end, they seem to agree that providence is primarily concerned with the universal, rather than individuals.

4 Final Remarks. Celsus on Providence: The Middle Ground between Epicureans and Stoics

I started with Origen arguing against the Epicurean rejection of divine providence. Celsus, considered an Epicurean by Origen, did not reject the doctrine

64 See Fazzo 1999, 33–34.
65 See Adamson 2018, 283.
66 See Sharples 1982, 198.
67 See Adamson 2018, 288.
68 Alexander of Aphrodisias, *On Providence* 23.

of providence itself, but rather Jesus' divine power, His standing out among men as well as the anthropocentric understanding of providence.[69] In his treatise Celsus admits the existence of the gods and of a kind of providence, but maintains that neither God nor a son of God has ever descended among men.[70] The culmination of Celsus' thought can be found in *Against Celsus* 4.99, according to which the providence of God is linked to the universe as a whole, to the world as a work of God, perfect in all its parts; individual man takes part in providence only incidentally and not in a position of supremacy in comparison with other animals. In the subsequent sections I focused on the Platonic background of Celsus' notion of providence and on the debate about providence at the end of the second century CE. Nonetheless, it is possible to acknowledge that Celsus' notion of providence has some points in common with Alexander of Aphrodisias' *On Providence* and Ps.-Plutarch's *On Fate*.

According to Jan Opsomer,[71] the belief in a transcendent providential god is one of the generally shared tenets that united the Middle Platonists. They occupied a middle ground between Epicureans and Stoics and, in some respects, so did Alexander of Aphrodisias. Unlike the Epicureans, Middle Platonists acknowledged the existence of providence; unlike the Stoics, they restricted the scope of fate, introducing the concept of conditional fate.[72] They rejected the determinism of the Stoics, but shared with them "the coherence and purposefulness of the world, governed by an intelligent and benevolent agent; the goodness and providential nature of god and the gods, their casual agency on humans."[73] According to Ps.-Plutarch, all things that conform to fate also conform to Providence, but not all things that conform to providence also conform to fate.[74] Also Alexander of Aphrodisias subordinated fate to providence, asserting that providence affect the sublunary world only in a global way.

The texts analysed here offer different perspectives from which one can evaluate the notion of providence: either by focusing on the omnipotence of God – here the problems of the justification of evil and of the possibility of human freedom emerge – or, in a different perspective, focusing on

69 Origen, *Against Celsus* 4.54.

70 Origen, *Against Celsus* 1.57, 4.4, 4.99, 5.3, 7.68, 8.45.

71 Opsomer 2014, 137.

72 This doctrine is in Ps.-Plutarch's *On Fate*, 9.573A–574D, and is also mentioned in Apuleius, *On Plato and His Doctrine* 1.12, 205–207, Alcinous, *Didaskalikos* 26, and Justin Martyr, *First Apology* 43. Other shared tenets include "the belief in an immortal soul, the rejection of Stoic determinism and of Epicurean hedonism, an ethics based on the idea that one should assimilate oneself to god through virtue" (Opsomer 2014, 137).

73 See Opsomer 2014, 139.

74 See Ps.-Plutarch, *On Fate* 9.573A–574D.

the transcendence of God – in this case, human beings can freely face their fate, since transcendence allows for an overall determinism. In this version, God has "the last word", whereas men have a certain margin of spontaneity of action and freedom of thought.

In commenting upon the Euripidean verse, which I adopted as the title of this chapter, Celsus asserts that the sun and the night cannot be servants for mortals alone since even for the ants and flies night comes for them to rest and day for them to see and to work. Celsus' position is certainly not unique but it turns out to be entirely coherent with the second century debate in which the different philosophical schools and religious traditions were very much interested in the problem of fate and providence. Celsus uses the Euripidean verse to clarify that providence neglects not only individuals, but, to some extent, also the entire human race, since Celsus acknowledges only a form of universal providence that overcomes the problem of the existence of evil and discredits the anthropocentric view of the world.

Bibliography

Adamson, Peter. 2018. "Dialectical Method in Alexander of Aphrodisias' Treatises on Fate and Providence." *Oxford Studies in Ancient Philosophy* 54: 279–308.

Andresen, Carl. 1955. *Logos und Nomos. Die Polemik des Kelsos wider das Christentum.* Berlin: De Gruyter.

Babut, Daniel. 1969. *Plutarque et le stoïcisme.* Paris: Université de Paris, Faculté des Lettres et Sciences Humaines.

Bergjan, Silke-Petra. 2001. "Celsus the Epicurean? The Interpretation of an Argument in Origen, *Contra Celsum.*" *Harvard Theological Review* 94: 179–204.

Bobzien, Susanne 1998. *Determinism and Freedom in Stoic Philosophy.* Oxford: Clarendon.

Bos, Abraham P. 1976. *Providentia divina. The Theme of Divine Pronoia in Plato and Aristotle.* Assen: Van Gorcum.

Boys-Stones, George. 1996. "Plutarch, *De Stoicorum Repugnantiis* 1048D–E." *Classical Quarterly* 46: 591–595.

Boys-Stones, George. 2001. *Post-Hellenistic Philosophy. A Study of Its Development from the Stoics to Origen.* Oxford: Oxford University Press.

Boys-Stones, George. 2007. "'Middle' Platonists on Fate and Human Autonomy." In *Greek and Roman Philosophy 100 BC–200 AD*, edited by Robert W. Sharples and Richard Sorabji, vol. 2, 431–447. London: Institute of Classical Studies.

Boys-Stones, George. 2018. *Platonist Philosophy 80 BC to AD 250. An Introduction and Collection of Sources in Translation.* Cambridge: Cambridge University Press.

Cataudella, Quintino. 1937. "Tracce della sofistica nella polemica celso-origeniana." *Rendiconti del Reale Istituto Lombardo di scienze e lettere* 70: 185–201.

Chadwick, Henry. 1947. "Origen, Celsus and the Stoa." *Journal of Theological Studies* 48: 34–49.

Chadwick, Henry, tr. 1953. *Origen. Contra Celsum*. Cambridge: Cambridge University Press.

De Simone, Pia. 2018. "L'epistemologia di Celso tra Platone ed Epicuro alla luce del concetto di *enargeia*." *Rivista di Filosofia Neo-Scolastica* 110: 245–258.

Diggle, James, ed. 1994. *Euripidis fabulae*, vol. 3. Oxford: Oxford University Press.

Dillon, John. 1996 [1977]. *The Middle Platonists. A Study of Platonism (80 BC to AD 220)*. London: Duckworth.

Dragona-Monachou, Myrto. 1994. "Divine Providence in the Philosophy of the Empire." In *Aufstieg und Niedergang der römischen Welt*, edited by Wolfgang Haase, vol. 2.36.7, 4417–4490. Berlin: De Gruyter.

Fazzo, Silvia, tr. 1999. *Alessandro di Afrodisia. La Provvidenza. Questioni sulla Provvidenza*. Milan: Rizzoli (BUR).

Ferrari, Franco. 1999. "Pronoia platonica e *noesis noeseos* aristotelica: Plutarco e l'impossibilità di una sintesi." In *Plutarco, Platon y Aristoteles. Actas del V Congreso Internacional de la I.P.S. (Madrid-Cuenca, 4–6 de Mayo de 1999)*, edited by Aurelio Pérez Jiménez, José García Lopez, and Rosa M. Aguilar, 63–77. Madrid: Ediciones Clásicas.

Grube, George M.A., tr. 1997. "Republic." In *Plato. Complete Works*, edited by John M. Cooper, 971–1223. Indianapolis: Hackett.

Lanzi, Silvia. 2000. Theos Anaitios. *Storia della teodicea da Omero ad Agostino*. Rome: Il Calamo.

Longo, Angela. 2016. "La maschera di Epicuro sul volto dell'avversario in tema di provvidenza e piacere nello scritto di Plotino, *Contro gli Gnostici*: alcuni paralleli con Celso, Attico, Alessandro di Afrodisia e Ippolito di Roma." In *Formen und Nebenformen des Platonismus in der Spätantike*, edited by Helmut Seng, Luciana G. Soares Santoprete, and Chiara O. Tommasi, 81–108. Heidelberg: Winter.

Magris, Aldo, tr. 2009. *Cicerone – Pseudo Plutarco – Alessandro di Afrodisia, Trattati antichi sul destino*. Brescia: Morcelliana.

Nehamas, Alexander, and Paul Woodruff, tr. 1997. "Phaedrus." In *Plato. Complete Works*, edited by John M. Cooper, 506–556. Indianapolis: Hackett.

O'Brien, Carl S. 2015. *The Demiurge in Ancient Thought. Secondary Gods and Divine Mediators*. Cambridge: Cambridge University Press.

Opsomer, Jan. 2014. "The Middle Platonic Doctrine of Conditional Fate." In *Fate, Providence and Moral Responsibility in Ancient, Medieval and Early Modern Thought. Studies in Honour of Carlos Steel*, edited by Pieter d'Hoine and Gerd Van Riel, 137–168. Leuven: Leuven University Press.

Runia, David T. 2017. "From Stoicism to Platonism: The Difficult Case of Philo of Alexandria's *De Providentia* 1." In *From Stoicism to Platonism. The Development of Philosophy, 100 BCE–100CE*, edited by Troels Engberg-Pedersen, 159–178. Cambridge: Cambridge University Press.

Sharples, Robert W. 1978. "Alexander of Aphrodisias, *De Fato*: Some Parallels." *Classical Quarterly* 28: 243–266.

Sharples, Robert W. 1982. "Alexander of Aphrodisias on Divine Providence: Two Problems." *Classical Quarterly* 32: 198–211.

Sharples, Robert W. 1987. "Alexander of Aphrodisias: Scholasticism and Innovation." In *Aufstieg und Niedergang der römischen Welt*, edited by Wolfgang Haase, vol. 2.36.2, 1176–1243. Berlin: De Gruyter.

Torrijos-Castrillejo, David. 2017. "Alexander of Aphrodisias on Fate, Providence and Nature." *Forum. Supplement to Acta Philosophica* 3: 7–18.

Valgiglio, Ernesto, ed., tr. 1964. *Ps. Plutarco, De Fato*. Rome: Signorelli.

Vimercati, Emmanuele, ed. 2015. *Medioplatonici. Opere, frammenti, testimonianze*. Milan: Bompiani.

Zeyl, Donald J., tr. 1997. "Timaeus." In *Plato. Complete Works*, edited by John M. Cooper, 1224–1291. Indianapolis: Hackett.

CHAPTER 16

Providence, Free Will and Predestination in Origen

Mark Edwards

The doctrine of divine providence is an indispensable article of Christian belief.[1] For this we have to thank Paul, but his apostle in the early church was Origen, who was conscious in all his dealings with philosophy that the only acknowledged 'atheists' of his time were not those who disbelieved in the gods but those who denied them any superintendence of mundane affairs. He was also conscious that even those who affirmed this superintendence might restrict it to the sending of omens, the allocation of rewards and punishments after death, or simply the ordering of the world with a view to the general good of his denizens. For him, as for his co-religionists, providence implied not only all of these things, but the direct intervention of the deity in mundane affairs in response to the prayers of his church and for the sake of each individual who belonged to it. Such tenets brought with them difficulties regarding the certainty and precision of divine foreknowledge, which had not been faced by any Greek philosopher before him.[2] In the course of the present paper, I shall set the texts in which he formulates his own beliefs against the teachings of the schools with which he appears to be best acquainted; I shall go on to examine the further problems that were raised for him by his refusal to admit predestination, by his universalism and by the apparent contradictions in the scriptures. I hope to show at the end that his eschatology is not so much one branch of his theology as the trunk of, as it determined his exegesis of the scriptures which in his view were the only appointed means of knowing God.[3]

---

1 The subject of free will in Origen has recently attracted the interest of classicists, e.g. George Boys-Stones (2007), who, like Michael Frede (2011), is chiefly concerned to set Origen in his place in the history of Greek philosophy, and therefore takes the *First Principles* as his centrepiece. The present study raises questions that fall under the rubric of theology rather than philosophy, and therefore consults a different range of Origen's works.

2 Plutarch, in such works as *On the Delays in Divine Punishment* (548–568) and *On the E at Delphi* (384–394) seems to affirm divine cognition of the contingent future even for individuals, but he is more concerned with ethical conclusions than logical niceties, and at *On the E at Delphi* 6.387B–C he considers the possibility that the oracle reveals only what will occur if a certain precondition is realised (cf. Cicero, *On Fate* 32).

3 The following editions of Origen's works have been consulted: Koetschau 1897–1899, Klostermann 1901, Baehrens 1920, Harl and Junod 1976–1983, Limone 2012, Behr 2017.

© KONINKLIJKE BRILL NV, LEIDEN, 2020 | DOI:10.1163/9789004436381_018

1 Divine Foreknowledge

There are two texts of some length in the surviving Greek works of Origen which undertake to prove that God's omniscience does not compromise the freedom that he vouchsafes to us as creatures. In the treatise *On Prayer* an unnamed interlocutor, citing numerous verses from scripture to prove that God foresees our petitions, concludes that it is therefore unnecessary for us to present them (5.2). This is a version of the "lazy argument", according to which if a man is destined to beget children he will do so even if he refrains from sexual intercourse. In his work *Against Celsus* Origen shows that he is familiar both with this sophistry and with the ridicule that is poured upon it (2.20);[4] in the case of prayer, however, he has also to disarm the objection that, whether or not we seek the good from God, he is bound by his nature to bring it about, so that any request on our part will be at best superfluous and at worst profane. We can scarcely suppose that he whose will is sovereign in all affairs will foresee any good that he himself has not foreordained; therefore, while we rightly deride the man who thinks that his orisons have caused the sun to rise, we should deem him even more a fool if he importuned God to arrest its motion (5.3). Scripture itself informs us that the prescience of God implies predestination, for if a sinner is "estranged" from the time of conception (Psalm 58.3) and the righteous man "set apart" from his mother's womb (Galatians 1.15), no human overtures will turn an Esau into a Jacob, and no act was open to Judas which would have overruled the prophecy, written long before his birth, that his days would be short and his estate would pass to another (Psalm 90.1–2). It is therefore futile to engage in prayer, as we cannot hope to countermand the will of God (5.4).

Origen begins his reply by distinguishing three orders of motion: that of the inanimate, which comes entirely from without, like the quarrying of a stone; that of a plant, which proceeds inevitably from the internal working of nature; and that of a sentient being, which is attributable to the agent inasmuch as it had the power to do otherwise (6.1). It is worthy of note that, while Origen elsewhere concurs with the Stoics in restricting the faculty of rational choice to human beings (*Against Celsus* 4.74), he acknowledges no difference here between humans and other animals. By contrast, the Stoics appear to have credited humans with a capacity for initiating motion which they did not ascribe to animals, while Alexander of Aphrodisias argues that we are set apart

4 For a full discussion of the definition of prophecy and the role of the prophet in this apologetic text, see Ramelli 2017.

from beasts by our ability to resist the object of appetition when it is presented to our senses.[5] Nevertheless, it is evident that the Christian author too believes human beings to be uniquely endowed with the power of choosing freely in the teeth of all temptations to vice and virtue. God's part, he maintains, is to have disposed the world so that our wills encounter these influences, while the goods or evils that he foreordains are strictly proportioned to the merit that we display in our responses (6.3). When, therefore, he answers the prayer of a righteous man, his purpose is to encourage merit by bestowing on it a visible reward; when the believer grows more lukewarm in service, he will be rebuked – and, if he is not yet insensible, edified – by the denial of his prayers (6.4). When he decides to exalt Josiah, knowing that he will prove more pious than his father Amon, God does not compel the son to be pious, any more than he compels Judas to fall into wickedness after making a noble start. He does not create Paul's character but, because he discerns that character, he permits him to connive at the murder of Stephen so that when he repents his zeal for Christ will be all the more intense (6.5).

This last illustration betrays the limits of Origen's curiosity. God, he says, allows an act conducive to the ripening of Paul's character: if, then, he had not allowed it, might Paul have become some other man than the apostle to the Gentiles? If we admit that God had a hand in the shaping of his character, we must grant that this is equally true for all human beings, since God has the power in every case either to intervene or to abstain from intervention, and he must know the consequences of either choice. The Christian God is not a Platonic spectator,[6] and his activity or quiescence must be at least an auxiliary cause (as the Stoics would say) of anything that he foreknows. We might argue that God arranges the train of affairs to bring out what is most salient in the agent's character; yet this hypothesis raises further questions that he seems not to have pursued. Must God, for example, not take some of the blame for the depravity of a person whose existence he might have prevented? And can he be sure of effecting the best of all possible outcomes unless he foresees not merely the one thing which will come to pass by his own permission but every other contingency that he might have permitted? If the number of such contingencies were infinite – and how could they not be? – God must be able to comprehend an actual infinity, which Origen, following

5 *On Fate* 15.186.6–20.189.21 Bruns. I use the text as revised by Sharples 1983.

6 The Platonic God (more properly, in most texts, the supernal νοῦς) is a spectator in the sense that he/it does not intervene in the affairs of individuals. Plotinus, of course affirms that νοῦς governs the world with regard to its moral harmony and physical equilibrium: *Enneads* 3.2–3, 5.8, 2.9.16 etc. See further Deck 1967.

Aristotle, holds to be impossible (*First Principles* 2.9.1). And even if the number of foreseeable counterfactuals is finite, the perception of that which does not exist was generally regarded in the ancient world – and not only in the ancient world – as a contradiction in terms. At the very least, it excludes the common argument that God's foreknowledge is not after all foreknowledge but simple cognizance, like his cognizance of the present or the past.

Prescinding for the moment from these questions let us turn to the second passage, which is preserved in his *Philokalia* and in Eusebius as a fragment from his *Commentary on Genesis*. As ever, his problem commences with a text: if the sun and moon were given as signs, as Genesis 1.14 declares does it follow that what they signify will inevitably come to pass (*Philokalia* 23.1)? Origen's first reply is that, by robbing us of "that which lies with us" (τὸ ἐφ' ἡμῖν), this doctrine renders exhortation useless, and leaves us no rationale for punishment and reward. The adversaries to whom he directs this argument are heretics whose mentors in the pagan world are astrologers and sceptics; in such company it is lawful to borrow even from Epicurus (*Gnomologicon Vaticanum* 40), who had urged against the determinists of his day (that is, the Stoics), that if their reasoning were true they could not know this, since the same reasoning entails that they believe only what they are fated to believe (*Philokalia* 23.2). Origen also holds with the Epicureans that no true oracles can be obtained from the shrines of the gods; whereas they argued, however, that it would compromise the serenity of such lofty beings to meddle in our affairs, he avers that, being no gods but demonic impostors, they possess no faculty of precognition (23.21). At the same time, it is they who have spread the falsehood that the stars are causes and not merely signs (23.6). Yet signs they are, because God cannot be ignorant of the future, as reflection on the concept of divinity teaches us even in the absence of the scriptures (23.4). For those who require empirical proof, the anticipations of Christ's coming in Daniel, Isaiah and the First Book of Kings will suffice;[7] the treachery of Judas was foreseen not only by Christ on earth but by the Psalmist, writing under inspiration centuries before. Both Stoics and astrologers reasoned that if what is foretold is necessarily true the event itself is necessary: a Peripatetic can deny the premiss, but a Christian, while denying the validity of the inference, takes the premiss as an article of faith.

The solution lies for Origen in Aristotle's antithesis between the "necessary" (ἀναγκαῖον), which could not have happened otherwise, and the "possible" (ἐνδεχόμενον), which could have happened otherwise until the agent's choice

7 *Philokalia* 23.4–5, adducing 1 Kings 12.32 and 13.1–5, Isaiah 45.1–4, Daniel 2.37–40 and 8.5–9.

determined the outcome.[8] The crime of Judas, like all historical facts, is now unalterable and hence in one sense necessary, but not in a sense that shows it to have been predetermined (23.9). Just as our awareness of past choices which are now irrevocable does not render these choices inevitable at the time when they were made, so God's infallible knowledge of the future, which is analogous to his own knowledge of the past, does not impair the freedom of those who populate this future because it is one thing to witness an act and another to cause it (23.3). Origen does not explain how God sees the future or ask whether he should be said to will acts of which he is cognizant when he does not choose to prevent them; it seems to be enough for him to argue that if we can predict a person's future conduct from his character, it should be possible for God to this at all times (23.8). We may feel that he strays into hyperbole by crediting God with an "as it were" infinite knowledge of both past and future contingents (23.20); the qualification is needed because he himself, as we have seen, denies elsewhere that there can be any actuality which is infinite.

The symmetry of past and future furnishes Origen with the strongest part of his case against the astrologers. They admit that a person's destiny is, in part at least, the product of antecedents which are woven into the causes of the astral configurations which predict these antecedents; these configurations therefore bear infallible witness to the past but it would be absurd to argue that they cause it. (23.5). They do in fact signify both past and future: the only written evidence for this is an extracanonical text, the *Prayer of Joseph* (23.19), but it is reasonable to assume that the God who sets the way of life before us in scripture should communicate his ordinances to the angels through this medium (23.21). The words of Genesis 1.4 on which Origen is commenting imply that God makes use of the heavenly bodies as a cipher, just as on another occasion he made Pharaoh a sign to the nations – though again it must be understood that he hardened the heart of Pharaoh only insofar as he attempted to persuade him by miracles, knowing in advance that they would fail of their effect (23.20). To ordinary denizens of this world the heavenly alphabet is illegible, since knowledge of the future would induce lassitude or despair (23.10); the pretensions of the astrologers are false because they presuppose an accuracy that no human can attain (23.17). That which God foresees in his omniscience, by contrast, cannot fail to occur (23.8), but that is a consequence of the logical relation between all knowledge and truth, not an index of any necessity in things themselves.

8 Origen, like Alexander of Aphrodisias, inherits his terms and the premises of his argument from Aristotle, *On Interpretation* 9, 18a28–19b4.

2 Origen and the Philosophers

Can these arguments be aligned with those of any Greek school? The maxim that "the fault lies with the doer; god is blameless", cited from the *Republic* half a century before by Justin Martyr, could have served as the superscription to any passage on foreknowledge and freewill in Origen's writings.[9] Yet Plato, unlike Origen, opined that the soul is by nature both immortal and designed for the animation of a body. In the *Phaedrus* he hints that the soul's descent from heaven to earth is predetermined by celestial revolutions, while both the *Republic* and the *Statesman* declare that human societies rise and fall in accordance with the recurring alignments of the stars.[10] The soul, once released from its corporal frame, is free to choose its lot in the next embodiment, but, since this decision is based upon experiences of which it retains no memory, it enters each life with a character already formed, and all the more inescapable because no account of its origin lies to hand. In the *Timaeus* each new incarnation has its tutelary demon and its allotted star: to Plotinus this implied that when each of us comes into this world a pattern of life is set before us which we may at best attain but cannot transcend.[11] Even the treatise in which he maintains that the stars cannot rob the soul of its autonomy concedes not only that they may betoken future events but that that they may exercise some influence on the physical environment of the soul, not excluding its body.[12] His pupil and biographer Porphyry, while he professed to share his master's contempt for horoscopes (*Life of Plotinus* 15.21–26), teaches that the soul cannot be at peace until it placates its natal demon; in the treatise *On the Mysteries* by Porphyry's pupil Iamblichus, the paradigm to which the soul aspires can be realised only with the help of the *oikodespotēs*, or master of the celestial house which reigns at the time of birth.[13] Close students of Plato, therefore, were unlikely to hold that even our deliberations, let alone our resultant acts, were wholly independent of the stars.

It is true that more eclectic thinkers, writing before the rise of Neoplatonism, were closer to anticipating Origen's doctrine of providence. Both Plutarch and Numenius taught that divine concern extends to the rewarding and punishing of individuals – a doctrine that Plotinus expressly denies – and envisaged a future state in which the soul preserves a remnant of its body.[14] On the

9 Justin, *First Apology* 44, citing Plato, *Republic* 10.617e.

10 *Phaedrus* 248c, *Republic* 8.546b, *Statesman* 269c–275a.

11 *Enneads* 3.4, commenting on Plato, *Timaeus* 90a.

12 On *Enneads* 3.3 and related texts see Adamson 2008.

13 See Iamblichus, *On the Mysteries* 9.1–5, with Pachoumi 2013, 46–69, esp. 47.

14 Numenius, fr. 12.17–21 Des Places; Plotinus, *Enneads* 2.9.16.

other hand, Origen would have quoted Jeremiah and Ezekiel against Plutarch's obsolete doctrine that the penalty of a man's sin is sometimes visited on his offspring: since the coming of Christ, every sinner must bear his own reward.[15] Nor would he have said of the biblical prophecies, as Plutarch says of the oracle that had once issued from Delphi, that the progress of knowledge had rendered them superfluous; for him, as for other Christians and not a few pagans, the wilful ambiguity of these utterances proved their authors to be lying demons. When, by contrast, the plain sense of a scriptural prediction seems to fail, the reason is that it was given not to pre-empt exertion but to induce repentance. It is God, as the preface to Jeremiah explains, who desires the aversion of the threatened calamity, perfectly foreseeing yet not dictating the free response of those to whom it is addressed.

The foremost champions of divination in late antiquity were the Stoics, who agreed with Origen in attributing definite foresight to the gods and at the same time in upholding the freedom of their human suppliants to prevent or bring about the thing foretold. While the Stoics had a reputation as fatalists, it appears that they regarded only the chain of natural causes as inexorable, reserving for human agents a spontaneous power of choice between such actions as were consistent with their physical circumstances.[16] These circumstances might include the possession of a character that was not of one's own making, but even this was a limiting condition on behaviour, not in the strictest sense a cause. Now Origen was certainly at one with the Stoics, and opposed to certain Platonists, in denying to beasts a capacity for reasoned deliberation.[17] He could admire their fortitude, as many Christians did, but he also endorsed the common accusation of fatalism; indeed he is one of our witnesses – all of them Christian – to the Stoic doctrine of an infinite succession of identical worlds, in each of which the same Athenian son of Sophroniscus will imbibe the same toxic draught (*Against Celsus* 4.67). He would not have been wrong in imputing to the Stoics some theory of sidereal influence, for which we have not only Philo's testimony but that of Aratus, whose verses were more widely read than any but those of Homer. How then, according to Origen, is character formed, if not by fate or the stars? He holds, with Aristotle, that we develop virtue by

15 See Plutarch, *On the Delays in Divine Punishment* 1.548B–11.556D, 18.560F–22.563B; Jeremiah 31.29; Ezekiel 18.2; Origen, *Homilies on Jeremiah*, fr. 34, p. 251 Klostermann.

16 Frede (2011, 45) surmises that Epictetus credits human with the power of willing to will, otherwise called "liberty of indifference", as opposed to mere liberty of spontaneity, the freedom to act on our will. If so, it may be that Origen is indebted to Epictetus, as he proposes: see further Gibbons (2016).

17 *Against Celsus* 4.74–91. Contrast Plutarch, *Beasts are Rational* (1–10, 985D–992E) and Porphyry, *On Abstinence* book 3.

acting virtuously, but he adds that, since we contend not merely with our own desires but with the whole company of Satan, we cannot prevail without the help of Christ (*First Principles* 3.2 etc.).

Origen was a younger contemporary of Alexander of Aphrodisias, the first great commentator on Aristotle. In recent years both Panayiotis Tzamalikos and Ilaria Ramelli have furnished evidence that Origen was acquainted with his writings, notwithstanding the absence of any mention of him even in the work *Against Celsus*, which shows little knowledge even of Aristotle.[18] The latter's supposed denial of any providence below the moon will have seemed to Origen only one step from atheism, and it is possible (as Crouzel surmised) that his panegyrist Gregory Thaumaturgus is alluding to the Peripatetics as well as the Epicureans when he praises his reluctance to communicate impious doctrines to his students in Caesarea.[19] Alexander, however, may not have fallen under his disapproval, for his treatise *On Fate*, directed against the supposed determinism of the Stoics, assumes as a matter of course that the gods gives oracles and respond to prayer. For him, as for Origen (and indeed the Stoics) vaticination implies both knowledge of the future and a benevolent concern with our affairs that cannot be attributed to Aristotle's deity; on the other hand, Alexander is a faithful disciple of the Stagirite in epistemology, and considers it essential to the defence of human liberty that the future should not be definitely knowable even to a divine intelligence (31, 201.10–11). The premiss of this Peripatetic commonplace is that the truth of the thing known follows necessarily from our knowing it; the inference, which would now be considered fallacious, is that knowledge of a coming event necessitates this event and thereby robs the future of its contingency. And this, they continue, robs the human agent of the autonomy which consists in being able to bring about either of two events. Origen, for his part, is as stout as the Peripatetics in affirming the contingency of the future, but he is not prepared to surrender the omniscience of God, which for him is a biblical doctrine and the guarantee of victory for the saints. Hence he asserts what Alexander denies, that we can distinguish between the necessary relation of truth to knowledge and the necessary truth of the thing that is known.

In other respects we see evidence of a profitable reading of Alexander. Origen not only avails himself of the terms *anankaion*, *endechomenon* and *eph' hēmin*,[20] which had entered the lexicon of all the philosophical schools in the

18 See Tzamalikos 2005, 182, 189, 205, 219, 245, 323, 348, Ramelli 2014, Edwards (forthcoming).

19 See Crouzel 1969, 158.

20 On the significance that these terms acquire in Alexander, see Bobzien 1998. In citing this article, Gibbons 2016 opines without giving reasons that Origen was probably unaware of Alexander.

Roman era, but adopts Alexander's tenet that a rational agent demonstrates his freedom by acting at times in ways that are not uniformly predicable of the species (27, 198.18–23). Had Judas done only what every human being would be compelled to do under similar influences, he would not have been justly condemned. We may find it disappointing that in rejecting the Aristotelian deduction of the necessity of the future from our knowledge of the future, he does not rehearse the arguments which the Stoics had already brought against this position.[21] Since he is among our principal witnesses to the teaching of the Stoics on other matters, we should hesitate to ascribe his silence to ignorance. No doubt he saw as clearly as Alexander the inadequacy of the argument that the future is open so long as we do not know it to be determined (24, 194.8–17): but this establishes only our uncertainty, not the genuine indeterminacy of the future up to the time when the choice is made. Nor would he have reason to be more satisfied by the modern reformulation which establishes not only the epistemic but the logical possibility of either outcome so long as the factors preventing one have not yet come into play.[22] Origen, like Alexander, wishes to uphold an indeterminacy which is more than logical or epistemic; we might feel that it was all the more imperative, if the Stoics and Peripatetics could not remove his difficulties, to offer a Christian solution. Here as elsewhere, however, his theological convictions are independent of the philosophical reasoning which may elucidate, but can never prove, what has been revealed by the word of God.

3 Predestination?

But even the most faithful exegetes come to the Bible with their own prepossessions. Origen's prepossession in favour of divine benevolence forbade him to embrace the plain sense of any text which hinted either that God creates evil or that he takes no account of our deserts in his decrees of reprobation and election. It is well known that he traces the beginning of evil not to any defect in God's own handiwork or even to his bestowal of autonomy on his creatures but to the wilful abuse of that autonomy, first by the devil and then by human souls. According to the common account, derived from his detractors in late antiquity, the embodied soul and the demon have fallen from the same state of bliss, and differ only in the gravity of their transgressions. This

21 On the Stoic argument that if human agency is a cause, we are responsible for its consequences, see e.g. Sakezles 2007.

22 Sharples 1983, 135–136.

is a teaching not easily elicited from his extant works, and perhaps at variance with them. For example, at *Against Celsus* 6.43, Plato's myth in which the soul sheds its wings (*Phaedrus* 248a–b) is represented as a garbled account of Satan's apostasy, not as an explanation of human embodiment. In view of Origen's own asseverations that no being but God is strictly incorporeal, that even demons possess a rarefied body, that paradise even now is a place on earth, and that some vestige of the body will endure in the future state,[23] we can scarcely credit him with the belief that God created souls for any purpose but embodiment: his comments on the coats of skin which God fashioned for Adam and Eve imply that these were not the first vestments of the soul but the first which it was bound to relinquish (*Homilies on Leviticus* 6.1). He may not even have spoken of a human fall from absolute perfection, for he notes that at Genesis 1.27 God does not bestow his promised likeness on humanity, and concludes that, having the image already by grace, we are required to attain the likeness through the acquisition and exercise of virtue (*First Principles* 3.6.1).

Trends of Platonic thought in the time of Origen favoured the view that even the best souls are obliged to enter bodies so that matter may not remain bereft of form. It is possible that some of them anticipated Porphyry in teaching that the soul descends in order to learn the virtues which can be mastered only in adversity. Numenius, of whom Origen knew something, contrasted the demons who assist the soul with their wicked counterparts who haul it back to earth (fr. 37.1–4 Des Places). Origen's demonology, however, is supported by exegesis and ecclesial tradition, and is coupled with the exclusively Christian tenet that we are all descended from the first transgressor. The universal sinfulness of humanity, in Origen's view, is the consequence of our carnal share in Adam rather than any degradation of the soul in a previous life. His argument for the baptism of infants at *Homilies on Leviticus* 8.3.1 is that each of us enters the world in a state of "defilement" (*sordes*), with the exception of Christ who had no human father. Our personal culpability, however, is in no way lessened either by this congenital frailty or by the assiduity of Satan. Only by God's special dispensation can he wound us either by illness or by natural disaster; for the most part, his sole ploy is deception, which prevails because we are willingly deceived.

If Satan and the stars are not to blame, still less is God. So much would be obvious were it not for the admonition in Romans 9 that God spares only

23 *First Principles* 1.6.4, *First Principles*, proemium 10, *First Principles* 2.11.6, *Against Celsus* 5.18–23.

those on whom he wills to have mercy, creating us to be vessels of honour or vessels of dishonour as he pleases, and with no more right to gainsay him than the pot has to cry out against the potter. When he addresses these texts in his *First Principles* (3.1.16–21) and his *Commentary on Romans*, Origen takes what we now call the Arminian view that God creates us knowing but not determining the choice on our own part that will shape us as vessels of honour or dishonour. If the apostle seems to have forestalled this interpretation by adducing the case of Jacob, who was preferred to Esau even in the womb, we must understand him in a manner that does not belie the justice of God in apportioning his gifts to human merits. That is to say, we must presume that Jacob was reaping the merits of his previous life (*First Principles* 2.9.7). Since Origen did not believe that a "man of the church" could entertain any argument for the transmigration of souls from one human body to another (*Commentary on John* 6.11.66), it has generally been assumed that he alludes here to a fall into the corporeal realm from the intellectual cosmos. Since, on the other hand, he certainly held that the child in the womb is already a person, it is possible that Origen was alluding to the Rabbinic traditions which charged the foetus of Esau with impiety, emulation and attempted homicide. This is another case in which he is more concerned to proclaim the truth than to vindicate it by philosophy.

If Esau could be left to judgment, the case of Judas might tax even Origen's faith in the innocence of God. Christ said on the eve of his own betrayal that it was "written" (Mark 14.21), and the Psalm in which it is written – "let his days be short and his bishopric pass to another" – was cited by Peter as evidence that even the crucifixion was ordained (Acts 1.20). Furthermore, he appears not to be a free agent, for when Satan enters into a man, it is only the power of Christ that can deliver him; yet Christ is the one who opens his heart to Satan by foretelling his treason, and once he is vanquished says to him only "What thou doest do quickly" (John 13.26–27). Origen is thus at pains, in his *Commentary on John*, to refute the inference that Judas was already fated to be a sinner by his own nature or by divine ordinance. His perfidy flowed from his character (*Commentary on John* 32.6.68), but this is the meaning, not the negation of freedom; the fact that, when Christ predicted his betrayal, every disciple began to suspect himself is proof the mutability of *prohairesis*, the faculty of choice (32.19.255). Judas retained this faculty up to the point where the sop was handed to him, and Christ refrained from unmasking him in order to give free play to his own conscience. Recognising at this point his own unworthiness (32.22.283), he succumbed to the tempter and went out into the night which symbolised the fall of darkness upon his soul (32.24.313). Once Satan has gained his way, it is impossible to say whether he or Judas is the addressee of Christ's injunction "What thou doest do quickly" (32.23.297); at first, however, Judas was as capable as any other saint of repelling the darts that Satan loses at all of us many times a day (32.2.19).

Origen contends that we are all capable of showing the same resolution when we are moved by the spirit of anger, and that any woman can offer the same resistance to an assault upon her chastity, so long as it is Christ who rules the soul (*First Principles* 3.1.4). In the Latin of Rufinus we encounter the Latin equivalent to the Stoic term *propatheia*, which signifies the instinctive movement caused by an impression of an object of fear or desire.[24] According to the Stoics, it will not assume the definite character of fear or desire in the wise man, although there is difference of opinion, among modern if not among ancient commentators, as to how far his soul is susceptible to the first motion. Hence there is also difference of opinion as to how well Origen renders the Stoic position; he is not to be judged however, by his accuracy as a scholar, for his text is not Chrysippus but the Bible, his subject is not the wise man but the God-man, and his chief aim once again is to avoid sacrilege, not to settle a philosophical dispute.

Why does God permit Satan to bring about the death of the righteous with the complicity of the sinner? In his *Homily on Numbers*, Origen hints at an analogy between Judas and Balaam, the pagan diviner who blessed the people of Israel against his will (Numbers 22). Judas by meditating evil brought about the salvation of the world (*Homilies* 14.2.4); Balaam, because he was bent on disobeying God's express command, was permitted to carry out those of his enemy, and thus became a harbinger not only of Israel's victory but of the birth of Christ (13.7.4). Since the star whose rising he proclaimed was the one that led the Magi to Bethlehem, we can answer those who ask why God permitted this friend of demons to go on practising astrology with success and thereby drawing others into this superstition. God, who ordains no evil, may permit it so long as it serves his providential design: unwilling, therefore, to leave the Gentiles without some presage of Christ, he confided their instruction to fallen angels, who, in creating this false science from the remnants of their own knowledge, would inadvertently teach them more than the lawful prophets were able to teach the Jews.

Thus, as I remarked above, all predestination *to evil* is avoided. This qualification is necessary because if one is, as Origen seems to be, a universalist, one must hold that all beings capable of salvation will be saved, which is to say that their salvation is predestined. At *First Principles* 2.8 Origen allots to the

24 For a comparison of these *primi motus* in Origen with those of the Stoics (e.g. Seneca, *On Anger* 2.2–4, Aulus Gellius, *Attic Nights* 19.1.15–21), see Sorabji 2000.

majority of souls after death a long and painful itinerary, first to the earthly paradise through its fiery gates and then through the planetary spheres until it is purged of sin, of all that binds the soul to earth, and of all that renders the body intractable to the spirit: then at last God will be our "all in all". His ancient critics were right to complain that this eschatology pervades his writings, though they would seem to be in error when they allege that he extends salvation even to the devil. He himself averred that only a madman would believe this; at the same time, he surmises at *First Principles* 3.6.5 that the overcoming of death foretold by Paul means not so much the extinction of death but his ceasing to trouble the elect (cf. 1 Corinthians 15.26). As death is expressly equated with the devil in his *Commentary on Romans* (p. 70 Bammel), we may take him to mean that, although the devil will not be saved, he will make his peace with God. And if that is so, it will seem that no-one can remain in hell.

4 Universalism?

No modern scholar denies the universalism of Origen; had there been any doubt it would have been allayed by Ilaria Ramelli's diligent compilation of illustrative passages in her study entitled *The Christian Doctrine of Apokatastasis*.[25] It is also clear that in Origen at least the word *aiōnios*, when applied to punishment, never means "eternal" but only "until the end of an age". All this being granted, however, there are passages in his writings that, at first sight, are inconsistent with the thesis that all will be saved. One of his more infamous speculations is that a sinner may be so obdurate, notwithstanding all divine counsel and correction, as to go on hardening sinfulness by sin until at last he is no more capable of repentance than a beast. This follows, of course, from this principle that God never overrules the human conscience, and it is also a Christian analogue to the figurative reading which was often applied to the doctrine of transmigration. Nevertheless, it leaves us wondering how we can be sure that God will make peace with the devil if we cannot be sure that a time will come when all sinners are reconciled.

We have all the more reason to doubt the universalism of Origen when he expounds Jeremiah's simile of the potter (chapter 18), which is echoed in Paul's reasoning on divine mercy in Romans 9. As vessels of clay, he says in his eighteenth homily, we are equally malleable to the refining fire of God and the corrosive fire of Satan. Satan and God alike have power to break us and to

25 Ramelli 2013, 1–221.

mould us anew, one into beauty and one into deformity; whichever of these processes we undergo, the result cannot be undone (151.20 Klostermann). If this passage stood alone, we could only deduce that Origen believes our lot to be cast with hell or heaven at the moment of physical death. Yet this is not what we would glean from the recurrent image of fire in his other homilies on the same prophet. In the twentieth, for example, he contends that it is better to suffer the inward flames of chastisement in the present life than the cautery that awaits us after death, but he does not state that the latter will be eternal (192–194 Klostermann). In the sixteenth homily he foreshadows the doctrine of purgatory in his comments on 1 Corinthians 3.15, in which the holocaust of the stubble, wood and hay that weak believers build on Christ is not so much a penalty for the believer as a means of preservation (138–139 Klostermann). Why then does Origen threaten us in one place with undying torment, only to imply elsewhere that the pains of the future life will be transient and salutary?

I suggest that the answer is found in Origen's advocacy of "deception" (ἀπάτη) as a pedagogic tool, which is another leitmotif of the *Homilies on Jeremiah*. At the outset, as I have noted above, we are told that the desired effect of a prophecy of doom is to avert its own fulfilment (*Homily* 1.1, p. 1 Klostermann). In *Homilies* 18 and 19, the language of scripture is said to be a constant accommodation to our imperfect faculties, just as adults adopt a prattling mode of speech to make themselves intelligible to children; one example of this practice, he adds, is to issue threats without qualification, although we do not mean to perform them (159–174 Klostermann). In *Homily* 20.7, Origen looks for the truth in Jeremiah's exclamation, "O Lord thou hast deceived me and I was deceived." Divine dissimulation, he argues, resembles that of the doctor who administers a honeyed draught while keeping the surgical iron out of sight (180.15–18 Klostermann). Thus the thing concealed may be more or less formidable than the thing revealed, but in either case the thing concealed is the evidence of love. Origen's universalism was not the received belief of the church, and it is therefore not surprising that he should hide it from simple readers under an artifice familiar from the nursery, which God himself had not disdained to borrow.

Whimsical as it may appear, this notion of divine subterfuge is the cornerstone of his hermeneutics. In benighted age, the natural law becomes illegible; it was Moses alone who knew, as he laid down the ordinances for the slaughter of animals, that the service required by God was the immolation of the carnal appetites (*Homilies on Leviticus* 5.2.1, 6.3.5 etc.). Fifteen centuries later this had become apparent to Philo; with the death of Christ, however, and the burning of the temple which avenged it, the occult sense of the law has not only become intelligible but has superseded the practical observance. In addition to the higher sense of the law, discerned by few in Israel, there is a highest sense that was hidden even from them. At the same time, as the crucifixion was a paschal sacrifice, this highest sense may be said to redeem the literal construction. The same pattern, in which the literal subsumes the allegorical, is apparent in the first homily on Jeremiah, where Origen contends that the words must applied in their entirety either to the prophet himself or to the One whom he prefigures. Of Jeremiah it can be true only in a figure that he was commissioned to "root up and to tear down among nations"; of Christ, these words are literally true, which is not to deny that they are richer still in their figurative import. And while it is not in the common sense true of Christ that he "knew not how to speak" (Jeremiah 1.6), it is true in the sense that our infantile discourse was not the tongue that he spoke by nature (pp. 4–5 Klostermann). God's mendacity differs from that of Satan as provisional evils differ from specious goods. His prophecies have two goals, revelation and edification: when one counteracts the other, the seer becomes for a time an instrument of deception, but only in order that others may be more readily undeceived.

Bibliography

Adamson, Peter. 2008. "Plotinus on Astrology." *Oxford Studies in Ancient Philosophy* 35: 265–291.

Baehrens, Wilhelm, ed. 1920. *Origenes. Homilien zum Hexateuch* [incl. *Homilies on Leviticus*]. Leipzig: Hinrichs.

Bammel, C.P. Hammond, ed., Brésard, L., tr. 2009–2012. *Origène. Commentaire sur l'Épître aux Romains*. Paris: Cerf.

Behr, John, ed., tr. 2017. *Origen. First Principles*. Oxford: Oxford University Press.

Bobzien, Susanne. 1998. "The Inadvertent Conception and Late Birth of the Free Will Problem." *Phronesis* 43: 133–175.

Boys-Stones, George. 2007. "Human Autonomy and Divine Revelation in Origen." In *Severan Culture*, edited by Simon C.R. Swain, Stephen J. Harrison, and Jas Elsner, 488–499. Cambridge: Cambridge University Press.

Crouzel, Henri, ed. 1969. *Grégoire le Thaumaturge. Remerciement à Origène*. Paris: Cerf.

Deck, John N. 1967. *Nature, Contemplation and the One: A Study in Philosophy*. Toronto: University of Toronto Press.

Edwards, Mark. (forthcoming). "Origen, Celsus and the Philosophers." In *The Oxford Handbook of Origen*, edited by Ronald Heine. Oxford: Oxford University Press.

Frede, Michael. 2011. *A Free Will. Origins of the Notion in Ancient Thought*, edited by Anthony A. Long. Berkeley: University of California Press.

Gibbons, Kathleen. 2016. "Human Autonomy and its Limits in Origen." *Classical Quarterly* 66: 673–690.

Harl, Marguerite, and Erich Junod, eds. 1976–1983. *Philokalie*. Paris: Cerf.

Klostermann, Erich, ed. 1901. *Origenes. Jeremiahomilien*. Leipzig: Hinrichs.

Koetschau, Paul, ed. 1897–1899. *Origenes. Gegen Celsus/Die Schrift vom Gebet* [i.e. *On Prayer*]. Leipzig: Hinrichs.

Limone, Vito, ed. 2012. *Origene. Commento al Vangelo di Giovanni*. Milan: Bompiani.

Pachoumi, Eleni. 2013. "The Religious-Philosophical Concept of Personal Daimon and the Magical-Theurgic Ritual of Systasis in the Greek Papyri." *Philologus* 157: 46–69.

Ramelli, Ilaria. 2013. *The Christian Doctrine of Apokatastasis*. Leiden: Brill.

Ramelli, Ilaria. 2014. "Alexander of Aphrodisias: A Source of Origen's Philosophy?" *Philosophie antique* 14: 237–289.

Ramelli, Ilaria. 2017. "Prophecy in Origen." *Journal of Early Christian History* 7: 17–39.

Sakezles, Priscilla K. 2007. "Aristotle and Chrysippus on the Psychology of Human Action: Criteria for Responsibility." *British Journal for the History of Philosophy* 15: 225–252.

Sharples, Robert, ed., tr. 1983. *Alexander of Aphrodisias. On Fate*. London: Duckworth.

Sorabji, Richard. 2000. *Emotion and Peace of Mind: From Stoic Agitation to Christian Temptation*. Oxford: Oxford University Press.

Tzamalikos, Panayiotis. 2005. *Origen: Cosmology and Ontology of Time*. Leiden: Brill.

Index of Passages

General Index

The entries in the index are meant to guide the reader back to the Greek and Latin terms in which the problem of fate, providence and free will was discussed in the early Imperial period and are thus as much as possible accompanied by the Greek or Latin originals. Entries of modern terms, such as free will, are entered with cross-references only, in order to draw the reader's attention to the terminology used by the ancients.

Printed in the United States
By Bookmasters